The Fifties Child

Also from Desert Hearts/Bennett & Bloom:

The Fifties Child

A Social History through the Songs of Barclay James Harvest

ALEX TORRES

DESERT ♥ HEARTS

First published
in 2013 by
DESERT♥HEARTS
www.deserthearts.com
www.bennettandbloom.com
PO Box 2131
London W1A 5SU
England

Typeset and designed by Desert♥Hearts

Printed and bound in Great Britain by
Marston Book Services, Didcot

British Library Cataloguing in Publication Data
A catalogue record for this book is available from the British Library

ISBN 978-1-908755-03-2

Every effort has been made to contact and obtain
permission from owners of copyrighted material
included in this book. In case of oversight
please contact the publishers.

For Les, John, Mel and Woolly,
with thanks for
a lifetime of music

"Fifties child was right to believe:
peace and love were our needs;
the need to be free"
—John Lees

Contents

PART 4: LIFE IS FOR LIVING

PART 5: ECHOES AND SHADOWS

Barclay James Harvest, 1968 – Mel Pritchard, Les Holroyd,
Woolly Wolstenholme, John Lees

Disclaimer

The song interpretations contained in this book are my responsibility only and, as such, there is no intention to present these views as factual opinions of the songwriters themselves. Associated with this is the fact that the punctuation provided in lyric excerpts is mine: this has been adjusted from the cursory punctuation provided in album lyric reprints in order to assist interpretation.

Readers may wonder why more extensive use is not made of lyric excerpts in support of the interpretations reached. Essentially, despite the fact that the lyrics to nearly all of Barclay James Harvest's songs are available freely online, one of the music publishing companies that owns the copyright to these songs insisted on payment. The way that the music industry works means that the other companies then followed suit. The anticipated sales of this book are such that they would not cover the cost of the purchase of all the licences: hence, lyric extracts are used more selectively than I would have liked.

Special Thanks

Keith Domone, for keeping the flag flying; Terry Luck, for being positive about early versions of the text; Stephen Roberts, for encouragement; and Nick Awde for practical help and encouragement.

Introduction

Taking a stand-back view at more than forty years of songwriting by Barclay James Harvest's three songwriters, it strikes one that, unusually for a rock band, there is a considerable body of songs that addresses societal issues. Rock bands have always addressed similar issues in their music—the "protest song" was certainly not invented by Barclay James Harvest—but what is unique in their instance is how societal subjects have occurred repeatedly over the course of a long career, reflecting a clear image of some of the major issues that affected the thinking and the lives of those growing up in Britain during the second half of the twentieth century. Of these songs, only a few are what one might truly term protest songs. The difference between these two types of song will become clear as we progress through this book.

The present intent therefore is to see how British society and its concerns are reflected through an interpretation of the songs of these three songwriters from Oldham: Les Holroyd (born 1948), John Lees (born 1947) and Woolly Wolstenholme (born 1947, died 2010). It will become clear that key social aspects of the period are covered by their canon of sociological songs, yielding a fascinating and valuable image of British society during a period of rapid change. In the aftermath of two cataclysmic world wars, how would the Fifties Child shape the world he was born into? Would he have the power to change it for the better? How would he cope with the morass of life's pressures? Barclay James Harvest's songwriters answer these and other questions.

Many of the songs covered will have deeply affected the hearts and minds of those who heard them. Whilst it is not possible to quantify the social impact of a song—and, heaven forbid, in this day of KPIs that is a heinous crime![1]— there is undoubtedly an effect. This arises not just by exposing listeners to issues they may not have known about—a deeper and perhaps more

1. I shall take my chances!

fundamental effect is in transmitting confidence to a mass of people that the views that they hold, whilst perhaps not being the "establishment" view, are nevertheless shared by others. The effect of such a force is not to be underestimated. Barclay James Harvest have sold over ten million records and have been playing to audiences in many countries throughout Europe for more than 40 years. Their songs, as well as describing various aspects of society, have undoubtedly had a social impact themselves.

This is not to imply that the band's songwriters were on a crusade to affect public opinion: there is ample evidence from their own songs, as well as from interviews, to the contrary. The prime objective for the band was to make money, whilst doing something they enjoyed, as Holroyd explained to an interviewer:

> I get annoyed, you see, about people who go 'we're in it for the art—we're not interested in the money'. The plain fact of course is that everyone likes the art side of it, that's what drives you forward, but you have to have a commercial side to it, in terms of going out there and performing and selling records. Of course you do it for the money, otherwise you wouldn't be doing it.

Lees is no slouch either: in 1997's autobiographical 'River of Dreams' he openly admits that the lure of money and glitzy fame were incentives for adopting the rock 'n' roll life. Interviewed in 1984, he had told *Kerrang!* magazine: "I hope no one sees me as a preacher. I wouldn't be shattered if a fan got off on the musical content of the song and never actually looked at or listened to the words."

This seems like an entirely reasonable stance: when listening to a piece of sung music, the mind is invariably alerted by the music first, including the melody of the sung part itself, rather than the words. It is only once the music has done its job that one might begin to focus on the words, but what then happens is that if the words resonate with us, they can give the song an appeal and longevity that it would otherwise not have had.

In practical terms, Barclay James Harvest's songwriters have inevitably affected others' thinking simply by writing about what mattered to them as individuals. Despite the inference that might be drawn from the previous quotations, this style of writing was not accidental for any of them, as is most obviously exemplified by what Lees said in answer to a contemporary interviewer's question about his song 'Hymn for the Children', from the *Time Honoured Ghosts* album: "(It's) like a follow-up to 'Child of the Universe', which is a follow-on from 'Summer Soldier', which is a follow-on from 'Dark Now My Sky'—there's always one statement-type song on each album." One "statement-type" song on each album there may be, but there are many more sociological songs than that! Of Barclay James Harvest's songwriters, Lees' is the most clearly autobiographical writing—he systematically wrote about his family, about the books and films that impressed him, about nature and, no less importantly, about his beliefs. In the same *Kerrang!* interview referenced above, he had said: "I like to write songs with a little depth to them, yet which can still be appreciated on the most superficial of levels."

It is clear that the lyrics meant much to Lees; and they were also a significant factor for Holroyd and Wolstenholme. This much can be surmised from the fact that the vocals were always clear and given prominence in the sound mix of Barclay James Harvest's music, which does not always happen for rock bands. Furthermore, from the time of the *Time Honoured Ghosts* album in 1975, all of their studio albums carried printed lyrics.

The number of their sociological songs totals more than 125.[2] The clarity and value of the resulting reflected social history occurs not only because of the length of the band's career but also because Holroyd, Lees and Wolstenholme, whilst sometimes sharing a common perspective, often wrote from different standpoints and about different topics.

The explicitness of their individual songwriting varied, with Lees being the most explicit and Holroyd the least. This, as well as the significant autobiographical nature of the writing, explains why the majority of sociological songs are of Lees' authorship.

Whilst some songs are easy to allocate to a sociological category, others are less so, and before considering them for inclusion one needs to view them in the context of the canon of other such songs written by that lyricist—this is what I will refer to as "contextualisation". Occasionally, the meaning may have been revealed by the writer. Sometimes, interpretation has been used but only when the risk of serious misinterpretation has been judged low—this is acceptable once a work enters the public domain. Hopefully, nothing as inaccurate as Ronald Reagan's misinterpretation of Bruce Springsteen's sociological songs has filtered through in this book![3]

Contextualisation and interpretation are useful in developing a fuller

2. The provenance of Barclay James Harvest's sociological songs is detailed in Appendix 2.

3. At the time of the US 1984 presidential election campaign, Springsteen had achieved massive popular success with his *Born in the USA* album and was selling out stadia across America, appearing onstage against a backdrop of a massive stars 'n' stripes flag. In a campaign speech in Springsteen's home state, Ronald Reagan associated himself with this apparent jingoism saying that his ambition was to bring to fruition the hope in Springsteen's songs. Springsteen was forced into a public repudiation of the president because, in actual fact, the intent of his sociological songs up to that time had been quite the opposite: to decry the erosion of American high values and the loss of the "American Dream".

societal picture, although it is clear that songs requiring it cannot always have contributed to their immediate social impact. Such an impact will have arisen from the many songs in which the meaning is either immediately clear or commonly misinterpreted. To give an example of the former, 'Child of the Universe' is not only abundantly clear but, when allied to the powerful music, has an immediate and lifelong impact on a listener with a mind that is fertile for its message:

> I'm a child of South Africa,
> I'm a child of Vietnam,
> I'm a child of Northern Ireland:
> I'm a small boy with blood on his hands!
> Yes, I'm a child of the universe.

Underlining this point is another quote from Lees, speaking at a progressive music forum in 2011:

> You never know how your music will touch people's lives, and also why. I remember at the height of the war in Lebanon, I got a message from a kid in Beirut thanking me for the song 'Child of the Universe', because that helped them to get through the troubles. That touched me.

The power of 'Child of the Universe's words lies in their simplicity and immediacy. It is no coincidence that the song has been a perennial fan favourite since its release in 1974. Its message can then be used, in association with that of other songs, to contextualize songs by Lees whose meaning may not be immediately clear.

Wolstenholme may have left the band in 1979, but his work under his own name and with his band Mæstoso into the twenty-first century is particularly incisive and contains much relevant and interesting material which enhances the sociological picture, and it is therefore included for consideration, as are songs from Holroyd and Lees released after the main band disintegrated in 1998.

In order to demonstrate that Barclay James Harvest's were not the only songwriters with a social conscience, I have included within each chapter the description of a small number of songs by other contemporaneous artists.[4] For the purposes of deriving a social history as from the eyes of a Fifties Child, I have defined "contemporaneous" as applying to British songwriters born

---

4. Generally, the provenance for these songs is given within the text, and the artists' place and year of birth are detailed in Appendix 2.

within five years of Barclay James Harvest's own songwriters. This gives us an approximate birth date range from 1942 to 1953. These are our "Fifties Children": they would have had, broadly speaking, a similar upbringing, and been subject to influence by a similar education and the same world events. You may quibble about the imperfections inherent in this definition but it is acceptable as a working guide. These examples from other artists are not intended to be exhaustive. They are sourced from my own musical collection, without resorting to research, and perhaps because of this I have had to occasionally break my own "contemporaneous rule". I have also occasionally strayed away from the rock scene towards folk: this is perfectly defensible on the basis that Barclay James Harvest's music is influenced by the English folk music tradition; indeed, you can imagine a number of their songs being perfectly suited for folk arrangements.

The social history that these songwriters describe is like a fascinating journey: the journey of the Fifties Child through life. I hope that you will enjoy it. The journey is enhanced if you know the music, so that you can play the songs in your mind as you are reading. May this book inspire you to plug any gaps in that knowledge!

Enjoy!

Part 1
Mill Boys

1

Family and Environs

During the Fifties the family was the stable unit of life: most Fifties Children were brought up in a home with two parents who were married and who will have continued living together even if they experienced marital difficulties. Divorce rates increased sharply during the remaining decades of the century; from an annual rate of about 27,000 divorces in the early Sixties, this increased more than fourfold in a decade, and reached over 150,000 by the early twenty-first century.

Oldham, Barclay James Harvest's home town, prospered in the nineteenth century as a mill town, growing from a village in 1801 to become the most important mill town in Britain, reaching a population of nearly 150,000 before the First World War. The start of the Fifties saw an acceleration of the mill industry decline that had started pre-Second World War, with the result that the population dropped by some 50,000 in the latter half of the twentieth century as people moved away to find work.

Barclay James Harvest's songwriters were deeply affected by their upbringing: their environs feature in songs by all three, whereas the family has a special place at the heart of Lees' writing. Thus, there are some specific and general societal observations that one can develop by considering their songs in this general area.

Family

The Fifties Child would live to see a significant degradation of that most fundamental of all units: the family. The changes would be so far reaching that he or she would stand little chance of grasping their true significance and implication as the decades advanced into the new century. Some Fifties Children would be personally affected by the social revolution that was manifested by the preponderance towards the dissolution of marriage, others not.

One of the consequences of divorce was the significant increase in lone-parent families, which was spectacular, rising more than fourfold from the beginning of the Sixties to about 25 per cent of all families with children by 2010. Divorce was not the only contributor to lone-parent families—the relaxation in sexual mores was another, with the number of children born out of wedlock rising dramatically. Less than ten per cent of children were born outside wedlock in 1971 but, by 2009, this applied to nearly half. This is a quite staggering change, considering the stigma attached to conceiving out of wedlock when the Fifties Child was born. Clearly, not all children born out of wedlock end up in lone-parent families, as another major change has been the reducing trend in marriages—down 30 per cent in the Fifties Child's lifetime—but that explosive change in out-of-wedlock conception must be a contributor to the dissolution of the Fifties Child's traditional family unit.

Whether these changes were driven by the weakening of the Church,[1] whether they were driven by some kind of more general rebelliousness against authority in the wake of the two World Wars, or whether they were an inevitable consequence of sexual permissiveness is a question that is beyond the scope of this book but the effect that they have had on society is significant, the repercussion tendrils wheedling their way into unexpected areas, pervading much of modern life.

Specific to John Lees' writing is a close focus on the home and family; his writing reflects not only the personal joys and sadnesses of family life but also how, during the second half of the twentieth century, aspects of that familial home life changed. This latter aspect of society is also reflected by Wolstenholme's twenty-first century writing for Mæstoso.

Chronologically, the first song explicitly dealing with Lees' immediate family is 1977's 'Our Kid's Kid', a celebration of his niece's birth. The musical arrangement is uncomplicated but joyous, as are the lyrics. Lees is excited by the news that his sister Edna has become the first of the two siblings to delight their parents with a grandchild. He jokingly offers his sister some advice to make sure that she sets little Ruth off on the right road to life by buying her a guitar.

A few years later Lees himself became a father for the first time and the birth of his daughter Esther is celebrated in 'How Do You Feel Now?'. Lees' description of the moments following the birth is deeply touching: moved to tears of elation at the sight of his baby daughter, he gently places her by his wife's side, delighting in the broadest of smiles which lights up her face. The significance of this moment to Lees may be gauged from the fact that he has

---

1. Divorce rates have also increased in the United States, which has not seen the same decline in church attendance as Britain.

often cited this song as a personal favourite from amongst his canon, at the same time as deriding his own performance on it. The moment clearly meant so much to him that he was seeking perfection.

Of greater concern to the listener, however, is the fact that there is a double-edge to the lyrics, which leaves the suggestion that there had been a strain on the marriage arising from the frustration of it being childless for so long. Indeed, this shadow appears immediately in the song's opening, even before Lees describes his delight at the birth. The inference is that the barren marriage was becoming increasingly frustrating and that it needed children to continue. This suggestion that his daughter's birth was necessary to save the marriage has the effect of slightly dulling the song's message of perfect joy, more so than any shortfall in Lees' performance. Societally, of course, it does reflect the fact that many marriages do continue solely because of supporting the children.

One must not over-dramatize such difficulties: over the course of a life together, frustrations inevitably arise. Lees' devotion and love for family would have assisted in overcoming such trials. The strength of the bond and the affection for his wife shines through in 'Midnight Drug', a song in which he describes how, when he is on tour with the band, he phones from the hotel after a concert to tell her how much he is missing her. Taken together, the sense from these three songs is that of a strong family unit.

While 'How Do You Feel Now?' exulted in the joy and strength that birth can bring to a family, by contrast 1993's 'Back to Earth' is replete with the intense sadness caused by the death of a parent. Lees' father—"Frederick the Great", as he is crowned in 'Our Kid's Kid'—died in 1992 and this sung eulogy is appropriately emotive. Sung as if he is actually speaking to his father, the song conveys the mutual love and friendship that enriched their relationship. The depth of their bond can also be adjudged musically: many fans would agree that Lees' overall performance on *Caught in the Light*, the album on which the song appears, fell short of his norm but 'Back to Earth' is as powerful as anything he has written; it is almost as if he had reserved all his energies for this one song. The song's final section develops a meditative, mantric quality that finally confirms to the listener that, not for the first time in Lees' oeuvre, the song is a prayer.

Reinforcing Lees' strong bond with his family is the fact that both of his children—daughter Esther and son John Joseph—have, very occasionally, performed live with Lees' current version of the band, John Lees' Barclay James Harvest. For Lees, therefore, the family is clearly one of the most fundamental aspects of life. These songs of his that we have just discussed immediately mark him out as the most autobiographical of Barclay James Harvest's songwriters.

Les Holroyd gives us no explicit clues relating to his family within his songwriting and Woolly Wolstenholme is coy. The latter's father receives a fleeting mention—too brief to be certain that it is autobiographical and therefore ascribe a wider social implication to—in 'Mr Sunshine' and despite a nagging suspicion that a number of his twenty-first century songs are cathartic by dealing with the break-up of his marriage, they are nearly all written generally, so that they arguably fall into the general gamut of love songs. The one exception is 'closure', but even with this there is some uncertainty, as it has been suggested that the song continues off from 'Ursula (The Swansea Song)' and 'Someone There You Know' (both from 1971), which were about an earlier relationship. However, the lyric "I broke my back for you / upon the rack of you" surely clinches the link to the marriage break-up. After leaving Barclay James Harvest in 1979 and subsequently abandoning the music business, Wolstenholme and Jill, his wife, took up serious farming, first in Lancashire and then on a 100-acre farm in Wales. Farming can be "backbreaking" hard work, and so the line "upon the rack of you" is a play on words, where "you" is used as a homophone of "ewe". Admittedly, ewe is more often used to refer to an adult sheep and the dish that's a perennial favourite on restaurant menus, then and now, is "rack of lamb" rather than "rack of ewe", but this nicety is pardonable given the clever twist on words. Wolstenholme appears to be saying that despite him grafting hard at the farming endeavour for the common cause of the marriage, still the relationship came to naught.

It may well be that in 'closure' Wolstenholme is clearing his mind of the debris of two failed relationships—it certainly will not be the last song of Barclay James Harvest's songwriters that we find with more than one meaning. In deference to the fact that it may deal with two relationships, the remaining quotation from the song comes from the verse that contains the play on "ewe", as this must pertain to the marriage break-up. The song continues:

Those years of misery
were not so good for me.
The loving songs I wrote
whose words stuck in my throat
now need one final note:
I did it to myself.

The two songs mentioned earlier, 'Ursula (The Swansea Song)' and 'Someone There You Know', cannot be the "loving songs" that Wolstenholme mentions in this lyric; in fact there are no "loving songs" from the keyboardist in the band's canon at that time (although, of course, he may have written them but not had them released). His "loving songs" came later and were written for his wife—'Harbour' is an example from 1978. So it would appear that 'closure' does, at least in part, cover the break-up of his marriage. This particular Fifties Child found it quite acceptable, much more so than his parents' generation would have done, to curtail the failed relationship with separation and divorce; a behaviour that is reflected widely in modern society.

Lees' own 'Children of the Disappeared' [1977] deals not with his immediate family but more generally with one aspect of how familial life has changed in the decades since his birth. Fifties Children, from toddlers up, would play on the streets: that was their playground. Bombed-out sites, building sites, derelict houses, hills and dales, streets and lanes, the Fifties Child would roam at will in fearless, carefree play. Without being able to define precisely why or when it happened, as the years rolled on from the Second World War, that aspect of carefree societal behaviour was replaced by an increasing risk-averse attitude and parents' control of their children's whereabouts became more acute. Kids were increasingly driven to and from school in private cars, rather than walking miles with their friends or on their own, and their roaming play was limited by short, tight leashes of parental discipline.

One can understand parents' concern for the welfare of their children. A series of grisly child abductions and murders in the Sixties would have been enough to instil terror into any parent's mind. The Moors Murderers, Ian Brady and Myra Hindley, perpetrated a series of horrendous sexual torture followed by murder on a number of teenagers and younger children, then buried their bodies on Saddleworth Moor, a location of natural beauty close to Barclay James Harvest's homes and so dear to their hearts. Brady and Hindley's arrest in the autumn of 1965 did not seem to stem this evil tide with two other serial child murderers, Raymond Morris and Ronald Jebson, active in the second half of the decade and the early Seventies. Horrific as these attacks and murders were, possibly the most bizarre of the child killers during this period was eleven-year-old Mary Bell, who killed two toddlers in separate attacks in 1968. Shaken by these events, the confidence of parents would never recover and indeed would erode still further as the decades passed. Little wonder: in twenty-first century Britain the combined rate for child murder and abduction by strangers is about ten per month! Notwithstanding the media's focus on the youngest child victims, which should serve to alert society to its wider problem, this is a shocking statistic.

'Children of the Disappeared' steers clear of analysing the reasons for the societal collapse of confidence seen by the Fifties Child and subsequent generations, choosing instead to express an intense sadness for the loss of those carefree days:

She grew up on easy streets;
danced so hard her feet they
never touched the ground:
love was all around.
No locks on their front door;
she'd stay out late and
they'd know she was safe:
no need to beware.
Now my, my, look at that sky
closing his eyes on a new tomorrow!
Hey, hey, heaven's in tears,
crying for the disappeared.

The above extract, which is the second verse followed by its accompanying version of the chorus, is straightforward enough to understand, as is the first verse,
which deals with a small boy's play but is otherwise thematically identical.
However, like in so many of Lees' songs, there appears to be a hidden depth of
meaning within 'Children of the Disappeared'. Readers may have picked up on
this fact already: after all, what does 'of the Disappeared' mean? It does not
quite make sense to say "of the" if all Lees is interested in is commenting on
the societal change relating to children playing in the streets. Sure, the first half
of the song deals with that and, crucially, the words in the first and second rendition of the chorus say "heaven's . . . crying *for* the disappeared". Then Lees
changes tack, the words twist and we have a new meaning.

So, what meaning does the song then encompass? Let us look at the repetition of the chorus which is sung immediately after the lyrics in the previous
extract:

My, my, look at that sky
turning his back on a generation!
Hey, hey, heaven's in flames
and no one wants to take the blame:
blame for children of the disappeared.

"For" has become "of": this is no slip of the pen to simply provide a tad of variety in the lyrics. Lees is saying something about "the disappeared": no one
wants to take the blame for the children of the disappeared. Who are these
"disappeared"? Arguably, the most common use of the term "the disappeared"
is applied to many people who have been abducted, principally for political
reasons, in South and Central American countries. These disappeared have
had a high profile within the rock music world: for instance, the Rolling

Stones' 'Undercover of the Night' [1983] and U2's 'Mothers of the Disappeared' [1987] both deal with the issue. My interpretation—based more on contextualisation than the lyrics themselves—is that it is not these disappeared who inspired this aspect of Lees' song, but those arising from the sectarian conflict in Northern Ireland, a conflict on which Lees had a close focus during his writing career, as we shall see later in our social history.

The disappeared of Northern Ireland were seventeen people who, over the three-decade period of the Troubles, were suspected victims of Republican paramilitary groups. Although a couple of teenagers are included in these disappeared, most were adults, including some who were parents. Jean McConville, for instance, a 37-year-old mother of ten, disappeared in 1972 and her remains were not found until 2003, some six years after Lees' song was released. Some of the disappeared still remain missing to this day and, despite intensive campaigning and lobbying, their families have been unable to lay their loved ones to rest in a fitting manner.

Should this sorry situation have been part of the motivation for 'Children of the Disappeared' then the twist in the lyrics in the song's second half (and in the song title) would not only make grammatical sense—*children of the disappeared*—but the fact that "heaven's in flames" would also make more sense. Heaven is angry that the families of the disappeared cannot lay their parents and other relatives to rest because the perpetrators of the crimes will not accept the blame and identify the locations of the bodies (this has now happened in the intervening period in some, but not all, cases). Heaven is in flames![2] Heaven . . . that safest of all havens . . . flaming with the fury of a burning hell . . . for what? Because children no longer play carefree in the streets as they used to? It is possible, but it is much more likely that such anger is reserved for a more shocking cause—the continuing silence of the murderers of the disappeared of Northern Ireland's recent history.

Irrespective of whether this interpretation has hit the bulls-eye or missed the dartboard altogether, 'Children of the Disappeared's treatment of its principal theme remains an eloquent indictment of a sad situation that has developed during the lifetime of a Fifties Child. Incidentally, the song features an impressive middle section with effective vocal-layering and harmonies followed by one of Lees's trademark guitar solos, which are more usually reserved for live performance. As such, it is one of Barclay James Harvest's most "progressive" late-period songs.

❦

2. The power of this metaphor is enhanced even more if we bear in mind Lees' strong Christian beliefs at this time. His spirituality is a recurring theme of his songwriting, as we shall soon see.

Family life and its place in society both find its way into other artists' songs: the couple highlighted here reflect topics also covered by Lees.

Jon Anderson is best known for his work with Yes but 'Animation', a song celebrating the joy at the birth of his daughter, is to be found on his solo album of the same name from 1983. Anderson's joy at the wonder of the birth is boundless. He equates it to a deeply spiritual experience; indeed, the experience of the birth approaches an epiphany, a rebirth of the spirit.

The ability of children to play carefree as a measure of societal success also captured the attention of Yusuf Islam at a time when he was still performing as Cat Stevens. His 'Where Do the Children Play?' [*Tea for the Tillerman*, 1970] overlaps with some of Lees' concerns on the topic, although Yusuf does identify a cause for the decline in carefree play. Yusuf's argument is that technological progress is potentially a good thing, but in the headlong rush to develop we must not lose touch with our humanity which, within the song, is symbolised by children's play. The inference is that if the children have nowhere left to play—we are losing our quality of humanity—then all this brilliant technological progress is actually having a negative impact on us all.

In this respect, one can argue that 'Where Do the Children Play?' is a song with, as a minimum, a spiritual undercurrent. There are spiritual elements also within Anderson's 'Animation', as well as in Lees' 'Back to Earth' and 'Children of the Disappeared' (its spiritual element is compassion *for* the "disappeared"). These three songwriters have written many songs with spiritual themes throughout their careers, often to the chagrin of some of their fans, and can be considered amongst the foremost spiritual writers in popular music.[3]

The songs discussed in this chapter are important in establishing the importance of family to many Fifties Children. They describe not only the love for one's own children, which is one of the greatest universal constants, but the affection and bonds to one's parents, siblings and consequent extended family. We have also seen how marriages can come under strain and how, for Fifties Children, it has been possible to accept the dissolution of that historically sacrosanct bond, despite the hurt that marriage break-up can cause. Finally, we have experienced some of the sadness that Fifties Children experienced as, growing older, they see that the new generation of children will not enjoy the carefree play of their own youth.

3. Yusuf caused some controversy when, after he had become a Muslim, he made remarks that were interpreted as supporting the fatwa against Salman Rushdie. However, that is a discussion for another book . . .

Environs

Being born and raised in a mill town north of Manchester, in an environment close to open countryside, was a factor that deeply affected the band's song-writers. Looking out from Oldham towards the moors brought a strong fascination and respect for nature that they were never to lose. This is exemplified by, for example, the many times that official band photographs were taken with the neighbouring countryside as a backdrop.

The band's members never lost connection with their roots for long. In this respect they were possibly unfashionable for a Fifties Child, in particular in their profession, where the strong gravitational attraction was to London. This predilection for their home surroundings reflects the general human trait of retaining a fondness and connection with the place of one's childhood, even when work or family forces a move away.

The band's local city environment is reflected most clearly in the 'Poor Boy Blues/Mill Boys' song cycle, which deals both with the inevitability and drudge of work in the cotton mills, as well as with the lure of the rich life away from them as the industry declined. The songs' meaning becomes clearer if one analyses them out of their playing order on the *Everyone Is Everybody Else* album, by taking Lees' 'Mill Boys' first.

The bleakness of Lees' depiction of work in the mills is accentuated by his very cinematic description of the morning weather in Oldham:

> Sky was black, Lord, rain came pouring down;
> number 12 bus shuffling down Shaw Road way.
> Mules keep spinning, black-faced lifers peck the ground;
> sun comes up like lightning over Tandle Hill's grey.
> We are mill boys, stuck on the hill boys;
> stuck in the mill boys, till our dying day!

Shaw Road and Tandle Hill are locations in close proximity within Oldham itself. A "spinning mule" was a machine used in the cotton mill industry. "Black-faced lifers" could be interpreted a number of ways: "lifer" is almost certainly used here to denote the fact that working in the mills was seen by many—and, as the song makes clear, not in a pleasant way—as a job for life, and "black-faced" might be referring to the protective masks provided to protect workers from cotton dust inhalation; "peck the ground" is a way of expressing the poverty these poorly-paid workers face—it is as though they have to scrabble around for crumbs. This situation clearly leads on to the urge for enhanced economic prosperity and is consequently reflected in the following advice to youngsters faced with the prospect of work in the mills: "Cotton mill will get you, boy, she'll take you to your grave / tell you, boy, to use your head, apprentice out your days!" Whether this is advice that Lees received from his father or whether it is his own advice to others is open to interpretation, but regardless it is worth noting that Lees followed it himself and steered clear of mill work. He studied and then worked in commercial art before accepting impresario John Crowther's offer of financial support,which allowed him to become a professional musician along with the other members of Barclay James Harvest.

Lyrically, Holroyd's 'Poor Boy Blues' is not set in any particular location, but its sense of place is definitely given by 'Mill Boys', with which it is musically enmeshed. The song, which is structured in two distinct parts, resonates with the message shunning hard labour for small wages, which is also heard in 'Mill Boys'.

The opening section of the song is sung virtually a cappella, and in the third person; it observes how easy it is to see how an impoverished worker is depressed by having to graft continuously to survive but also makes the point that it was always his fate to become like that. The societal point that this draws out is how the parents of the Fifties Child would have found it normal to have followed on in their own parents' line of work, and the second section of the song then demonstrates how the Fifties Child begins to reject that historical imperative. The song switches to the first person: the protagonist breaks from tradition by leaving this life of slog behind and goes off searching for the easy times of the rich man.[4]

This short but effective song cycle acts as an impressive reflection, not just of the drudgery of work in Oldham's cotton mills, but of the decline that the industry was facing. One can infer from these songs that the factors affecting its downturn were not just external (cheaper cotton available from abroad). The significant internal factor was that people did not want to work there anymore—they had heard of better pay and better conditions elsewhere and they wanted to be away, away from the chore of hard graft. Of huge sociological significance, the 'Poor Boy Blues/Mill Boys' song cycle is the hymn for the funeral of Oldham's mill industry. Furthermore, by being prepared to break the chains tying him to graft forever in the place of his birth, the Fifties Child is, perhaps unwittingly, exerting further pressure on the traditional family unit that had sustained countless generations before him. Away from home, away from the mill, away from the farm, who would there be to look after the young babes, who would there be to care for the elderly, who would there be to tender the business? The Fifties Child's new-found freedom would have implications for his cherished family, one more pressure weakening its bonds. One can be even bolder and extrapolate the song cycle's implications into the following generations, and in so doing one can

---

4. Perhaps our songwriters should have become bankers instead of rock musicians . . .

see within it the genesis of the modern societal malaise that is manifested by the fact that—in a society with massive unemployment—employers often find it difficult to recruit conscientious workers in many manual labour areas.

'Our Kid's Kid', which we met in the previous section in connection with the family, also contains references to specific locations in Oldham, demonstrating the importance that Lees attaches to the sense of place and home: he urges his sister to foster a love for Oldham in her daughter as she grows up.

Another locality referenced by Lees is the Saddleworth village of Delph, where he lived for a time. 'Delph Town Morn' is a straightforward love song inspired by a pretty woman that Lees and Holroyd are on the look-out for, hoping to catch a glimpse of her beauty as she walks by.

'Ballad of Denshaw Mill' has added interest by virtue of the fact that this is probably as close to pure folk that Barclay James Harvest have ever come. Lyrically, this tells the Saddleworth legend of an angel appearing to three fathers during the First World War. Their sons are on the continent, fighting in the front line trenches. The three are gathered around a derelict mill one night, speaking of their shared yearning to see their sons home for Christmas, when a bright angel appears and allows them a brief glimpse of their sons in a rare happy moment during a lull in the fighting, the sound of their laughter filling the air around them. Their sons would die in the conflict, but the fathers truly believed that the angel had brought them home that night, allowing them to share one last moment of happiness together. In true folklore fashion, Lees borrows a line for his lyrics from local poet Ammon Wrigley, and packs his rendition of the song with subdued, hair-raising emotion, in the best traditions of genre masters such as June Tabor.

Wolstenholme also has a couple of songs dealing with the local environs. The first, 'Sunday Bells', is a sensitively arranged evocation of a Remembrance Day in a Saddleworth village, overlooked by Alderman Hill and Alphin Pike: the song's musical opening is peaceful, respecting the occasion, then develops majestically, highlighting the grandeur of the location. He then takes us just a few miles up the road to 'Hebden Bridge',[5] whose musical and lyrical delight and whimsy reflect the quaintness of the village, stuck in time.[6]

There is general warmth of feeling and love of location pervading these songs, despite the local weather—as constantly reflected by the lyrics themselves—not being the best!

5. 'Hebden Bridge' is a joint composition by Wolstenholme and Mæstoso's guitarist, Steve Broomhead, but it is likely that Wolstenholme wrote the lyrics. He also takes the lead vocal on the song.
6. Wolstenholme would have been stunned, like many of us, by the snap flooding that hit the village in the summer of 2012.

Similar emotions pertaining to local environs are to be found in the work of artists such as Van Morrison and Chris Rea.

Van Morrison is an artist with lyrical synergies with Barclay James Harvest, particularly in the areas of location, nature and the environment, and spirituality. Within Morrison's writing—as, indeed, within Barclay James Harvest's—one gets the sense that it is the spiritual force itself which underpins these other aspects and gives them the prominence of feeling that makes the songwriter want to sing about them. His 'Coney Island' [*Avalon Sunset*, 1989] is a superlative example, musically and lyrically, the emotion bursting through the music as Morrison *recites* his poem. He describes a trip from his native Belfast to the seaside, during which he takes immense delight in simple pleasures: birdwatching, local food delicacies, autumn sunshine. 'Coney Island' is a pearl of a song, making you wish you were there on the trip. In this sense, it echoes the same lure of location such as we have found in 'Our Kid's Kid', 'Sunday Bells' and 'Hebden Bridge'.

On the other hand, listening to Chris Rea's songwriting, it is easier to find synergies with the theme of industrial decline covered by the 'Poor Boy Blues/Mill Boys' song cycle. Rea's Middlesbrough roots often find their way into his music: for instance, 'Steel River' [*Shamrock Diaries*, 1985] and 'It's All Gone' [*On the Beach*, 1986] both deal with his disillusionment with the way that the town has declined over the years.

'Steel River' is heart-breaking in its depiction of the demise of Middlesbrough's industrial heritage. So great was the town's prowess that it became a major target for German bombers during the Second World War. It survived their onslaught but it could not survive the peace. Rea considers himself fortunate that he was able to find success elsewhere but it clearly does not lessen his hurt at the town's fall from grace.

'It's All Gone' takes a different approach but continues the theme: Rea's father concedes the town is finished and advises him to move on, leave it behind, in a very similar fashion to the advice given in 'Mill Boys', and the protagonist's intent in 'Poor Boy Blues'.

This theme of industrial decline will re-occur in our social history of the Fifties Child but, for now, what we take from these songs is how they underlie his sense of home and sense of place. This attachment to a locality yields a feeling of belonging that was clearly important for the soul of these Fifties Children. It was with some sadness that they witnessed the decline in prosperity of the locations dear to their hearts but, crucially, this did not pre-vent them from exercising their freedom by leaving the traditions of the past behind in the search for greater fortune.

2

Nature and the Environment

Children of today may criticise their parents because of the media-fuelled perception of the disrespect that they showed for the environment but, on the contrary, it should be obvious—but it is seldom said—that many Fifties Children do possess a great respect and love for nature and the environment. In any case, the perception that earlier generations were to blame for our environmental problems pales in the face of historical realities. The first half of the twentieth century was no time for environmental fantasising: two World Wars and their industrial consequences were enough, virtually by themselves, to ensure that fact. Then, from the Fifties, in parallel with the war-torn economy trying to rebuild the nation, we begin to see concerns about our environment creeping into society: smog—a combination of fog mixed in with domestic and industrial smoke—reputedly killed thousands in London in the early part of the decade. Such events gained prominent national coverage via popular media avenues such as Pathé newsreels, which were shown in cinemas nationwide. This focus on pollution and the effect of heavy industry developed over this decade and into the Sixties to become a more general concern about man's effect on his environment.

The British people are known for their love of animals, indeed it is a national characteristic, part of our identity as a country. The world's first animal welfare society, the Society for the Prevention of Cruelty to Animals, was formed in London in 1824 and it was not long before the Royal Family lent its support: the Society received its royal patronage in 1837 and Queen Victoria gave her permission for the royal "R" to be added in 1840, from which time the society has been our beloved RSPCA. Another campaign group that was quick to gain its royal charter was the Society for the Protection of Birds. Originally

formed in 1889 as a response to the destruction of birds for plumage to deco-
rate ladies' hats, the Society became the RSPB in 1904. Like the RSPCA, the
RSPB has since become a British national institution; both charities have continued to be popular throughout the life of the Fifties Child.

International groups campaigning on behalf of nature and the environment
began to form in the Sixties. The focus was initially on animal life: the first
major international group to be formed was the World Wide Fund for Nature
(WWF), which formed in 1961. Concern about humankind's impact on his
environment continued to grow during the Sixties, leading to the formation
and globalisation of Friends of the Earth and Greenpeace at the beginning of
the Seventies. All of these groups took skilful advantage of the burgeoning
growth of the media through a series of newsworthy campaigns. This era was
the dawn of what we now recognise as the environmental movement.

Despite the noteworthy efforts of these campaign groups, it was not until
the Eighties that the implications of humankind's impact on their environment became systematic front-page news. The rumble before the eruption
was the discovery announced by the British Antarctic Survey in 1985 that
ozone levels above Antarctic regions were becoming significantly depleted for
part of the year—the now famous "ozone hole".[1] The cause was thought to be
due to emissions of CFCs (chlorofluorocarbons), a man-made compound used
in refrigeration and other applications. The potential of CFCs to harm the
ozone layer—which protects us from harmful solar ultraviolet radiation—had
already been theoretically predicted in the Seventies and this had led the USA
to be the first country to ban CFCs from aerosol sprays in 1978, although their
use in other applications continued as a result of pressure from industry. The
ozone hole continues to grow in extent and magnitude.

The real headline-grabber, however, was to be climate change. Studies into
humankind's impact on the planet began in earnest during the Fifties. For
many years scientists struggled to construct sufficiently reliable models of the
earth's atmosphere and several theories, encompassing the whole range of
possibilities from the onset of a new ice age to global warming, were vigorously debated. By the late Sixties, more scientists were becoming convinced of
the greenhouse effect of carbon dioxide, one of the major industrial waste

---

1. The discovery was a major coup for the British Antarctic Survey, whose ozone
measurements were all undertaken manually in situ from the Antarctic by scientists
with frost-bitten fingers—I should know, I was one of them. At the same time
NASA were also monitoring the ozone concentration from satellites but, crucially,
they had a routine in their software that threw out data that was considered too low,
on the basis it must be instrumental error! Subsequently, the NASA scientists
argued that they had indeed spotted the depletion and had been preparing a paper
for publication in 1986 . . . bad losers, I say!

gases, although others argued that the increase in man-made aerosols would counterbalance this effect by cooling the atmosphere. Concerns about the melting of the ice caps in the Arctic and Antarctic regions, and the consequential increase in sea levels, were also raised at this time. The debate in the scientific community was such that the media began to notice, in particular as its newsworthiness was enhanced by a series of major droughts around the globe in the first half of the Seventies. The press fancied a new ice age, but the majority of scientists were not so sure. The factor that possibly tipped the balance towards the understanding that the greatest risk came from global warming was the realisation that deforestation would have a major impact on the climate: without the forests, the ability to limit atmospheric carbon dioxide was severely compromised.

So, at the close of the Seventies, the majority of scientists believed that human-driven global warming was a significant threat. The next problem—to convince the politicians to do something about it—would, in many ways, prove to be more difficult than the scientific calculations. Ronald Reagan's presidency of the United States brought with it a backlash against the environmental movement in the early Eighties, as powerful businesses successfully lobbied for no action. The international scientific community continued its research as best as it could and, by the time that the ozone hole was discovered, the evidence for human-influenced global warming was becoming overwhelming. The political turning point came in 1988, with a high profile conference organised by the Canadian government in Toronto called 'The Changing Atmosphere: Implications for Global Security'. British prime minister Margaret Thatcher's subsequent support for the scientific evidence and call for action were crucial in placing climate change on the political agenda, a (possibly dubious) distinction it has maintained ever since.

Despite this higher profile, political action was slow to arrive. It was not until 1992 that a United Nations conference in Rio de Janeiro—the Earth Summit—produced a Framework Convention on Climate Change, and even then, the United States blocked calls for serious action. In the wake of further scientific and natural evidence for global warming, the Kyoto conference of 1997 drafted a protocol aimed at combating the threat. The United States again refused to support the protocol, partly because China was excluded from its provisions for being classed a developing country, despite being one of the world's greatest emitters of greenhouse gases. To this day, the United States has consistently failed to take significant action against global warming, bowing to pressure from oil lobbyists and shielding itself behind scientific dissenters. Its political inaction can have done little to encourage other nations, and a concerted global response to the threat has yet to materialise.

In the twenty-first century few scientific dissenters remain: there is now virtual scientific unanimity that humankind is causing global warming. What remains to be seen is exactly what magnitude and on what timescale the effects will be felt. Today, with our constant focus on climate change, almost everyone is concerned about the environment. Today, we criticise those countries whose environmental practices are not as fine as our own for destroying the environment. Yet, having stolen an early economic advantage through our own polluting industries in decades past, these criticisms will sound hollow to these emerging nations.

The world is a competitive place with an explosion in population growth: from less than three billion when the Fifties Child was born, United Nations median projections are that by 2050 nine billion people will share the planet. That is a mind-boggling increase within the lifetime of some Fifties Children! What chance for the environment then? I want space, food, water, warmth; and so do you. Can we deny the other eight billion, nine hundred and ninety nine million, nine hundred and ninety-nine thousand, nine hundred and ninety-eight the same desire? It may well be that we are currently living *the* golden days for the world's environment, at least until such a time as mankind's numbers on the planet reduce dramatically or—to borrow a phrase from science fiction—we learn to terraform our own planet.

✺

Barclay James Harvest's home, Oldham, may have been one of the great industrial centres of Britain, but it was the proximity and beauty of the surrounding countryside that wormed its way into our songwriters' minds and hearts. The value of nature's beauty in inspiring the human spirit and the consequent respect for the environment in general has, from the very first, been a constant feature of their songs, presaging the interest in that environmental movement which kicked off in mainstream society in the Seventies.

We have already mentioned in the previous chapter how frequently promotional photographs showed them regaling in the glory of the local countryside. As a further demonstration of the importance of nature and the environment to them—despite the fact that it may sound gauche if you're not an established fan of the band—is their logo, which throughout their entire career has been a butterfly. With one exception, all of their studio albums have included a butterfly as part of the album art. Designers worked with this emblem to create a variety of attractive motifs, for instance the stained glass windows of the debut album or the "winged woman" that appeared on album labels for a period in the Seventies. The importance of such details to fans can be gauged from the fact that there were mutterings when—for the *Everyone is Everybody Else* album—a butterfly design was omitted. This fan reaction underlies the importance of the image and of the lyrics of a band: there is an affinity by association with its *principles*, even when they are not explicitly or intentionally stated. These principles form an important factor in keeping the fans coming back for more, even in the face of occasional musical hiccups and, ultimately, they help the music itself endure.

The fact that the band's links with nature were present from their earliest days is reinforced in this extract from Roy Hollingworth's[2] humorous sleeve notes to 1971's *Barclay James Harvest and Other Short Stories* album:

> If you've ever travelled on a sleezy football special,[3] ankle deep in brown ale and Woodbines,[4] and through a peek-hole in the window, caught a glimpse of a field of Yorkshire sunshine—you'd be getting close to what Barclay James are all about. Not that the Barclays are Woody-chuffing boozers (although some may dispute that!)—they are the other, that field of warmth, that causes the eye to squint a little, makes the present atmosphere frost, stand still, fall away.
>
> . . .
>
> Barclays . . . create peaceful, lotus emotions. They are that field of sunshine, that slow, graceful movement. Laze down real low. Pump it through your ears. Let out the day, and slip in the Barclays. Hope you understand.

Hollingworth's lucid assessment would still "fit the mould" forty years later (although you would have been arrested for smoking on the train).

It is already clear, then, that Barclay James Harvest were at the vanguard of the fledgling environmental movement. Their canon is replete with songs about nature and the environment, and these songs appear constantly throughout their long career. The first such explicit example is 1969's 'Brother Thrush', with lyrics written by Lees. This is an extremely appropriate song, given the point just made about the explosion in population growth and the consequent, inevitable pressure on the environment. The song is a glorification of nature through the imagery of birds: the thrush, the gull and the lark are held in wonder for their flight and their song.[5] Lees effectively predicts man's demise, but is confident these birds, through their natural bond with nature, will endure after the cities have crumbled to dust. It is a strong environmental song which, musically, might be rooted in the Sixties yet its message—the power and beauty of nature compared with man's works—is so

2. At the time Hollingworth was a reporter with the *Melody Maker* music newspaper. He later released a record himself. He died in 2002, aged 52.
3. i.e. a train for football supporters travelling to a match.
4. For those too young to recall: a brand of cigarettes.
5. The verse which captures the flight of the gull seems almost prophetic to me, in pre-empting Richard Bach's *Jonathan Livingston Seagull* by some years. It is almost as if Bach heard the song and was then inspired to write his now famous book. Anyway, the fabled Jonathan appears again later in our social history.

simply delivered that it becomes timeless. In a sense, the song—the band's second record release, following 1968's 'Early Morning', also nature-friendly—set up Barclay James Harvest's sociological agenda, from which they would never deviate.

The focus on the imagery of birds within 'Brother Thrush's lyrics typifies the bond with nature and the environment that would drive their environmental "protest songs". Fans of the band would soon find this imagery filtering through in many more songs, from all three songwriters, even when the message was not explicitly environmental: 'Mocking Bird', 'Little Lapwing' and 'Jonathan' being just three examples. Taking these bird-imagery songs as a group, they reflect that perennial—and very British—fascination with birdlife that we mentioned earlier.

The year after 'Brother Thrush' was released as a single, the band's first album, the self-titled *Barclay James Harvest*, hit the record shops. This debut contained another environmental statement from Lees in the musically formidable closing number, 'Dark Now My Sky'. The song, which had been written a couple of years earlier and had already become a staple of the band's live set, was inspired by Rachel Carson's influential environmental movement classic *The Silent Spring* [1962], a book that is often credited with leading to the banning of DDT.[6] There is a stark musical and lyrical contrast with 'Brother Thrush' where 'Dark Now My Sky' is clearly sombre and lacks the environmental optimism of its companion song. Lees borrows a couple of phrases from Carson for his lyrics which, within their ambiguity, act as a lament on the loss of love as well on the destruction of nature.

The title of Wolstenholme's 'Happy Old World' is sarcastic and that humour pervades a little of its chorus. The two verses, however, are straightforward: the first tackles conflict and injustice in the world and the second deals with the environment. It is an intriguing song, sung in the first person, infused with an element of science fiction. The protagonist gives a clue that we have come from somewhere in space and been put on this planet—almost in a von Daniken-esque way—by someone with great power.[7] This "he" would be quite happy for us to stay here if only we could live peacefully and gracefully with each other, but our behaviour towards others and towards the

6. DDT—dichlorodiphenyltrichloroethane, a pesticide blamed by Carson for decimating fish and bird populations. She was not the first to identify its dangers but the eloquence of her argument inspired immense popular support, and this is why she is often ascribed the credit—or blame, depending on your perspective—for the banning of DDT. Carson died from cancer at the age of 56, a mere 20 months after her book was published.

7. As this is a Wolstenholme song, I am not contextualizing this greater power as God, despite the use of the word "Lord" once within the lyrics: the reasons for this will become evident further on in our social history.

environment is deplorable and likely to see us evicted off the planet. The protagonist is so distraught by humanity's greed, hate and wanton destruction that he falls into depression and becomes suicidal. Like 'Dark Now My Sky', 'Happy Old World' lacks optimism, perhaps because, unlike 'Brother Thrush', both these songs focus on man's impact rather than on natural beauty itself.

This pessimistic theme continues as the band's earliest run of songs with an environmental theme comes to an end with Holroyd's 'Crazy City', a song which firmly establishes the band as "Country Mice". Within it, Holroyd decries the dehumanizing effect that cities have on people. His solution is simple: he is leaving, returning to the countryside where he can feel a synergy between nature's rhythms and that of the human soul.[8]

Just as being environmentalist was becoming fashionable, this kind of explicit protest on the environment disappeared from their songs for nearly twenty years: it would be 1992 before Barclay James Harvest again protested against environmental malpractice. This is not to say that the intervening years were without comment on nature and the environment. Far from it. One can sense that Holroyd, Wolstenholme and Lees all absorbed spiritual energy from nature as they write about the impact of its glory, wonder and beauty in 'Jonathan', 'A Prospect of Whitby' and 'Paraiso dos Cavalos'. A seagull in flight at one with the winds, storm waves crashing on the shore, horse riding through the surf, all these demonstrate the band's close bond with the natural world.

Cementing this idea that the power of nature and the environment is able to invigorate one's spiritual force is Lees' 'Knoydart'. Lees may have left explicit environmental campaigning off his songwriting agenda after 'Dark Now My Sky', not because he fell out of love with the countryside, but because other worthy topics caught his attention. 'Knoydart' [1993], inspired by a trip to the Scottish highlands, is another straightforward celebration of the majestic beauty of nature and the environment. Listening to the song, it is easy to see how the trip recharges the battery pack of Lees' spirit: the stiff breeze has the effect of cleansing his mind of all its worries and the wildlife and scenery then make him feel as if he has arrived in paradise. Mind you, he was lucky during his visit with glorious blue painting the skies—not all visitors

8. 'Crazy City' is yet another song written in the first person. One cannot consider each such song as autobiographical or even semi-autobiographical—indeed, there are plenty of first-person songs in the band's canon that are clearly neither of these—but when there is weight of contextualisation, as there is for each of the band's songwriters on the topic of nature and the environment, one can at least consider that the song's protagonist's views match those of the songwriter at the time.

to the west coast of Scotland can boast that. The power of 'Knoydart' at explaining the healing force of nature is further enhanced by an understanding of the psychological problems that Lees experienced during his life, which will be covered in detail in later chapters.

Saying that "protest on the environment disappeared . . . for nearly twenty years" may have been semantically accurate but it is perhaps misleading, as two of our three songwriters did protest about abuses against animals during that period. The *Gone to Earth* [1977] album included Holroyd's ethereal 'Spirit on the Water', which criticises the shallowness of those prepared to wear animal fur. The year before the song's release the environmental group Greenpeace had begun their much-publicised campaign against the culling of harp seals, in particular by Canada. Holroyd would undoubtedly have been aware of the campaign and the song may even have been inspired by Greenpeace's action. On the basis of 'Spirit on the Water', he supported their aims:

A sacrifice for the coat he's wearing;
a paradise for the lady who dares
colour him red upon the snow.
We carry the burden upon our shoulder,
we carry their lives in the palm of our hand.
Don't you care about the state you're in
or don't you understand?

The "he" in the first line is the harp seal, and he is sacrificing his life for the woman who has the audacity to wear his pelt as a coat: the responsibility for spilling the seal's blood on the snow rests with her. The "burden [on the] shoulder" is a scarf or wrap made from fur; the "lives in the palm of our hand" refers to gloves—Holroyd is incredulous that our vanity leads us to kill these animals. The questioning style within this excerpt is typical of Holroyd's protest songs: he is perplexed by the fact that others cannot plainly see, or are prepared to turn away and ignore, the injustices that we perpetrate against nature and against each other. Other examples of this songwriting style can be found in 'Who Do We Think We Are?', which we will discuss in a moment, as well as in 'Victims of Circumstance' and 'Copii Romania', which appear in later chapters.

Wolstenholme's 'The Will to Fly' has a lyrical depth which requires some interpretation but the song's subtitle 'Sport ohne Mord', translating as "sport without murder", along with Wolstenholme's own website notes, make clear that the song is also anti-hunting. The shooting of birds is used as the anti-hunting example in lines such as "The birds die screaming, 'Once you were our friend!'; / how come there's pleasure found in so much pain? . . . / Warm bodies lying on the bloody ground; / they'll shoot you up, but they'll never shoot you down", because this lends itself best to the metaphors that Wolstenholme wants to use to develop his deeper message, which appears to be about the "sportsmen" themselves: "It seems they've lost the will to fly; / I wonder if they ever try. / They think they've reached the very top; / there are no mountains left to climb."

The suggestion here is that the "sportsmen" lack the will, or the ambition, or drive, or imagination even to search out more worthy pleasure pursuits; ones that will not cause suffering to other living creatures. There is possibly more depth to the lyrics than that even: when you put the line "they'll shoot you up, but they'll never shoot you down" from the previous example—which was used to illustrate the imagery relating to birds, and in that example it means that "sportsmen" will not fire at a bird on the ground, but only when it is in flight—back in the context of its order in the lyric, then it picks up ambiguity: "They took your theme of flight and made it ring; / now there's another song they choose to sing. / Warm bodies lying on the bloody ground: / they'll shoot you up, but they'll never shoot you down."

Whilst these words might still be interpretable directly as relating to a bird-shoot, they are untypically clumsy for Wolstenholme if that is the only meaning to the song. However, "shoot you up" is also interpretable in terms of recreational drug use, and if one follows this clue then other, still not absolutely clear, meanings open up elsewhere in the song relating to the sportsmen.

'The Will to Fly' was written nearly ten years before its eventual release on disc, and by that time Holroyd had already returned to the theme of anti-hunting with 1990's 'Shadows on the Sky'. The lyrics and music evoke the magical beauty of Africa's endless plains: the song is filled with compassion for the plight of the animals and disdain for the hunters who pursue their prey in the lust for profit. Then, as now, illegal poaching was a major threat to the populations of elephant and rhino.

This three-song anti-hunting suite is interesting from a societal aspect because support for hunting and blood sports in Britain is greatest amongst the countryside community and, given that we have established these song-writers as Country Mice, one might have expected a different stance. However, what will become clearer as we progress through this book is that Barclay James Harvest's love of nature and the environment helped to foster an extremely strong spiritual ethos and, in this particular case, this manifests itself in compassion for living things. In these three songs one can sense that both Holroyd and Wolstenholme feel the unnecessary suffering caused to the animals simply for motivations driven by pure profit or fun, and it is that frivolous aspect which is anathema to them.

Holroyd's 'Spirit on the Water' had resonances with Greenpeace's harp seal campaign and Wolstenholme was another who publicly supported such environmental action groups, with his 'Quiet Islands' being dedicated to Friends of the Earth in the album sleeve-notes for *Mæstoso*. Again, the song requires some interpretation but appears to go even further down the absolute environmentalist path than Holroyd:

> Bird sounds on quiet islands,
> warning of our intrusion.
> Dream on, you quiet islands,
> morning will find you woken,
> broken where you lie.
> "Disturb us if you dare;
> we will not sleep again."

Wolstenholme seems to be alluding to natural wildlife habitats being disturbed by people—tourists, for want of a better word—coming to observe nature and the animals. Many of these habitats are extremely sensitive and the implication is that man's intrusion will endanger the animals' continued existence.

Due to Wolstenholme's break-up with the band in 1979, he did not participate—although he would surely have approved—with Barclay James Harvest in a project initiated by the Bolland brothers. Working from the Netherlands, Rob and Ferdi Bolland invited the band to participate in their *Darwin: The Evolution* album, which was released in 1991 and featured performances by a number of invited artists, including famous contemporaries of our songwriters, such as Ian Gillan and Colin Blunstone. Barclay James Harvest performed one song written by the brothers, 'Stand Up'. The following year, 'Stand Up' was released as a single under the band's own name. The song is unique in their history as being the only track released by them not to have been written by a member of the band, but its inclusion as a sociological song under the band's "brand" in this social history is entirely justified on the basis of its strong environmentalist message, which resonates with much of their own writing.

Listening to the song, it becomes immediately clear why they agreed to participate in the project: the lyrics are forthright in their denunciation of man's destruction of nature and the environment, recognise that the world is now in a situation of crisis and call for everyone to stand up and take action to save the planet. It is a clarion call for the environment that fits that Barclay James Harvest brand perfectly.

Perhaps the band had stopped writing such protest songs of their own by the mid-Seventies because they felt that the burgeoning environmentalist movement would bring about a change for the better. By the start of the Nineties, however, it was clear that this was not going to happen, as mankind's greed was too great, hence the return to protest with 'Stand Up'. Holroyd himself was sufficiently concerned to follow that song in 1993 with his own forthright composition 'Who Do We Think We Are?', for the *Caught in the Light* album.

Through its directness, 'Who Do We Think We Are?' becomes the most powerful lyrical attack on man's disregard for the environment in the Barclay James Harvest canon—and almost certainly the most powerful condemnation amongst their contemporaneous songwriters.[9] Holroyd effectively argues that we have lost our humanity by losing touch with our place in the scheme of the universe, that we abuse what power we have, spend our time fighting wars, imperilling innocent children through our unthinking actions and, all the while, we are destroying the planet for future generations. Who do we think we are? Do we think we are so important that we can destroy this wonderful gift that nature has given us? Despite the stylistic questioning that we mentioned earlier, there is no doubt where Holroyd's views stand on the matter. It is also reasonable to assume, contextualizing from Lees' and Wolstenholme's career songs on this theme, that these views are common to all of Barclay James Harvest's songwriters.

The final song—so far—with an environmental comment from these three visionaries is 'Festival!'. Despite this comprising essentially a single comment within a song about revisiting one's youth by attending an outdoor summer festival in the rain and the mud, it is still an illuminating one in two important respects. The first is that the comment refers to a concern about the rise in sea levels, one of the dire consequences of global warming, demonstrating that, after more than thirty years of writing (campaigning?) about man's destruction of the environment, these songwriters were now conceding that the worst had come to pass. Secondly, the song's protagonist says that it is just a fleeting concern: the societal comment here is that, yes, people are concerned about global warming, but they are just too busy leading their lives to worry and take action about something which may happen in a few years or decades from now. It is a one-liner with a wealth of meaning, encompassing in a microcosm the frustration of these songwriters over the years with man's disrespect for nature and the environment.

Taken together, these career-spanning songs form an impressive and unique

9. It is a pity that, because of concerns over the running time of *Caught in the Light*, the first verse was omitted from the recorded version, although the lyrics were printed within the album's booklet.

statement on the theme of nature and the environment and demonstrate all three songwriters' deep-rooted affinity for all things in the natural world. They took up the cause of nature and environmental protection before it became trendy and never abandoned it, writing some of their least ambiguous protest songs in the process. A large portion of society would join the cause in the mid-Seventies and beyond. Postulated climate change and its associated issues is now an ever present concern of governments and millions of people but the pressures that led Holroyd to write 'Who Do We Think We Are?' continue to exist. Greed, egotism, population growth and other factors continue to put pressure on nature and the environment. Despite the successes of the environmental campaign groups many setbacks repeatedly occur: for example, the banning of the culling of the "whitecoat" young harp seals was definitely a success, but the culling of older harp seals continues and the numbers being killed in the present day are as high as 300,000 a year. That's *not* a typing error.

And the year of a worldwide population of nine billion approaches inexorably . . .

It is interesting to note that there were not many environmental protest songs—or even more general songs about nature and the environment—written by contemporaneous artists to the extent that the selection presented here more or less chose itself. One of the earliest to appear was 'Messin' ', written by Mike Hugg for Manfred Mann's Earth Band's 1973 album, for which it became the title track. As its title implies, the song recognises the mess that we are making of the planet with pollution, a fact we blithely ignore.

Often the songs that do exist are written by songwriters who, like Barclay James Harvest's, possessed a strong spiritual side to their nature, and often found communing with the environment a means of strengthening that spirit. Jon Anderson was one such artist and his 'Don't Kill the Whale',[10] for Yes's 1978 album *Tormato*, is a song which amply demonstrates the influence of the environmental groups' campaigns during the Seventies—Greenpeace's campaign against whale hunting had begun in 1975. Despite initial successes, nations such as Japan and Norway have continued systematically hunting whales, and have even increased their quotas in recent years. That this can happen in the modern age is testament to the degree of danger that nature and the environment face against the onslaught of man.

Another artist to find a spiritual link with nature is Van Morrison: as an

---

10. This is jointly credited to Anderson and Yes's bass player Chris Squire [born London, 1948] but the lyrics have Anderson's stylistic hallmark. 'Don't Kill the Whale' was also released as a single and was a minor Top 40 hit in the UK.

example, his *Common One* [1980] album is replete with spirituality. One finds, however, that the scope of Morrison's writing on the theme of nature and the environment is narrower overall than that of any of Barclay James Harvest's individual songwriters. For instance, despite often getting the sense from his songwriting that he feels at one with nature, he was not one for extolling the beauty of animal life or protesting about its wanton killing. Or, for that matter, voicing his distaste—did it in fact upset him?—for man's treatment of his fellow man, or for filling his songs with compassion. Personally, I find these omissions make Morrison's songwriting spiritually inconsistent and therefore, despite its musical qualities, less rewarding for regular listening than Barclay James Harvest's offerings.

There is no doubt—Barclay James Harvest were the champions of nature and the environment. Is there anyone, in today's age, who doubts that they were right?

Societally, support for the environmental protest movement was high in the Seventies. In the Eighties, as the power of the media increased, the focus shifted to helping the victims of famine and, subsequently, children's charities became the focus of much media attention. Nature and environment protest groups continue to exist and win support from some sections of society but their struggle is a tough one against the more general human characteristics—egoism, greed—identified by our songwriters, as well as against an expanding worldwide population. More and more species have become extinct or are coming under dire threat. Fur items are still available for sale in UK shops—the worldwide trade in furs was worth over £8 billion in 2010. The illegal ivory trade is flourishing: in 2011 25,000 elephants were butchered to satisfy man's lust for ornately carved objects. More and more rainforest is destroyed even as you read. More houses, more roads, more and cheaper airplane flights. More, bigger, better. Better, bigger, more. More, more, more.

Enjoy nature and the environment whilst you can, these might well be the last of its halcyon days.

John Lees

Preface to Barclay James Harvest's Conflict Songs

Children of the Fifties faced a very different legacy to those of today. The Second World War had followed not long after the calamitous First: these horrific conflicts and the ensuing Cold War between the Western Allies and the Soviet Union left a huge imprint on their lives. There was rationing on a national scale, not lifted until 1954. There was the rebuilding of scarred, bombed-out cities. There was the rebuilding of an industry that had been turned over to armaments during the war years. There was the rebuilding of an economy. Post-war, this meant luring vast numbers of Commonwealth citizens, as well as those of other nationalities, to the UK to bolster the workforce. The demographic face of Britain would be changed forever. All of this was happening in the shadow of a nuclear weapons race, with its vivid threat of MAD, or Mutually Assured Destruction, the tactic which dictated that the best way of avoiding a nuclear attack by the enemy was to have the capability to annihilate him in return.

Barclay James Harvest's songwriters may not have lived through the terror of frontline action or the threat of civilian bombardment themselves, as their own parents had done, but this modern threat of nuclear attack, perpetrated by an unseen and distant enemy, was a real and frightening one. On a lesser but still frightening scale was the fact that attacks on civilians were not just a vapid threat. Indeed, they became a constant source of terror, with Irish Republicans undertaking a war of attrition against Britain.

As time passed after the Second World War, these and other traumas began to invade ordinary people's lives as never before: first with the onset of newsreel films, and then by the increasing, pervasive invasion of television during the Fifties and beyond. Amongst the most shocking images to invade the comfort of people's daily lives were those from the conflict in Vietnam, where the United States was attempting to staunch the advance of its communist foe.

The threat of a nuclear holocaust may have lessened following the break-up of the Soviet Union in 1991, but anyone thinking world peace was returning was to be in for a nasty surprise when small conflicts erupted across the former Soviet bloc as ethnic groups sought to create new nations and unleashed great waves of sectarian hatred towards each other.

Conflict was everywhere, its images raw with menace, affecting the lives even of those not directly involved. This was a major influence on the Fifties Child, and so it is not surprising that it was a fertile one for Barclay James Harvest's songwriters, with conflict-related songs appearing throughout their careers.

Some of these conflict songs deal with a war theme but, interestingly, they are not generally true "anti-war" or "protest" songs, but deal often more with a deep concern for soldiers who are seen as victims of abusers of power, as well as for more obviously innocent bystanders of the conflicts such as children. Hence, even in Lees' 'For No One', which has the very explicit plea "please lay down your pistols and your rifles", the actual focus is on the individual, as we shall see in due course. There is almost a temptation to treat these songs solely under the subject heading of "compassion" (which is covered in the chapter on Spirituality) but, insofar as the relevant detail goes, they are also dealt with as conflict songs.

It is worth emphasising that this songwriting approach of Barclay James Harvest's is different to that of a true anti-war song. For example, Buffy Saint-Marie's 'Universal Soldier' [1964] pins the blame firmly on the soldier: "He's a Catholic, a Hindu, an atheist, a Jain / a Buddhist, and a Baptist and a Jew / and he knows he shouldn't kill and he knows he always will kill /. . . and without him all this killing can't go on / He's the universal soldier and he really is to blame." True, Saint-Marie tempers this by admitting that we—you and I—give the orders, but it is still a long way from Barclay James Harvest's usual treatment of soldiers as victims themselves.

This distinction makes Barclay James Harvest's songs no less powerful, since what they do is herald a movement in society, evident as the decades passed on from the Fifties, which manifests itself in, for instance, increased concern for the welfare of soldiers in battle.

Barclay James Harvest's songs about conflict are dealt with in the following two parts of this book: the first deals exclusively with the Cold War, and the subsequent one deals with other conflicts.

Part 2
Cold War

3

The Soviet Threat

The Cold War conflict between the Soviet Union and the Western Allies lasted from the end of the Second World War until the demise of the Soviet Union in 1991.[1] Its consequences loomed large in the minds of many Fifties Children.

One of the ironies of the Second World War was the fate of Poland. Britain had entered into war with Germany because of the invasion of Poland, ostensibly to liberate it. When it came, Poland's "liberation" was by Soviet forces in 1944, as they surged westward to wreak their revenge on the retreating German armies. For many Poles, this was a worse fate: Marshal Edward Rydz-Smigly, the commander-in-chief of the Polish armed forces, had expressed the sentiment of his people as early as 1939, thus: "With the Germans we run the risk of losing our liberty. With the Russians we will lose our soul."

The Soviet Union's alliance with the Western Allies during the Second World War had been an uneasy one. In fact, many analysts trace the beginning of the Cold War all the way back to the Bolshevik Revolution of 1917, which instituted the communist Soviet Union state. In reality, during the war, the Soviet Union was fighting a common foe, rather than being an ideological ally in the fight. This distinction was vital when the main combatants in the European war theatre against Germany—the United States, Britain and the Soviet Union—met in 1945 to discuss the future governance of the battleground.

It was the partition of Germany between the Allies that was the focus of these discussions but in the aftermath of the conflict it soon became apparent that other countries which had been liberated by the Soviets would remain

---

1. During the Second World War the term "Western Allies" referred principally to Britain and the United States, the countries that negotiated the state of post-war Europe with the Soviet leader, Stalin. Afterwards, it included countries such as France, West Germany and others allied to their cause.

under—at best—its strict supervision. This was bad news for Poland, the country that Britain had entered the War to liberate. The Soviets would exert their iron grip over Poland: there would be no liberation, no freedom. Many Polish combatants fighting for the Allied cause, spread throughout the world, decided not to return home. One of their major destinations became Britain; this was the first great wave of Polish "migration" to our shores.

The lands encompassing the Soviet Union had suffered badly from invasions throughout their history and Joseph Stalin, their wartime leader, was keen to protect the new nation from further encroachments by building a surrounding buffer zone of countries under its control, resulting in pressure to extend the Soviet empire. It was able to achieve the desired growth with comparative ease given that its armies had pushed westwards during the German retreat in the final part of the war in the European theatre. As well as Poland, other countries becoming Soviet states or falling significantly under their influence were Latvia, Estonia, Lithuania, parts of Finland, Romania, the eastern parts of Germany which it had overrun—which were to become East Germany in 1949— as well as Bulgaria, Hungary and Czechoslovakia.

Yugoslavia was to be a notable exception, with its powerful leader Josip Tito maintaining a non-aligned position, despite being communist. Ultimately this is a combination that saved Tito as other states that dared attempt some sort of liberation from the Soviets' grip fell foul of the Soviet leadership. As an example, in 1948, fearing the Czechoslovak government was attempting to steer away from communist doctrine, the Soviets staged a coup d'état. In fact Stalin's death in 1953 brought no reprieve to the Soviets' stranglehold on their satellite states: Hungary was invaded by the Soviet army in 1956 for straying politically and Czechoslovakia suffered an identical fate in 1968 for the same reason.

These Soviet invasions were, clearly, significant events that were widely reported by the media and became infamous in Britain and the West, reinforcing the popular view that the Soviet empire was "The Enemy" and a ruthless one at that. The Western Allies' view of the Soviets representing ruthless evil was given credence in 1956 by Soviet leader Nikita Khrushchev's astounding public revelations of the worst excesses of Stalin's ruthless rule, which had included dozens of assassinations of members of the ruling Central Committee of the Communist Party itself.

International tensions caused by actions such as these meant that for a Fifties Child, growing up in post-War Britain into his teenage years, Eastern Europe was a constant point of focus. The Cold War yielded many incidents that were covered by the media: amongst the most prominent were the Berlin Blockade (1948-49), the construction of the Berlin Wall (started in 1961), the Cuban Missile Crisis (1962) and the nuclear weapons race, which became a permanent fixture of the period. Some of these incidents—the Berlin Wall and the nuclear weapons threat—and their effect on Barclay James Harvest's music are dealt with in more detail in subsequent chapters, whereas this current chapter concerns itself primarily with the more general aspect of the Soviet threat.

As a conflict, the Cold War did not involve any direct fighting between the two superpowers of the Soviet Union and the United States, nor between the countries most closely aligned to them through the respective military alliances of the Warsaw Pact and the North Atlantic Treaty Organization (NATO).[2] What did happen, however, was that the superpowers became involved in proxy conflicts around the world, supporting one or other of the participants depending on how they perceived their political alignment. The Korean War (1950-53) was an example of this, as was the Vietnam War (1955-75).

These proxy wars were expensive. Some commentators attribute the eventual collapse of the Soviet Union in 1991 to economic difficulties exacerbated by its involvement in Afghanistan, which it had invaded in 1979 in order to support the existing communist government. It is another of the ironies of history that, during that conflict, the Western Allies supported the Afghan resistance whereas today, post the Soviet withdrawal and the subsequent implosion of its state and post the Twin Towers attacks in New York in 2001, it is we who are entrenched fighting in that vast country. As Lees says: will we ever learn?

Amongst the standard apparatus of any totalitarian state such as the Soviet Union is the secret police. For the Soviets, it was the KGB that kept the populace under the state's control. Amongst those dissidents that came to the attention of the Western media were Alexander Solzhenitsyn, a writer, and the nuclear physicist Andrei Sakharov. Extensive media coverage in the West of their persecution in the face of attempted free speech reinforced the image of the Soviet empire as a brutal bully.[3]

At this stage we should remember, crucially, that the Cold War was not being waged over the issues of freedom, democracy or even free speech. Far from it. Indeed, the Western Allies in the Cold War included European countries, very close to Britain, that practised totalitarianism. Both Spain and Portugal sported ruthless right-wing dictatorships, with all of the associated

2. Czechoslovakia was a member of the Warsaw Pact when invaded by the Soviet Union in 1968! This demonstrates the extent of the Soviet stranglehold!
3. Solzhenitsyn was deported from the Soviet Union in 1974 and lived in the West for 20 years, before returning to Moscow in 1994, after the fall of the Soviet empire. Sakharov spent many years under tight Soviet state surveillance. He died in Moscow in 1989.

trappings, including secret state police, well into the Seventies. Additionally, amongst the various alignments and proxy wars in which the Cold War adversaries engaged, there were some dubious choices on the Western side, such as the United States' backing during the Eighties, under President Reagan, of the Contra rebels in Nicaragua.

So, what *was* the Cold War really about then if not freedom or demoracy? Ideology? What ultimately is ideology about? Money, control, power? The lyrics from Lees' 'African'—"Far left, far right, centre / it's power they crave!"—provide a possible answer. Whatever the answer really is, freedom it isn't.

Ideologically, there were certainly many people in Britain who supported the Soviet philosophy. That much is clear from the very fact that many of the most high profile spies for the Soviets—Philby, Burgess, Blunt and Maclean—were Cambridge University-educated members of the upper class, working in the higher echelons of government. And, as you will surely know, ninety per cent of the iceberg lies under the water and so, extrapolating to the rest of society, one may infer that the Soviets will have had many more sympathizers in Britain.

Empathy for the Soviets would have arisen in a number of ways. Workers in hard-grafting, low-paid industries may have felt oppressed by the seeming injustices of our economic system and been lured by the idealistic view that workers were held in higher regard under the communist system. This factor led many people in Britain to believe that the left wing of the Labour Party as well as many trades unions were sympathetic to Soviet ideology. This much will have been obvious from the fact that even after the USSR's intervention in Czechoslovakia in 1968, the Communist Party of Great Britain retained some 30,000 members. In the early Seventies, the newspaper that it controlled, the *Morning Star*, could be seen hawked for sale along Britain's High Streets every Saturday morning.

Other echelons of society would have been lured in different ways. The example of George Blake, the MI6 agent who switched allegiance, becoming a double spy who provided a wealth of intelligence to the KGB, is illuminating. His experience whilst a captive of the enemy in North Korea was enough to convince him that a redressing of the balance was in order, as he himself explains in his autobiography, *No Other Way* [1990]:

> It was the relentless bombing of small Korean villages by enormous American flying fortresses. Women and children and old people, because the young men were in the army. We might have been victims ourselves. It made me feel ashamed of belonging to these overpowering, technically superior countries fighting against what seemed to me defenceless people. I felt I was on the wrong

side . . . that it would be better for humanity if the Communist system prevailed, that it would put an end to war.

Blake's treachery was eventually discovered. Tried in 1961, he was sentenced to 42 years in prison. He was helped to escape in 1966 by three former inmates whom he had befriended. He subsequently succeeded in making his way to the Soviet Union, where he has been feted by the authorities, before and after the fall of the Soviet empire.

Who knows? Perhaps treason such as this . . . reviled as it is by all nations—and, let's not forget, there were also Soviet citizens betraying their Empire by passing crucial information to the Western Allies . . . perhaps treason such as this played a crucial role in maintaining the balance of power in the world during the Cold War, ensuring that no one side felt confident enough to launch an attack on the other, and therefore was key in maintaining the "peace". Who knows? In the final analysis, the spies did what they did for what they believed was right, the same that you and I do every day. *To every action there is an equal and opposite reaction*: remember that? Maybe that's not just a law of physics.

In between the opposites just discussed—the manual workers and the spies—there will also have been many people who will have found their own rationales for being attracted to the communist ideology. Notwithstanding, the majority view of Fifties Children in Britain will have been that portrayed by the bulk of the media: that the Soviet Union practised a vile form of government, preyed upon its people and those of neighbouring states, and it was the enemy of Britain. It was for these people, then, that the Soviet Threat was pertinent. Their concern was to prevent communist sympathisers from garnering such a "critical mass" of support that the Soviet authorities would be encouraged to attempt infiltrating and subverting Britain's democratic government. That such a concern could have existed in the Seventies now seems almost incredible. Nevertheless, whilst not as accentuated as in the United States, it was a real concern for many people in Britain.

This was the popular view that was reflected through the music of Barclay James Harvest via two Lees songs: 'May Day' and 'Rebel Woman'. Neither song explicitly refers to the Soviet Union, and 'Rebel Woman' in particular is lyrically opaque, but it does give sufficient clues to reveal that the source of Lees' frustration is the insidious damage that the Soviet Union's stance implicated.

The title of 'May Day' [1976] refers to the traditional celebration of the working classes' Labour Day, which remains a public holiday in many countries. It is a holiday with a political left-wing association, and in the Soviet

Union it would be celebrated with huge displays of military prowess as thousands of soldiers, tanks and military paraphernalia were paraded through Moscow's Red Square.

In common with many other of Lees' songs, 'May Day' takes the form of a story: it is a fictional account of what might happen should Britain suddenly fall to a communist revolution. The protagonist is a citizen who is overcome with confusion at the new norms, which are those that Lees perceives as applying in Soviet-controlled countries. 'May Day's totalitarian regime is very reminiscent of that in Orwell's 1984 [1949] where simple facts are distorted by the regime and anyone not subjecting to its will is dispatched to correction centres. The echoes are not just Orwellian, of course, but also of brutal state police practices, such as those of the KGB in dealing with Soviet dissidents. Lees' Orwellian hyperbole provides a superb storyline:

> But every time I think I'm right, they say I'm wrong:
> "This day is night and night is day—
> it's there in black and white."
> Night is light and dark is day—
> if I disagree they say I'm insane
> and the treatment will begin!
> If I say that the day is light
> they just point my eyes to the blinding night, saying
> "We can't set you free, if you always disagree,
> so the State is going to pay your doctor's fee."

As in 1984, there is no happy ending. The protagonist eventually succumbs to the will of the State after his "treatment": finally he knows what is right and wrong—it is simply what they tell you it is. Another equivalence with 1984 is that the government in the 'May Day' story is by "the Party"—the clue comes in the final verse when, after his cure, the protagonist witnesses another "confused" individual being helped by an official:

> I saw a man in the street today
> ask another man "Is it night or day?"
> He just stared in disbelief!
> He said: "Friend, it's your lucky day:
> I'm a Party man, won't you step this way?"

The Orwellian parallels are not surprising as both writers are attacking totalitarianism. The distortion of truth was seen as one of the prime consequences of such regimes; for Lees it is exemplified by the contrast "night is light and dark is day", whereas for Orwell it is "War is Peace. Freedom is Slavery." However, it would be misleading to overplay the similarities between these two pieces of fiction, which arise as a result of the topic. The 'May Day' title and Lees' interview statements from the time are ample evidence that his focus was specifically on the Soviet Union and the choice of words such as "Party" is entirely consistent with that.

The song has an intriguing musical ending that is relevant to its story. Lees had wondered how the populace of Britain might react to the Soviet-style totalitarian takeover, and concluded that people would attempt to keep their spirit alive by, amongst other things, singing traditional patriotic songs. 'May Day's latter section consists of a number of these songs performed in unison to a lofty overlayered keyboards backing. One can clearly hear snippets of 'Land of Hope and Glory', 'There'll Always Be an England' and 'It's a Long Way to Tipperary'. The first line of the socialist anthem 'The Red Flag'— "the people's flag is deepest red"—is also heard a couple of times, but is swamped out by the multitude of patriotic singing as the voices and keyboards reach a climax.

It is an interesting, powerful and emotive musical effect but one that requires the listener to immerse himself deeply in Lees' concerns as well as his story, so perhaps it may have been lost on many casual listeners because, at around three minutes in length compared to five for the story part of the song, it is not one that immediately and obviously enhances the song's overall guitar-driven effectiveness.

'Rebel Woman' is another guitar-driven song and features a catchy, gutsy riff from Lees, but it is more difficult to interpret lyrically than 'May Day'. Lees himself gave the necessary clue to its meaning in an interview to the fan club's magazine in 1985, revealing that the song had been inspired by the Soviets' shooting down of a Korean Air Lines Boeing 747 in 1983, killing the 269 passengers aboard, including a United States congressman. The plane had strayed into Soviet airspace and their drastic retaliatory action led to increased military spending by the Reagan administration, ratcheting up the pressure in the Cold War. With Lees' clue, the lyric "Another plane in the ocean / another wall in the sky" then anchors the song firmly into the Cold War. The "(an)other wall" is clearly a reference to the Berlin Wall, which has become one of the most famous symbols of the Cold War—and which we shall later discuss in the 'Berlin' chapter. Lees is implying that the Soviets are closing themselves in even more as time passes; closing themselves to the outside world behind impenetrable barriers.

It then becomes clear through contextualisation that the "rebel woman" is simply a depiction of Mother Russia—a national patriotic personification—in the period after the 1917 Bolshevik revolution.[4] The remainder of the song then opens up to interpretation. Lees' Eighties stance, with the Cold War still raging, is that this "rebel woman" has been scorned by the world and we are now all suffering the consequences of her reaction. Having suffered many invasions throughout history, culminating in the Nazi invasion during the Second World War years, she is now unleashing her fury upon the world, giving us the song's opening lyric, which echoes the popular saying, "they say that hell hath no fury". However, Lees' breadth of vision encompasses the realisation that it is both her own people, not just those of the Western Allies, who are suffering the consequences of her fury:

> This mother's scorn is a strange thing;
> she pays her children for love.
> She heeds the cry of their innocence:
> they pay her with their blood.

So, it is they, and us, who become the "victims of circumstance / convicted without a trial".[5] By contextualizing from other songs by Lees, one can say with confidence that it is the subjugation of individual freedoms within the Soviet system that makes it so unpalatable to him.

❦

The suppression of freedom is a theme that finds its way into the songs of other artists commenting on the Soviet system. Typical of the particular songwriter is Donovan's 'Love Will Find a Way'[6] where somehow he manages to weave indignation very similar to that expressed in 'Rebel Woman' into his typically sweet song about the power of love. He taunts both the superpowers of the day—the United States and the Soviet Union—by saying that for all their mighty deeds, they can never stop love finding its true course. The verse that deals with the United States relies on metaphorical interpretation but the one dealing with the Soviet Union is explicit. Donovan depicts it as suppressing, subduing and deceiving its people, as well as quashing individuality. But, if you are in love, then not even the Soviet might cannot stop you. That's Donovan. And why not? Love, truth, can they be hidden forever?

The Soviets' repression of their own people also came to the attention of

---

4. During the Cold War period—the years of the Soviet empire—"Mother Russia" became "Mother Motherland", to subsume within its patriotic embrace the people of countries beyond Russia itself.

5. The album's printed lyrics alternate between this and "convicted without a crime" but Lees never actually sings the alternative.

6. 'Love Will Find a Way', *Rising* [1990], a live album which featured some previously unreleased songs of which this was one. It was released under various guises and names in different countries—my copy is titled *Rising*.

Betty Thatcher, the main lyricist for the Annie Haslam incarnation of Renaissance during the Seventies. In 'Mother Russia' [*Turn of the Cards*, 1974] she evokes visions of the difficulties faced by Solzhenitsyn and other dissidents, as it paints the harsh and inhumanely slavish conditions of the labour camps which is where those who dared to question the Soviet State— "the day is light"—were sent for "treatment".

These songs demonstrate how evident the Soviet Threat was at the height of the Cold War. The Fifties Child was cognisant and wary of its menace yet nevertheless able to feel compassion and empathy for the people subjected to its repressive rule.

We therefore now move on to look at specific aspects of the societal impact of the Soviet Threat.

4

Spectre of a Nuclear Holocaust

The Second World War ended after the United States dropped two atomic fusion bombs on Japan. On August 6, 1945, Hiroshima was devastated by the first explosion and, three days later, Nagasaki suffered the same fate. More than 100,000 people died from the immediate effects of the explosions. Japan, fearing its apocalypse, surrendered. Photographs of the explosions and their effect were to become iconic for the Fifties Child generation.

The Americans had been only one of the combatants working furiously to develop atomic weapons during the course of the war: they just happened to reach that goal first, whereas Germany and Russia trailed behind in their research and development. Germany's research fell to its defeat in the war whereas Russia, as co-victors, continued theirs, culminating in the test detonation of an equivalent bomb in 1949.

Russian and American distrust went back many years. Long before their uneasy, forced alliance against Hitler's Germany the two powers were at odds over ideological issues following the Bolshevik revolution of 1917. There was no rapprochement between them post-Second World War, and the atomic weapons issue exacerbated the tension. Here now was a weapon with which, if one gained an advantage in development, one could eradicate the enemy completely. Hence, with the end of the Second World War, the race for nuclear weapons supremacy began.[1]

Explosive yield, number of warheads and tactical design acuity were key factors. Over the next four decades this gruesome race would present mankind

---

1. At some point in time the word nuclear became the norm for describing what started out as atomic weapons. I shall use this term from now on.

with such wonders as the hydrogen fission bomb, multiple independently-targeted re-entry vehicles (MIRVs), neutron bombs, mutually-assured destruction (MAD), the Strategic Defence Initiative ("Star Wars") and much more.

Advocates of MAD may well argue that it is precisely that tactic which averted a nuclear holocaust in the second half of the twentieth century. As a tactic, MAD relies on the assumption that neither of the superpowers (the United States and the Soviet Union, together with their respective allies) would launch a nuclear attack against the other because to do so would trigger an apocalyptic counter-attack. The tactic necessitates a couple of pre-conditions for each side: first, the ability to detect an incoming attack and, second, a sufficient number of warheads targeted at the enemy to obliterate them, even allowing for the possibility that many systems will have been destroyed by the enemy's pre-emptive attack, despite the early warning capability.

This in turn led to the requirement for overkill: you needed to have far more weapons than it would take, in a defenceless attack, to destroy the enemy. Add to that the fact that old weapons were not always decommissioned as more modern ones were developed, and you have a situation where both superpowers amassed sufficient nuclear weapons capability to destroy the planet many tens of times. Even now, in the twenty-first century, the United States and Russia have combined overkill capabilities of about fifty. Yes, that's right, today they have enough nuclear weapons to destroy the world fifty times over. Of course, this is to say nothing about the nuclear weapons held by other nations such as Britain, China, India, Pakistan . . .

One of the objectives of the nuclear arms race was to develop a sufficient advantage over the enemy to the extent that surviving a nuclear warhead exchange, at the same time as destroying them, would be feasible. As an example, Reagan's Strategic Defence Initiative (SDI) of 1982 was criticised by many, including allies, for its destabilising effect. Opponents of the initiative were concerned that having the ability to destroy the Soviet Union's nuclear missiles *before* they hit their targets would give the United States a winnable position. Hence, the Soviets might be pushed into a politically uncomfortable situation whereby it felt forced to launch a pre-emptive nuclear attack before the United States had deployed the system, even if it risked its own annihilation in the inevitable retaliatory strike.

Imagine the cost of this madness. Imagine what could have been done with such vast sums of money. And if such mind games over a planet critical issue seem like madness, that's probably because they were. It is a picture of the world that the Fifties Child lived in.

Or was this detente? Was this just the charade that was needed to keep the peace? Was it all an intricate game played by well meaning, skilful politicians and generals? After all, massive shows of strength have always been a part of diplomacy, all the way back to Henry VIII and the Field of the Cloth of Gold, and beyond. And, unlike the adversaries on that particular occasion, at least the United States and the Soviet Union did not end up fighting each other directly. Perhaps, then, the Fifties Child should really thank them all for being so clever in their machinations.

Perhaps . . . or . . . perhaps not . . .

These are not merely hypothetical considerations. The world came perilously close to experiencing the apocalyptic scenario of mutually assured destruction as a result of the Cuban missile crisis of 1962 when many people, my parents included, thought there would be a nuclear war.

Cuba is a close neighbour of the United States: it lies less than one hundred miles from the coast of Florida. A revolution in 1958 saw the overthrow of the incumbent dictator Fulgencio Batista by Fidel Castro. The Soviet leader Khrushchev wooed Castro, whereas the US president Eisenhower had shunned him, amidst fears that his politics were communist-leaning. Whether as a result of this American indifference or not, Cuba became allied to the Soviet regime.

American alarm grew at the close proximity of this Soviet ally. The now infamous "Bay of Pigs" incident—a failed United States-backed attempt by Cuban exiles to invade Cuba and overthrow Castro in 1961—heightened tensions. Another long-running attempt at sabotage and subversion, with the intention of concocting the overthrow of Castro—Operation Mongoose—was a failure, producing no tangible change in the Cuban government's power base. Then, in October 1962, a U2 spy plane took reconnaissance photographs showing evidence of Soviet nuclear missile sites being built in Cuba: crisis time!

Politically, if not strategically, it is inconceivable that the United States could have ignored such a provocative move on the part of the Soviets. Initially, the whole of the American presidential team favoured launching an early aerial attack against the nuclear missile sites being prepared in Cuba. However, President John F. Kennedy soon realised the high potential for the Soviets to respond to any such attack directly with nuclear weapons or to retaliate against other prized Western ally targets, such as West Berlin[2] or American nuclear missiles based in Turkey. Such retaliation would almost certainly have escalated into nuclear war, leading Kennedy to decide that a less aggressive initial response was required. Accordingly, on the evening of October 22, and against the advice of many of his advisors and military staff

---

2. "Berlin is the testicles of the West", said Khrushchev, "Every time I want to make the West scream, I squeeze on Berlin."

who favoured a more robust response, he announced in a television address to the nation that the United States was imposing a naval blockade of Cuba in international waters, and demanded that the Soviet leadership take immediate steps to remove the offending nuclear missile bases.

Kennedy's televised announcement served to bring the crisis to the attention of the public, who became convinced that nuclear war must inevitably follow. They—and the president himself—were concerned that if a ship was challenged and failed to stop, this could lead to an exchange of fire that would quickly escalate into a war between the superpowers. Unbeknownst to them all at the time was the fact that Khrushchev's immediate response to the imposition of the blockade had been to order an about-turn of his militarily-critical ships and submarines. Like Kennedy, Khrushchev did not want to escalate the conflict into a nuclear war.

Negotiations were conducted amidst some confusion, exacerbated by the fact that diplomatic traffic between the two leaders took many hours to reach its destination and that Khrushchev appeared to harden his negotiating position before the American administration had responded to an earlier proposal. Meanwhile, preparations for an all-out invasion of Cuba were urgently progressed in parallel with the softer diplomatic approach. At Kennedy's instigation, the Strategic Air Command's alert level was raised to DEFCON-2, one short of an actual nuclear exchange, meaning that thousands of nuclear weapons were made ready to fire at short notice. These comprised not only ground-based ballistic missiles but also many weapons continually in the air aboard bombers, ready to respond with a massive strike against the Soviet Union should the conflict escalate. The military continued to press to begin a preparatory, week-long aerial bombardment of Cuba, presaging an invasion, as soon as possible. Kennedy struggled mightily to postpone the start of this campaign by two days until October 30. His generals were keen to engage the enemy early, even if it implied an all-out nuclear war, as exemplified by the Chief of Staff of the Air Force General Curtis LeMay, whose conviction was that the Soviets could not totally wipe out the Americans' nuclear weapons and, therefore, in his opinion the United States would "win"—regardless of the fact that millions might die on either side.

Somewhat bizarrely, as if in a work of fiction, it seemed that negotiations brokered between a Soviet spy acting on his own initiative and an American ABC News reporter with high-level contacts in the government finally showed promise, allowing Khrushchev and Kennedy to reach a secret agreement to diffuse the military tension. The Soviets would remove the offensive weapons and installations in exchange for an American commitment to not invade Cuba. That much was made public but, crucially, there was a secret part to the deal—a sweetener for the Soviets—in that the Americans agreed to remove its own—Soviet-targeted—nuclear missiles from bases in Turkey.

That is the story according to the common lore associated with the Cuban Missile Crisis. However, new research published in 2008 demonstrated that it was unlikely that the spy-reporter-brokered route could have succeeded, because of the delay in the spy's message reaching Khrushchev after the Soviet ambassador in Washington had refused to send it via his own encrypted route, leaving the spy to take the more circuitous messaging route via his KGB superiors. Kennedy did indeed secretly concede the Turkish missiles—a public admission would have been politically impossible for him—but the key negotiation was almost certainly brokered between the president's brother Robert Kennedy, who was the Attorney General in the government administration and a close aide to his brother, and the Soviet ambassador. The fact that such an apocryphal story could have survived as the definitive account for nearly fifty years after the event is indicative of the confusion and secrecy surrounding the negotiations.

Khrushchev announced the Soviets' decision to withdraw the missile sites from Cuba on open air via a Moscow Radio announcement on the 28th, fearing that the hours-long delay of using a formal diplomatic route would mean that the conflict would already have escalated beyond his control by the time the conciliatory message was received in Washington. The two sides had come as close to a nuclear holocaust as it was possible to come without actually unleashing Armageddon. They had, in fact, come closer than the respective leaderships had wanted—it is naive to think that one can always control everything that happens in a tense situation such as this once forces on both sides are armed and deployed in the field, psyched and ready for battle. Events often take a course of their own.

Three particular incidents during the crisis posed serious threats to escalating the conflict into a nuclear exchange: they all occurred on October 27, the day that became known as "Black Saturday". The first of these was the shooting down of an American U2 spy plane over Cuba by a Soviet soldier operating beyond the permissive boundary that Khrushchev desired. The pilot was killed in the crash. The second incident involved another U2 plane. Both the Unites States and the Soviet Union had continued undertaking atmospheric nuclear weapons tests during the crisis and this particular U2 had been sent over the Arctic region to collect air samples for radioactive spectral analysis. The pilot was navigating by the stars but the auroral display confused him and he strayed deep into Soviet airspace. MiG jets which scrambled to intercept the U2 failed to down the American aircraft only because it was flying above their operational ceiling. The pilot eventually managed to regain some sense of direction and left Soviet airspace whilst gliding his aircraft—he had insufficient fuel to return to base. He was then spotted by American surveillance, approached by friendly aircraft and guided to make an emergency landing in Alaska. On hearing that a U2 had strayed into Soviet airspace, Kennedy's reaction was: "There's always some sonofabitch who doesn't get the word!"

The third example occurred when the American navy, who had been hunting down Soviet submarines in the proximity of Cuba during the crisis, located one. Signalling depth charges were dropped to indicate to the submarine that it should surface as part of the naval blockade's rules of engagement. Unfortunately, the Soviet authorities had not informed their submarine captains of these rules and the distressed captain of the B-59 ordered the arming of his nuclear missile with the intention of destroying the American ships that were assailing it. Fortunately for us all, other high-ranking officers onboard the submarine—the Chief of Staff of the Soviets' submarine flotilla happened to be on board—persuaded the captain not to fire his missile. The submarine surfaced and was kept under observation by the American navy for a couple of days before—with batteries fully recharged during the time on the surface—diving and making its escape. On returning to the Soviet Union, the captain of the B-59, together with the captains of two other vessels that were subsequently forced to surface by the Americans, was told by the deputy minister of defence: "It's a disgrace. You have shamed Russia!"

Tensions eased as the Soviets began to dismantle their bases. The United States removed its own missiles from Turkey the following year. One of the spin-offs of the crisis was the introduction in 1963 of the hot-line telephone between the Soviet and American heads of state—communications during the crisis itself had been subject to shambolic delays and confusion, clearly not a desirable situation when the stakes are so high.

Also of interest is the fact that both Kennedy and Khrushchev were criticised by powerful elements of their own governmental machines for their poor leadership. Kennedy was criticised by General LeMay for embarrassing the United States. "It's the greatest defeat in our history! We should invade today!" he told the president after the Soviets had conceded. For his part, Khrushchev was ousted from power in 1964, accused of megalomania, adventurism, damaging the international prestige of the Soviet Union and taking the world to the brink of a nuclear war.

Despite the criticisms of Kennedy from within his own administration, the consensus of people who value peace is that the world was lucky that he was in power at that particular moment in history and that he had the fortitude to resist the pressure for immediate and direct military action. Had he not been so resolute, it is unlikely that neither he nor Khrushchev would have been able to prevent their respective military machines escalating the conflict into a nuclear war. The public's recognition of this aspect of his presidency is certainly a contributing factor to the near-mythology that has built up around the legend of Kennedy. His charisma reached far and wide, before and after his assassination, affecting many British Fifties Children. This particular societal impact does not feature in Barclay James Harvest's songs but it does in the work of contemporaneous songwriters who appear elsewhere in this social history: for instance, both Peter Gabriel's 'Family Snapshot' [*Peter Gabriel (3)*, 1980] and Ray Davies's 'Give the People What They Want' [The Kinks' *Give the People What They Want*, 1982] take part of their inspiration from Kennedy's assassination in 1963. The fact that these Fifties Children were still affected by the legend of a foreign leader nearly twenty years after his untimely death is an eloquent testament to the power of the myth built up around him.

Whilst there were no further close-calls such as the Cuban missile crisis during the rest of the Cold War—or, at any rate, none that we know of—the two ideological enemies accelerated in their race for nuclear supremacy, continuing to amass many more sophisticated nuclear weapons in their bid to out-manoeuvre each other.

This gruesome competition, and not just the Cuban missile crisis itself, led to the threat of nuclear war being felt deeply by many people across many nations. In Britain, the effect was felt particularly sharply for two reasons. The first was that, given its close alliance to the United States, there were American nuclear warheads stationed at bases in Britain. Secondly, Britain had itself tested nuclear weapons as early as 1952 and had subsequently developed an "independent deterrent" capability, consisting of nuclear missiles deployed on Polaris submarines. Despite being under British control there can be little doubt that during the Cold War the Soviet Union would have seen these "independent" weapons as part of the American threat, as well as any other American weapons based in Britain—this small island was a prime target for a Soviet nuclear attack.

These facts were unpalatable to many people in Britain and a popular movement, the Campaign for Nuclear Disarmament (CND), began in early 1958. CND quickly organised mass demonstrations against Britain's possession of nuclear weapons: the first Aldermaston march taking place in April of the same year. The campaign gathered its support from a broad range of society, from Labour Party activists as well as from academics, journalists, writers, musicians and actors. One of its most famous faces in the early years of the campaign was the philosopher Bertrand Russell who, as early as 1955, had signed alongside other notables such as Albert Einstein a manifesto highlighting the worldwide dangers of nuclear weapons.

The profile of these nuclear weapons in society was high and, for a Fifties

Child, reaching the opinion-forming teenage years in the maelstrom of their wake, they were an inescapable and grim fact of life: the stuff that nightmares are made of. It is no surprise to find then that these fears of Armageddon were played out in a number of forms in the media and in popular culture. Newspapers carried detailed coverage. There was radio coverage of the factual events and, certainly by the time of the Cuban missile crisis in 1962, television news coverage. Pathé newsreels covered relevant events in their cinema showings. In 1965 the BBC made *The War Game*, a drama-documentary covering the after-effects of a nuclear attack on Britain. The programme was deemed too horrific for general transmission at the time and was not shown in its entirety on television until 1985, although public screenings were arranged by the likes of CND to bolster membership throughout the intervening period: I saw it myself whilst at university in the Seventies.

In popular culture, the concerns expressed themselves through books, film and music. Amongst the most notable examples of these are *On the Beach*, Nevil Shute's 1957 book which was made into a successful film two years later with a star-studded cast featuring Gregory Peck, Ava Gardner and Fred Astaire, and Walter M. Miller's science-fiction classic *A Canticle for Leibowitz*, first published in 1960.

It is interesting that of Barclay James Harvest's three nuclear weapons-influenced songs, Lees' two are written as fictional stories, reflecting his own love of science fiction. In these two songs, it is almost as if popular culture is reflecting itself, rather than the nuclear horror. Holroyd's song is more factual, more politically direct.

Both of Lees' songs must have been originally written around the same time. The first to be released was 'After the Day' [1971], and this was followed by 'Death of a City' ten years later. Whilst sections were rewritten for the 1981 release, 'Death of a City's demo goes back to 1968, and it was on the live set list at the time.

Lyrically, whilst none of these three songs is explicit—not one uses the word "nuclear", nor are there references to "mushroom clouds" as in some other artists' songs relating to this topic—it is clear that they relate to concerns over nuclear war.

'After the Day' is perhaps the most musically evocative of the trio. On its first appearance on the *Barclay James Harvest and Other Short Stories* album it segues seamlessly from Wolstenholme's pastoral-symphonic 'The Poet', a brooding composition, and its slow musical crescendo builds up to a final cataclysmic explosion, giving the tale even more impact. That final explosion of sound is actually one of the clues that the apocalypse has been nuclear; the other lies in the lyrics:

The eyes of night march slowly by;
the last grain falls,
the kneeling man just sighs.

"The last grain falls", referring to radioactive fallout, is that second clue. The suggestion within the remainder of the lyrics is that the "kneeling man" has survived because he has been protected from the effects of the blast by a massive wall. This wall has many stained glass windows and, amongst the rubble of the nuclear devastation, a cross remains standing. The man's posture, as well as the description of his surroundings suggests that he is sheltering amidst the ruins of a church or a cathedral.

This depiction evokes the isolated monastery existence of the nuclear war survivors in the first part of *A Canticle for Leibowitz*. Lees' enjoyment of books often finds its way into his songwriting—we have already seen parallels between his 'May Day' and Orwell's *1984* in the previous chapter, and we shall be coming across more such comparisons in future chapters. Neither 'May Day' nor 'After the Day' retells the story of the book and it is possible that neither influenced Lees. However, what one discovers as one becomes more absorbed in his songwriting is that, even in those songs that are clearly known to be influenced by specific works, Lees always alters the story or its perspective, to the extent that the result is an entirely new, original piece of fiction.[3] 'After the Day' has the feel of a preface to *A Canticle for Leibowitz* if, indeed, there is more than pure coincidence linking the two fictions.

'Death of a City's story is told in the first person and 1968's rewritten lyrics for the 1981 release bring to mind the effects of the more modern neutron bomb, a weapon designed to kill humans but leave buildings relatively unscathed—Soviet leader Leonid Brezhnev dubbed it a "capitalist weapon". Within the lyrics, Lees again accentuates the description of the destruction, and he even refers briefly back to 'After the Day'. The song's descriptions of nuclear fallout are chilling, evoking memories of the unnerving photographs from the Hiroshima and Nagasaki destruction:

Time is like dust and the dust is like snow
as it covers the ruins of the life that you know.
Trees once green now turned to stone;
objects that look like ghosts . . .

The protagonist in the story is near death, suffering from the effects of radia-

3. Or music, where the originating influence is a song, rather than a book or film.

tion; his sight is fading, his mind confused; he knows he will soon be joining his friends in the next life.

Notwithstanding the fact that both Lees' contributions are written as fiction, they nevertheless reflect the high societal impact of the threat of nuclear warfare. It is important to note that they are both non-judgemental: Lees is certainly not condemnatory; rather, his standpoint on this topic is fatalistic, which makes the fictional approach extremely suitable. Indeed, considering Lees' canon in context, there are songs in which he voices an opinion that might be deemed political—'The Great 1974 Mining Disaster', 'May Day', 'The Closed Shop'—when it is not actually left-wing, which in Britain is the political faction most often associated as being against nuclear deterrents.[4] Despite writing many songs relating to the conflict topic, a close examination reveals that Lees is never explicitly judgemental with regard to the specific issue—his concern invariably centres on the innocent victims of the conflict, individual responsibility and the abuse of power.

Holroyd's contribution to this topic dates from 1984 and is completely different in its approach. 'Victims of Circumstance', the song which gave its name to the album, is direct in its complaint and is, in effect, a protest song, possibly the only one of Barclay James Harvest's conflict songs of which this can be said. Holroyd wrote the song during the recording of the album itself, having taken inspiration from Lees' "victims of circumstance" lyric in the demoed version of 'Rebel Woman'.

In the late Seventies and at the beginning of the Eighties there were a number of developments in the nuclear weapons race that caused significant debate in Britain, as well as elsewhere. The first of these was the American intent to deploy neutron bombs across bases in Europe. Protests led to President Carter abandoning these plans in 1978 but Reagan restarted development work on the system in 1981. Also in 1981, the proposed deployment of American cruise missiles to their bases on British soil led to significant opposition, spawning the Greenham Common peace movement. Then, in 1982, Britain reached an agreement with America to purchase nuclear-warhead equipped Trident missiles for deployment on Vanguard submarines, as a replacement for Britain's ageing Polaris fleet. There was a strong body of opinion against this move. Finally, in 1983, Reagan announced the Strategic Defence Initiative, aka Star Wars, which was, as we have already mentioned,

4. It might be more accurate to say that the three songs just referenced deal with the theme of individual freedom but, nevertheless, they stray into areas that can be deemed political. Lees himself has said, "I'm not really political, I've got a social conscience", and we have already seen that in his song 'African' he sings "far left, far right, centre / it's power they crave!"

an attempt to obtain a strategic superiority over the Soviets by nullifying their ability to strike at American soil.

These various nuclear initiatives contribute to the angst in 'Victims of Circumstance', much of which is written in Holroyd's questioning style. Holroyd is angry that he has read about these major decisions—i.e. acquiring new weapons systems—in the newspapers and feels that there should have been a referendum on the issue. By not informing the people beforehand, by ignoring their views, by deploying the weapons without consultation and by making us a direct target in any confrontation that might occur, the government has made its people "victims of circumstance". The Trident decision is referred to directly—although Holroyd uses the word "ships" rather than "submarines"—whereas it is left to one's own interpretation as to which of the other three issues, or indeed all of them, he rails against in a sarcastic tone.[5]

The song is despairing of politicians who fail to seek out or act on the wishes of the people. This means that 'Victims of Circumstance' has two principal themes—victims and abuse of power—both of which re-occur throughout Barclay James Harvest's songwriting. And, as if in answer to the debate that we were having earlier in the chapter as to whether the nuclear weapons escalation was madness or brilliant detente, Holroyd is in no doubt : he thinks it is insane. This therefore is a powerful song from Holroyd who, by this stage in his life, like many of his contemporaries, having seen violence and conflict in a myriad of forms, had developed a certain world-weary scepticism of those in government.

'Victims of Circumstance' is unique in the Barclay James Harvest canon, in that it is the only one of their sociological songs to have reached No. 1, going to the top of the singles charts in France.

🦋

Reflective of the wider impact on society of these horrendous weapons is the fact that there are very many songs from which to choose a few to highlight here.

We shall start with Black Sabbath's 'Electric Funeral', from their *Paranoid* album [1970]. Black Sabbath's songs are all credited to the band as a whole, but it is known that bass player Geezer Butler wrote most of the lyrics from this period.[6] On 'Electric Funeral' they are dark and brooding, with an easy rhyme

---

5. "Submarines" doesn't fit in the song's rhythm and, in any case, Holroyd may not have wanted to be too explicit; it's not his usual songwriting style.

6. Geezer Butler: born Birmingham, 1949. All of the other band members are contemporaneous with Barclay James Harvest's songwriters. The producer of *Paranoid*, Rodger Bain, later did an excellent production job on Barclay James Harvest's 1974 album *Everyone is Everybody Else*, giving it a cohesive sonic quality that has lasted well down the years: it remains a firm fan favourite.

somehow adding to the feeling of despair caused by the lyrics' explicit description of the ghastly effects of the nuclear strike. This is a far more literal approach than Lees' and, as in his own writing, a twist of science fiction also creeps into Butler's 'Electric Funeral'. The closing verses reveal that an all-powerful consciousness is watching over the earth, takes control at the sight of our peril and condemns all evil people to burn in hell forever. This consciousness is electric, hence its mass execution of the evildoers gives the song its title.

Ian Anderson's 'Protect and Survive' for Jethro Tull's *A* album [1980] was inspired by the government pamphlet of the same name, which had also been published in 1980.[7] This was an official document advising people how to shelter from a nuclear attack. It was subsequently derided by E. P. Thompson, an eminent historian and peace campaigner, in his parody *Protest and Survive*, which enabled the CND to attract new membership. Anderson is a master in the use of satire and the government's leaflet comes in for a hefty dose, musically and lyrically. The music's lilt and the lyrics' jokey sarcasm heap scorn on the government's patronising advice which, unfortunately, Anderson does not receive because the postman has been splattered to the wall by the nuclear blast. The dustmen and the milkman suffer similar grisly fates, as do the rest of us, leaving the apparatchiks, ensconced deep underground, waiting to reclaim a devastated wasteland.

The inspiration for Donovan's 'Neutron' [*Neutronica*, 1980] is also clear from its title. This straightforward ditty lacks the story-telling aspect of Lees' 'Death of a City' but has a certain appeal nevertheless: "I was born in the rubble of World War Two, / played ball where the tall buildings once grew, / But today there's a way to make war pay: / A new toy from the boys in the USA. / Neutron, you're a real estate bomb! / The property stays but the people are gone!"

The bitter humour of these last two songs demonstrates how many Fifties Children, in a world with the capacity to destroy itself with nuclear weapons many times over, were tiring of governments continually spending on yet more weapons whilst at the same time handing out puerile advice to their populations

It is clear then, through all of these lyrics, just how deep the nuclear threat gouged its mental scar on the Fifties Child. Irrespective as to exactly how the fear was played out—and later in our social history we shall come across

7. *Protect and Survive*'s advice was to "use the cellar or basement if there is one", otherwise to construct a shelter within one's own home. Concurrently, the public's concern about the nuclear threat was such that fallout shelters for the garden were commercially available.

other avenues of relief other than the protest, humour and depiction of devastation that we have already seen—to those with their eyes open, it was a decades-long concern. This really was the "peace that is no peace" that George Orwell had predicted in 1945 in the wake of the Hiroshima and Nagasaki bombings.

5

The Vietnam War

Vietnam warrants just two fleeting mentions in Barclay James Harvest's lyrics but, despite that, it deserves inclusion in this social history. Why? Precisely because the inclusion of those fleeting mentions indicates that the world was changing significantly around the time that the war was being fought. Consider: why should a British Fifties Child, in early adulthood, care in the slightest about a war being fought more than five thousand miles away between two foreign powers? Britain was not involved. Fifties Children certainly were not concerned with the remaining colonial wars going on in Africa. What was so special about the Vietnam War?

First and foremost was the fact that America was involved and Britain was—and remains—in its lap. Second, what happened with the Vietnam War was that its images were streamed almost constantly into the consciousness of still impressionable Fifties Children by a media keen to exploit the shrinking of the post-Second World War globe. Photographs, newsreels, television: the Vietnam War was the first "television war", and many commentators ascribe the public's growing antagonism towards it to the coverage they saw on their screens. Atrocities were committed by both belligerents—are they not always in war?—and some of these made a televisual impact on Fifties Children.

Arguably, this was the first time in history that the primeval brutality of war was made evident to the populace not directly involved in the conflict. Sure, the parents of Fifties Children lived through the Blitz but, murderous and destructive as bombing of cities is, that killing and destruction has an element of randomness about it and is primarily intended to instil fear and loss of morale leading to a pressure to surrender the fight, whereas there is often a more calculated and sinister aspect to the atrocities committed in a conflict. As that sensitive, psychedelic, flower-power, summer-of-love generation began to ponder what was happening, there was an explosion of revulsion against the war that was reflected strongly in popular culture, particularly in music. True, the reaction was greatest in the United States, as one would expect, but as American music was hugely popular with British Fifties Children, they too became affected by the strength of the American revolt against the war.

Thus, the growing power of the media, together with British affinity for all things American, conspired to make the Vietnam War an issue for many British Fifties Children. Its impact was significant, and some of the photographs from the conflict became icons of the age for us all, with a power to shock that lasts to this present day.

The Vietnam War was, of course, a Cold War conflict. What had started off for the Americans, at the beginning of the Fifties, as a low-key attempt to stem the march of communism in the French colony, soon developed within the next decade into a morass from which they would not extricate themselves, humiliated, until 1973. By the mid-Fifties, the French had been ousted from Vietnam and the country split into two sections, north and south. Ho Chi Minh's northern government of the Democratic Republic of Vietnam was backed by communist powers—initially China, then the Soviet Union—whereas South Vietnam[1] was backed principally by the United States. In the second half of the Fifties, the communists in the north instigated those sympathetic to their cause who had remained in the south—the Viet Cong, who were significant in number—to begin a campaign of attrition against the government's rule. This infiltration became more violent and deadly as the decade drew to a close, leading to regular invasions of military aid and personnel from the north as the Sixties dawned.

In the Sixties' morning light, President Kennedy resisted sending in actual fighting troops, but the number of American military "advisors" in South Vietnam had increased to more than 15,000 by 1963. Despite this involvement, the authorities in the South implemented a despotic rule over their people, were rife with corruption and infiltration by communist sympathizers, and suffered militarily from an inefficient army. Eventually, following encouragement of rebel generals by the CIA, the United States' inept puppet-leader, Ngo Dinh Diem, was overthrown and killed in November of 1963. Hopes that the coup would improve matters were soon dashed: the country was thrown into even greater turmoil which, in turn, prompted the northern Vietnamese regime to intensify their destabilising activities.

1. After French colonial rule ended, the country was known as the State of Vietnam, then it became the Republic of Vietnam, but was more commonly known by the name South Vietnam. I shall use this name to avoid confusion with the northern, communist Democratic Republic of Vietnam.

The ascendancy of Lyndon Johnson to the presidency following Kennedy's assassination in November 1963 brought about a change of emphasis in the level of engagement in Vietnam. Initially, this was subtle, but escalated when US warships skirmished with North Vietnamese boats in the summer of 1964. American troop numbers then increased rapidly and in March 1965, when the United States despatched 3,000 Marines to Vietnam and began a massive aerial bombing campaign—it lasted over three years—they were effectively at war.

Their enemies were everywhere. Against the Viet Cong they were fighting an internal battle in South Vietnam with communist sympathizers trying to overthrow the government. In the northern Democratic Republic of Vietnam, they were fighting a Soviet-backed enemy that was not only surging across the border but also providing military support to the Viet Cong. If that was not enough, they also had to fight communist sympathizers in neighbouring Laos and Cambodia, the countries through which the famous Ho Chi Minh logistical supply trail to South Vietnam's communist fighters passed. The United States' commitment to Vietnam became total, with about 200,000 Marines on the ground by the end of 1965.

Although viewing events from a distance, and with an inevitable sense of detachment due to Britain's non-involvement in the war—the British government had refused the United States' pleas for assistance—the Fifties Child could not help but be perturbed by the events unfolding across the world in the name of freedom. Amongst many recurring anti-war demonstrations worldwide—including in the United States of course—was the one in London in March 1968, which ended with chaotic rioting at Grosvenor Square, the location of the American Embassy. Pathé News described it as "a bloody riot such as Britain has never before witnessed".[2]

As the war and the United States' involvement intensified, so did the strength of its opposition. During the presidential campaign of 1968, Richard Nixon promised an honourable end to the war. Under his presidency the Americans began a process of returning the responsibility for the defence of their country to South Vietnam's authorities. The withdrawal of fighting forces was complete in 1973, although the United States continued to provide support to South Vietnam until it fell to the communist north in 1975. Since then, Vietnam has been a unified country.

The human cost of the war was immense. Nearly 60,000 American soldiers died in Vietnam and more than 150,000 were seriously wounded. Despite a

---

2. The Fifties Child knew all about the link between demonstrations and riots; he did not have to wait for twenty-first century babies to teach him.

series of cathartic attempts to relieve the pain through movies, books and song, the war left a putrid, festering sore on American consciousness for decades. Vietnamese casualties were even greater, with civilian casualties throughout the north and south estimated to be in the range between a few hundreds of thousands to a couple of million.

Lees' 'Child of the Universe' and 'Psychedelic Child' are the two Barclay James Harvest songs to feature Vietnam. Of the two, 'Child of the Universe' is the most revealing.

> I'm a child of Vietnam
> . . .
> I'm a small boy with blood on his hands!
> Yes, I'm a child of the universe!
> . . .
> You can see me on the TV every night:
> always there to join in someone else's fight.

The significance of the lyric "you can see me on the TV every night" will be covered in the 'Politics and The Media' chapter, where a review of the song in that context reveals an interesting sociological observation. Here, however, we shall simply note that Lees was clearly affected by the images of violence beginning to appear regularly on our TV screens.

The song's lyrics also refer to Northern Ireland and South Africa. Thus, even without the all-embracing "I'm a child of the universe" lyric, one can say that the song is as much about innocent children's war-suffering in any part of the world as it is about these specific conflict-torn areas. Unfortunately, there continue to be many conflicts in the modern world in which children are inextricably embroiled. Each of these conflicts is a frosty nip on the Fifties Child's post-Second World War flower of hope. Yet, as the message that Lees received from the Lebanese child shows,[3] the song's very existence, and its lyrical power, is a potent reminder that the flower of hope, though withered, is strong and still survives. The force of that hope, expressed through the still-relevant 'Child of the Universe', acts to galvanize all those who want to change our world for the better and is a nutritious food for needy children's spirits.

For its part, 'Psychedelic Child' is a recollection of many aspects—almost in a list form—of the psychedelic scene of the Sixties: Vietnam receives a namecheck and no more.

---

3. See the book's Introduction if you skipped it.

Whilst it was American musicians who raised awareness and led the charge against the Vietnam War, British musicians were not far behind. Folk singers will usually be at the vanguard of any protest movement: in Britain, Donovan was the foremost of these to be concerned over the Vietnam War and, as early as 1965, his second album *Fairytale* contained two powerful songs on the issue.[4]

The first of these, 'Ballad of a Crystal Man', is a lyrically complex, but thinly-veiled attack on what he saw as American abuses, with an explicit and venomous attack on Vietnam coming in the final verse. For Donovan, this was the worst of their blackest deeds. He is sick of the hypocritical smiles of Americans and rejects the American Dream and its brand of deceit-shrouded freedom, both of which are tarnished by the Vietnam War and other misdeeds.

The second Vietnam-related song on *Fairytale*, 'The War Drags On', is not Donovan's own—it was written by his folk-singer friend Mick Softley,[5] who had previously released it just a few months earlier on his debut album, *Songs for Swingin' Survivors*. It complements 'Ballad of a Crystal Man' well, by virtue of its hard-hitting message, told through the eyes of an American soldier. Softley also reflects on how reality is corrupting the American ideal of freedom: the soldier goes out to fight for all the values that the American Dream exalts but that lofty ideal is vanquished amidst the blood and the gore, the bodies and the refugees. The song ends with the nightmare of a nuclear bomb explosion.

It is interesting to note how both these songs, in which Vietnam is a main theme, are totally lacking hope or compassion: these are true protest songs, unlike Lees' 'Child of the Universe', which is lyrically simple, thematically complex and offers both compassion and hope.

Black Sabbath's 'Hand of Doom' [*Paranoid*, 1970] also references Vietnam but, like Lees' 'Child of the Universe', its principal subject is not the conflict itself. It is an anti-drugs song—we shall address this aspect in the 'Drugs' chapter—in which the shocking and spirit-demoralising images from the conflict are one of the reasons that might lead an individual to shun reality and be caught by the lure of drugs.

4. The original British release contained only one, 'Ballad of a Crystal Man'. It was the second American printing, still in 1965, that added the equally powerful 'The War Drags On'.

5. Born Essex, 1941. The song qualifies as "contemporaneous" because of its adoption by Donovan.

Four disparate artists, all equally affected by the horrors of the Vietnam War—a war with no British involvement and fought thousands of miles from our shores—that reflect a society, empowered by knowledge from the media, shifting away from expansionism, away from Empire, away from carnage. The Fifties Child had come of age.

6

Berlin

Berlin itself became an icon of the Cold War, symbolizing the deep divisions between the communist and capitalist ideologies. The German capital was conquered by Soviet forces at the beginning of May 1945 and at the War's end, only a few days later, it was well behind the front-line, deep within Soviet territory.[1] However, despite Berlin being under their control, the Soviets had already agreed in 1944 that the city would be split into four quarters: one for each of the main combatant victors in the European theatre, including France. The city soon became a huge source of contention between the Soviet Union and its former allies.

The Soviet strategy towards the portion of Germany which it controlled was to emasculate its economic base by removing its factories to the Soviet Union. It exerted a strict ideological grip on forms of government of all the lands under its control, resorting to force when this failed. In the years immediately after the end of the War, this policy resulted in a significant migration of people westwards, towards the more liberal ideologies of the other victors. Berlin was a key point for these political and economic refugees, given its part-Western governance and transport links to countries controlled by the Western Allies, including the western part of Germany.

This and other factors led the Soviet Union, in the spring of 1948, to restrict the rail and road access to the parts of Berlin not under their control, in the hope that this would strengthen their grip over the city. The so-called "Berlin Blockade" was the first major crisis of the post-war Cold War. The Western Allies responded by undertaking a major airlift of food into its own sectors, at a huge economic cost, and with the loss of many lives in various air accidents. However, the airlift was successful in supplying the Western-held

---

1. Parts of the Soviet army had continued to push westwards whilst others fought for Berlin.

sectors of the city with food and fuel, to the extent that the Soviets' blockade was lifted about a year later. The political damage was severe though, and led to the formal creation of the German Democratic Republic (East Germany) and the Federal Republic of Germany (West Germany).

Migration westwards continued throughout the subsequent decade. Following the closure of the border between the two German states and the erection of the inner German border in 1952, Berlin became the migration's focal point. By 1961 approximately 20 per cent of the East German population had moved across to the west. The Soviets, by now governed by Khrushchev, could tolerate no more and, in the summer of 1961, Khrushchev himself ordered the East German government to erect a wall within the city of Berlin to stem the tide of emigration.

The Berlin Wall closed off East from West. The border closed to migration and, for nearly thirty years, the Wall became a symbol of the ideological divide between the superpowers. It was a daunting physical barrier, built with guard towers, anti-vehicle trenches, fakir beds and other defences.

Such was the desperation of many living in the east that attempts at crossing over to the west continued. The Wall's notoriety spread as it became known that those attempting the crossing were being shot and killed by border guards. These people were being treated as if they were attempting to escape from a war-time concentration camp. Over one hundred people died attempting to reach the west over the Wall, attempting to attain the freedoms that we so often take for granted. Many more made the escape successfully, employing a variety of ingenious methods, ranging from underground tunnels to hot air balloons.

Despite the fact that the Wall contravened war-time agreements, the Western Allies effectively accepted it as a fact of the Cold War. Perhaps the allied leaders were cognizant of the fact that the Wall was a propaganda disaster for communism. Playing on this, two American leaders, separated by a quarter of a century, made keynote speeches within media-distance of the Wall.

Kennedy's 1963 speech has become famous for his 'Ich bin ein Berliner' keynote statement. It was an emotional speech, typically stirring stuff:

> There are many people in the world who really don't understand, or say they don't, what is the great issue between the free world and the Communist world.
>
> Let them come to Berlin.
>
> . . .
>
> Freedom is indivisible, and when one man is enslaved, all are not free. When all are free, then we look—can look forward to that day when this city will be joined as one and this country and this great Continent of Europe in a peaceful

and hopeful globe. When that day finally comes, as it will, the people of West Berlin can take sober satisfaction in the fact that they were in the front lines for almost two decades.

All—All free men, wherever they may live, are citizens of Berlin.

And, therefore, as a free man, I take pride in the words "Ich bin ein Berliner."

Reagan's 1987 speech might have lacked Kennedy's oratorical lustre but enhanced its impact by being delivered with the Brandenburg Gate—one of Berlin's enduring, emblematic sights—as a backdrop. By 1987 Mikhail Gorbachev had come to power in the Soviet Union and had begun a series of reforms ("perestroika") that over the next few years—as so many informed commentators believe—led to the breakup of the Soviet Union and the consequent end of the Cold War. President Reagan used this media opportunity to encourage Gorbachev to remove one of the most visible signs of the Cold War:

We welcome change and openness;[2] for we believe that freedom and security go together, that the advance of human liberty can only strengthen the cause of world peace. There is one sign the Soviets can make that would be unmistakable, that would advance dramatically the cause of freedom and peace. General Secretary Gorbachev, if you seek peace, if you seek prosperity for the Soviet Union and Eastern Europe, if you seek liberalization, come here to this gate. Mr Gorbachev, open this gate. Mr Gorbachev, tear down this wall!

Of course, Reagan was addressing the population of the Soviet empire as much as its leaders, stirring the mood for change, adding to its inertia.

For Berlin, when that change did come, it was inspired by its own people. The event that triggered a domino effect of changes that would bring down the Wall occurred when Hungary—a Soviet bloc country—disabled its physical border with Austria in the summer of 1989. Thousands of East German "tourists" to Hungary defected across the border into Austria. The media, by now a powerful beast, regaled in the images of jubilant East Germans celebrating happily: it was powerful television.

The Hungarian and East German authorities tried to stem the new emigration but the tide had turned. The people were strong and there was no longer the political willpower in Berlin, Moscow or elsewhere for the mass disobedience countermeasures that would have been required to quell the surge for greater freedom. Huge demonstrations in East Germany began in September, continuing to grow in strength into October. The political pres-

2. Openness = "glasnost". "Perestroika" and "glasnost" were Gorbachev's key promotional phrases.

sure was such that on the 18th of that month the longstanding leader of the country, Erich Honecker, resigned.[3] Early in November, the demonstrations reached their peak when about half a million people gathered in the city's Alexanderplatz. The emigration of East Germans to the west via various routes had continued and, a few days after the Alexanderplatz demonstration on November 9 the new government made plans to open up the borders to West Germany, including the crossing in West Berlin, on November 17.

However, the official responsible for announcing the new provisions to the press had not been directly involved in the government's decision and had been inadequately briefed. In response to questioning at the end of his formal announcements, he effectively stated that the border crossing from East to West Berlin was open with immediate effect, and West German media began reporting that particular information almost immediately. Crowds then began to gather on the East German side, demanding to be allowed through. The border guards were unsure how to proceed and their orders were unclear but the human pressure was insurmountable. Relenting, they opened the border.

East Germans swarmed through, to be greeted warmly by their compatriots on the other side. The date was November 9, 1989. For a Fifties Child, that was a truly memorable day, one to be savoured and remembered, cherished and celebrated, and not just in Berlin but throughout the world. The significance of the re-opening of the border between East and West Berlin, together with the unofficial and official dismantling of the Wall that followed soon after, cannot be overestimated. It is no exaggeration to say that the fall of the Wall on November 9 felt as though it was the beginning of the real end of the Second World War. An icon of evil had been destroyed and, no matter what the future brought, it was a tremendous day for humanity.

Today, Berlin stands proud as one of the great European capitals, with famous landmarks such as the Brandenburg Gate and the Reichstag revitalised and its people again as one.

🦋

The story of Barclay James Harvest is intimately linked with Berlin. The band first played in Germany in 1970, at a progressive rock festival in Köln, although it was not until 1975 that they became regular visitors. Their first visit to the city of Berlin itself came in 1976 and the band quickly developed an affinity for it. Over the next three years their reputation in Germany grew immensely, to the extent that the country became their main commercial market. In the summer of 1980 the Berlin Senate's Cultural Committee was looking to promote some special summer events in the city and Barclay James Harvest agreed to perform a free concert on the steps of the Reichstag, the old

3. He had become leader in 1971.

parliament building that had remained—just, it was very near the Wall—within West Berlin. The concert was a huge success, with a massive crowd estimated at up to 250,000 people turning out to witness a specially extended set.

The Reichstag's proximity to the Wall meant that fans on its eastern side would also have been able to enjoy the music. As a testament to the band's popularity in Germany, as well as the effects of perestroika and glasnost, Barclay James Harvest were the first Western band invited to play an open-air concert in East Berlin, performing in 1987. Due to ticket demand, the concert was held at Treptower Park, another venue very close to the Wall. The huge number of fans that turned up on the day meant that the authorities were forced to abandon the ticketing arrangements and let people in for free. Another massive audience of around 200,000 saw the band perform.

Given the band's empathy for the city and its people, as well as the immense significance of the Wall, it is not surprising that Berlin features prominently in the band's recorded music. The first song to appear was, appropriately, 'Berlin'. Written by Holroyd, this charming ballad would become one of the band's most popular and enduring songs. The song is full of hope and love for the city, to the extent that Holroyd personifies it. Much of the song's lyrical power stems from Holroyd's presentiment, even as early as 1978, that the shift of control away from communism had already begun, filling him with hope for the city's future: he can see that its days of great sadness are in the past, that the darkness that has enveloped it is clearing. No wonder the Berliners liked it.

In 1981, the *Turn of the Tide* album was to provide two Berlin-inspired songs: 'Back to the Wall' and 'In Memory of the Martyrs'.

The meaning of the lyrics of Holroyd's 'Back to the Wall' is more obscure than those of 'Berlin', courtesy of some intended ambiguities, although its opening half fairly clearly points to the desperate situation of those living in East Berlin, feeling trapped by the situation there, wanting to cross to the west:

Stranger at the gate: let him in!
. . .
He's been waiting on the other side;
he's been waiting for the turn of the tide:
. . .
won't you let him in?

The "stranger" is the East Berliner. The "gate" could be specifically referring to a couple of things, both of which essentially mean the impenetrable East-

West border. The first is the Brandenburg Gate, one of the city's most famous landmarks, which was situated very close to the Wall, but on its eastern side. The second is one of the crossing points between East and West through which dignitaries might cross, such as Checkpoint Charlie. This particular crossing was made famous in John le Carré's thriller *The Spy Who Came in From the Cold* [1963], which was later made into a film starring Richard Burton.

The East Berliner has been waiting for the political "tide" to turn so that he can cross to the West, thus fulfilling the hope that Holroyd had so famously expressed in 'Berlin'. 'Back to the Wall' then shifts up a political gear in its second half. My interpretation is that Holroyd is telling the people in the East that it is they themselves who now have to rise up and make the political changes that will lead to the Wall's demise. Again, as in 'Berlin', there is hope: Holroyd had clearly seen the "turn of the tide" which would allow them to take this populist step:

> Back to the wall:
> have you seen the light?
> Is your soul worth saving?
> . . .
> Can you pay the price?
> Then your life is waiting!

The "stranger" in the East has his "back to the wall", i.e. he is in a desperate situation, but the tide is turning and he has "seen the light". Whereas there might be a high "price to pay" for greater freedom, this is the "life that is waiting". In the final lyrics, Holroyd explains that we in the West can help no more, implying that the impetus for political change has to come from within the East:

> Down by the shore
> we can help you no more;
> standing with our back to the wall.

Note that Holroyd has personified the people of the West as Barclay James Harvest themselves, who, during the Reichstag concert of 1980, literally had their "backs to the wall". Like 'Berlin', this is a song full of hope for the people living in the East. Once their tide had come in a little higher, they then took it upon themselves to force through the changes in 1989 that brought down the Wall—almost as if they were following Holroyd's advice.

Holroyd returned to a similar topic, almost prophetically, on 'Halfway to Freedom'. In the short period between this song's recording and release in

March of 1990 the Wall had finally been breached. The sleeve notes on the album dedicated the song to the people of Germany and the lyrics urge them on to follow through the changes needed to bring down their totalitarian regime. Holroyd later explained that, whilst generally applicable to those enslaved by Soviet systems in Eastern Europe, the original inspiration for the song had been the dire situation in Romania, which was also ripe for turning. Holroyd would revisit Romania's problems in 'Copii Romania', a song which we shall come to later.

The other song concerning Berlin's plight to feature on *Turn of the Tide* was Lees' 'In Memory of the Martyrs', which was inspired by those people who had died in their attempt to cross the Wall. It had been especially written for the band's extraordinary concert at the Reichstag in 1980, where it was premiered. Lyrically, there is no clue that it was the East Berliners who were the inspiration, but fans were left in no doubt when the concert video was released in 1983. Evocative sepia footage accompanying the song showed Berliners, the Wall, and then East Berliners attempting to flee across it. Watching the footage whilst listening to the sensitive accompanying music and lyrics, is a spine-chilling experience.[4]

The song's message is told through a number of metaphors whose meaning is unlocked with confidence given the visual clue from the video footage. Like many of Lees' other songs, 'In Memory of the Martyrs' has a deep spirituality which is easy to miss on a casual hearing. In fact, through the oft-repeated chorus lyric "we are love", it is arguably this aspect which is the core of the song. I shall cover this nuance in context and in the necessary detail in the 'Spirituality' chapter. For now, however, we shall focus on what Lees is saying that is relevant to the city of Berlin. Here is one metaphorical sequence:

> I dreamt I held a baby,
> I dreamt I held a child.
> I dreamt I held a young man,
> a prisoner in my hand.
> My hand I could not open:
> the man grew up inside—
> a prisoner without reason,
> just on the other side.

The protagonist is looking from outside the city into East Berlin. Through

---

4. It gives me goosebumps every time! This experience underlies the power of Barclay James Harvest's music, which has helped it to endure down the years. Its power doesn't just come from the beauty of the music, it comes from the "soul"—I use the word in its broadest sense—and it enhances one's spirit.

the joint policies of politicians in the East and the West, through the many years of growing from a baby into adulthood, these policies have yielded a city—represented by the protagonist's hand, indicating that the whole of mankind, including the Western Allies, have some responsibility for the situation—in which people are "prisoners without reason", just on the other side of the Wall within East Berlin. The following metaphor is equally as attractive:

> The blood red rose of summer
> grows elegant and tall
> in memory of the green grass
> beyond the guardian wall.
> The green grass grows forever
> beneath the bloody sky:
> in memory of the martyrs
> she'll cover when they die.

The scene has switched; the perspective is now from within the city. The rose is representing the hope that the "green grass"—meaning the better, "free" world on the Western side of the Wall—will one day be attained. Its buds close at each life lost in the attempt to cross the Wall—a setback for the flower of hope—but freedom is a powerful force and will endure forever.

The "guardian wall" is, of course, the Berlin Wall. Note how Lees has sub-tly enmeshed the common British proverb "the grass is always greener on the other side of the fence" into the fabric of his metaphors by using "guardian" as a near-homophone of "garden" and substituting "fence" for "wall". The use of this proverb is significant within the context of the overall message of the song because its prime intent is to convey the sense that people in general will always aspire to what they do not have, thinking—often erroneously—that it is better, instead of concentrating on living their own life well. Later, when we open up the spiritual aspect of the song, it will become clear that Lees' intent is to suggest that the attainment of political freedom is a hope worth fostering but, in the meantime, there is a life full of enriching experiences to lead, even within the constraints of East Berlin. One can even push this interpretation a little further (perhaps too far?): this "freedom" that he means—the green grass that grows forever—has a spiritual aspect. It is the freedom that comes with strength of spirit—giving, for instance, liberation from anxiety—which one can begin to foster equally well in East Berlin—"the green grass grows forev-er beneath the bloody sky"—as on the other side of the g(u)ard(ia)en wall, where the political advantages might turn out to be not as great as they seem.

In essence, 'In Memory of the Martyrs' is a spiritual song addressed to the people of East Berlin. It carries an extremely powerful message but, of course, it is doubtful whether anyone understood its full ramifications at the time, given that it is written in metaphors and deciphering it requires a substantial understanding of Lees' spiritual journey. What the East Berliners will have taken from the song, though, is as powerful, or more so, than an understanding of Lees' exact intent. They will have felt the compassion for them within the song, in the same way that they will have felt the compassion in Holroyd's three songs.

The earliest three of these four songs—'Berlin', 'Back to the Wall' and 'In Memory of the Martyrs' (collectively, let's call them Barclay James Harvest's Berlin Suite)—are also quite extraordinary in a sociological way, in that they demonstrate their compassion in the face of the societal norm of the time, which was still, thirty-plus years after the War's end, predominantly anti-German, certainly in popular culture. Despite being raised on a fodder of comic book stories glorifying the defeat of the Germans and despite the continuing belittlement of Germany through film, television and other media into the Seventies, these two songwriters brought us all a humanitarian vision of Berlin and of Germany and, in so doing, bucked a trend. Holroyd and Lees used their personal experiences of the city and the country to bring us all a breath of fresh air, a wonderful gift of hope.

Berlin and its Wall are rarely covered by Barclay James Harvest's contemporaneous musicians and never with our songwriters' compassion.

David Bowie spent some time living in West Berlin in the Seventies, releasing a famous suite of albums: *Low* [1977], *Heroes* [1977] and *Lodger* [1979]. The inspiration for his move to Berlin may have been more to do with musical innovation than compassion and empathy for the city or its people, but the city's divisions inevitably affected him. 'Heroes', the title track of the second album of the trilogy, is a fictional account of two estranged lovers beating the system by meeting surreptitiously next to the Wall.

Neither Camel's 'West Berlin' [*Stationary Traveller*, 1984], written with the Wall standing in its might, nor Pink Floyd's 'A Great Day for Freedom' [*The Division Bell*, 1994], written after its fall, quite hits the "contemporaneous" tag: the lyrics for 'West Berlin' were written by Andy Latimer's wife, Susan Hoover, who is rightly keeping her age a personal detail, whilst those for 'A Great Day for Freedom' were co-written by David Gilmour's wife Polly Samson, who was born in 1962. However, as the bands themselves and their leaders do meet the criterion, I shall overlook the shortfall.

'West Berlin' is a fictional story sung in the first person about someone planning to escape over the Wall from the East: in fact, the whole *Stationary Traveller* album is a concept based around this escape. As in many other Camel albums, some of the tracks are instrumentals, but even these have titles that fit in with the story, as does the album's artwork. 'West Berlin' is itself ambiguous about whether the escape is from the East to the West or—bizarrely—the other way round; it takes clues from other songs such as 'Refugee', in which the protagonist says she wants to be free to disagree, and the subterfuge of 'Cloak and Dagger Man' to assure the listener that this is indeed the direction of travel. Sociologically, of course, it does not matter since the significance in this regard is that the problems of this divided city have come to the attention of this lyricist. Back to the story: our protagonist makes her escape over the skyline by hanging onto a steel cable line. Afterwards, coming to terms with her new life, she yearns for the loved ones she left behind, knowing that it is impossible to return.

Gilmour and Samson's 'A Great Day for Freedom' goes a little deeper in that, having celebrated the Wall's demise, it reflects on the betrayal of the hope that accompanied that momentous event once Eastern Europe began to split asunder as old rivalries and hatreds were unleashed. As in some of Barclay James Harvest's songs, there is an ambiguity about the song's complete lyrics, as Gilmour and Samson also bring in a personal element that many Pink Floyd fans have interpreted as referring to Gilmour's soured relationship with former bandmate Roger Waters, who was the principal motivator behind that band's famous *The Wall* [1979] album. Of course, *The Wall* was not about the Berlin Wall, and Gilmour denies that 'A Great Day for Freedom' has anything to do with his relationship with Waters—perhaps, as in Camel's 'West Berlin', the individual is a fictional character.

Berlin symbolized the Cold War, its Wall was an icon of evil. Everything it represented was anathema to the Fifties Child who had grown up fostering hopes for a peaceful world in which men were free to pursue their own endeavours. Over the years, its divisions and its problems wormed their way into the minds of many Fifties Children, especially those who were fortunate enough to see it firsthand. At its fall, the Fifties Child celebrated like never before: at last, war was over and peace finally on its way. The failure of that hope to live up to its promise was a crushing blow. Let us now see in greater detail how the dream of peace floundered.

7

Break-up of the Soviet Empire

As time wore on, the passing away of the Soviet Old Guard and tough economic realities combined to weaken the communist grip on its empire. A popular uprising swept through the region from the late Eighties on, transforming the face of Eastern Europe in a way that the Second World War had never done. Hatred left simmering from old atrocities was rekindled, unleashing ethnic violence of the kind that the free world had thought was consigned to the history books.[1] The fall of the Soviets did not bring peace and happiness everywhere.

The Soviet empire had been built on the backs of strong, and at times uncompromising, leaders. Stalin, its leader through the Second World War, had been in power for some thirty years, with only his own death managing to oust him from power in 1953. Political wrangling followed: his successor, Malenkov, had barely settled into the role when he was deposed by Khrushchev in 1955. However, Khrushchev suffered from his perceived embarrassment by Kennedy in the Cuban Missile Crisis and was replaced by Brezhnev in 1964, whose own reign lasted nearly twenty years until his death in 1982. Then, as it appeared to a Fifties Child in Britain, it was as if this great fearsome force of dinosauric, longevous leaders had been vanquished: Andropov and Chernenko followed in quick succession, each lasting less than 18 months. This, at a time when the world was beginning to change, when the force of hope throughout Eastern Europe was beginning to flower—not auspicious for the Soviet empire. It somehow gave the appearance that its politi-

---

1. Keen observers, such as Lees, would point to Northern Ireland, even today, and say that such hatred has, unfortunately, never disappeared. It is in our own garden.

cal will was crumbling. Could this great, evil beast not find leaders that were not already half dead?

The answer was Mikhail Gorbachev. To our Fifties Child, the appointment of Gorbachev as leader in 1985 was like the appearance of the first snowdrops in a deep winter. It was immediately apparent that he seemed to be from a different breed. For a start, he was relatively young and had the audacity to smile. Communists did not smile. What was happening? The Fifties Child had never seen a Soviet leader smile. Extraordinary!

Gorbachev possessed a strong charisma that was clearly evidenced on TV screens across the world as he sought to woo Western leaders. The empire that he inherited may already have been crumbling beyond repair, but the new leader had the wit to begin the reforms that led to its relatively peaceful dismantling rather than wait for a violent implosion or, worse still, manufacture a cataclysmic Cold War conflict with his ideological enemy so that both of them—together with the rest of the planet—could wallow in each other's death throes.

Perestroika ("restructuring") and glasnost ("openness") were the tools that began the deconstruction process. It is almost certain that, once started on this course, Gorbachev was not in full control of events. That much is clear from the attempted coup by hardliners in the summer of 1991.

As in war, events take on a life of their own and some of those uncontrollable events occurred in countries under the Soviet umbrella, with consequences that subsequently fed back into the maelstrom leading to the Soviet Union's collapse. Poland's force of hope had flowered as early as 1979 when the pastoral visit by Pope John Paul II acted to galvanize the unification of the people. Luckily for them, they then found another charismatic leader at this key moment of history. Lech Walesa was able to use his position as leader of the trade union Solidarity to challenge and begin to weaken the strictures of the Soviet-backed stranglehold in the country. The struggle for Poland was bitter but, with the impetus given by Gorbachev, its government could not hold back the ripples of perestroika and glasnost washing at its shore, and Soviet Poland fell in the summer of 1989. Crucially, the Soviet Union did not intervene to stop the formation of the first non-communist government within its sphere of control.

The East Germans were watching of course—the Poles' fashioning of hope into a potent political force undoubtedly inspired them and bolstered their own confidence, leading to the fall of the Berlin Wall.

The Soviets' uncharacteristic reluctance to react served as a catalyst to enhance the revolutions of other Eastern European countries. Romania's fall from communism was violent—its feared leader Nicolae Ceausescu was executed by the victorious revolutionary forces on Christmas Day, 1989. Czechoslovakia's new non-communist leader Vaclav Havel took hold of power four days later.

The desire to break free of the Soviet strictures also applied to people in many of its own states, to the extent that the three Baltic states of Latvia, Lithuania and Estonia achieved their independence in the summer of 1991, before the final dissolution of the Soviet Union itself. However, to some Western observers, the clearest sign that the Soviet dissolution was coming was the opening, in late winter 1990, of the first McDonald's fast-food restaurant in Moscow. Just think, one of capitalism's greatest icons lighting up the Moscow night.

The dissolution itself came not long after in another Christmas Day event, this time in 1991. Gorbachev resigned and on the following day the relevant remaining ruling bodies governing the country dissolved themselves, formally recognising the end of the Soviet Union.

These were momentous times for a Fifties Child. The Second World War, finally, properly over. The liberation of Poland had at last been achieved and this fearsome, evil, decades-old foe, who had once been an unwilling ally, vanquished. The forces of good had won. The world was now free. Huge sigh of relief!

Looking back now, and despite the horrors that we have all witnessed since, and continue to witness, my perspective is that the tension of the Cold War has indeed been dissipated. Lees was right, in 'Rebel Woman', to infer that it was we who were the "victims of circumstance" of the conflict. At its root, the circumstance was the Cold War, and the Fifties Child was suffering the consequences—the threat of a nuclear war, a divided Europe, proxy wars throughout the globe, espionage intrigues and more. Who worries about the threat of a nuclear holocaust now? The nuclear weapons overkill factor is still incredibly high, so why does no one worry any more? The nuclear spectre is not the demon that terrorised the Sixties, Seventies or Eighties. That fear, that demon, was the progeny of the Cold War, of the Soviet Threat. Whether today's sense of security is a false one or not is in many ways irrelevant to the perspective of this book, which is concerned with the impact on Fifties Child's society. Today's horror is more medieval, driven by racial and religious hatreds, as opposed to ideological ones, and people's assessment of the threat is based on their perception of the weapons deployable in this new arena of conflict.

This sort of tension affects many people less deeply than that of the Cold War. An illustration of this fact can be seen from an interview conducted with Holroyd in which the interviewer from the *Middle Bavarian Daily* newspaper

started a question on Lees' 1990 song 'Cheap the Bullet' with the statement
that "the world is getting more and more peaceful", prompting Holroyd to
interject:

> Oh, really?! I wouldn't exactly call the world peaceful at this point in time,
> with situations as they are in the Middle East. That's just a prime example of
> how cheap the bullet is—life doesn't mean anything, it's all to do with power
> and at this point in time it's to do with oil. It's nothing to do with saving the
> Arabs or saving the country, it's to do with saving oil and that's all, so life is
> still cheap.

Holroyd's reference to oil indicates that he was thinking of the First Iraq War
(the "Gulf War") when he answered. Mind you, he could just as well have
taken his pick from other recent conflicts in the area: Iraq had only just ended
its bitter eight year-long war with Iran before it decided to invade Kuwait,
triggering the conflict that he refers to, and the long and bloody Lebanese
civil war was just petering out. More pertinently, if Holroyd had said this to
an interviewer only yesterday, his words would still have seemed entirely
appropriate. Sad.

Irrespective of whether one wholeheartedly agrees with Holroyd's statement or not, it exemplifies that for outward-looking Fifties Children, such as
the band's songwriters, the hope fostered in the lead-up to the Soviet
dissolution was being cruelly dashed, even before it had become fully realised.

Another example was how in the summer of 1991, before the final collapse
of the Soviet Union, ethnic wars began in Yugoslavia that would be the source
of horrific, barbaric events. Yugoslavia theoretically fell beyond the Soviet
Union's reach. Historians may debate and judge why Stalin and his successors
allowed this but, as we have said, a significant factor must have been that the
country was led by Tito, a powerful communist leader who had modelled his
post-war country on the Soviet Union, with a number of republics controlled
by a federal government. These republics were, roughly, the same as the independent countries that we know today.

The 'Yugoslav Union' was perhaps even more volatile than the Soviet one.
Fresh in the minds of many of its peoples were ethnic atrocities that had been
committed during the Nazi occupation in the Second World War.
Furthermore, the wartime resistance movement had consisted of two factions,
one led by Tito and backed by the Soviets, the other backed by the Western
Allies: these factions had often ended up fighting each other rather than the
Nazi occupiers. The Union had acted like a bandage over these wounds, but
once removed on its demise, the world was to discover that the wounds had
not only not healed but were still festering. The events unfolding in much of

Eastern Europe during the late Eighties had the same catalytic effect on these disenchanted Yugoslav people, who began to crave independence ever more vigorously. The resulting conflicts were protracted, vengeful and bloody.

✻

We have already seen how Barclay James Harvest's writers had a focus on the Eastern European situation, and this post-Soviet-influence period was no different, being reflected in three of Holroyd's songs. Two of these songs were featured on the band's 1993 album *Caught in the Light* and both deal with negative aspects of the aftermath of the Soviet collapse.

The first, 'Copii Romania' ("children of Romania") is inspired by the plight of Romanian orphans, whose dire circumstances were latched onto by Western TV media in the aftermath of the death of totalitarian leader Ceausescu. The in-depth media coverage provoked a wave of compassion and assistance, not least from Holroyd, who donated all the royalty proceeds from the song to the response fund. The song is one of Holroyd's more lyrically straightforward ones: his desire is that collectively we should not ignore the plight of these needy children, as we have ignored others in the past. He muses on the fact that whereas the fight for Romania's freedom from the darkness of its repressive regime had only just recently begun, these children's fight for life was an ongoing one. We should all respond and help them, yet Holroyd is frustrated by the fact that people no longer seem to care: surely we cannot again pretend that we didn't know?

Like its predecessor on the album, 'Cold War' is filled with world-weariness, in this instance that of someone who has seen his pre-Cold War hopes dashed by the horrors that human beings can perpetrate. Holroyd's cousin was living in Yugoslavia during its vicious civil wars, sharpening his focus all the more. The frailty of hope is a feature of Holroyd's later writing and contrasts sharply with the optimism which he had held for the people of Eastern Europe only a few years previously, as exemplified by 'Halfway to Freedom'. Clearly, the events that followed the break-up of the Soviet empire were sufficient for him to lose confidence in the human race—it was not just the ethnic hatred that exploded in Eastern Europe, it was also the indifference of many people in the Western world to the plight of innocents, such as the Romanian children, and even mankind's continual mistreatment of nature and the environment, as we saw in his 'Who Do We Think We Are?' earlier in our social history. *Caught in the Light* is the album on which Holroyd most clearly demonstrates his conviction that his ideals will not be replicated by the human race. In 'Cold War', despairing in the bravado songs of the militias going off to fight and preparing to martyr themselves for their cause, he sings forlornly—repeatedly—that nothing will change for mankind. The music to 'Cold War' is haunting, the song's significance that of a sadness without bottom.

Eight years later Holroyd was able to call on the whimsical side of his nature for the gorgeous 'January Morning', a song inspired by a friend's visit to the Russian city of St Petersburg, known as Leningrad for most of the Soviet era. The end of the Cold War had opened up the former Soviet Union to mass tourism and it had become a popular tourist destination. Despite the song's whimsy, the underlying message reflects a similar world-weariness to 'Copii Romania' and 'Cold War'. The whimsy comes in the form of Holroyd's depiction of street artists painting imaginative pictures on the snow but then, moving into the realm of metaphors, he equates the artists' imagination with their dreams for a better tomorrow. These dreams are similar to those which others in the recent past will have had for a better future: they are similar to the floundered hopes for the post-Soviet world, both within and outside its former borders. Will the dreams of these artists of today suffer the same fate as their pictures, now melting with the snow? 'January Morning' demonstrates that Holroyd's flower of hope had not bloomed again since the disappointment of the post-Soviet debacle: this Fifties Child, like many others, was now travelling his life's journey against the pungent headwind of mankind's deeds.

By the time that the Soviet Union collapsed many of Barclay James Harvest's peers had ceased releasing new songs. Nevertheless, the Romanian orphan situation drew a significant compassionate response from many contemporaries, including George Harrison and Van Morrison, who contributed songs to the 1990 album *Nobody's Child*, which was released in support of raising funds to help the orphans.

Younger songwriters could not help but be affected by the consequences of the break-up of the Soviet empire: an example of one such song is the Cranberries' 'Bosnia' [*To the Faithful Departed*, 1996], penned by lead singer Dolores O'Riordan. The lyrical style may be very different stylistically to that of Barclay James Harvest's songwriters but O'Riordan manages to convey a depth of feeling and compassion that is often missing from the writing of Barclay James Harvest's contemporaries. O'Riordan contrasts our cosy security with the barbaric terror of Sarajevo, highlighting the impact on young children and babies. There is also a strong thematic synergy with Holroyd's sentiments: she feels that we really could change things if we wanted, but are clearly too comfortable to take an interest.

And so we conclude this part of the book dealing with the Cold War. As we have seen, this was a highly significant issue for many Fifties Children. As teenagers, the spectre of a nuclear war loomed large in their minds. Conflicts broke out around the world involving the two opposing nuclear weapons superpowers. Closer to home, in Europe, the Berlin Wall was a reminder of the deep divisions affecting their world. Finally, as they approach their fortieth year, the enemy begins to crumble. There is hope! Then, as they pass that persaonl milestone, the Cold War is finally over: peace at last!

. . . Peace? Their hopes lie in ruins and, as time passes, the awful realisation embeds itself in their souls that the world is not, never will be, as they wish it to be. This disappointment, deep as the flaming hell, will linger forever in the Fifties Child's mind.

Woolly Wolstenholme

Part 3
Cheap the Bullet

8

The Troubles in Northern Ireland

The conflicts that have so far been at the centre of our social history all originated a long way from home: Berlin, Eastern Europe, Vietnam, the hypothetical threat of a nuclear strike from afar. The roar and terror of real violence, however, was right on the Fifties Child's doorstep.

Young adults living in Britain in the late Sixties and early Seventies cannot
have avoided being affected at some level by the Troubles in Northern
Ireland, irrespective of whether or not they understood the issues impinging
on the situation. In fact, it is almost certain that the vast majority, if not all,
did not understand the situation fully, given the complexity of its history.
Mainland Britain had meddled in the governance of Ireland since the twelfth
century, while the origin of the Troubles themselves goes back to at least the
early seventeenth century, when predominantly Protestant Scottish and
English settlers were given land confiscated from predominantly Catholic
Irish people. Four hundred years later and—despite the fact that we are currently living through a relatively peaceful period in the region—the fundamental questions of sovereignty and equal human rights remain unresolved in
the minds of many people.

The Irish Republic was partitioned off in the early Twenties, finally becoming an independent state in 1948. Sectarian unrest in mainly Protestant
Northern Ireland, which had remained part of the United Kingdom, was sporadic through the following two decades, fuelled by prejudicial attitudes
against the minority Catholic population.

There was a sharp acceleration in this sectarian unrest from the late Sixties.
The resulting period of systematic conflict was to last about thirty years, abat-
ing following the signing of the Good Friday Agreement in 1998. Broadly,

there were two distinct sides in conflict as the Troubles erupted. On the one side were the Unionists, who were associated with Protestantism, held power in Northern Ireland and supported the province as part of the United Kingdom—their allegiance was to the Queen. Bitterly opposed to the Unionists were the Catholic Republicans, who felt downtrodden by the authorities, and who sought a unified Ireland, ruled as a republic. This tension still exists today. The first years following the re-eruption of this ages-long conflict are of particular interest to us here, insofar as they appear to have deeply affected many Fifties Children.

The Ulster Volunteer Force (UVF), an illegal Protestant paramilitary organization, was formed in 1966 in response to a perceived increase in the Catholic Irish Republican Army's (IRA) activity at the time of the fiftieth anniversary of the Easter Rising. The Rising was a failed attempt in 1916 by about a thousand republicans to set up an independent Irish state. Their hope was that Britain's involvement in the First World War would leave it vulnerable to direct action. As it turned out, British forces were immediately sent in and after five days of fighting the rebels were defeated, in the process giving birth to what came to be known as the IRA. The UVF's formation statement was this:

From this day, we declare war against the IRA and its splinter groups. Known IRA men will be executed mercilessly and without hesitation. Less extreme measures will be taken against anyone sheltering or helping them, but if they persist in giving them aid, then more extreme methods will be adopted . . . we solemnly warn the authorities to make no more speeches of appeasement. We are heavily armed Protestants dedicated to this cause.

Their actions were even more violent than their words might suggest. They began operating immediately, targeting Catholic civilians if known IRA members could not be found. On June 11, 1966, a 28-year-old man was shot whilst walking home, dying two weeks later, and on the 26th, three men were shot at a pub in Belfast. One of them, 18-year-old Peter Ward, died.

In 1967 the Northern Ireland Civil Rights Association (NICRA) was formed. This organisation was based on principles similar to those of the American Civil Rights Movement and its intent was to see anti-Catholic legislation repealed. However, suspicions were raised that NICRA was really just a front for the IRA. A march through Londonderry, planned for October 5, 1968, was banned by the British home affairs minister after a rival Protestant group, the Apprentice Boys of Derry, announced their intention to march along the same route at the same time. NICRA went ahead with the march regardless, and the Royal Ulster Constabulary (RUC) was sent in to break it up. Their tactics were televised and deemed by many to have involved excessive use of force. About 30 people were injured, including the Labour MP for Belfast West, Gerry Fitt, who was struck by a police baton. Fitt, who had to be treated in hospital for his injuries, later said: "I was a marked man before the march started. These were stormtrooper tactics at their worst. They hit me once, but that wasn't enough—they had to have another go." The RUC's tactics led to Catholics increasingly mistrusting them. Many observers mark the beginning of the Troubles as the violence that beset the October 5 march, which was followed by two days of rioting in Londonderry.

Unionist marches celebrating victories in the centuries-old conflict represent a significant tradition in Northern Ireland. The tensions between Catholic and Protestant communities continued to mount during 1969 as the time for the main Protestant marches, July and August, approached. On August 12, the Apprentice Boys of Derry marched through the majority Catholic city of Londonderry and right into the Catholic Bogside area. There were clashes that led to intervention by the RUC. Rioting ensued, which continued for another two days. Police were stoned and petrol-bombed. NICRA called for other Catholic communities to take pressure off the Bogside residents, leading to the rioting escalating as far afield as the Catholic areas of Belfast and elsewhere. For their part, the RUC deployed armoured cars mounted with machine-guns. Amongst the resulting casualties was a nine-year-old boy killed in his bed by a tracer bullet. There were other deaths and many injuries. Many Belfast families, the vast proportion of them Catholic, were forced to leave their burnt-out homes. Those commentators who do not accept the beginning of the Troubles as being NICRA's march of October 1968 opt for the events occasioned by the August 1969 Londonderry march, known as the Battle of the Bogside, as marking their onset.

The riots led to the British Army being called in to support the RUC. They arrived on August 15, 1969, and the period from their arrival to the end of 1972 was violent to say the least. In 1972 alone, 500 people, half of them civilians, lost their lives. One of the factors for the escalation was the splitting of the IRA into two groups, one of which, the Provisional IRA, took on itself the role of militarily "defending" the Catholic population. In 1971 its Army Council sanctioned attacks on British troops. In 1972 the Provisional IRA killed approximately 100 soldiers, injured many more and carried out around 1,300 bombings. Civilians were often caught up in the violence.

Some of the major incidents from that era have become notorious. The following list is illustrative of those occurring until July 1972, the most likely period to have influenced Barclay James Harvest's early writing on the subject:

June 1970: Premature explosion of IRA bomb in Creggan. Two children amongst the five victims.

Feb 1971: Five civilians killed in County Tyrone when their Land Rover is mistaken for an army vehicle.

Dec 1971: 15 civilians killed in a bombing at McGurk's Bar, Belfast

30 Jan 1972: Bloody Sunday—13 civilians killed during an anti-internment demonstration. This incident has been the cause of two British government inquiries.

Feb 1972: 7 civilians killed during an attack on the British mainland at Aldershot barracks.[1]

March 1972: 7 deaths due to bomb in Donegall Street, Belfast

May 1972: Short Strand, Belfast—8 killed.

July 1972: 3 civilians and 2 republican paramilitaries shot by snipers in Belfast

21 July 1972: Bloody Friday—22 bombs explode in Belfast. At least ten dead, amongst which two children and two soldiers.

July 1972: 3 simultaneous car bombs in Claudy—9 dead.

This ghastly wave of violence had prompted the British government to suspend Northern Ireland's own home-rule government in March 1972 and impose direct rule from London. This move did not stem the violence, either immediately or in the longer term. Deaths continued to accumulate throughout the Seventies. British prime minister Edward Heath was targeted on a couple of occasions but the bombs exploded when he was not at the scene. The IRA's audacity was astonishing: one of their bombs exploded at the Houses of Parliament in 1974, injuring eleven people, and in 1979 another of their attacks killed the shadow secretary for Northern Ireland, Airey Neave, as he was leaving the Palace of Westminster car park. Then, only a few months later, the Queen's cousin Lord Mountbatten was killed in another IRA attack.

The Eighties saw the political wing of the IRA scoring a significant propaganda victory courtesy of hunger strikes in Northern Irish prisons. In 1976 the British government had withdrawn special prisoner status for those imprisoned for political acts, and so, following a number of failed protests seeking to reverse the decision, a number of prisoners went on hunger strike, starting with Bobby Sands in 1981. Sands and nine other prisoners died, becoming martyrs of the Republican cause. The government may not have made any concessions but support for the IRA soared: more than 70,000 people attended Sands' funeral in Belfast. In an ambitious attack in 1984 the IRA narrowly failed to kill the prime minister Margaret Thatcher and her cabinet ministers, who were staying at a hotel in Brighton during the political party conference

---

1. In this chapter "mainland" is taken to mean England, Wales and Scotland.

season. Thatcher might have narrowly escaped injury but MP Anthony Berry was killed, along with four others.

In 1985, the governments of Britain and the Republic of Ireland began to work together more closely and to co-operate on resolving the Troubles. The resulting Anglo-Irish Agreement was an attempt at giving the Republic of Ireland more say in Northern Ireland's affairs. The agreement outraged the Unionists, who scuppered plans for any real change. The Republicans were against it too, since for them it was well short of the changes they wanted to see for Northern Ireland.

The atrocities continued. However, if the hunger strikes had been a propaganda coup for the IRA, then the Poppy Day Massacre was the exact opposite: 11 people died, 10 of them civilians, and dozens more were injured in a bombing at a memorial service in Enniskillen in November 1987.[2]

Finally, there was a dawning of hope. First with the 1993 talks between the British and Irish governments, which led to the issuing of the Downing Street Declaration, proposing that the people of Northern Ireland should be free to decide on their own future. And then with multi-party talks beginning in 1996 chaired by US senator George Mitchell. The road through the Nineties to peace was fraught with setbacks and yet more violence but finally, in July 1997, the IRA announced a ceasefire. The stalled negotiations resumed and a peace agreement was reached in 1998. The Good Friday Agreement had the backing of the majority of people in Ireland, however some dissatisfied Republicans continue their struggle to this day and terrorist attacks, though much less frequent than during the Troubles, still occur.

The Bloody Sunday incident from 1972 became particularly significant in deepening divisions in the region since it reinforced the Republican Catholic community's conviction that the authorities were siding with the Unionist cause. As a result of the accusations at the time, an inquiry was held during 1972, led by Lord Widgery, the Lord Chief Justice of England. It lasted a mere three weeks and ended by exonerating the army of any wrongdoing, but was instantly dismissed as a whitewash by the Republicans. The resulting rancour continued to cause division down the years and, finally, the British government decided in 1998, following staunch campaigning by the families of those affected, to hold a second inquiry led by Lord Saville. This version was wide-ranging and deep in its investigation, taking twelve years and costing £195 million to complete. The report's conclusion states that:

There was a serious and widespread loss of fire discipline among the soldiers

2. If you happen to be too young to remember the shock, just try and imagine Wolstenholme's peaceful 'Sunday Bells' shattered by explosion and carnage.

of Support Company . . . The firing by soldiers of 1 Para on Bloody Sunday caused the deaths of 13 people and injury to a similar number, none of whom was posing a threat of causing death or serious injury. What happened on Bloody Sunday strengthened the Provisional IRA, increased nationalist [Republican] resentment and hostility towards the Army and exacerbated the violent conflict of the years that followed. Bloody Sunday was a tragedy for the bereaved and the wounded, and a catastrophe for the people of Northern Ireland.

Of course, to an observer of the time, living on the British mainland, none of this would have been evident. What would have been clear, from the media reporting, was the deep hatred and bitterness that the sectarian divisions in that society had created over the years. What was also clear was the disturbing nature of some of the violence that was unleashed: beatings, maimings, torture, the targeting of innocent civilians. And, as is clear from the illustrative list of incidents, the violence was beginning to affect—and would continue to do so for many years—people living on the mainland.

It would have been only too easy for such an observer—no, more than observer, because by now there was the threat of terrorist attacks affecting potentially everyone through the British Isles—to start apportioning blame. Many people almost certainly did this, indeed they may well have been justi-fied in doing so, as the conclusion of the Widgery Inquiry, for example, was that the British Army soldiers had been fired on first and that there was no reason to suppose that they would otherwise have opened fire themselves. Subsequently, as the IRA extended their bombing campaign onto the main-land, killing many more—their terrorist threat was greater than that which we experience today—there can have been few Fifties Children who did not unequivocally blame the IRA for the Troubles.

In the face of this situation confronting the Fifties Child, it may seem quite extraordinary that in all of Barclay James Harvest's songs that deal with the Troubles—all by Lees—there is not even a hint of apportioning blame. The way that Lees responds is in typically compassionate fashion. Not for him the reflex of countering violence with violence. No. Instead, he opens up and addresses the deeper issues: for instance, how a child born into that situation, on whatever side of the divide, almost inevitably becomes drawn into the conflict, as the following quotation from 'Summer Soldier' [1972] demonstrates:

I feel sorry for the children who with open mind are willing
to fight for ideals aged and past their time.

I feel sorry for the children who will join the vicious circle
of instinct fear bred from their parents' minds.

'Summer Soldier' is a song of exceptional vision: it is both hugely perceptive and deeply spiritual and I am convinced it is without parallel in British rock. Unsurprisingly, its depth of meaning means that it will make recurring appearances throughout this book. In 'Summer Soldier' Lees expresses his compassion for *all* of the victims of the conflict. What is most remarkable, and what helps to make this such a powerful and memorable song, is that he recognises that it is not only those killed or injured that are victims, but also the perpetrators of the violence itself:

I feel sorry for the soldier, who is shot and stoned in anger;
I feel sorry for his wife and child at home.
I feel sorry for the bomber, who all life and limb dishonours;
for the people that he's maimed and left alone.

Astonishing words. "I feel sorry for the bomber"—astonishing! This stance stems from the clear recognition that those born into a deeply antagonistic situation such as the Troubles find it difficult to extricate themselves from the norms of their peers. This exemplifies the broad vision of a peacemaker, the sort of vision that Senator Mitchell would have had to apply in bringing the bitterly opposed parties together in brokering the Good Friday peace agreement. Lees also had his own recommendations for the peace process within 'Summer Soldier':

The Lord God said love thy neighbour:
break the circle, free the hater,
call him a friend.

The song has a strong humanitarian thrust, in calling for an end to the divisions, an end to the reprisals. It calls on everyone to stand up for peace, making the point that we are each and every one of us responsible for achieving it:

Wake up! Wake up! There's a man by your side
with a knife and a gun in each hand!
Wake up! Wake up! You're one and the same!
It's time to stop and decide:
is it love or hate?
Is it peace or war?
It's for sure there's no in-between.

Politicians point views
but they're pointing for you—
the solution has to be seen!

"You're one and the same"—Lees is saying that if you do nothing to alter the cycle of violence then you are as culpable as the "man . . . with a knife and a gun in each hand". This is what he means by "break the circle, free the hater, call him a friend". Effectively, the "hater" is the person(s) to whom Lees is addressing this section of the song, the ones who are caught up in the "vicious circle of instinct fear bred from their parents' minds". He is urging them to stop the "vicious circle", to stop the violence. There is an ambiguity in the "you're one and the same" lyric which is perhaps intentional. Two possible meanings are "why are you fighting someone who's the same as you?" and "if you do nothing to stop the vicious circle of violence, then you're as bad as any actual perpetrator of that violence". The ambiguity does not affect the crunch—"they're pointing for you"—there is no escaping it, the responsibility is individual, it is with us all.

We shall revisit and discover more about this phenomenal song a little later, as we have still only uncovered a part of its meaning—it really is an absolute gem.[3] However, despite its complexity, it still has an immediate and life-lasting impact, if only by virtue of the depth of compassion behind the immortal line "I feel sorry for the bomber, who all life and limb dishonours".

'Summer Soldier's call for each individual to assume responsibility and take action to work for peace is repeated in another of Lees' songs inspired by the Troubles. 'For No One' is one of Barclay James Harvest's most popular songs and it is one which, despite probably never being interpreted exactly how Lees meant it, has always had an immediate and very powerful impact as an anti-war song, courtesy of its kick-arse opening music and lyric "please lay down your pistols and your rifles".

'For No One' is, however, much more than a simple anti-war song: in fact, arguably, it is not a true anti-war song at all. Rather, as in 'Summer Soldier', Lees makes a direct call on individuals—the "no ones" of the song's title—to make a difference by bringing about a change for peace by standing up for what is right. The list of changes targeted by Lees continues on immediately

---

3. The song's power has not diminished with the years. John Lees' Barclay James Harvest played 'Summer Soldier' in December 2010 at the live show recorded for the *Rock Legends Filmed Live at Metropolis Studios* DVD: the audience's ovation was emotional and prolonged, causing the band's keyboards player—Jez Smith, a relative newbie—to exclaim an impressed "follow that!" when it eventually subsided. Sadly, the mavericks at Metropolis edited it out. That's why you should go to live shows!

from that famous opening: "Please lay down your colours and your creeds." This is the lyric that keys the song into the Troubles, the "colours" referring to the gaudy banners carried by Protestants during the marching season, which the Catholic community always found provocative, and the "creeds" referring to the feud between those two creeds of Christianity. Lees itemises further items for change but, crucially, the crux of the song comes in the lines that follow on from the opening couplet, as well as in the chorus

> Please lay down your thoughts of being no one:
> concentrate on what you ought to be
> . . .
> Take a look at what lies all around you:
> then pray God we can live in peace!
> Everyone's a loner 'til he needs a helping hand;
> everyone is everybody else.
> Everyone's a no one 'til he wants to make a stand!
> God alone knows how we will survive!

By being trapped in the "colours and creeds", the individual being addressed is effectively in the same "vicious circle" as those in 'Summer Soldier' and, as such, he is described by Lees as a "no one". He is a "no one" because, in order to feel that he is "someone", he has to seek the acknowledgement and praise of his peers by following the established norm of his family and friends ("everyone's a loner till he needs a helping hand"). He just reacts to peer pressure and has become trapped in the circle of violence "bred from . . . parents' minds". Lees tells him to "look . . . all around you", can't you see that "everyone is (the same as) everybody else": we are all the same, why are you fighting? "Concentrate" on what is right, change into "what you ought to be" and then "we can live in peace". God alone will decide how the world will evolve. By making this difficult change, by resisting the peer pressure and "make(ing) a stand", they cease to be "no ones"—they have stood up for what is right by rejecting "pistols and rifles . . . colours and creeds . . . bullshit and protest . . . governments of greed". The "everyone is everybody else" line is also interpretable—perhaps more securely in the context of the chorus—as meaning that by succumbing to the peer pressure viewpoint you just become a "no one" amongst all the others who follow an unworthy cause for the principal—and very human—reason of wanting to be accepted as part of the crowd, part of the gang, part of the tribe. The song is addressed to all the individuals caught by this "vicious circle"—which is why it is called 'For No One'.

These calls for individual action are what make 'Summer Soldier' and 'For No One' stand out from the normal anti-war song. They are anti-war songs, yes, but first and foremost they are calls for all of us to seek out compassionate truth, stand up for the fact that we are all equal and put an end to violence. We are all accountable, you and me.

'Summer Soldier' is even more complex than this, and in the earlier analysis I omitted any mention of the second half of the song. Why? Why not mention a major portion of such a significant song? To have analysed it earlier in the chapter would have detracted somewhat from the flow of the argument, which is helped by some of the analysis of 'For No One'. The second part of 'Summer Soldier' is a dream sequence in which two contrasting personas appear; the "summer soldier", who is intent on war, and the "angel bright", who favours peace. It will become clear later in our social history, when we revisit the song, that these opposing caricatures are, in fact, a manifestation of the inner psyche;[4] they are Lees' way of saying that, within us all, there is both the potential for perfect good and for perfect evil and, throughout our time on earth, the battle between these opposites—which we may or may not be aware of—is ongoing in our minds and continually dictates our actions. In the context of 'Summer Soldier' and the Troubles, then, what he is saying is that *each one of us*, placed in the same situations, with the same pressures, could be capable of the same atrocities. Which is why Lees does not condemn: he understands the fine line between being a peacemaker or a warmonger. This is why he can feel "sorry for the bomber who all life and limb dishonours": he understands that, in another life, it could be him—or *you*, or me—planting that explosive device. The exemplification of the duality of the psyche leads to yet another possible meaning of the lyrics: "Wake up! Wake up! There's a man by your side / with a knife and a gun in each hand! / Wake up! Wake up! You're one and the same!" Lees is addressing the actual perpetrator of violence directly and pleading with him to work within his own mind to seek the "angel bright" of his nature. It is possible that Lees did not intend all three meanings that I have identified for this section of the song, but I am sure that they are all consistent with the intent of both 'Summer Soldier' and 'For No One'.

These two songs, inspired by the Troubles but applicable to so many situations of conflict, are absolutely monumental in their scope and psychological insight. They are undoubtedly two of the most extraordinary songs of the Fifties Child's classic rock era.

Equally inspirational is another of Lees' songs from the same period, 'Child

---

4. My use of the term "psyche" throughout this book is not consistent with that of most philosophers or psychiatrists. Instead, it is driven by Lees' own writing in a number of songs, in which he seems to suggest an internal mental battle between the forces of good and evil. Metaphors are used in these songs, so to avoid calling this battle one for the "mind" or "soul", which many people have specific ideas about, I have called it the "psyche".

of the Universe',[5] which we have already met a couple of times. The song relates to the way that children become innocent victims of adults' conflicts— one of Lees' recurring themes—and Northern Ireland gets the necessary and inevitable namecheck: "I'm a child of Northern Ireland . . . I didn't ask to be born and I don't ask to die!"

In 'Cheap the Bullet', another song which is at least partly influenced by the Troubles in Northern Ireland, Lees intimates at his belief in a link between the violence on the TV and that on the streets. This excerpt is taken from the song's stirring musical bridge:

> I'm baptised in your prejudice;
> I'm confirmed with your hate;
> I'm ordained into violence:
> I'm a child of the modern world,
> of the media world,
> of the TV world.

Whilst one might be tempted to consider that the clear religious imagery, delivered with bile, anchors the song firmly into the Troubles, there is—as ever—another possible interpretation that makes us hesitate. Like 'Summer Soldier' and 'For No One' before it, 'Cheap the Bullet' never explicitly mentions Northern Ireland. However, although the song could apply generically to the riots and other street violence that had wracked Britain for a period in the Eighties, there can be little doubt that the continuing Troubles were a factor in its thinking. We hear Lees returning to themes already familiar from 'Summer Soldier':

> Our children wake to the bomb and the body-search:
> we fill their ears with the drums and the battle cries.
> They burn your car when you stray; it's a game they play.
> They're fed on hate—it's a circle we don't want to break.

The "drums" are, of course, those played on the Unionist marches, which were also referenced in 'For No One' through the use of the word "colours".

---

5. 'Child of the Universe' was probably written around the same time as 'Summer Soldier', as it was first recorded during 1972 for Lees' solo album, *A Major Fancy*. The solo album itself was not released until 1977 due to contractual issues, so that the song's first appearance was on the *Everyone is Everybody Else* album. Also, there is probably less than two years between 'Summer Soldier' and 'For No One'; the comparatively long gap between the two consecutive respective albums being due to the same contractual issues.

"They burn your car when you stray" is about the violence perpetrated on members of their own community by paramilitary groups when they decide that a particular individual is not aligned to the cause and this feeds neatly into the "circle of hate" theme again. Contrast the lyric from 'Cheap the Bullet' with the one from 'Summer Soldier':

['CTB']   They're fed on hate—it's a circle we don't want to break
['SS']   The vicious circle of instinct fear bred from their parents' minds

Anyone who has ever doubted that 'Summer Soldier', 'For No One' and 'Cheap the Bullet' were inspired by Northern Ireland will surely now see, having looked at them closely together like this, how the synergies between them indicate unequivocally that the Troubles were indeed a major source. There is a great sadness in this though, despite the songs' brilliance, and it is that Lees felt compelled to write 'Cheap the Bullet' some twenty years after 'Summer Soldier', 'Child of the Universe' and 'For No One'. Only the sickening, persistent violence, the ongoing circle of hate, could be responsible for that.

This suite of songs—the "Troubles Suite"—is one of the most significant sociological statements in British rock history. Had Lees never written any other songs than these, then his legacy would have still deserved a unique place in that history.

In 2012 Lees revealed—without giving the reason—that he had struggled to convince the other members of the band to include 'Summer Soldier' within the *Baby James Harvest* album. Clearly, Lees' response to the situation in Northern Ireland, in particular the non-attribution of blame, is his own individual stance, but it is possibly one that was shared by many people in Britain. After all, this sectarian violence was between Christians, ostensibly people who believed in the same God. Irrespective of how widely his personal view was shared, the fact of the matter is that the situation in Ireland was high on the agenda for all Fifties Children, taking up a high profile during some thirty years of their peak adulthood.

Possibly the most well-known song inspired by the Troubles is U2's 'Sunday Bloody Sunday'. However, its lyricists—The Edge (David Evans) and Bono (Paul Hewson)—were born in 1961 and 1960 and were both brought up and educated in the Republic of Ireland, so they are too far-off being contemporaneous with our songwriters. My personal favourite song from an artist who meets the criterion is the Sutherland Brothers' 'Ireland' [*Lifeboat*, 1972], composed by Iain Sutherland. The Sutherland Brothers are another act whose music, like Barclay James Harvest's, was underappreciated by the British public. However, unlike Barclay James Harvest's writers, Iain

Sutherland did manage to pen one huge Top 10 hit ('Arms of Mary', from the *Reach for the Sky* album, reached No. 5 in 1976), while his brother Gavin wrote the song 'Sailing', which appears alongside 'Ireland' on the *Lifeboat* album, and which topped the charts for Rod Stewart in 1975.

Sutherland's contextual approach on 'Ireland' is, unlike Lees' stance, explicitly politicised, although he also covers similar compassionate ground. Like Lees, Sutherland draws out images of the Unionist marches, singing sardonically that people are dying whilst this flamboyant and ostentatious display is happening; and he feels pain for the plight of children and their mothers caught up in the fighting. And why, why all this fighting, when all men are equal? These aspects have a high synergy with Lees' writing but Sutherland also launches a scathing political attack on "England", blaming the British government for the problems and saying unequivocally that the troops should be withdrawn. If England really is such a wonderful, free country, why does it not show everyone in the world how it can bring about peace? That is the real test!

Despite the sporadic violence that has continued since, the Troubles are generally accepted as having ended with the Good Friday Agreement. More than 3,000 people died. At its height, some 30,000 British soldiers were stationed in the province, many more than have been deployed to Afghanistan. Attacks on the mainland were common: the Houses of Commons, 10 Downing Street, the military, pubs and shopping malls were all attacked. The threat of terrorist attack was high and real, claiming many lives on the mainland, as well as in Northern Ireland. There is no doubt that for a British Fifties Child, the Troubles were a big issue, a great cataract in his vision of hope.

9

South Africa under Apartheid

South Africa plays a role—albeit not always a happy one—in Barclay James Harvest's history, as well as being the inspiration behind a number of songs, and so it is proper that it should feature in our social history.

Like many countries of the world, South Africa was the subject of European colonization from the fifteenth century onwards. Home to some of mankind's earliest settlements, South Africa was "discovered" by the Portuguese as they made their way around Africa to their colonies in the east. It was the Dutch however who first settled the area—in what would become Cape Town—in the mid-seventeenth century. Conflicts with indigenous African people, migrating southwards from further north, began almost immediately. Their enmity with the colonizers meant that the Dutch imported slaves from Madagascar, Indonesia and India to supply them with cheap labour. It also meant that in order to secure sufficient food supplies, farming development was encouraged, which necessitated expansion northwards and eastwards from the Cape area.

As Dutch power waned in the late eighteenth century, the British moved in, taking control in 1806. Farming expansion had continued apace under Dutch control: the adventuresome farmers—whose numbers had been added to by emigration from Germany, Scandinavia, and France—were to become known as the Boers. Discrimination on the basis of race was already prevalent by the time of the British takeover. British immigration concentrated on urban areas; hence, they formed a distinct population from the mainly rural Boers.

Despite the abolishment of slavery in 1834, discrimination against the non-white population continued. Like the Dutch before them, the British sought cheap labour from overseas. The British Empire was then flourishing and resource-rich: about 150,000 workers would arrive from India before the turn of the century.

The nineteenth century as a whole was a time of strife in South Africa as Boers, British and indigenous Africans came into conflict. The tension was exacerbated by the discovery of diamonds in 1869 and eventually the Boers' resentment of the British erupted into war in 1880 over control of one of the republics of the region, Transvaal. The Boers quickly repelled the British, who nevertheless continued in an attempt to consolidate other republics under their rule.

The discovery of gold in 1886 again increased the animosity between the two European-originating factions. Inflamed by a British incursion into Boer territory in 1895, tensions escalated to the point that a second war with the Boers broke out in 1899. This time the conflict was longer and bitter. Finally the British emerged victorious and, at the beginning of the twentieth century, the Boers resigned themselves to British sovereignty.

Despite having lost land and cattle to the colonizers, the indigenous African kingdoms managed to retain their independence for most of the nineteenth century. It was only through the British push for unification during the latter part of the century that the Xhosa, the Zulus and other tribes finally fell under colonial rule. By the turn of the century, all of the African kingdoms were under British control. These black people would be granted as few rights as those others who had already been living in colonial-controlled areas.

However, by 1909, home rule had been granted. Under Boer and British-settler administration, the new parliament passed race segregation legislation in 1913 that would become the basis of apartheid.[1] Further apartheid legislation would follow, each new law reducing still further the rights of non-white people. Discrimination against all non-whites was significant, with restrictions on land ownership, voting, freedom of movement, employment, use of public services, etc.

A significant step in the internal opposition against the repression had been taken in 1912 when the disparate efforts of various black tribes were unified by the formation of the African National Congress (ANC). This organisation would grow in influence after the Second World War, becoming the main focus in South Africa's internal struggle against apartheid.

1. Apartheid is now defined by the International Criminal Court. The crime includes within its definition similar policies and practices of racial segregation and discrimination as those implemented in South Africa. It must be "committed in the context of an institutionalised regime of systematic oppression and domination by one racial group over any other racial group or groups and committed with the intention of maintaining that regime".

Independence from Britain was granted in 1931, though South Africa remained part of the Commonwealth until 1961. Governments shifted steadily to the right over the course of the century, with the radical Afrikaner-controlled National Party dominating politics.[2] South African support for Britain and the Allies during the two World Wars was begrudged by many and, post-Second World War, the moderates who had placed the country on the Allied side were marginalised. Further tightening of apartheid regulations followed as the Boers tightened their grip on power.

By the start of the Sixties, the policy of apartheid had become increasingly controversial both within and outside South Africa, and international protests against it had begun. The Anti-Apartheid Movement in Britain had its origins in 1959 and was intensified after the 1960 Sharpeville Massacre, when 69 black protestors were shot by police. Anti-apartheid support came from the Labour and Liberal parties, the British Communist Party, the trades unions, some churches and other, non-aligned organisations such as Amnesty International (founded in 1961). The Musicians' Union was another non-aligned organisation taking action—as early as 1957 it was preventing its members from performing to segregated audiences; in practice, a ban against playing to audiences in South Africa. In 1962, the United Nations passed a non-binding resolution calling for the imposition of economic and other sanctions against South Africa but this was not supported by the British and other Western governments.

Let's just stop there. Consider the situation for a moment. Arguably, Western civilization owes much of its economic strength to the exploitation of indigenous peoples during the colonial era. Often, the indigenous people paid a much heavier price than that levied through apartheid, the people of the Americas being a prime example. Elsewhere, indigenous wealth was raped for Western profit whether by exploitation of slave or ultra-cheap labour, or by commandeering economically-rich land. South Africa provides such an example: cheap labour was imported from India and China and the profits from diamond and gold mining operations went to the colonizers. The focus of Britain's interest in the area only sharpened once diamonds were discovered. At the time of the United Nations resolution in 1962, the British still retained significant economic investment in South Africa. In these sorts of situation, one is often left with the impression that government decisions on whether to take military action or impose economic sanctions are based on self-interest, rather than on any humanitarian considerations. For instance, who remembers Tiananmen Square now? The April 1989 protest movement against the

2. Afrikaners, the ethnic group which includes the Boers, are of Dutch, French and German descent; their language is Afrikaans, related to Dutch, and they are considered to be distinct from South Africans of British descent.

Chinese government was focused around Beijing's Tiananmen Square, where at certain times as many as 500,000 people gathered in protest at their government. After seven weeks, the army—the People's Liberation Army—cleared the Square using live ammunition. Guestimates of the death toll range from several hundreds to the thousands. And what did the world do? Impose token, short-lived economic and military sanctions. Ultimately, the repressive Chinese government was strengthened by the events. China was then given the prestigious Olympic Games to host and we continue to do a roaring trade with the country as it grows economically. Was the Tiananmen Square movement so different from the protests of the Arab Spring?[3] From a humanitarian standpoint, no, but anyone trying serious intervention in China was going to end up with a very bloody nose! Plus, look at all the money that we are now making from China. On the other hand, the conclusion was that we could intervene in Libya without suffering too badly militarily or economically—so let's all support the Arab Spring. Our foreign policies are a combination of economics allied to bully-boy bravado, while humanitarian considerations come in at a very low second place.

Exploitation of "lesser" peoples was thus inculcated in colonial—in Western civilization—culture and this was still prevalent in the Britain of the early Sixties, despite the erosion that its empire had by now experienced. Elsewhere in the Western world, these attitudes also still prevailed—let us not forget that the dismantling of legal segregation of black people in the United States did not begin until the mid-Fifties and the process of implementing it would last almost two decades. So it is perhaps not surprising that Britain and the United States refused to support the implementation of economic sanctions against South Africa in the Sixties. In fact, disinvestment in South Africa by the nations with the power to hurt it economically did not begin until more than twenty years later, when the Republican-controlled United States senate finally voted in favour of sanctions.

In summary, even as the years rolled by and apartheid was entrenched, opposition to its existence came principally from pressure groups, rather than from governments.

🦋

Into this maelstrom of confusion and conflicting opinions stepped Barclay James Harvest. In the autumn of 1972, after the recording of—but prior to—

---

3. Arab Spring is the name given to a series of anti-government protests affecting Arabian countries that started in Tunisia in December 2010 and which dominoed across the region thereafter. Western nations, including Britain, intervened militarily in Libya, assisting to overthrow the previous regime—major oil companies from leading interventionist countries stand to make hefty profits from partaking in the country's rich oil industry.

the release of the *Baby James Harvest* album,[4] they undertook a seventeen-date tour of South Africa. This move was met with incredulity by many of their own fans and outright hostility by many campaigners against South Africa's apartheid regime.

Whilst the band were not members of the Musicians' Union at the time, they would surely have known of the resistance to performances in South Africa. The Musicians' Union ban was high profile, not just because of the abhorrence of apartheid, but because it was not unanimously supported by musicians, and had therefore generated much debate. The Rolling Stones had cancelled a tour to South Africa in 1964 because of the situation. Admittedly, their profile may not yet have been high enough for the cancellation to have been noticed by our songwriters—who would have been in their mid to late teens at the time—or their managers but there was plenty of publicity surrounding Dusty Springfield's decision to include a "no segregation" clause in her contract to play in South Africa in 1964.

At that time, there was a loophole in South African law which allowed live performances in theatres to play to integrated audiences. Springfield took advantage and played one such show in Cape Town. The authorities were incensed and deported her back to Britain, subsequently closing the loophole. The singer was lauded for her actions by the House of Commons but some performers, such as Max Bygraves, were angry with her for having annoyed the South African authorities, fearing an impact on their own potential income there. Cliff Richard, too, played in South Africa during the Sixties, and often repeatedly after, in order "to bring Jesus into people's hearts and so change them and society". So a Musicians' Union ban there might have been, and the lack of consensus in the performing industry meant there was plenty of "noise" surrounding it.

Barclay James Harvest's rationale for undertaking the tour is not well documented and remains perplexing. There can be little doubt that the tour lost the band many British fans, possibly forever. The impact may have been exacerbated by the fact that, even at this early stage of their career, Barclay James Harvest were a band with principles: as we have already seen in previous chapters, they had already released a number of environmental protest songs, as well as 'After the Day', which may well have been interpreted as an anti-nuclear weapons song. Therefore, they attracted fans with principles, just the sort to have found news of the South African tour distasteful. Additionally, the

4. The exact timing is important because this places the writing of 'Summer Soldier' before the tour took place, cementing the band's "principles" credentials: in other words, the tour was ill advised; a mistake for these four young adults who—as well as wanting to make some money—wanted their idealism to translate into positive action.

band's fan-base was strong within the universities, which were a bastion of anti-apartheid sentiment. Some forty years after the event, it is possible to find comments on the internet still decrying their decision.

The inevitable happened as the British tour in support of the *Baby James Harvest* album, released soon after their return from South Africa, was badly disrupted by student protests against the band. Wolstenholme's comments in a 1988 interview are not helpful in clarifying the decision-making process:

> We went out there, did a few scrappy things like playing with the Durban Symphony Orchestra, and it was not anything big deal; an audience is an audience, so I don't think anyone asked what colour they were . . . if the principle was right to pillory us, why weren't they pillorying everyone else? It was only because we were a college band. Naivety comes into it—we were less aware of things then, we just wanted to play a few gigs in some funny country somewhere, and then you come back and it's like all hell's broken loose. I'm still not absolutely convinced what to do about South Africa—I don't have that kind of information.

One can only surmise that if naivety had been a major part in the decision to go to South Africa—and how could it not have been?—then Wolstenholme had not lost it.

Certainly, anyone conversant with Barclay James Harvest's sociological songs will be sure that their motives for the trip would not have included any thought of promoting or defending the apartheid regime. One only has to consider songs such as 'Summer Soldier' and the *original* version of 'Child of the Universe', both of which were written around the same time as the tour, to begin to grasp that fact. This view is supported by evidence from one of the band's managers at the time, Dave Crowe, who says that the band "were saying things on stage [whilst in South Africa] which could have got them into trouble—they did in fact get fined".

Eventually, in an attempt to restore some normality to their working arrangements after returning home and facing the disruptive protests, the band joined the Musicians' Union and issued the following statement to the press in November 1972:

> Following the tour of South Africa by Barclay James Harvest, during which they performed largely before segregated audiences in agreement with South African law, students at Leeds, Liverpool and Portsmouth have protested at performances due to take place at the universities and colleges by this group. We have now joined the Musicians' Union and agreement has been reached with the Union that no further visits to South Africa will be made while the present South African government laws prevail. Agreement has also been reached with the Anti-Apartheid

Movement to the effect that, whilst Barclay James Harvest went to South Africa with the intention of helping to bring a new culture to the young people of the country, they now realise that the international cultural boycott is a more effective method of opposing the South African government's abhorrent policies.

Notwithstanding this message—which, forty years' worth of songs later we know with confidence to have been sincere—Barclay James Harvest's visit to South Africa remains a blot in their history despite the fact that consensus on cultural boycotts—or, indeed, boycotts or sanctions of any sort—was never reached and that other British artists—Queen, Status Quo, Rod Stewart and others—continued to play in South Africa during the apartheid era.

The force that was to dismantle apartheid came from within South Africa itself. In the late Eighties, it sometimes seemed as if the world was awash with angels determined to correct some of mankind's wayward wanderings.[5] One of those angels came in the guise of the man known as F. W. de Klerk: a staunch conservative climbing the rungs of the South African National Party, he took over its presidency in 1989 when long-time leader P. W. Botha fell ill.

De Klerk was as skilful as Gorbachev in the Soviet Union: as early as February 1990 he made a speech to the South African parliament in which he declared his intent to not only release Nelson Mandela from his 26 years of incarceration, but also to legalise the ANC—along with its military wing, Umkhonto we Sizwe—as well as the South African Communist Party. The announcement was met with some incredulity: the right wing of his own party responded with protests and boos. But de Klerk was no fool: he could understand the way the world was developing and that, if nothing in South Africa changed, then in twenty or thirty years the country would be totally isolated and with a civil war on its hands. This in no way diminishes the brilliance of his courage and breadth of vision: that de Klerk was then able to implement his strategy so successfully is a massive testament to his skill.

The release of Mandela, the leader of the ANC's military wing, who, despite—or perhaps because of it—his incarceration in 1962, had come to symbolise the whole of the anti-apartheid resistance movement, was as significant for South Africa as the fall of the Berlin Wall had been for Europe. Television images of his release were beamed live across the world: here was the man the world had been waiting to see for a quarter of a century. And wow, what presence. Mandela's charisma was *immense*. Never mind angels, this was the stuff of fairy tales! No wonder that the ANC handed him the responsibility for leading negotiations with the South African government.

5. . . . the one assigned to China must have crashlanded . . .

What Mandela and de Klerk, together with their respective negotiating teams, achieved in the course of the next four years—the peaceful transformation of South Africa into a democratic society with equal rights for all—was nothing short of miraculous given the open inter-racial bitterness that existed. Much of this success will have been down to Mandela's charismatic leadership and his remarkable, oft-repeated call for reconciliation.

Free elections with voting rights for all were held in 1994 and the ANC won more than 60 per cent of the vote, going on to form the new government, which it has held in all subsequent elections to date. South Africa continues to have its problems, as many other countries do, but its situation would surely have been far worse had de Klerk not taken his brave course of action back in 1990.

Interestingly, apartheid and cultural boycotts are still very much on the agenda today, and the same debates are played over again. This reflects the circularity of history to which Holroyd refers in 'Ring of Changes'—by 1983 he had seen enough of the world to realise that what happens tomorrow will in essence be a replay of what has gone on before. This time around, the focus is on Israel, and its treatment of Palestinians, a situation that is one of the great unresolved problems of our world but one that Barclay James Harvest are unlikely to become embroiled in.

✻

South Africa features in three of Barclay James Harvest's songs: Lees' 'Child of the Universe' and 'African', and Holroyd's 'African Nights'.

'Child of the Universe' will have been written around the time of the South African tour, or perhaps even earlier, as an early version was included on Lees' solo album *A Major Fancy*, which was recorded in 1972, but not released until 1977 because of contractual reasons.[6] Of course, we have already met 'Child of the Universe', being as it is a timeless powerhouse of a song, its enduring message a vibrant reminder that, in this modern world, all of us have to take responsibility for its injustices: "I'm a child of South Africa . . . you can see me on the TV every day / I'm the child next door, three thousand miles away!"

Written some fifteen years later, 'African' is one of the most overtly political songs penned by Lees. Whilst its lyrics offer no solutions to the South African problem, they have sufficient depth to suggest that Lees had lost that element of naivety that had influenced the decision to tour South Africa. He was prompted to write 'African' by the Kinross mine disaster of 1986, in which more than 175 people died and over 230 were injured, causing the mine workers' union to stage a massive protest against working conditions. The specifics in the song relate to the situation in South Africa:

6. In 2010 an even earlier demo version—with partially different lyrics—found its way as a bonus track onto the re-release of the remastered *A Major Fancy*.

> The politics of apartheid—
> the politics of shame!
> The cold abuse of human rights,
> of torture and of pain
> are only part of the action
> when you're an African . . .

But Lees also generalises the situation into other contexts where similar abuses of power occur and he takes the opportunity of venting his anger. This excerpt seems to align with a line of argument developed earlier in this chapter:

> The politics of making more,
> the politics of greed:
> the cold abuse of poverty
> to keep your labour cheap
> are only part of the action
> when you're a working man.

The final generalisation in the song brings its most powerful moment, as the blame is firmly placed with greedy, power-hungry people, of whatever nominal ideology, who make their way to positions of control:

> Far left, far right, centre:
> it's power they crave!
> The politics of buying arms
> when there's no food to eat;
> the politics of digging gold
> instead of planting seeds.
> The leader with his private golf course
> and his flashy cars
> sits playing with his diamond wrist watch
> while the people starve!

One can see that Lees' stance is apolitical: 'African' may have been inspired by a specific incident but becomes a rant against abuses of political power in general. Its musical arrangement is perfectly aligned to the message; one can easily sense Lees' anger through the powerful guitar-driven rock.

Holroyd's 'African Nights' is entirely different in approach, being an exultation of the beauty of Africa, told through some pleasant memories from that infamous South African tour. This song's synthesized bird sounds, lilting rhythms and happy melody will resonate particularly with anyone who has been lucky enough to visit Africa and experience its majesty. There is no contradiction in deriving so much pleasure from a tour that proved so controversial. Irrespective of the controversy when they returned home, the beauty of Africa will have been sufficient to linger long in the memory of our songwriters who were, let us remember, instinctively drawn to the beauty of the natural environment. This aspect of the tour will have charged their spirits: an effect that the stress of the anti-apartheid protestors on the subsequent British tour could not have entirely dissipated.

A reflection of the British ambivalence in the fight against apartheid in South Africa is the fact that there are very few examples of songs on the topic by other artists, with Peter Gabriel's 'Biko' [*Peter Gabriel (3)*, 1980] being probably the most famous example. Stephen Biko was a high-profile black South African anti-apartheid campaigner. He was arrested by the authorities in August 1977 and suffered significant injuries, including head wounds, under interrogation. He died from those injuries in September, shortly after a 1100km drive—he was transported naked and manacled in the back of a Land Rover—to a prison with hospital facilities. Two journalists who were close friends of Biko's publicised the truth behind his death, leading to outrage throughout the world at the brutality of the police, and the incident helped to boost the international campaign against apartheid. Gabriel's song is one of many written worldwide to mention Biko. If you are after a literal, but very powerful, account of the event then listen to American folk singer Tom Paxton's 'The Death of Stephen Biko' [1978]. Gabriel's own attempt is equally as compelling but takes a different approach, concentrating on evoking the African spirit through the music, including the rhythm of the words. Essentially, he argues that the incident has finally changed the world's perception of the apartheid system's brutality against black people and that now the international pressure against its injustices will mount: Gabriel's powerful music almost seems to invoke Biko's spirit in pursuit of this aim.

Barclay James Harvest's own interactions with South Africa, through the controversy of their 1972 tour and through song, reflect the societal impact on British Fifties Children. Drawn to the country through its majesty and beauty, many Fifties Children found the South African government's legislation of apartheid deeply distasteful. There was less consensus about what type of action to implement against South Africa's policy: many people and organisations favoured boycotts and sanctions but many others, including the government, were doubtful about their effectiveness and worried about any negative impact they might have on South Africa's deprived population. Ultimately, whilst economic sanctions never did bite South Africa deeply, the continuing international debate about the evils of apartheid and South Africa's near-isolation were amongst the factors that persuaded de Klerk that change was needed.

One final word on the South African tour controversy: let me just offer you a personal perspective on how easy it can be to make decisions that could "break the boycott". As a teenage student at university (1978-81), I supported various "principle" groups, such as CND and Amnesty International (which was anti-apartheid). I often went along to concerts by my favourite bands at the Students' Union—amongst the contemporaries of Barclay James Harvest that I saw there were bands such as Procol Harum, Renaissance and Strawbs. If I suspected those groups or, indeed, Barclay James Harvest (whose popularity in Britain meant that by that time they had moved on to playing bigger theatres and only the odd students' union gig remained on the tour schedule) of touring South Africa then I would almost certainly not have gone to see them or bought their albums. It was only by the accident of my age that the first time I became acquainted with Barclay James Harvest was in 1975, and it would be a few years before I would find out that such a controversy over their tour had existed. Had they toured South Africa in 1976, my reaction might well have been as adverse as that of some fans in 1972.

On leaving university in 1981, I joined the British Antarctic Survey and was initially stationed at South Georgia, an island claimed by Britain that was administratively linked to the Falkland Islands. Then, in April 1982, the Argentinians invaded and my colleagues and I were flown back home to Britain after some shenanigans in Argentine detention. Travelling back to the Antarctic in the autumn of 1982, the British Antarctic Survey supply ship called in for supplies at Cape Town. So what did I, this "principled" young man, do? Stay on board the ship for the three days that we were in port and sulk? No, out I went with friends, travelling, seeing the sites, and buying *large* quantities of delightful South African wine—"the cold abuse of poverty"—from the vast and beautiful vineyards of the region. What a cad. So, there I am, supporting apartheid . . . but please don't tear up this book!

So, you are a musician in a band and you are deeply in debt. Someone offers you the chance to earn some money in a faraway country. You know there is a problem with the mistreatment of black people but you are told you will be playing to mixed audiences. So, you are bringing your music to these deprived people *and* making some money. Win-win, must be . . .

10

The Second Iraq War

The birthplace of Islam is Arabia where, during the seventh century Muhammad was praying in the mountains near his hometown of Mecca when God revealed himself to him. Muhammad preached widely about God's teachings, which would eventually be written down in the Quran, the Holy Book of Islam. After an initially hesitant response to Muhammad's mission, his followers, the Muslims,[1] grew rapidly to form the international religion that we know today.

Arab leaders expanded into new territories far afield in a desire to convert new peoples to the Islamic faith. Expansion to the east of Arabia was as swift as it was westward and then north into southern Europe, where large portions of Spain and Portugal stayed under Islamic control for centuries. Inevitably, tensions rose between Christians and Muslims as each sought to expand their religion to new territories. Worse still for the Christians was the fact that, in their expansion, the Muslims had conquered Jerusalem—a holy city for the three main Western religions of Christianity, Islam and Judaism—as early as 637.

This led directly to the Crusades, a series of war campaigns starting from the late eleventh century and sanctioned by the Roman Catholic Pope with the original objective of ousting Muslims from the Christian Holy Places. By the start of that First Crusade, Arabian supremacy had already begun to wane in favour of other Muslim forces, as Turkish peoples began to migrate from distant Central Asia. In the thirteenth century, it was the turn of the Mongols to sweep through vast parts of the region, then in the fifteenth it was the Ottomans. European power had grown with the wealth garnered from their conquests in the Americas and by the seventeenth century it was ready to start challenging the Ottomans militarily and economically. This shift of power

1. The word "Muslim" means "one who offers himself to God" in Arabic.

began to reflect itself in the European domination of Middle Eastern territories from the nineteenth century, during which the French seized Algeria and Tunisia and Britain took control of Egypt and the Persian Gulf. This trend continued as more lands fell directly under European control or influence and they were the dominant force in the region at the start of the twentieth century.

The First World War brought no dramatic change in this situation. Towards its close Britain gave its backing, through the Balfour Declaration of November 1917, to growing Zionist demands for a Jewish state in Palestine, on land that, whilst it had been occupied by the ancestors of the Jews in the millennium before the second century AD, had itself been the home of Arabs for well over one thousand years since the seventh century. Whilst the state of Israel did not actually come into existence until after the Second World War, the seemingly insoluble "Palestinian problem" dates back to this British stance.

In between the two World Wars, a number of countries, such as Syria and Egypt, began to push for independence from European control. The political muscularity of the region was enhanced by the discovery that the Middle East lands were oil rich, making them one of the most important geopolitical areas in the oil-hungry world of the twentieth century.

Conflicts in the region continued during the Second World War, including a British invasion of Iraq in 1941. By the war's end, whilst there had been a significant overall reduction in European control, the pressure for a Zionist state had become immense. Eventually, when the British Mandate in Palestine expired in 1948, Zionist leaders autonomously declared the State of Israel. Their armies then defeated combined forces from a number of Arab countries in the conflict that resulted as a direct consequence of this unilateral declaration of independence. Sporadic conflicts and wars between Israel and its neighbours continue to this day, with the Palestinian problem being a super-fermenter of deep hatred.

And so, as we can see, European and Islamic conflict is as old as the centuries, with religion at its root. It might seem as if, for most humans, religion has always been a reason for conflict. The question thus arises: is this propensity for conflict intrinsic in the nature of religion or of humans? It cannot be religion. First, the fundamental set of laws of each of the major religions prohibits killing: there is no ambiguity here, the prohibition is absolute. Man may have come along later and distorted this for his own purpose; even shrouded such confusion with false legalities, such as the infallibility of Popes, but the religious law is absolute. Second, within major religions themselves, such as Christianity and Islam, there has been—and still is—bitter hatred and killing between different creeds. In Christianity, conflict between Protestants and

Catholics dates back centuries, as do conflicts between Shias and Sunnis in the Islamic religion. This second factor indicates that conflict is also not intrinsic in cultural differences: there being little or no cultural division at the root of the Islamic intra-religious conflict. Thus, it is more likely that the propensity for conflict is simply intrinsic in human nature: indeed, it is this characteristic, amongst others, which religions seek to subdue by the power of the mind, in order to alleviate suffering in the human condition. But we digress . . .[2]

Into this simmering cauldron of millennia-festered mistrust enters the Fifties Child, almost certainly too freckle-faced to take note of the debacle over Britain's involvement in the Suez crisis of 1956 and probably too full of the preamble to the "summer of love" to worry over the deeper meaning of Israel's blitzkrieg victory over Egypt in the Six Day War of June 1967. By this time, and despite the fact that, as elsewhere, enmities in the Arabian world were becoming enmeshed by the Cold War, the British Fifties Child will have had his attention distracted by other arenas (Vietnam) of that conflict. He may, however, have wondered about, but not for too long, the seemingly interminable war between Iran and Iraq that started in September 1980 and which featured sand-trench warfare as stagnant and as bloody as some of the fighting in the First World War. The alert Fifties Child will even have picked up on the fact that Iraq was using chemical weapons against its adversary and perhaps mused over the fact that the United States and its allies, including Britain, were supporting the Iraqi regime, led by Saddam Hussein, during that war.

The Iran-Iraq war petered out in 1988, the combatants unable to break the deadlock and finally deciding to sue for peace, agreeing more or less on the retention of the pre-war borders and status quo. Then, as the Cold War itself was petering out amidst Gorbachev's reforms, Iraq invaded the small kingdom of Kuwait in 1990, the pretext being that Kuwait was slant-drilling oil from Iraqi reserves.

Faced with this unprovoked aggression, discussions were held at the United Nations, culminating in a Security Council resolution which empowered states to use "all necessary means" to obtain an Iraqi withdrawal. The Western Allies, led by the United States, who also had support from a number of Arabian states for this venture—Saudi Arabia, Egypt and Syria—organised military forces with the intention of ousting the Iraqi armies and liberating Kuwait. The United States deployed massive and technologically advanced firepower in the operation, codenamed Desert Storm, which was overwhelming in its effect. More so than any other conflict before it, Desert Storm almost seemed to be being played out for the benefit of the 24-hour TV news

2. . . . although one could have an interesting conversation with Lees about this.

cameras and, as the one-sided nature of the battle played out on screens worldwide, the action was eerily reminiscent of the role-playing computer games eagerly sought after by teenagers. What many observers failed to understand was why, having pushed the Iraqi armies out of Kuwait as far back into their own territory as the proximity of Baghdad, Saddam Hussein's capital, the Allied armies decided to stop and then withdraw, leaving Saddam Hussein in power. If they had hoped that the Iraqi leadership would be overthrown in a popular revolt, then they were to be disappointed.

The Iraqi land armies and air force had been clearly outmatched in the Allied attack, leaving the Iraqis with the sole—but potent and portentous—tactic of launching Scud ballistic missiles from within their territory, mainly towards Israel. Historically, Israel was the source of much Arab, not just Iraqi angst, and one had the impression that Hussein's tactic of involving Israel was designed to muster Arab support for his cause. That failed and, post-war, the Iraqis had to submit to United Nations inspections of many of their industrial installations. The world had become spooked by their ability and willingness to use chemical weapons and ballistic missiles, and there was a suspicion that they had, or were close to having, biological and nuclear weapons capability.

This issue of Iraq's "weapons of mass destruction" was to have a high profile during much of the remainder of the century and the early years of the twenty-first. Iraqi co-operation with the inspections was begrudging. Opinions differed as to how great the threat was. Eventually, in December 1998, frustrated by progress, the United States and Britain launched a series of cruise missile and air bombing attacks against various Iraqi targets, concentrating on military targets but also including various others designed to disrupt Saddam Hussein's power base, including one of his presidential palaces. The attack broke the near unanimity that the policy of the United States—and Britain hanging on its coat-tails—against Iraq had enjoyed up to this point, with Arab nations and others now critical of the abandonment of international consensus-seeking that the unilateral action implied.

Whether or not this resentment at the United States' adopted role of self-appointed international policeman, jury, judge and executioner led directly to the devastating September 2001 attacks on the United States by al-Qaeda is uncertain, but it undoubtedly helped to recruit many followers to the terrorist cause. Amongst the many victims of those al-Qaeda attacks were the withering shred of hope remaining from the end of the Cold War and the still flowering hope that the new century would bring a new dawn of peace for mankind.

Al-Qaeda succeeded in doing what no other adversary of the United States had ever done: inflict a deep wound on Americans on their own continental patch. The American reaction was predictable, seeking to understand who had perpetrated the attack and how it had been planned in order to then be able to eradicate the threat. A number of countries were accused of harbouring terrorists including, in the run-up to the 2003 invasion, Iraq.

United Nations inspections for weapons of mass destruction had restarted in 2002 and were making progress in spite of the Iraqis' unhelpful stance. With issues unresolved, US president Bush and British prime minister Blair talked up the need for military intervention in Iraq. They failed, however, to persuade the United Nations to give its backing for such action but, regardless of that and much other opposition, launched an invasion in March 2003.

In Britain, the crux of the justification used to send troops into action was the claim that Saddam Hussein had the capability to launch weapons of mass destruction within 45 minutes of an order. The "45 minute" claim was clearly designed to impress and frighten the public. The basis for this extraordinary claim was investigated, along with the government's overall intelligence reporting on Iraqi capability, by the Butler Inquiry (2004). The conclusion with respect to the claim is that it should not have been made without explaining specifically what it referred to. Furthermore, MI6 was now stating that the source of the claim was dubious.[3]

Arising from the 45-minute claim is one of the greatest conspiracy theories of modern times. David Kelly, a government scientist who had been active in the United Nations inspection programmes in Iraq, had an unauthorised meeting with Andrew Gilligan,[4] a BBC journalist, who later transmitted a TV news report claiming that the government dossier on Iraq's weapons capabilities had been "sexed up" by the government itself. Infamously, Gilligan's journalistic source was inadequately protected and Kelly was eventually brought before a government foreign affairs select committee, where he was questioned aggressively. On July 17, 2003, two days after his inquisition, Kelly's body was found in woods near his home. Despite the coroner's verdict of suicide, later corroborated by a public inquiry under Lord Hutton, some remain convinced that Kelly was murdered by the authorities themselves.

The March 2003 invasion of Iraq was extremely unpopular. If Fifties Children had been uncertain about the wisdom of the 2001 intervention in Afghanistan—they could still remember the Soviet Union failing in its own intervention there—then they were highly dubious about the reasons why their government had sent troops to fight—and die—in Iraq.

3. At the time of writing yet another inquiry, under Sir John Chilcot, is investigating a number of issues pertaining to the conduct of the Iraq War, including its justification. Findings are not expected until the latter half of 2013.
4. Having signed the Official Secrets Act, any meeting with the press should have been sanctioned by his superiors.

The military intervention very quickly ousted Saddam Hussein from power. The invasion began on March 20 and the capital Baghdad was under American control by mid April. Despite an intensive search, there was no cache of weapons of mass destruction to be found. In the anarchic and violent aftermath of the invasion, American and British troops suffered many deaths and had significant difficulties extricating their troops from Iraq. The last British troops were not withdrawn until July 2009 and American troops were still being deployed in 2011. Whether Iraq and the world are better or worse places as a result of the invasion, or just different, is too deep a question for this particular book. The answer is certainly open to debate.

❦

At the time of the Iraqi invasion, none of the Barclay James Harvest song-writers were active in releasing new songs, although this was soon to change as Wolstenholme returned to active recording, issuing three studio albums within a four-year period from May 2004. These yielded two songs that touched on issues raised by the Iraq war: '2 a.m.' and 'Soldier of Fortune'. Also, on the 2010 British tour by John Lees' Barclay James Harvest, the band played an unreleased song, 'Ancient Waves', that Lees himself introduced on stage as being about the 2003 Iraq war, and which was first available as a recording on the *Rock Legends Filmed Live at Metropolis Studios* DVD in 2011.

In fact, the existence of 'Ancient Waves' was known to ardent fans from as early as a 2006 interview for *Record Collector* magazine:

> One I'm working on now is "Ancient Ways" [sic]. I started it when Britain invaded Iraq . . . it starts with waves crashing on a shore and then all the souls of the dead of all the conflicts there have ever been shouting "Not again! Not again! Not again!" It's almost finished.

Lees has not always been prepared to explain his songs' metaphors but, on this occasion, he seems to have been particularly keen to do so. He explains it again in the interview accompanying the live footage in the *Rock Legends* DVD:

> This is where I was at four years ago. The song basically is about history and how we never listen to, or take notice of this history that they teach us in schools . . . There's all these ancient souls trying to speak to us from wherever they are— all the souls of dead soldiers, and people who've been killed in wars actually saying "Don't do it again! Don't do it again! Don't send any more here!" . . . That's the waves crashing on the shore.

The song's central metaphor would have been potentially interpretable, given the references to the politicians towards its close, but the explanation helps.

'Ancient Waves' is also interesting in that it is the closest that Lees ever comes to naming the victims of his songs. In the past, even an obvious reference to Tory prime minister Edward Heath in 'The Great 1974 Mining Disaster' was disguised as "a sailor oh so gay" but, in 'Ancient Waves', Lees barely cloaks his target. This change of emphasis is perhaps demonstrative of how strongly he opposed the intervention, as well as the nature of its justification, making the song a strong candidate for the most politically direct of his career. It certainly does not signify a diminishing in his writing capabilities—the song is lyrically sharp, with some canny nuances. For instance, the actual naming of American president Bush and British prime minister Blair is done craftfully, with the subtle touch of a master:

> A flaming bush sows seeds of fear
> that grow so fast no one can hear to the end of truth;
> a blare of silence drowns the sound
> of endless protest crashing down in pieces on the sand.

The British government at the time placed significant emphasis on media management and one of its aides, Alastair Campbell, was dubbed the "Spin Doctor". Suspicion was (or is?—despite the fact that the Butler Inquiry exonerated any particular individual from blame) that Campbell played a crucial role in the "sexing up" of the report on weapons of mass destruction that lies at the centre of the David Kelly controversy. Campbell comes in for some stinging criticism from Lees: "The prince of darkness spins a knife / that silences dissent with lies / and everyone's deceived." It does appear, however, that Lees has merged his characters here since "the prince of darkness" was in fact the nickname for one of Campbell's prior colleagues, the equally infamous Labour politician Peter Mandelson, who had left the government team in 2001. Irrespective, Lees' condemnation is acute.

Despite the explicit nature of the political attack, the song retains Lees' more usual characteristic of understated observation, only that by now it is tinged with a sprinkle of world-weariness. He rues the fact that those in power say that they fear the destruction of their own society, yet go out destroying others, using history to justify their actions without actually heeding its lessons. Within the song there is a clear reference to David Kelly, as the "quiet man" who "lays down his life". Lees, like many in British society, seems clearly convinced that Kelly's unauthorised discussions with the press were driven by a concern that the justification being presented for taking the country to war was unsustainable.

David Kelly's tragic case also appears as the single, fleeting Iraq-related reference in Wolstenholme's '2 a.m.', a song which deals primarily with insomnia. It is an acerbic and cutting lyric, all the more powerful for its brevity. Wolstenholme first muses on the vast numbers of people suffering from insomnia; they grasp in vain for peaceful sleep as their thoughts spiral out of control, threatening to send them spinning over the cliff of depression. Then, damning by its contrast, comes the swipe: is Tony Blair able to sleep soundly after David Kelly's suicide? The inference is, of course, that the prime minister himself is tainted by the scandal.

Wolstenholme's 'Soldier of Fortune' is an extraordinary composition.[5] Musically immense, it draws from a number of influences including folk and progressive rock, and oozes Englishness, a precious quality in Barclay James Harvest's early music. The erosion of this quality as the other band members began to immerse more American influences into the band's music was one of the reasons that caused Wolstenholme to become dissatisfied with his role within the band and eventually leave. Lyrically, 'Soldier of Fortune' condemns the Iraq war to the radioactive dustbin of conflicts in which the soldier becomes fodder to the whim of politicians. As in '2 a.m.', the song's principal theme is not the Iraq War—in this case it is the victimisation of soldiers, a theme we shall address fully in the following chapter. However, one of the things which Wolstenholme does within the song is associate Basra with Flanders and, contextualizing from his songs dealing with themes of the First World War, it then becomes clear that he viewed British involvement in the Iraq War with disdain.

One has to consider that three songs with references prompted by the Iraq war, written towards what must be the final stages of a forty-year-plus career, is significant as a reflection of the huge wave of public outrage and anger that Britain's invasion of Iraq caused. Clearly, there will have been people who supported the invasion, but the protest movement against it was one of the largest ever mobilised in Britain. As an illustration of the public's depth of feeling, a demonstration was held in central London on February 15, 2003, as part of a coordinated worldwide protest against the possibility of war, which attracted between 750,000 and two million protestors, depending on whose estimates you accept. It is fair to say that public support for the military intervention did not increase during the occupation as it became clear that many Iraqis—perhaps obviously but in contradiction to what the British government's and Bush's spin would have the public believe—deeply resented the occupation troops.

5. The song was written in partnership with Mæstoso's drummer Kim Turner. On the album, *Soldier of Fortune* is superbly, seamlessly segued into 'The Road to Nowhere', and it is particularly the conjunction of these two songs—whose sum is more than the individual parts, in much the same way that 'The Poet' and 'After the Day' resonate on the . . . *and Other Short Stories* album—which makes one search for the superlatives dictionary.

Accentuating the impression that the societal impact of the Iraq invasion was significant is the fact that, despite only a fraction of Fifties Children continuing to write into the twenty-first century, it is possible to find songs by Barclay James Harvest's contemporaneous artists that address the situation.[6] Notable examples are Strawbs' 'The Call to Action' [*The Broken Hearted Bride*, 2008] and Asia's 'Holy War' [*Omega*, 2010]. The approach to both songs is similar to Wolstenholme's holistic approach of treating these modern Arabian conflicts as part of a whole aspect of, for want of a better term, historical "Western" foreign policy, rather than focusing on Iraq specifically. Dave Cousins' 'The Call to Action' does not mention Iraq specifically but one can infer that it is the real subject of the song. He contrasts the current conflict with the religion-inspired Crusades and, by mentioning the desire to develop a democracy, Iraq falls squarely into the target of the song. It is a subtle song lyrically—my interpretation of Cousins' message being that constructing a democracy might be a laudable aim but God cannot be on your side when vanity drives your actions. The inference that can be drawn is that vanity *is* a factor, hence the rationale for the invasion is flawed.

In John Wetton and Geoff Downes' 'Holy War', Wetton's lyrics echo 'Soldier of Fortune' by providing reference to famous battles of the past— Kerak, Hattin, Crecy and, like Wolstenholme, Agincourt—in the course of making his argument. Reflecting on how God has often been used to justify these various conflicts, Wetton says that one thing that life has taught him is that all men are fundamentally the same: enough of war!

One of the interesting factors about these three modern songs dealing with the conflicts in the Arabian lands (and in Afghanistan)—'Soldier of Fortune', 'The Call to Action' and 'Holy War'—is not just the recognition historically placed on God as a justification for going to war but, more importantly, its rejection as a valid justification. This is a crucial societal change. A significant proportion of British Fifties Children, perhaps the first generation for centuries to do so, is rejecting one of the foremost time-honoured reasons for going to war, because it has come to realise—having abandoned the dogmatic aspect of religion—that inside our souls, all humans are the same, and this realisation demands a new approach to the world.

This last aspect raises another interesting point. The rhetoric used by the

6. The inconsistency with the dearth of songs on Yugoslavia is illusory. Many contemporaneous artists stopped working in the Eighties, thus missing the break-up of the Soviet empire, but then resumed activity in the twenty-first century, buoyed by the communications explosion of the internet, which resparked interest in their fans (whose families had by now grown up, work was steady, etc, and so they had time to spare to once again focus on rock music).

United States and Britain to justify going to war demonstrated the widening gap between the two Allies with respect to formal religious observance. Britain is indebted to the United States for its help in assuring defeat of Germany in the First and Second World Wars. Even as recently as the Eighties the United States provided key assistance during the Falklands War. However, there is a concern, which is reflected in these songs by Strawbs and Asia, that the greater religious fanaticism in the United States can have an undue effect on its foreign policy. Some of the rhetoric used by Bush in the aftermath of the Iraq invasion is perilously close to sounding like religious fanaticism and undoubtedly coloured the quasi-Crusadic lyrical approach to 'The Call to Action' and 'Holy War'. Here is just one example, something that Nabil Shaath, who was the Palestinian foreign minister at the time, claims that President Bush stated to the Palestinian delegation at a summit in Sharm el-Sheikh in 2003:

> I am driven with a mission from God. God would tell me, "George go and fight these terrorists in Afghanistan." And I did. And then God would tell me, "George, go and end the tyranny in Iraq." And I did. And now, again, I feel God's words coming to me, "Go get the Palestinians their state and get the Israelis their security, and get peace in the Middle East." And, by God, I'm gonna do it.

It would appear that an ideological gap has developed between us and our American allies; it will be interesting to see how this affects the "special relationship" in decades to come.

Attentive readers will have noted, of course, that Lees' "flaming bush" in 'Ancient Waves' is also a possible reference to this characteristic of the United States president—in the Bible story, God appears to Moses as a burning bush. The word-play in Lees' lyric is quite cunning!

The Iraq invasion in 2003 had a deep, and divisive, societal impact. It was a war that left many people, including many Fifties Children, as we have seen through their songs, resentful of what British troops were being ordered to do in the country's name. The decision to go to war, the way it was made and the deceit which was involved in the justification, also had the effect of alienating many from democratic government. There is still much healing to be done.

11

The Soldier as Victim

As the twentieth century ebbed away and the twenty-first washed in, one could sense within society a growing concern for the welfare of, and fairness towards, soldiers. This turning of the tide does not yet have a name that I know of, but it has not gone unrecognised by others, whether it be here in Britain or amongst our close allies in the United States. Some observers refer to it simply, and disparagingly, as "casualty fatigue" but I believe that is actually a symptom of a more encompassing public mood. What it really feels like to me is that it is the coming of age of a post-empire emancipation of the spirit.

The roots of this change began to stir in the soil of society during the First World War. The earth was barren and growth would be problematic and slow, but the roots of this movement would not wither. At the dawn of the twentieth century Britain was still living through its Age of Empire. The Empire was celebrated, a justified boast. In 1911 the Festival of Empire was held to celebrate King George V's coronation. A sporting competition between teams representing the empire—participating were sportsmen from Australia, New Zealand, South Africa and Canada—was held: this event is now seen as the forerunner of the modern Commonwealth Games (which were originally known as the British Empire Games when first held in 1930, and in fact the word "empire" was not dropped from the title until 1970). To be British meant entitlement to the Swagger of Rulers.

At the outbreak of the First World War—the Great War—people understood fairly clearly *who* Britain was fighting, and why. Men enlisted voluntarily in huge numbers, driven by the perceived cause, and by the glory of war. For God, King and Country. Duty—remember that word?—was also a factor: it was their duty to go and fight.

And yet their masters failed them. Their generals abandoned them to the front line of the trenches. Safely ensconced well behind the line, out would go the indisputable order to go over the top. They were treated as cannon fodder, as a disposable commodity, a plaything of their masters' war-room games. Upstairs and downstairs, only these were no stately home pleasure grounds, they were the battlefields of Flanders, the Somme and so many more killing fields.

The terror of the First World War's trench warfare has travelled stealthily down the generations, a shadow on our collective consciousness. Many soldiers suffered psychologically during the battle itself from the stress of the particular horror of that warfare, a condition they termed shell-shock. Indeed, despite the fact that soldiers during the American Civil War are also thought to have suffered from shell-shock, this was the first time that this condition had been recognised to the extent of being given a name. It was, we now know, a misnomer: during that war the condition was thought to be due to the effect of the repeated, strong pressure pulses from near-proximity shell explosions on the brain, whereas it is in fact a purely psychological condition arising from repeated exposure to indescribable human suffering and carnage, including that perpetrated by the soldiers themselves in action, such as bayoneting an enemy soldier in the face during a raid on the opposing trenches, or emptying a weapon's magazine into soldiers giving themselves up for surrender because the commander's order was to take no prisoners.

The battlefield condition of shell-shock often resurfaced as further psychological illness months or even years after the battle was over: these time-lapsed illnesses are now known as acute and post-traumatic stress disorders. Yes, their masters failed them. Their masters failed to show any humanitarian feeling towards these soldiers, as though the strictures of empire had deprived them of all feeling, individual thought or ability to reason. The prime concern during the conflict was to return those suffering the affliction to the front-line as quickly as possible. Paraphrasing the treatment for shell-sock sufferers as "get on with it, you coward!" gives a fair impression of the prevailing attitude of the time. It was no different for those whose illness continued, or even started for the first time, on returning home. The poet Siegfried Sassoon used his own experience of the trauma within the haunting 'Survivors':

> Of course they're 'longing to go out again'—
>
> . . .
>
> They'll soon forget their haunted nights; their cowed
> Subjection to the ghosts of friends who died—
> Their dreams that drip with murder; and they'll be proud
> Of glorious war that shatter'd all their pride . . .
>
> . . .
>
> Children, with eyes that hate you, broken and mad.

Yes, their masters did fail them. And so post-war society failed them. The experience of many fell far short of the expectations set by prime minister David Lloyd George's promise to work for "a fit country for heroes to live in". This failure to support all of our First World War heroes caused a wound so deep that its festering scars are visible to this day, now evident as the falling away of respect for authority of any kind. And, just round the corner, a few short years, from the bloody horror of trench warfare came the economic slump that turned into the Great Depression of the Thirties. Jobs, what jobs? Deprivation beyond imagining. Was this the prize for all the death, the reward for all the suffering?

Then: Hitler and the Second World War. The empire, the foundation rock on which Britain stood, which had been on the wane, was, to all intents and purposes, dismantled during the years of that conflict. Victory . . . ?

Then: Hiroshima and Nagasaki. Whoa! The devil incarnate, unleashed.

Then: enter the Fifties Child, who, growing to consciousness, looks all around, looks back at the recent wars of his fathers' making and it makes him retch with sickness from the depths of his being. He rejects the lot. This is not just a generation-gap change: this is a mind-set revolution that brings distrust for authority, distrust for artificial divisions between people and contempt for the values of the past. Down the plughole with the empire went duty, went servitude, went respect: the upstairs, downstairs society was finished. With the new mind-set come rejection of etiquette, rejection of elocution, of the Queen's English, and the rejection of social mores grounded in false spirituality. Praise the Lord who took us into these two World Wars? No, thanks! "Thou shall not . . .", whether commanded from God or Man, was rejected. This diminution of authority is important in our consideration of society's view of the soldier as a victim because it provides a clue that this societal shift is not due to casualty fatigue or loss of heroic qualities in the British character.

Strangely perhaps, the monarchy survived the onslaught on authority. It has wobbled under the Fifties Child's gaze, for sure, but it still stands. One can speculate that a reason for this might be that as its real authority was stripped away centuries ago, it never quite fell centrally into the sights of the Fifties Child's revolution. Moreover, the monarchy is a symbol of Britain and, despite whatever changes have occurred, patriotism has not waned. Some observers have commented that many people in the modern age struggle to identify what exactly constitutes Englishness. As the dominant nation within the British United Kingdom, the English have perhaps suffered more from the loss of empire than the Welsh, Scottish or Irish, all of whom were originally unwilling partners in that union and, despite much cultural and population assimilation over the centuries, significant independence movements remain within their countries. Under such circumstances, the monarchy continues to provide a clear focus for the human need of belonging to a home, to a place of birth, to the patriotic sentiment. The Queen's dignified reign has managed to retain the appeal of the monarchy not just within England but also in Wales, Scotland and Ireland, as well as in many countries throughout the former British Empire, demonstrating that the umbilical cord to grace, civility, decorum, poise and steadfastness—archetypal values of England, of Empire—has not quite yet been fully severed.

Before we continue our discussion, let us just develop some casualty perspective by reviewing the human cost, in terms of British military deaths only, not including wounded, of some of the more recent engagements:

Napoleonic Wars (early nineteenth century)—300,000ish
Boer War (1899-1902)—less than 10,000 in combat
First World War (1914-18)—nearly 900,000
Second World War (1939-45)—nearly 400,000
Korean War (1950-53)—about 750
Cyprus (1955-59)—nearly 400
Northern Ireland (1969-98)—over 750
Falklands War (1982)—over 250
First Iraq War (1990-91)—less than 50
Second Iraq War (2003-09)—about 200
Afghanistan (2001—present)—about 400

One can see at a glance that the conflicts that British troops have been involved in since the Second World War have not been as significant in terms of human loss as previous engagements: in fact, they're not even in the same league. The British Fifties Child has indeed had the great good fortune of living through a period of comparative peace.

By the time that this Fifties Child had reached his later years, society's attitude towards soldiers was drastically different to that of his grandfather's time. Concern for soldiers' welfare, and its understanding of the psychological impact of battle, is almost certainly currently higher than ever. However, even now, some senior officers returning from Afghanistan still bemoan the lack of understanding and support for soldiers suffering from post-traumatic stress disorder. I suspect that what this lack of complete societal understanding now reflects, rather than an indifference targeted at soldiers that it considers cowards, as in the First World War, is the continual misunderstanding and intolerance of psychiatric disorders in general.

Concern for soldiers is reflected in other behaviours. For instance, we have seen, in our newspapers and on our televisions, every returning coffin from Afghanistan being greeted with awesome displays of deference and honour.

The repatriation corteges through Wootton Bassett have become symbolic of our age. In context, British military deaths in the First and Second World Wars were a thousand times greater, and the volume of such losses meant that such comparative behaviour was not logistically possible, even if society had wished it.

Strong public sentiment such as this has been converted by campaign groups into pressure on the government to ensure that it provides a sound infrastructure and sufficient funds for the delivery of adequate and reliable equipment in sufficient quantities for our soldiers in the field. Pressure for change has even come from the law, as coroners presiding over the inquests of soldiers killed in Afghanistan have formally ruled that their training and equipment were inadequate. As a result of this mounting pressure from society, the government in 2011 set in law an armed forces covenant that specifies its and society's responsibilities with respect to all armed forces personnel, not just during but also after their term of service.

Are these new behaviours symptomatic of the fact that we expect to fight a conflict without loss of life, or that we have lost our bravery or our patriotism? Surely not. A more likely explanation is that, even in a shrunken world where foreign travel is commonplace, these modern conflicts are being fought in far-off, remote places that few people have ever visited and many have perhaps never heard of. How many of us, even today, can readily identify the location of Iraq or Afghanistan on a globe?

When society is sceptical of government, cannot easily identify the enemy and when it is uncertain about the reasons for engaging in battle, it is no wonder that any losses are more keenly felt. Don't forget that the Fifties Child is the first in history to have actually seen—through television and other images—the carnage and suffering of war; prior to his generation only the soldiers themselves had to suffer the shock. Does the Fifties Child want his sons and daughters to suffer that pain? For what? There were no weapons of mass destruction in Iraq. We have not won the hearts and minds of the Iraqis or the Afghans, and how can we, when we do not know their proud history or understand their culture? When so many government—i.e. authority—promises turn to dust, modern society balks. And that is why there is so much current sentiment over casualties and pressure on authority to enhance soldiers' conditions: we lack trust in our leaders, we lack trust in those in authority. The Fifties Child and his own children will no longer tolerate it.

There is no loss of patriotism, no loss of bravery. We still have our heroes. And we will not tolerate them being abused by those in authority—the Fifties Child has slowly, but surely, ensured that fact.

The songs of the Barclay James Harvest songwriters that can be confidently interpreted as applicable to this topic are all of Wolstenholme's authorship. Indicative of his strength of feeling caused by injustices towards soldiers is the fact that these five songs span nearly thirty years of his career. In this particular topic area the more literal of these songs turn out to be the most revealing; taking them slightly out of chronological sequence helps in this regard.

We have already seen from our sociological analysis that the First World War was the point at which shell-shock became recognised as an illness. The horrors of the butchery of that war echoed down the decades and were still deeply affecting many Fifties Children, Wolstenholme amongst them. 'Gates of Heaven (14/18)' and 'Soldier of Fortune/Road to Nowhere' deal explicitly with the First World War from the perspective of the effect on soldiers, who are clearly identified as victims of society.

'Gates of Heaven (14/18)' [1980] expresses shock at the extreme youth of many of the soldiers going out to fight in the trenches and is unequivocal about the fact that they were betrayed by their society. Wolstenholme notes the hypocrisy of those who sent them out to die, singing and waving them along as they left. Their dreams of England would be shattered by the cacophony of the murderous battlefield, to be replaced by more soothing sounds as they arrived at the gates of heaven. In Wolstenholme's song, the youths going out to fight are only seventeen but it was almost certainly even more shocking than this, of course, as many youngsters joining up in the volunteering frenzy lied about their age in order to be allowed to fight.

Nearly thirty years later, the First World War's killing fields also make an appearance in 'Soldier of Fortune', a song that we introduced in the previous chapter. Sung in the first person, Wolstenholme traces how an individual— the "soldier of fortune" at any stage of history—might become trapped into being a soldier through lack of other opportunities in life, through machismo, and through love of God, king and country. The soldier has faith in God, who will help him to get through the fighting . . . but our soldier, who represents a melding of all soldiers through time, now lies dead on the fields of Flanders, of Basra, of Helmand—does it matter which? He now knows, having seen the gore of the battlefield, that God will not save him from the hell of combat. "Hell"—the last word in the song—is printed on the lyric sheet but is left unsung; instead, the band provides a barrage of controlled heavy rock that leaves no doubt as to the brutality of the carnage. The song implies a depth of failure of authority to support its soldiers of such great a magnitude that not even God can overcome. We, the soldiers fighting for our Country—which we thought was our common cause—have given our lives. What have *you*, society, given?

As implied in a footnote in the previous chapter, 'Soldier of Fortune' is most effective when listened to—or considered—together with its companion song, 'Road to Nowhere'. Musically and lyrically this song continues to evidence the folk-roots of its predecessor. It tells the tale of Jack, an average man happily leading a simple life, working for a modest salary to support his family, who immediately answers the call to go out to fight in the First World War. On his return home to the "land fit for heroes", he finds that half of the town's men have died in the fighting. Nevertheless, a victory parade is held, full of empty words and pomposity. Wolstenholme's descriptive condemnation is acute: Jack is given a seat at the back, from which he cannot see the service because his injuries prevent him from using his legs. Then, when he tries to find a job he is rejected because he has lost a hand in the fighting. Society has deserted him; he ekes out a pitiful existence until his death.

The "land fit for heroes" is a reference to Lloyd George's infamous promise. The reality for many, particularly for those who had been wounded physically or psychologically, and for those who developed post-traumatic stress disorder after the end of the War, was far from that expectation. Even those who were fully fit found that the economic reality of the Twenties and the Thirties was hardly reward for the strictures and sacrifices of the war.

The two remaining songs that are interpretable as considering the soldier as a victim are 'In Search of England' [1978] and 'Patriots', which appeared on Wolstenholme's first solo album, *Mæstoso* [1980], which was released soon after his departure from the band. Unlike the previous three songs, these two are not identifiable as belonging to any specific conflict, but they do convey a sense of the abandonment of the soldier by a society unappreciative of the individual sacrifices they make in all of our names.

The gorgeous 'In Search of England' takes the form of a metaphorical conversation between "the boy"—representing the soldier—and "the old man"—representing the leadership and authority of society. The old man tells the boy that his sacrifice is needed to ensure a safe haven for everyone but the boy rues how he has been abandoned, without support, without a hope of survival.

'Patriots' is packed with intense musical and lyrical emotion virtue of the fact that these heroes are being blithely mistreated and misled by their leaders. The soldiers are blind to the truth of why they are being sent to fight, and they obey silently, as though dumb, unable to speak their protest:

We who stand and wait still serve,
on us you can rely.
We are the blind, we are the dumb,
and in our hundreds we will come:
though we'll never say a word,
like patriots we'll die!

The excerpt's strong echo of the upstairs, downstairs mentality—"we who stand and *wait* still *serve*, on us you can rely"—is probably not accidental, as it would have been from this echelon of society that the front-line troops would have been drawn. Additionally, one could debate whether there is a sense in the song to suggest that Wolstenholme intended a double-play on the word "dumb", which would imply an overall meaning nearer to that of Motörhead's 'Sword of Glory', which we shall come to in a moment. Irrespective, it is clear that they are made dumb and blind through unquestioning allegiance to the strictures of God, King and country.

These five songs constitute a powerful description of the victimisation and societal marginalisation of soldiers sent to fight in conflicts from the First World War all the way through to Afghanistan.

Reinforcing the picture of the turn of the tide in the favour of the soldiers is the fact that it is quite easy to find songs by other artists dealing with the topic, from across the musical spectrum.[1]

Taking folk music first, we stay with the horrors of the First World War with Bill Caddick's 'The Writing of Tipperary'. My favourite rendition of this song is to be found on June Tabor's *A Quiet Eye* [1999], where it is segued by the standard 'It's a Long Way to Tipperary', the First World War song that troops sang as they left their loved ones for the front. The musical twist that comes at the end of the vocal part is one of the most eloquent and emotive touches to be heard anywhere; it is more subtle than, but as impressive, as Wolstenholme's blitzkrieg in 'Soldier of Fortune'. Caddick's lyrics are unambiguous in their description of the victory—which cost millions of lives—as dubious. The fact that this conflict elicits such emotive musical writing and performance from these sensitive musicians is powerful evidence that the horrors of that War were still able to haunt the dreams of many Fifties Children.

The power of Fifties Children's feelings on the subject of the victimisation of soldiers during the First World War may be gauged from the fact that in 2006, nearly ninety years after the end of that cataclysmic conflict, the Shot at Dawn pardons campaign—supported by the British Legion amongst others—succeeded in its objective of obtaining a formal pardon from the British government for all of the soldiers executed for military offences during the War.

As in all things, there is another side to the argument: there are some historians, for instance, who will argue that, in the context of the age, there were some clever strategic manoeuvrings in the First World War and that the

---

1. And one only has to remember a sit-com such as *Blackadder Goes Forth* to recognise that the concern is manifested in other cultural art forms also. The writers of *Blackadder* were Sixties Children, demonstrating that the effect persisted further into the century.

popular culture concept of "heroes led by donkeys" is a fallacy. It was really all a good thing. The Fifties Children of our social history, however, have rejected this kind of cold, calculated logic and replaced it with an enhanced emotional, or spiritual, force. No doubt they look at the geopolitical shape of modern Europe and find it difficult convincing themselves that those millions of combatant deaths on both sides of the war front—together with the civilian cost of these horrendous wars—were really worth it.

Moving on chronologically, as well as musically towards a more progressive vein, finds us arriving at Pink Floyd's 'When the Tigers Broke Free' [single A-side, 1982], in which Roger Waters' opprobrium, with an impressive force of sarcasm, is reserved for leaders during the Second World War. A deeply personal song, 'When the Tigers Broke Free' recounts how Waters' father died in fighting at the Battle of Anzio in 1944, in a sacrificial bid to delay the advance of the enemy. Realising the situation was impossible for his men, the forward commander sought permission to withdraw but this was refused by the generals, consigning the force of a few hundred men to death. Waters feels equal disdain for the King, who sent his mother a condolences message, in an impressive gold-leaf adorned scroll, signed with a rubber stamp! In this song, this Fifties Child consigns King and Country (personified by the generals) to the realms of the past.

There is no shortage of examples in the heavy rock field either. As early as 1970 Black Sabbath's 'War Pigs' [*Paranoid*] left us in no doubt as to how the Fifties Child apportioned the blame: Generals and politicians; abusers of the poor, who are sent out as cannon fodder. At least Black Sabbath gave their fans the satisfaction—even if only fictitious—of seeing these evil leaders punished: as in 'Electric Funeral', they are consigned to hell, this time it would seem by a more "conventional" God.

Much more recently, Motörhead's 'Sword of Glory' [*Kiss of Death*, 2006]—lyrics written by band leader Lemmy—provides one of the more interesting perspectives on the soldier as a victim. In this song, the onus for stopping unnecessary carnage is placed with the soldier (or, to be more exact, with those budding heroes *wanting* to become soldiers) and it therefore has echoes of Buffy Saint-Marie's more famous 'Universal Soldier'. There are also synergies with Wolstenholme's 'Soldier of Fortune', in that the protagonists in both songs are the spirits of soldiers killed in battle through the ages. The spirits of the dead soldiers directly address these budding heroes, saying that all of history is there for them to learn from. All of their deaths—millions of them—should serve the purpose of educating them that the carnage is in vain, and make them turn away from being soldiers. Read history, learn its message, don't be the same fools that we were, otherwise the same mistakes will be just repeated over again.

The difference with 'Universal Soldier' is that the song is addressed at tough, young men, whose blame lies in the fact that, through wanting to become heroes by grasping the soldier's "sword of glory", they fail to see all the deceptions that have led to the hundreds of millions of soldiers left dead on battlefields throughout mankind's history. 'Sword of Glory' is not a call to arms, it is a call to empowerment through historical knowledge. A quite extraordinary song! It is interesting to note in passing that Lees, in 'Ancient Waves'—another song which features the spirits of dead soldiers warning against yet another conflict—also places value on the lessons of history and rues the fact that our leaders deny its lessons.

These Fifties Children songwriters' call for young men, soldiers and leaders to empower themselves through historical knowledge is a manifestation of their own realisation and rejection of the flawed leadership to which, in their perception, mankind has been subjected.

Afterword to Barclay James Harvest's Conflict Songs

This rejection of authority that we have highlighted—of Man and of God—is one of the most important legacies of the Fifties Child.

The rejection of Man's authority is evidenced through many facets, one of the more sinister of which is apathy towards government elections. The standard that the Fifties Child has enshrined in Britain is encapsulated by the adage "it doesn't matter who you vote for, the government always gets in". General election turnouts have dropped to below 70 per cent this century—this at a time when millions of our neighbours in the Arab world are risking their lives for a chance of democracy. It may have its faults, but democracy is still a better option than much of the rest of the world has the luxury to enjoy, most of whom still live under Orwellian states!

The Fifties Child did not turn his rejection of authority into a political revolution—only a social one—which is why, during his life, he has been left floundering at the whim of those in power, pressurising here and there as he goes along, with varying degrees of success. Some of the Fifties Child's initiatives, such as the Shot at Dawn campaign and the pressure leading to the armed forces covenant, have been successful. When celebrities become involved there is even more chance of success: just as relevant to our recent discussions on the soldier as a victim is the high-profile campaign—given particular press interest by the involvement of that Fifties Child actress Joanna Lumley—to allow all Gurkha soldiers who fought for the British to be allowed to settle in Britain. Is this rocket science? You ask a group of friends to risk their lives for you, some of them die fighting your battles and then, when the war is over, you turf them out of your house. Eh? No wonder the Fifties Child rejected the authority of Man.

His greatest disappointment is, perhaps, not having been able to abolish conflict from the world. The impetus needed to deliver such a change was far more than the Fifties Child could muster, particularly as his was not a united front. One only has to look at the writing of our three songwriters to see the different perspectives they took. Arguably, Holroyd and Lees were more concerned about the violence that was occurring in the world at the present time than Wolstenholme, whose conflict songs remain largely rooted in the sins of the past. They also differed over what action to take. Exemplifying this factor, we have the vastly different approaches in strategy between Sutherland's directness on 'Ireland' and Lees' cloaked appeals for individual responsibility. Those who yielded power were too strong against such well-meaning disunity, too easily able to shape many minds towards conflict, thus continuing the "circle of hate".

However, despite the continuing propensity for conflict in the world, things could perhaps have been worse. One has to remember that these songs we have been discussing, and many others, had a profound effect on a great number of people. Indeed, many teenagers first realised that there were alternative opinions to those being voiced by politicians on television when they heard them in these songs. Thus, the power of the songs was immense not just in informing young people but in giving them the confidence that they were not alone in the world when they were shocked at Vietnam, abhorred the nuclear deterrent or really wondered why there was so much violence originating from Northern Ireland. This effect, in turn, may have given like-minded politicians more confidence that their vision of a better world was worth lobbying for and would not lose them too many votes, perhaps even win them some. We have the world that we have, and we will never be able to quantify the effect of these conflict songs in shaping that world, but the positive energy that they generated will surely have had a significant effect, not just on the individuals who heard and loved the songs but on many others as well.

The contrast between Sutherland's 'Ireland' and Lees' Troubles Suite also exemplifies the difference identified in the 'Preface to Barclay James Harvest's Conflict Songs' between true protest songs and the band's sociological songs. 'Ireland' is, undoubtedly, a protest song. The Troubles Suite? Sure, many people think that 'For No One' is a protest song—it is arguably but, as we have seen, it is actually much more than that, in that it is a call to all individuals who are caught in the "circles of hate" to resist and reject the violence. It is not a protest, it is a plea. That call gives it added depth and, together with the fact that it does not have an easily identifiable target, I would argue therefore that it is not a true protest song. 'Summer Soldier' is equally, if not more, complex. In its essence, 'Summer Soldier' is a spiritual song, as is 'For No One'. Of the songs that form the Troubles Suite, 'Cheap the Bullet' is the only one which departs from this theme, in that it is mainly observational in nature, placing partial responsibility for the continuing circle of hate on television and the media—it is therefore the closest that comes to a pure protest song.

Similar subtleties appear elsewhere in Lees' conflict songs; 'In Memory of the Martyrs' being an example. Holroyd's fatalism and Wolstenholme's weighting towards the First World War also generally preclude their songs from consideration as true protest songs—'Victims of Circumstance' is a possible exception but perhaps requires too much interpretation.

Moving on now to think about the Fifties Child's rejection of the authority of God: that rejection is actually far more problematic than the rejection of the authority of Man. Do as I say and you will be saved and find everlasting happiness in heaven, reject all that pre-War truism and . . . and what? Doomed? This life is all you have? Why put up with all the suffering then?

The effect that the rejection of God's authority had for the Fifties Child was to open up his whole life as a spiritual quest without bounds. Whether he has realised it consciously or not, the Fifties Child has replaced faith with a quest for a meaning to life; and it has been a life's journey without the promise of an answer. Without the rock of faith to guide them, everyone's quest would take such individual twists and turns as life and mind dictated, each shift capable of shaping the spiritual road ahead for years at a time. And, without the rock of faith, there would be no safety net.

So, let us take a look at how that lifelong quest for a satisfactory spirituality is mirrored by Barclay James Harvest's songwriters. First, however, we must share some of the vistas that shaped their life's journey . . .

Les Holroyd

Part 4
Life Is for Living

12

Politics and the Media

As we have just noted, the Fifties Child's rejection of the authority of Man did not turn into a political revolution. So, some of the significant events shaping his life's journey would be completely outside his control and, as they exerted sufficient influence to be reflected by Barclay James Harvest's songs, they merit inclusion in our social history.

Seemingly disparate, these two aspects of life—politics and the media—became intertwined during the Fifties Child's lifetime, to the point that it now seems impossible to disentangle, or even cut through, the strong vine knots that bind them together. Holroyd expressed all our fears as far back as 1990—my God, was that really more than twenty years ago?—in 'Welcome to the Show':

> and they [musicians] surely do well
> for the politicians who sell them
> on TV today:
> makes me uncertain
> of who runs the world.

Most of us, Fifties Children and others, are still uncertain on that aspect, as our lives are constantly buffeted and shaped by the whims of politicians' fancies and the media barons' drive for the reward of private yachts bobbing in the calm waters off tropical island paradises. Try as we might to avoid the tendrils of their influence, try as we might to pretend we are not interested or affected, we are inevitably ensnared by some aspect of their success or failure. Perhaps it was always thus . . .

Politics

Explicit political commentary was not a common topic for rock musicians of the Fifties Child generation. It was not until after 1976's punk revolution that, fuelled by younger songwriters, it began to feature more prominently as a topic for rock lyrics. It is therefore atypical of the genre that Barclay James Harvest's songwriters' most explicit political intervention until the twenty-first century came in 1974, as a result of the battle over wages between the government and the National Union of Mineworkers (NUM). The songwriter, Lees, returned to a similar topic, union law, a few years later and these two instances—which, whilst they are clearly small in number, did surprise and even disappoint many followers of the band for the nature of what was said—do justify the inclusion of a brief review of the period's politics, with a particular focus on the government's relations with the unions within this social history.

Although he might not have realised it, the Fifties Child found himself living in one of the more unusual voting systems of the democratic world. The British government election system—in which the country is subdivided into about 600 land areas, called constituencies, with an elected member of parliament for each of those constituencies chosen on a "first-past-the-post" basis—has a tendency to yield governments of greater political dogmatic strength than the electorate itself. Supporters of the system argue that it is only in this way that one achieves strong, stable government, whereas alternatives to the system—so they say—such as proportional representation, result in weaker governments in which coalitions between differing dogmas are required in order to be able to actually pass legislation through Parliament and thus be able to rule. Advocates of different systems can point to various parts of the world as proof that their argument is the superior one, with Germany and Italy often being used as examples in favour and against systems which incorporate an element of proportional representation.

In practice, what this voting system has meant during the Fifties Child's lifetime is that there has been a fairly constant and regular change in government leadership between the Conservative and Labour Parties, to the total exclusion of the Liberal Party who, despite holding on to a sizeable percentage of the actual electoral vote, have been an emasculated force compared with the nineteenth century and the pre-First World War years. It is perhaps no surprise, therefore, that the most ardent campaigners for a change to proportional representation, or other voting systems other than the established one, are supporters of the Liberal Party, who believe that such a change would grant them more governmental clout. Lees' words come to mind once again: "Far left, far right, centre / it's power they crave!"

It is also interesting to note—getting into dangerous ground here because politics is always a thorny subject—that, irrespective of whether the government is of Conservative or Labour persuasion, once the politicians actually ascend into power, there is a smoothing of the worst of the pre-election rhetoric. When the realities of actually running a country—without an empire and without a large manufacturing infrastructure—in the modern world hit home, then to a great extent the options for manoeuvre are limited. The cynic would say that the main aim of government is to achieve some kind of economic good news just prior to the next election so that the existing rulers continue in power. Others argue that, to a large extent, it is the Civil Service that runs the country, providing much of the continuity that ministers of government cannot. The breaking of election promises has become notorious but is partly due, certainly for governments coming in to power from opposition, to the new ministers suddenly being faced with a whole set of new factors they did not previously know about or fully comprehend. Nevertheless, such behaviour reduces the electorate's faith in the political system.

As the Fifties Child grew into his thirties, Mrs Thatcher's leadership of the Conservative Party finally brought about long-term stable government of the country. The Conservatives would hold power for eighteen years from 1979, more than eleven of them with Thatcher in charge. However, far from being a government of unity, the leadership during those years served to polarise society—not that, according to Thatcher, there was one (in 1987 she famously declared "there is no such thing as society")—in a way that had not been seen since before the Second World War. Buoyed by the jingoistic fervour of an empire-recalling victory against Argentina in the Falklands War, the government went on to inflict an equally famous—and more societally significant—victory against the NUM, which in turn enhanced its ability to complete a series of ever more restrictive union legislation, seriously curtailing Unions' ability to conduct strikes in the way the NUM had in the Seventies. Or, depending on your perspective, the legislation was aimed at reducing the unions' ability to protect the working class from the excesses of the capitalists.

Who was right? Who was wrong? Given the economic globalisation forces already making themselves felt at the time, did it, in fact, make any difference whatsoever? Some things are certain: a significant proportion of our national infrastructure is actually now owned by foreign companies rather than by the British public. We may have a choice of supplier but our bills are still large, and is the quality of service any better now than then? Did the unions price our labour force out of the market and drive most of our manufacturing industries out of business, so that we rely on cheap imports from near-slave condition factories overseas? Possibly. Or did the government not protect our industries to allow us, as a country, to retain some control, keep employment opportunities for our workforce at home and thus retain a greater national pride? In essence, defence minister Michael Heseltine's fight for Westland Helicopters in 1985/86, which led to his resignation from the Tory government due to differences of opinion with Thatcher, was about retaining more control within Britain and Europe, rather than further overseas—but the Prime Minister was then irresistible, sweeping all before her.

The kind of quasi-dictatorial demeanour that a long spell in power yields is not well appreciated by the British character and was undoubtedly a factor, not only in Thatcher's ousting by her own party in 1990, but then also of the electorate's ousting of her successor, John Major, at the 1997 election. The electorate's counter-reaction was so severe that Tony Blair, the incoming Labour prime minister, was able to hold on to power for so long that he, too, though his reign was not as societally divisive as Thatcher's, became likened to a dictator.

Slightly odd, don't you think, this aversion for dictators when we shy away from the coalition governments that a proportional representation system would bring? Clearly, the kind of democracy that the Fifties Child likes is that which delegates the government sufficient power to rule, but retains enough to allow him to quickly rein it in by its electoral choke-chain.

The fudging of dogma that comes with the responsibilities of government, together with the innate suspicion of authority of the Fifties Child and his generational successors—sharpened by well publicised sleazy scandals involving high-ranking politicians—are amongst the factors that have led to the downturn in election turnouts in recent years. It is almost as if the electorate has decided that its individual vote does not make sufficient difference (which, under the current system, is very true in many constituencies) or that it does not matter which political party is elected to govern because, irrespective of their differing ideologies, the practical form of legislation is sufficiently similar.

Contrary to the inference drawn from this recent electoral apathy, Fifties Children have seen enough governments to realise that it does clearly matter which political party is elected to govern. Fudging of dogma there may be, but there are clear and essential philosophical differences in the way that Conservatives and Labour have governed. One of the most fundamental of these has been the approaches of the differing political dogmas to the working class, as represented by the trades unions. Throughout the lifetime of the Fifties Child, the Labour Party has in general had the support—including a substantial financial element—of the trades unions, whereas there has often been conflict between the unions and Conservative governments. Some of these conflicts—in particular the battles involving the NUM in the Seventies and Eighties—have had significant, divisive and long-lasting impact. Many academic studies, books, poems, films and songs have been inspired by these cataclysmic societal events—the sketch given here will purely remind us of the facts so that we may later place the songs in their context.

Younger readers may perhaps wonder why I am referring to battles between workers and *government*. In the Seventies, infrastructure industries, such as coal supply for power stations, were nationalised, which is to say they were owned by the people as a whole, with the government in formal custodianship. The coal supply company was called the National Coal Board (NCB) and, like other manual labour industries at the time, was approaching full unionisation, with closed shop agreements in place at many work locations between the NCB and the NUM. This meant that anyone that was employed by the NCB *must* be a member of the NUM. Just think about this for a while: one of the implications was that, if you were expelled from the union, you would then lose your job. So, the union had power over you, not just your employer. Also, when the unions fought the employer they were, in effect, fighting the government, the custodian of the people.

Whereas coal only contributes 30 per cent or so of electricity generated in the UK in the twenty-first century, in the Seventies its contribution was more like 70 per cent, meaning that its production and delivery to the power stations was crucial to maintaining the electricity supply. Miners had not been on strike since the Twenties but by 1971 they had become deeply dissatisfied with the level of pay for what was not only a difficult and dangerous job but also one that was vital to the country's economic health.

At the NUM annual conference in 1971, the miners voted through a demand for a significant annual pay rise, which was well in excess of the government's maximum target of 8 per cent. When the NCB brought in private contractors to cover lost shifts following the NUM's overtime ban, the union, fearing anarchy within its ranks and the breakout of wildcat strikes, announced that an official strike would begin in January. All 289 of the NCB's pits were closed from the first day of the strike. The depth of ill-feeling amongst the mineworkers was such that—against the wishes of the NUM's leadership—they refused to provide safety cover in the coal pits. Such cover was required to maintain the pits' long-term integrity and safety and without it, there was the possibility that some pits would be unsafe to mine once the strike was over. One miner, questioned on television about putting the future integrity of the pit at risk, replied: "So what? Who wants to go down the bloody pit again anyway?"

Clearly this extraordinary response, made in the adrenaline-fuelled high emotions of the moment, could not have been representative of the miners as a whole, who needed the jobs to feed themselves and their families. More importantly, what it signifies is the bitter anger that had welled up in these workers. Frustration builds up over years, ebbing and flowing, but when its causes are not addressed, it eventually causes an explosion of feeling that is not easily controlled, precisely as happened on the streets of Britain in early 1972.

Picketing of all sites associated with the fuel supply for power stations was intense, aided by workers of other industries out to support the miners. It is estimated that, during the 1972 strike, 500 separate work locations were picketed around the clock by some 40,000 miners and other workers. A key battleground in the strike was the Saltley coke distribution depot. The struggle to keep its fuel moving out to the nation's power stations was intense, leading to injurious clashes between pickets and the police.

Whether it is because of his role in the miners' fight with Mrs Thatcher's government in 1984, or whether it is because it was his actions that provided the pivotal moment in the dispute, I shall leave it for sharper sociological commentators to decide, but what is true is that many accounts of the time identify Arthur Scargill—who was organising the picketing at Saltley—as being a key figure in the 1972 strike. On February 9, with fuel still leaving the depot, Scargill addressed a meeting of the Amalgamated Union of Engineering Workers (AUEW) in Birmingham demanding that they come out on strike in support of the miners and join the pickets at Saltley. The response to Scargill— a sharp, rhetorical speaker—was decisive: the following day the 3,000 miners already there were joined by more than 10,000 other workers. To shouts of "close the gates!" this picket army continually surged against the police cordon until the chief constable of Birmingham, who had assured the Home Secretary that such a thing could never happen, ordered their closure, thus preventing the vital power station supplies from being distributed.

The dearth of fuel soon caused the first power cuts and, on February 12, the government announced that from Valentine's Day non-essential industrial users would not be able to use electricity on Sundays and three other days of the week. Less than a week later, 1.6 million workers had been laid off by their companies because of the lack of power. The industry secretary told Parliament that, even with these restrictions, fuel supplies for power stations would last only a couple of weeks more, with enough left only for essential services after that. In effect, the entire country was without the electricity needed to put its labour force to work.

The government had convened an urgent inquiry under Lord Wilberforce to review miners' pay, which reported on the 18th, suggesting increases of between 15–31.6 per cent. The NUM held out for more, and the government eventually agreed to all of its demands after meeting the union leadership at Downing Street. The seven-week strike was called off on February 25, leaving miners amongst the highest paid workers of the working class.

These events have been described here in a fair amount of detail, not just because of the effect they came to have on some of our songwriters, as we shall see, but because they were momentous events with long-running repercussions for the country, the effects of which can still be felt today.

What may now seem surprising is that, not much more than 18 months after achieving their aims in 1972, the miners were again in dispute with the government over pay. How could they become dissatisfied so quickly?

The answer reveals as much about the inability of governments—irrespective of their originating ideology—to control events as it does about the specific reasons for the renewed turmoil. Inflation in the early Seventies had more than doubled from Sixties levels. Under these circumstances a worker's pay could quickly become eroded in real terms or become disproportionate in relation to the pay of others if those others had higher annual pay rise awards. One of the government's tools in the attempt to curb inflation was, perhaps not unreasonably, a limit on annual pay awards but this was set below the level of inflation and caused inevitable frustration, not just because of the absolute level of pay but because differentiation between the nationalised and private industries more than likely would follow. However, the destabilising factor that upset what was, after all, a state of normal dissatisfaction—the vast majority of workers always want more pay—was completely outside the control of any government.

On October 6, 1973 the Egyptians and Syrians invaded Israel in a surprise, coordinated two-pronged attack. The ensuing war, which has become known as the Yom Kippur War because the Arabian forces elected to attack on the holiest day of the Jewish faith, became a Cold War conflict, with the United States and the Soviet Union backing Israel and the Arab States respectively. A ceasefire was enforced prior to any direct engagement between the superpowers but the conflict's economic aftermath for the Western Allies was to prove punitive as, in vengeance for the West's support of Israel, oil-producing Arab nations imposed restrictions on production and embargoes against the United States and other Western ally nations, causing the 1973 energy crisis. Oil prices quadrupled, and the repercussions on inflation in the oil-hungry Western economies were severe to say the least.

The miners' dissatisfaction led to the NUM's executive ordering an overtime ban on November 12, shortly followed by equivalent action from electricity workers. Note: an overtime ban, not a strike. Clearly, the expectation of the government was that miners should have to routinely work overtime—rather than this being used as an occasional measure to cover unforeseen eventualities—because, on the following day, prime minister Heath declared the country to be in a formal state of emergency. In mid-December, with the overtime ban still in force and the effects of the oil crisis being keenly felt, Heath announced that, from January 1, 1974, electricity for non-essential industry users would be limited to three consecutive normal working (no overtime) days. This was the infamous Three Day Week, and it would last the remaining tenure of Heath's government.

In late January 1974, as fuel supplies dwindled and tempers frayed, the secretary of state for energy—Lord Carrington—warned of a possible two-and-a-half or even two-day week. In response to the threat, Mick McGahey, the vice-president of the NUM and a member of the British Communist

Party, said that the miners would make a plea to British troops, who had been deployed by the government to assist in maintaining some semblance of normality, to defect to the miners' side and support the strike. There was general outrage, not just amongst the government and its supporters, but from many miners and the Labour Party also, pressurising McGahey into retracting his mistimed revolutionary call for troops to disobey orders.

Now, admit it, when you read 'The Soviet Threat' chapter, you thought that Lees was being slightly extreme in dreaming up 'May Day' as a fictionalised account of Britain under a totalitarian communist regime, didn't you? Think again, dear reader, this was the Cold War: the positions of the United States and the Soviets over the Yom Kippur War had been a factor in the British crisis of the 1973–74 winter, during which it was abundantly clear that sections of British society were keen admirers of the communist ideology, and would have happily replaced our democracy for a similar regime to Moscow's. Let this be a warning: ignore Lees at your peril!

The government came under increasing pressure when the NUM voted in favour of a strike on February 4, leading Heath to announce, just three days later, that a government election would be held at the end of the month. Desperate attempts continued to prevent the miners' overtime ban becoming a strike during the election campaign. These efforts failed and the miners' strike began on the 9th.

The beleaguered Conservative government, hoping to receive a reinvigorating mandate from a dejected electorate, fought the election campaign to the clarion call of "who governs the country?" The country was clearly uncertain and returned a hung parliament. On that occasion, the Liberals and Ulster Unionists backed the Labour Party, which had won the largest number of seats, forcing Heath to resign. The incoming Labour administration quickly settled with the miners and the Three Day Week ended during the second week in March.

The disruption that the Three Day Week caused to normal life was significant and left many people feeling bitter towards the miners. Even today, nearly forty years on, one still finds political commentators deriding their actions in the press. However, the fact that it was the Labour Party that won the greatest number of seats in the Houses of Parliament in the February 1974 election must also tell you that, despite the hardships, there must have been many people who were sympathetic to their cause.

Labour's government, under prime ministers Harold Wilson and, from 1976, James Callaghan, was unable to control the oil-fuelled inflation. If price rises had caused discontent in the early Seventies, then they would certainly not sate tempers in the second half of the decade. Inflation hit a record high in 1975, peaking at over 25 per cent and would stay at well over ten per cent until the early Eighties. In the maelstrom of pay-rise fury that this caused, anyone watching from afar would have never believed that the unions and Labour were meant to be natural allies. In fact, a series of crippling strikes during the 1978-79 winter—the Winter of Discontent—would prove fatal for both the government and the unions. It was the lose-lose action of all time, presaging a Conservative government under Margaret Thatcher that, having pondered the lessons of the Conservatives' own defeats at the hands of the NUM in the early part of the decade, hastened to alter union legislation with the intent of making it increasingly difficult for unions to call and implement effective strike action.

It was almost inevitable that the miners would clash with the Thatcher government. When it came, the timing of the dispute was inauspicious for the miners, who would be battling a government enjoying unusually high levels of public approval. Starting in March 1984 with a dispute over pit closures, the strike, the most divisive societal event of recent British history, would ultimately have the effect of accelerating the decline of the British coal industry. The government was better prepared than a decade previously: coal stocks had been garnered at the power stations, extra supplies put in storage in safe locations as far as Rotterdam, and the mix of nuclear power within the country's overall supply had increased. At the head of the Central Electricity Generating Board was Walter Marshall, appointed by Thatcher's government, and who would be rewarded by them with a peerage for his services to the country in helping to keep the lights on during this year-long strike.

This section's Barclay James Harvest-derived focus on the miners provides a slight distortion on the society of the time. It was not just that industry's workers that had disputes with the governments during the Seventies and Eighties—many others also expressed their growing frustrations by staging strikes. However, the Thatcher government did not just defeat the miners in 1985, it crushed the whole of the labour movement in Britain, and with that defeat crippled the hopes of many Fifties Children. The post-Second World War emancipation of the working classes, together with the consequent shrinkage in the disparities of the class system, were now for nought. The consequences are that, today, the disparity between rich and poor is at greater levels than at any time since the Second World War, the greatest that the Fifties Child has seen.

One of the significant differences between then and now is that in the modern world, as we saw in the chapter 'The Soldier as Victim', there is not the respect for God, King and Country—the respect for authority—that there was then. Societal cause and effect often takes decades to unravel, and it is likely that we have yet to see the full consequences of the miners' defeat in 1985.

Quite what you think of this polarisation in society largely depends, firstly, on your own status within it and, secondly, on where you live. Certainly, if you live in England and south of Birmingham, unless it is in a deprived area of London, it is highly likely that you either do not recognise a polarisation at all, or that it is an issue of low importance to you. North of the line I have drawn, both reactions become acutely opposite to that. This type of divide is certainly not new, but the Fifties Child had hoped to temper it: however, it has sharpened again since the Seventies.[1]

❦

Barclay James Harvest's songwriters, of course, were not only born, but also lived north of that societal demarcation line, and one might therefore expect their songwriting to reflect a political slant that recognises the hardships of working class people. To a great extent, it does just that. We have already discussed songs such as the 'Poor Boy Blues/Mill Boys' cycle and 'African' that empathise with the daily hard grind that many working people face in order to make a living, and further on in our social history we will meet the moving 'Three Weeks to Despair', a compassionate look at the plight of homeless people. And yet, two of Lees' songs—'The Great 1974 Mining Disaster' and 'The Closed Shop'—caused some controversy and led fans to question Lees' political stance and support for the working class.

Personally, I find it difficult to interpret 'The Great 1974 Mining Disaster' satisfactorily. One thing is abundantly clear, however, and that is that there were no major accidents in the mines in that year, so that the "disaster" of the title can only refer to the NUM's battle with the government, an inference from the choice of that word then being that Lees was not supportive of the miners' stance in the dispute. Another aid to interpretation is Wolstenholme's introduction to the song, recorded for posterity on the Radio 1 broadcast of their 1974 concert at Golders Green Hippodrome in London:

> John decided that musicians—especially popular ones—were rather like politicians: whatever they say, you do. The first person we mention is the Bee Gees—sorry the BBC, slip of the tongue—and David Bowie, and Edward Heath and, finally but most important, Joe Gormley, who did such good work for the miners and made us shiver for such a long time. This song is then dedicated to him really.[2]

1. I remember, as a student at Leicester University, attending a speech on the 1979 election campaign trail given by Edward Heath on precisely this subject. Heath's views on society, of course, were not shared by Thatcher and her government—he was already yesterday's man.
2. The relevance of Wolstenholme's Bee Gees jest is that 'The Great 1974 Mining Disaster' is a deconstruction of their 1967 chart hit 'New York Mining Disaster 1941'. We shall discuss Lees' deconstructions in the chapter 'Rock 'n' Roll'.

Along with the inference from the title, the sarcasm pervading the dedication to NUM leader Gormley enhances the interpretation that Lees—and Wolstenholme—did not support the miners' action. The song's mention of Edward Heath—"a sailor oh so gay"[3] refers to Heath's predilection for yachting and is an allusion to the popular belief that he was homosexual—comes almost in passing but Gormley—"Mr Groan"—merits the chorus:

> Have you seen my life, Mr Groan?
> Do you know what it's like to be outside?
> All you have to do is smile to cause a landslide,
> and you do, and you do, Mr Groan.

Whilst it is impossible to be clear exactly what is meant by these words— beyond the admission of Gormley's charisma in the words "all you have to do is smile"—the title, Wolstenholme's sarcasm and Gormley's metaphorical depiction as Mr Groan are sufficient to underline the song as being critical of the NUM's stance in the winter of 1973-74.

Interestingly, Gormley himself was a comparative moderate within the NUM's executive.[4] One has to consider that leaders—including prime ministers—often have difficulty controlling large organisations—including government—and shaping them to their exact will. Often, as leader, one's best efforts are directed into tempering the excesses of one's organisation. There is ample evidence from the miners' dispute of 1972 to show that Gormley attempted to moderate the uglier mood and militancy of the miners, and it is believed that one of the major reasons he clung on to the NUM leadership for as long as he did was in an attempt to prevent the communist McGahey from becoming its leader. The popular media would not have portrayed his moderating aspect thus, certainly not during the Three Day Week when Gormley had the media's focus as leader and all the talk was about moving from an overtime ban to a strike. It is almost certainly the popular media's image that Lees and Wolstenholme were happy to mock as Mr Groan. Clearly, the media was a major influencer of opinion, even able to affect those who would often berate it.

'The Closed Shop' [1978] is easier to understand: an attack on the union practice that restricted a company to only employ members of the union.

---

3. On the *Legacy* live album's version of the song—recorded in London in 2006—Lees sings "a major oh so gay": I am not certain if this was a slip of the tongue or if he was making an oblique remark to someone in the news at the time. If it is the latter then I have failed to unmask the target of his wrath!

4. So much so that in 2002 the BBC series *True Spies* claimed that he was a Special Branch informant.

Supporters of the closed shop claimed that it assisted in ensuring that workers' rights were safeguarded by preventing employers from bypassing negotiations with the unions. Employers also liked some aspects of the arrangement—negotiating terms and conditions with one union was a lot easier than the alternatives. Critics, however, said that the practice infringed an individual's right to free choice and that it gave the unions too much power. Margaret Thatcher's government made restricting its legality and power a priority of its legislative programme, beginning as early as 1980 with a requirement that 80 per cent of workers entitled to vote should do so in favour of a closed shop agreement for its provisions to be considered legally binding.

In 1978, however, it was still an unassailable bastion of the working class labour force and Lees' song—bearing in mind the band's "principles" standing as we have already discussed—caused some consternation amongst its fans, amongst which was the popular Radio 1 disc-jockey, John Peel, who complained during a broadcast that one could not tell whether Lees was pro or anti the closed shop practice. In fact, in this instance, the lyrics are unambiguous. As in a number of other of Lees' songs, the lyrics are sung from more than one perspective: the verses and chorus are sung in the third person but the bridge verse is sung from the perspective of the union workers themselves, and it is clear that they are in a dispute with their employers. Both perspectives reveal Lees' dissatisfaction with unions' tactics: the former suggests that they are in dispute over outdated issues and the latter—the workers' bridge verse—is an angry rallying call for unity in the dispute, which is seen as a battle of will, not reason. In fact, the workers admit they are so fired up for battle that they have lost their reason. This last criticism is one that could be levelled at participants in any antagonistic dispute. We have already identified in our social history how conflicts are difficult to control once the opposing sides have joined in the fray, and these union-government disputes were simply a form of conflict. The rules of engagement were clearly different to those of a military conflict, but a conflict is what they were nevertheless and, as such, they evoked all the usual human failings from participants.

The fact that 'The Closed Shop' was regularly interpreted as an attack on the trades unions prompted an interviewer in 1989 to question Lees as to where he stood on the issue of his support for the working class:

It's misinterpreting what I said in the first place. I wasn't against the working class, I wasn't against the unions—I was against the closed shop. I thought it was a destructive force, and I still do. If you look back through all the songs I've written in that kind of vein, they're all pro-working class, because that's what I am, and you can't change where you come from. I'm not really political, I've got a social conscience.

Misinterpretation is an issue that Lees will often have had to deal with—but hopefully not too significantly within this book. We have already seen how songs such as 'For No One' can be misinterpreted, or not fully understood, which is perhaps not surprising given the intentional ambiguity and obfuscation inherent in much of his writing. However, by this stage, we have learnt sufficient about his style to understand that he stays close to a number of themes, one of which is "victims". The understanding of 'The Closed Shop' is then reinforced if we consider some of the most crucial lines from his writing, from 'Fifties Child':

Fifties child was right to believe:
peace and love were our needs;
the need to be free.

"The need to be free." Clearly, in the closed shop system, an individual is not free to choose. So far as Lees is concerned, taking away that choice immediately condemns the practice as unfair. The individual coerced into joining the union is a victim, in the same way that the child caught up in the Troubles is a victim, the same way that we were the victims of circumstance of the Cold War, and the same way that we were victims of the consequences of the NUM's dispute with the government. That—the fact that we were all victims of the dispute—was the real "disaster" inherent in the title of 'The Great 1974 Mining Disaster'.

'The Closed Shop' is not an anti-union song, it is a song in defence of freedom. "Freedom" was one of the prized values of the Fifties Child, who wished to lead his life unencumbered by interference from politicians and other rulemakers (just two examples of these are the Church and simple peer pressure—'Summer Soldier', 'For No One' and 'Cheap the Bullet' all describe how an individual can be trapped by peer pressure). This concept of freedom also appears in Holroyd's songwriting; we have already discussed his 'Victims of Circumstance' and later, in the chapter on Spirituality, we shall analyse 2001's 'Revolution Day'. Quite whether the Fifties Child's notion of freedom is naive or not is a subject for philosophical debate that could fill several books, so it is best that we just leave it at that in this social history—suffice to say that the corruption of the freedoms that they aspired to in their idealistic hopes for the world was a factor that bred disillusionment and sadness.

Finally, before moving on, it is perhaps worth just saying that, despite the fact that he was seen as a moderate, Gormley was a supporter of the closed shop, which perhaps explains Lees' depiction of him as Mr Groan.

There are two other Lees songs which we have previously discussed which need representing here for completeness: 'African' and 'Ancient Waves'.

The politicisation of 'Ancient Waves', a song whose main intent, as we have already learnt, is to decry the Second Iraqi War, comes through the naming of leaders Blair and Bush. Lees is not as obvious as that, of course, although he is more direct than when writing about Edward Heath as the "sailor oh so gay". In 'Ancient Waves' he talks about a "blare" of sound and the "flaming [burning] bush" of the Biblical story.

There is no subtlety about the language used in 'African'. Despite being inspired by events and the apartheid system in South Africa, there is much about the song that appears to be universally applicable, for instance:

> Slave labour, working class:
> what's in a name?
> Far left, far right, centre:
> it's power they crave!

These are some of the most direct and hard-hitting lyrics in Lees' canon. The first couplet effectively equates the working class to slave labour. One is tempted to speculate that, some thirteen years after the event, Lees had developed a different view of the British miners' disputes with Edward Heath's government. The second couplet demonstrates the apoliticisation that Lees hints at in the interview just quoted above. Lees' distinction between being political and having a social conscience is an interesting one and it is perhaps symptomatic of the Fifties Child's innate distrust of authority. This distinction also appears in Holroyd's writing: for instance, his 'Victims of Circumstance' provides social commentary with little or no explicit political content. Lees' distinction almost certainly explains that the relative dearth of political comment in his songwriting is more than just reticence at expressing explicit political views within songs. In life, of course, he will have had to make a voting choice at election time, the same as the rest of the electorate. Even if the choice is not voting—and lowering government election turnouts suggest that is what more and more people are choosing to do—that is still a choice with consequences.

It is clear that, societally, the political reticence of Lees' and Holroyd's songwriting is reflective of a significant portion of the electorate. Hopefully the trend to distrust politics and politicians will not worsen. One only has to observe the events of the Arab Spring to realise the high value that one should ascribe to democracy. And, despite the fact that there might be a lot of truth in the lyric "far left, far right, centre: it's power they crave", the resulting ideologies are very different. And, surely, we would all like our politicians to have a social conscience! Democracy requires participation: you get nowt for owt. The ability to vote has always been one of the Fifties Child's greatest strengths.

Barclay James Harvest's contemporaries—perhaps even more so than they themselves—largely stayed clear of explicit political writing. One can contrast the different political approaches of the Fifties Children generation with the one immediately following by contrasting Strawbs' 'Part of the Union' [Single A-side, 1972; *Bursting at the Seams*, 1973] and the Style Council's 'Walls Come Tumbling Down!' [*Our Favourite Shop*, 1985].

'Part of the Union', written by Richard Hudson and John Ford after the 1972 miners' strike, exudes musical and lyrical joy at the power of the unions; rejoicing in the fact that a simple working man can defeat the government through being part of the union. The song is undoubtedly the lyrical antithesis of both 'The Great 1974 Mining Disaster' and 'The Closed Shop', though its somewhat frivolous musical treatment meant that it was probably not taken too seriously; indeed, some people thought that Hudson and Ford meant it sarcastically, which they denied.[5] 'Part of the Union' was a No. 2 hit for Strawbs, although one must not be tempted to draw any inferences from that with respect to the record buying public's support for the miners!

By the time that Paul Weller had disbanded the Jam and gone on to form the Style Council at the beginning of 1983, he had already—along with a number of other musicians surfing music's New Wave—written a number of political leaning songs. The Style Council's politicisation was even more overt than the Jam's: 'Walls Come Tumbling Down!' is one of a number that he wrote for that band explicitly criticising the policies of Thatcher's government. There are no Leesian nuances here, he just goes ahead and explicitly states the political point he wants to make. Arguably, this was rock music connecting with its most primeval political roots: Weller refers back to the unions' famous victories against the government in the Seventies, states that the enemy is at No. 10 (Downing Street, the prime minister's official residence) and that unity can bring about the government's fall again. Why revolt? There is conflict because of class divisions and those in power reap the profits whilst suppressing the pay of the workers: are you just going to carry on scrabbling at your pitiful job or make the revolution work? 'Walls Come Tumbling Down!' is a cry for action if ever there was one. There were others in this vein from Weller and his generation of musicians, clearly fulfilling as much of a societal need for their fans as Barclay James Harvest's more apolitical, but equally socially conscious, music had done for their own fans just a time-slice before.

We shall finish off with a couple of more recent songs reflecting the divisions that the Fifties Child has seen re-emerge in his later life. In 2008, Gavin

5. The song's lyrics are clearly borne of Woody Guthrie's 'Union Maid' (first recorded 1941), showing that Lees was not the only one to be tempted by such antics.

Sutherland muses about what an alien traveller, observing the earth from space, might think about the stark contrasts between people on our planet, some driving around in limousines whilst others shuffle along in bare feet, some living in mansions whilst others make do with a cardboard box: 'Strange!' [*The Deal*].

The plight of the working classes is eloquently described by Jonathan Barrett in his song 'Shoot Them Down' for the Tangent's album *COMM* (2011).[6] This song's powerful lyrics unify a couple of themes of our social history: the soldier as a victim and politics. Barrett's argument is that governments manipulate the working classes for their own purposes both in times of war and in times of peace. In war, they are sent off to the front line, treated as little more than cannon fodder; and, in peace, they are drained of their strength, working at whatever suits until it suits no longer, then unceremoniously dumped. These people, the working class who have built the empire, are now exhausted: exhausted from war and exhausted from the depression caused by the prospect of no work—they are spent, mere husks, and they have nothing left to give. Complete with a poetic reference back to the miners' dispute with the Thatcher government, 'Shoot Them Down' is a stonking sociological song.

The predilection of significant parts of the working classes to vote Conservative—which they must do, otherwise that party's share of the vote would not be what it is—has always struck me as rather at odds with that political party's ideology. It is a bit like turkeys voting for Christmas. This nuance of democracy must have as much to do with the ability of propaganda and the media to persuade people than it does with calculating and maximising one's own opportunities. Let us now see what our songwriters cause us to delve into within that world of manipulative wizardry . . .

The Media

I exaggerate, you say? You have probably forgotten the Michael Foot dufflecoat incident. Champion of the working classes, lovely man, amongst the most dignified of post-war politicians, elected to leader of the Labour Party in 1980, he goes along to 1981's Remembrance Day Service at the Cenotaph, a formal state occasion, wearing a short length overcoat. It was cold, after all. Gets ridicule and a huge panning in the media for wearing, at best, a dufflecoat and, at worst, a donkey-jacket. At the next government election some 18 months later, loses by a landslide. You think there is no correlation between these events?

Question: why do companies spend millions on advertising? Answer:

6. Barrett is a Fifties Child follower—he is even younger than me!

enough of us are sufficiently influenced by the subliminal and explicit messages to go out and buy their products, and they make a profit. Money! Question: why do political parties spend millions on propaganda? Now, write your own answer in the space below . . .

....

The first memory of many Fifties Children will be that of crowding around a small television set, along with their families and neighbours, to watch the Queen's coronation. In 1953, few homes possessed a television—indeed, it had only been about thirty years since the BBC started radio broadcasting. These timespans—between the onset of radio and television, and between then and now—may seem lengthy to us, but in generational, and therefore societal, terms they are tiny. The advance in communications of the last one hundred years, now that we can also include the worldwide web, is of staggering proportions, the full consequences of which will take time to filter through and which we have only begun to understand.

For the Fifties Child, it was the advance in television that dominated that technological advance. Less significant, but still of considerable impact, have been advances in newspaper printing: a black and white photograph first appeared in a newspaper in 1880, but they were not regularly introduced until well into the twentieth century while colour photography would not become commonplace until the Eighties. Tabloid journalism was also popular with the Fifties Child, in particular from the end of the Sixties when *The Sun* switched to the tabloid format and began its fierce rivalry with *The Daily Mirror*.

Images enhance the power of advertising, whether it be for commercial or political purposes, and these advances in printing and television would change the Fifties Child's world in ways unimaginable to his parents. Television in particular, with its power to enter people's homes across the social classes, had a societal changing impact that was witnessed firsthand by the Fifties Child. When Princess Elizabeth became Queen in 1952, only around ten per cent of all households had television but, by the turn of that decade, the proportion was already nearer two-thirds. *That* is societal impact! Growth continued during the Sixties and, by the time that Lees wrote 'Child of the Universe', the percentage of households with television was 90 per cent or more—in effect, almost everyone in Britain would have had access to a television by that time.

But why mention 'Child of the Universe' in this context? The Vietnam War, which we discussed in an earlier chapter, has been called the first "TV war" and it is interesting that the Barclay James Harvest song that triggered our review of that conflict—'Child of the Universe' of course—also provides us with a vital clue as to when the step-change in television's influence occurred.

The first version of the song that was known about for many years was that recorded in 1972 for Lees' solo album *A Major Fancy*, with the familiar lyrics that have been known to us for nearly forty years, although the song had previously been demoed—and rejected—for an earlier Barclay James Harvest album. That earlier demo version was recently unearthed and issued as a bonus track on 2010's CD remastered version of *A Major Fancy*; the key aspect, in the present context, is that the lyrics are substantially different to the established version. The song still contains the same "I'm a child of . . ." sequences but, elsewhere, the lyrics concentrate on the inner feelings and emotions that the child experiences through living in his desperate situation—it is a hauntingly spiritual rendition. The relevance, then, is that, whatever it was that prompted Lees to alter the lyrics drastically, he chose to replace the originals with lyrics that describe the power that television was beginning to yield over people's lives, almost as if he had suddenly realised that step-change in impact that it was having. Therefore, given that the demo must have been written at the outset of the Seventies, 'Child of the Universe' places this key sociological transition around the turn of the Sixties.

Television's influence would not just have an effect on politics and world affairs through the transmission of news programmes and investigative documentaries. Many commentators argued that the implicit power of suggestion within entertainment programmes also had the effect of altering people's attitudes and behaviour. As early as 1963, Mary Whitehouse,[7] a school teacher, began campaigning against what she perceived as the adoption of low moral standards by the BBC in its programmes. She perceived that viewers would mimic the behaviours they saw broadcast as entertainment, leading to a mass lowering of morality. Whitehouse campaigned against enhanced sexual content and pornography, as well as the increase in profanity, blasphemy and depictions of violence. She launched the Clean Up TV campaign in early 1964 and then formed the National Viewers' and Listeners' Association (NVALA) in 1965, using it to continue her resolute campaign against the decline in moral standards for over three decades. Despite there being many who were sympathetic to her cause—the NVALA garnered about 150,000 members—she was subjected to abuse and ridicule from sections of society along the way. Whitehouse had been born pre-First World War and the clash between her and the broadcasters was a reflection of the more general societal

---

7. Whitehouse was born from a different mould to that of the Fifties Child. Born in Warwickshire in 1910, she lived through two World Wars. Very different indeed! A true lady of the Empire, formally appointed a CBE in 1980, she died in 2001.

clash between the Fifties Child and pre-war society and culture. Nevertheless, the NVALA developed a respectable standing as a pressure group; it was renamed as Mediawatch-uk in 2001 and continues its work to this day. However, the temptation remains to judge Whitehouse's campaign as a failure. The force of Fifties Children's push for freedom of expression in the wake of their rejection of authority was just too strong to withstand and this led to increasing permissiveness in moral expression on television, which remains to this day.

Whitehouse's legacy, perhaps more so than the success or failure of her campaigning, are the many sympathisers who live on convinced that the content of television programmes can and does influence behaviour. After all, if day after day, you see your favourite actors and actresses indulging and enjoying aspects of adulterous life, then you are going to think it is normal behaviour and want a taste of that lifestyle. If you see youths joyriding and delighting in setting cars alight, you might be tempted to try it out. Once hellfire and damnation no longer scare you, the vista opens up immeasurably. You are open to suggestion: hence we have the domino effect of the fall of the Soviet empire, of the copycat UK riots, of the Arab Spring. Perhaps these cascading events would have happened anyway, but the consensus of observers is that their likelihood is greater with ideas promulgated by moving image media. Moreover, compared with Whitehouse's campaign heyday, our modern world now has mobile telephones and the internet with which to assist that dissemination. Just don't say that she didn't warn you!

The depth of influence of television, and of the media in general, takes on a more sinister aspect when the owners of the media are either controlled by, or have a close association with politicians. It is no accident that a major priority of any totalitarian state is control of the media. Ask China. Even in a democracy such as ours, politicians who are able to manipulate the media or have a close association with its owners stand to gain a significant advantage over their rivals given their enhanced ability to get a multitude of messages across to the electorate, whether they are appealing to intellect or emotion. Re-reading Orwell's *1984* as part of the research for this book, I was shocked at how, so many years after its first publication, so many aspects of its society were reminiscent of our own.

Real life is, however, never exactly like fiction, and there will be some uncertainty about precisely where you place Rupert Murdoch on our politico-media gameboard of life. Is the media baron influencing the politicians or they him? In essence, it matters little; what is clear is that Murdoch—who clearly has the ability through his media empire to affect political public opinion—and politicians use each other for their own purposes in a way that you—the electorate—do not quite comprehend. The suspicion is that, in a world such as ours has become since the Sixties, democracy will always be liable to be fudged in this way; perhaps that is the best that we can hope for. Is that better than totalitarianism? Why do you think there is so much immigration to Britain? Even when the prime cause of immigration appears to be economic, deeper research exposes totalitarianism—or sham democracy—within the immigrant's homeland, either in the present or recent past. Totalitarianism is a factor not just in political migrants but in economic ones also.

Of greater concern is the disrespect of the all-powerful media for any law other than that of its own choosing, as demonstrated by the phone hacking scandal that has recently hit Britain. You have the media, a portion of which is controlled by a powerful leader with seemingly nepotistic tendencies, which has very good friends in government, and which is quite content to pry into the most intimate details of your private life. Did I just say that was the best we could hope for?

In the most recent times of our modern world, the bypassing of media control via the internet has the potential to disrupt the power base of the alliance between the traditional media and the politicians, which is why countries such as China place heavy restrictions on internet content. Perhaps, all things considered, Britain is not so badly off after all.

As a band, Barclay James Harvest almost always suffered from bad press in the British music papers and this was undoubtedly a factor that contributed to the relatively low status they achieved in their home country. Indeed, Lees' 'Poor Man's Moody Blues' was written in response to the mocking jibe of a journalist who had written a scathing review of an album without actually listening to it. The song's lyrics themselves, however, have nothing to do with the media.

Of the band's songs that do explicitly deal with the media, Holroyd's 'Welcome to the Show'—amidst taking a general swipe at the music business of the late Eighties—is the only one that, with a touch of sarcasm, deals directly with their own relationship with the media: "wrong place, wrong face." Within 'Welcome to the Show's embracing criticism of the music industry— part of the media world—Holroyd singles out the interaction between it and politicians. This is the extract with which we opened the chapter:

> and they [musicians] surely do well
> for the politicians who sell them
> on TV today:
> makes me uncertain
> of who runs the world.

This alludes to politicians and musicians using each other to further their own interests. Holroyd revealed in an interview that the specific example that had brought this form of profit by association to his mind was that of the Liberal MP Cyril Smith's appearance in a video promoting the all-girl group Bananarama's *Greatest Hits Collection* album in 1988. This may seem like a huge joke, and perhaps in this instance that is really all it was, but there is a serious aspect to such involvement in general, as Holroyd draws out in the excerpt's final sentence. As the politicians try to insinuate themselves with the media into prospective vote-winning situations, a suspicion arises that the media side may have more influence on the politicians than is ideal. Is it better if the media controls the government than if the government controls the media? At least you might have an idea of what is going on, even if your means of affecting it with a democratic vote is diminished, whereas in the latter instance you are simply misled. Perhaps we expect too much from our politicians.

We have already met Lees' 'Child of the Universe' and 'Cheap the Bullet'— as well as touching on the subject of the Troubles in Northern Ireland, both songs also deal explicitly with the impact of television on the modern world, as does 'Sideshow', which dissects their timeline.

With respect to the media, the key lyrics in 'Child of the Universe' are: "You can see me on the TV every day / I'm the child next door, three thousand miles away!" These lyrics portray how the medium of television is serving to shrink the world, by allowing events that are happening at almost inconceivable distances to appear as though they are taking place right next to us. This world-shrinkage effect was exacerbated by satellite transmissions— first demonstrated in 1962—which allowed events occurring around the globe to be viewed live. Arguably, television has done much more for world-shrinkage than air travel.

It is worth noting that the treatment of the media in 'Child of the Universe', written as television was beginning to flex its influential muscles, is purely observational and definitely non-critical. However, by the time we come to 'Sideshow', written a dozen or so years later, Lees has changed his attitude, now seeing television news coverage as a force for evil through its constant and insidious barrage of violence and world disasters. It is as if he is arguing that the skewed focus on bad news is sapping our spiritual strength, and he pleads for a change, he pleads that we be shown some of the love and joy that exists in the world. The vibrant musical performance on the song lends force to Lees' argument; there is a subtle but impressive lyrical and musical shift in the coda as Holroyd picks up the vocal from Lees and the attention shifts to a homely scene—husband and wife, girlfriend and boyfriend, family together, you decide—turning on to watch the TV news and weeping at the images of innocent victims transmitted into the unsuspecting comfort of their living rooms.

Unlike 'Sideshow', the media is not the sole topic of 'Cheap the Bullet'; nevertheless, its treatment within the song is unequivocal. Television is portrayed as a part of the pressure that adds to Lees' "circle of hate":

I'm baptised in your prejudice;
I'm confirmed with your hate;
I'm ordained into violence:
I'm a child of the modern world,
of the media world,
of the TV world.

As I mentioned in the chapter 'The Troubles in Northern Ireland', the temptation is to simply assign the religious imagery within this excerpt to the fact that the song is about the Troubles, but there may well be a deeper, less obvious meaning. Our social history will later reveal how church attendance has fallen steadily during the life of a Fifties Child. For the first time in centuries, the influence of the Church—which had once been strong enough to move kings and governments—was on the wane. It was losing its influence with those in authority and its faithful followers were deserting in droves. What societal force would replace religion as the influencer of kings and the great shaper of the populace? This excerpt from 'Cheap the Bullet' can be interpreted as saying that, for the Fifties Child and successor generations, it is television and the media that have ousted the Church from this power role: now, we see the prejudice, the hate and the violence on the television screen and we wallow in it, follow it, want more of it. Television and the media are the new religion: hence, we are baptised in its prejudice, confirmed with its hate and ordained into its violent world. It is possible to see how Lees could have arrived at this conclusion in the twenty years since he was prompted to write 'Child of the Universe', and everything that has happened since 'Cheap the Bullet' was released in 1990 has reinforced the power of the media, the power of the New Religion. Where, historically, the world once had the King-Church power axis, it now has the equally dominant Government-Media power axis.

One can observe that in these three songs by Lees the principal media focus is television news and that, in the decade or so since he first observed them having an influence on people's thinking, his opinion became that they had a detrimental effect on societal morale and behaviour. Interestingly, this concern about the deleterious shaping of society by television is, of course, the same one that Mary Whitehouse shared and campaigned against for so many years.

The link between politicians and the media was not one to have escaped the attention of Lees' songs. Referring again to 'Ancient Waves', we see that, like many people, he had become disturbed by the political spin that modern governments had begun to deploy. In this instance, the example was the deceit of the British public over the rationale for the Second Iraq War, as we saw in the earlier chapter dealing with that conflict: "The prince of darkness spins a knife / that silences dissent with lies / and everyone's deceived."

Taken as a whole, Barclay James Harvest's songwriters' songs which deal with the influence of the media demonstrate a shared concern for the power that it yields over societal behaviour. This concern has been shared by many in society down the decades from the Sixties, as is reflected in the writing of many other songwriters.

The lyrics of Chris Rea's splendid 'You Must Be Evil' [*Road to Hell*, 1989] have a strong thematic synergy with Lees' 'Sideshow', so much so in fact that, knowing how the music press have treated Barclay James Harvest over the years, it would have been no surprise to have seen accusations of plagiarism levelled at Lees, with our fictional reporter coming across 'Sideshow' in the Nineties unlikely to have bothered to check the fact that 'Sideshow' was written several years before Rea's song. However, Barclay James Harvest were by then sufficiently dim in the British music press's sights to escape this sort of attention. Like Lees, Rea is equally adamant that the broadcasters must change their policies. He arrives home to find his daughter crying at the horrific scenes she has watched on the TV news. He is furious, and lambasts the broadcasters for seeking sensationalist broadcasting: if it is news, just tell us, you don't have to screen these gory images which, given your bizarre approach, you sometimes even show in slow motion. You are affecting people's behaviour and you are evil.

One of the most interesting things about this particular pair of songs— 'Sideshow' and 'You Must Be Evil'—is how Whitehousian they are in their complaint. Either could easily form part of an advertising campaign for the NVALA. They are a powerful demonstration of the support behind some of Whitehouse's campaigning and hint at the possibility that, as some academics have argued, had her tactics and methods been more refined, she would have been more successful in her struggle to temper television's excesses.

The preponderance of TV news focus on strife has not diminished since the Eighties: one of the more forthright musical statements of this comes in Andy Tillison's 'Four Egos, One War' (2008), from the Tangent's *Not as Good as the Book* album, in which he voices expressively the concerns of many: "The press always get there in time for the flag-burns in every demonstration report /

the bombs always go off in the centre of the picture in an area the size of New York / and we don't see this as funny, just give awards to the TV crews."[8]

As a final example from a contemporaneous songwriter, Van der Graaf Generator's 'Every Bloody Emperor' [*Present*, 2005] offers what is undoubtedly one the most powerful condemnations in rock music of political spin. Peter Hammill's lyrics are clever, biting and delivered with venomous scorn. Our leaders are building a new empire off the back of countless lies; enmeshed, intertwined and repeated ad nauseam until they are taken for a default of the truth. Detractors are branded as traitors. These arrogant leaders believe themselves to be divine and treat us with disdain, manipulating the media and spinning deceit to the extent that, slowly and insidiously, the democratic process is emasculated. Our votes become worthless in the face of the growing power of these self-appointed emperors. Hammill has no words of comfort, no happy ending: the leaders' persistent subterfuge is sufficient to erode our own most precious quality—our faith in justice and human nature. As the Fifties Child approaches the end of his life, that faith, important to sustain a happy life, has become emasculated as he becomes enslaved by the new empire. The Fifties Child's sadness in the final lines of the song is palpable, his hopes eroded away by the decades, until all that remains is a media circus charade.

So, our first chapter in this 'Life is for Living' section of the book has proved to be full of dour societal implications. Barclay James Harvest's political songs presaged—unwittingly, I think—a disenfranchisement of the working class as, from the Eighties, chasmic divisions were reintroduced into our society. As these sociopolitical shifts were developing, so the media was enhancing its power to shape, manipulate and influence both public opinion and government.

Faced and often baffled by these changes, our sensitive Fifties Child's not uncommon response was to attempt to ignore this maelstrom of fluff and just get on with living. Which, for our songwriters, could only mean sex, drugs and rock 'n' roll. Couldn't it? Let's see . . .

---

8. Tillison is one of the foremost sociological commentators writing in rock today. He is not a contemporary of Barclay James Harvest. Born in 1959, he became a fan of the classic bands of the golden rock era and was inspired to follow in their wake. His work with the bands Parallel or 90 Degrees and the Tangent is sociologically rich, the lyrics both biting and humorous. 'Four Egos, One War' was first recorded by Parallel or 90 Degrees for an unreleased studio album, but does appear on that band's compilation *A Can of Worms* [2009].

13

Sex

Each new generation thinks it has discovered sex, drugs and alcohol. The Fifties Child was no different and, like his predecessors and followers, he was spectacularly wrong. The human condition itself seems to demand a mental release from the realities of life and it is often tempting to seek refuge in the quick release of sex, drugs or alcohol. Many argue that the spiritual path can provide a more satisfying and longer-lasting alternative to pacify the mind, but finding the right spirituality to suit one's individuality is often complex and not generally aided by organised religion.

Perhaps, of all the generations, that of the Fifties Child can be excused for thinking that it *did* invent sex, drugs and alcohol. After all, the First and Second World Wars had acted like an enematic cleansing of established values and the cataclysmic end to the Second World War, the nuclear devastation of Hiroshima and Nagasaki, demanded a new start, a clean slate. And then along came rock 'n' roll. Yes alright then, perhaps it was the Fifties Child who did invent sex, drugs and alcohol. It is to him that we will give the credit.

From the hidden, clandestine nature of sex and its associated industry during his teenage years, the Fifties Child will have witnessed a massive relaxation in moral standards and the sex industry's virtual acceptance in the early part of the twenty-first century. To a large extent this dizzying change has been driven by technological advances, in particular since the advent and subsequent popularity of the worldwide web. The last of Lees' songs dealing with the topic dates from 1983 and so misses the accelerating part of the changes. However, even by that date, the societal picture had changed drastically from his teenage years.

During the Fifties Child's childhood, sexual morality was strict. Sex before marriage will have been discouraged by many in society and cohabitation was virtually non-existent, as was childbirth out of wedlock. A stark, illustrative example of the magnitude of the change in mores can be seen from the attitude to homosexuality, which had been a capital offence until the mid-nineteenth century. It was not until as late as the mid-twentieth century that attitudes began to change. A high-ranking committee was set up under Lord Wolfenden to investigate the issue. Reporting in 1957, the Wolfenden Report's recommendation was that some aspects of homosexuality should be decriminalised:

> Homosexual behaviour between consenting adults in private should no longer be a criminal offence . . . Unless a deliberate attempt be made by society, acting through the agency of the law, to equate the sphere of crime with that of sin, there must remain a realm of private morality and immorality which is, in brief and crude terms, not the law's business.

Despite this, it was not until 1967, the year that Barclay James Harvest were formed, that the law in England and Wales was finally relaxed and some aspects of homosexual relations became legal. In Scotland, homosexuality did not become legal until 1980, and Northern Ireland had to wait until 1982. In the present day, same-sex civil partnerships, effectively equivalent to a marriage, are allowed in law. Now, that is head-spinning change within the lifetime of a Fifties Child! What would you have thought if the same liberalisation of attitudes had applied to murder? It has been an extraordinary change and one that, to a degree, applies to societal acceptance of sexuality as a whole.

The clandestine characteristic of sex during the Fifties Child's youth pervaded all of the media forms: books and magazines, theatre and film. What did filter through in the Fifties was replete with double meanings, such as the *Carry On* films. Furtiveness faded as the decades approaching the twenty-first century neared and moral liberalisation increased but Fifties Children would never be entirely free of the characteristic. This need to hide sex pervaded music also, reaching as far as some of Barclay James Harvest's songs; the double meanings in Lees' 'Loving is Easy' and Holroyd's 'Sip of Wine'—both from as late as 1978—being examples. In fact, according to the BBC, 'Loving is Easy' was too explicit and it refused to broadcast the album version of the song, meaning that the band had to record an even more temperate version for radio play. A single version was released on blue—there you go, there's another double entendre—vinyl but failed to make any impression on the charts. Perhaps the machinations over the versions did not help to get the song airplay, as it certainly had a catchy enough riff to be a hit. To be fair to Barclay James Harvest, this sort of subterfuge with double meanings was never a strong feature of their writing. We did not have to hear multiple references to "head" in various guises, nor was there such a strong predilection for double entendre in their songwriting as with, for example, Caravan (by the time

that band's sixth album was released, one had to carefully re-read its title—
Cunning Stunts—several times before being able to say it confidently out
loud). I have not included songs where double meanings are the only sexual
content within this social history, consigning them to the general subject area
of "love songs".

However, the sex industry itself does feature in Lees' writing—yes, there
are double meanings within those songs—and, as the subject is of sociological
import, the songs merit inclusion in our history. The four examples discussed
within this chapter have more depth than a standard rock 'n' roll track about
sex and are all worthy of analysis. Two aspects of the industry are dealt with:
prostitution and pornography.

Prostitution

The Wolfenden Committee that we mentioned earlier had also addressed the
issue of prostitution. Despite concluding that the state could not condemn
prostitution as being immoral in itself, the legislation that was implemented
more or less concurrently with the committee and subsequent to it did little
to resolve its perceived problems, principally nuisance to "respectable" citizens and the coercion of individuals into the trade. More than fifty years on,
it seems as if nothing has changed.

Throughout the nineteenth and twentieth centuries—and into this—there
has been continual debate regarding prostitution legislation, leading to several changes in the law and, perhaps more importantly, how it is policed and
dealt with by the courts. However, it is not entirely without reason that it is
often called the oldest profession in the world because, irrespective of its legal
status, it has often flourished. There can be little doubt that prostitution has
been a constant in society for a Fifties Child. There may be periods when,
driven by various motives, its policing is more strict than in others but, nevertheless, a constant it has been. Society's inability to deal with the issue effectively is strange, given its significant secularism. What also seems to be a constant is that, despite the actual framing of the legislation, it is often the prostitutes themselves that take the brunt of police and court action, rather than
pimps or clients.

There are some parallels between the issues of prostitution and recreational drugs: there are advocates for and against full legalisation; each side able to
identify some research that supports their position and pick the flaws in the
opposing camp's view. The complexities of the issue are undoubtedly significant, which is one of the facets that makes the incisiveness of Lees' first, and
perhaps most significant, foray into the topic so remarkable.

'One Night' [1975] addresses the issue from the context of the human
emotions that drive both the prostitute and the client into their respective

situations. Lees is in typically compassionate mode, replete with empathy for the prostitute. The song is sung in the first person but, cleverly, the narrator switches between the client (first and final verse) and the prostitute (middle verse). It is almost as though the two are having a heart to heart conversation about their lives and their motivations for finding themselves in this situation. The client is depicted as choosing prostitution as an easy way to love, only to be quickly disillusioned:

> You took all my money,
> I left you no name.
> . . .
> My eyes are now open
> but what do I see?
> One ride after midnight:
> had I thought it would mean that much to me?

In an ironic parallel, the prostitute had also seen the profession as the easy way, in her case that of earning a living, but had not accounted for some of the less appealing aspects of the profession:

> I thought it was easy,
> but what did I know
> of old men and first blood,
> or the drunk who gets taken blow by blow?
> The dice are all loaded;
> you pay by the throw,
> but you pay the loser . . .

One can imagine the song's refrain being sung as a duet, with both the prostitute and the client sympathetic towards the other's situation. The prostitute feels sadness that he has to resort to bought love in an attempt to fulfil his needs, whereas the client wonders whether she will ever satisfy her need for love whilst she is working in the profession:

> Everybody needs someone to love,
> everybody needs a friend.
> Everybody needs someone to care:
> do you think you can make it in the end?
> Do you think that you can make it . . . my friend?

In the song, Lees' pause—holding the previous note for a whole bar—before singing the "my friend" on the second and third iterations of the refrain has the musical effect of conveying a wealth of compassion, each for the other. This eloquent use of the music to convey deeper meaning is highly effective, enhancing the song and its message.

Despite the fact that, by virtue of its nature as a song, 'One Night' is comparatively simple in its treatment of the topic, it does nevertheless go straight to the essence of the problem facing prostitution, and it is one that receives a poor airing in the learned debates on the issue. The issue is that both the man and the woman have a need for love, they have a need for fulfilment in their lives, they need satisfaction for their soul. They find it difficult to find that fulfilment through their ordinary lives, so they go searching. Society is not giving them answers and, for both, prostitution seems an easy avenue to explore.

You may well be dismissive of that last paragraph—after all, surely the man is just after quick sex and the prostitute just wants her money. However, the empathy and compassion in the chorus lyrics show that such a short-sighted view does not hold sway with Lees, who sees that any satisfaction they might derive from prostitution is purely transitory and will not deliver the most basic food for the soul: love. The third verse's closing lyrics, sung by the punter— "we're dealt just the one card / but the dealer plays in every game"—convey a fatalistic sense that the prostitute has fallen into a rut in her life, cementing Lees' view of them as victims in not such a different way to all those others that he writes about so compassionately when dealing with other topics. The song has a particularly interesting resonance with 'Three Weeks to Despair', which deals with the plight of another group shunned by conventional society, that of people living rough on the streets.

In 1983, Lees returned to the issue of prostitution with 'Midnight Drug', but from a very different, and perhaps more personal, perspective. Whereas in 'One Night' it is the prostitute who is the main focus and recipient of Lees' compassion, in 'Midnight Drug' it is the client, who is cast as a personal friend of his, while the prostitute's role is a supporting one only—and she is simply characterised as a sex worker. In essence, however, the message of the song is the same as 'One Night's: it is not in prostitution that one can find comfort and love.

Lees' technique is to contrast his own life experience with his friend's, urging him to turn away from the "midnight drug" in an attempt to find fulfilling friendship and love. This is Lees' experience, presumably when he is out on tour with the band:

And in the evening when my work is done
I make a phone call from the hotel:
speak to my woman each day.

> . . .
> At least she knows that I'm not
> sharing out our love
> with the midnight drug.

Whilst that of his friend on the other hand:

> You make a phone call from the hotel:
> spending your life in the night;
> the kind of women who don't come for free
> but then I guess they know you'll pay the price.
> If they can keep you up
> they know you've got what turns them on.

Within the ambiguity covered by the song's "midnight drug" phrase, the "keep you up" is one of two references to the erectile function which indicate that this song's "drug" is principally prostitution, rather than recreational drugs or alcohol. For necessity in getting over the message of the song, the portrayal of the prostitute, as we can see from the verse above, is lacking in any compassion. This is reinforced by the closing lines: "they only pick you up then let you fall / 'til you come back for more / of the midnight drug." The "pick you up then let you fall" is the second reference linking the song to prostitution—it simply refers to the loss of erection after orgasm. Admittedly, Lees' words are ambiguous in that they could equally apply to the effect of recreational drugs. This is intentional, his friend is living out of bars and partaking of bought sex, drugs and alcohol. Lees' atypical approach in the song— a lack of compassion towards the prostitute—is forced by the need to persuade his friend to abandon his addiction and return to the realm of lasting friendship. This final excerpt from 'Midnight Drug's is crucial in understanding much of Lees' writing, in that it underscores much of his motivation:

> How many times must we tell you
> just how much we care?
> You must know how we love you,
>
> . . .
> I think you're worthy of a better cause.
>
> . . .
> I get my kicks from my friends and their love:
> it's the kind of love that comes for free.

Love of friends, love of family, love that endures and satisfies the soul. These themes have echoes in many other songs by Lees. It is clear that the overriding message in 'One Night' and 'Midnight Drug' is compassionate; Lees is empathising with the human frailties that can lead one into prostitution, from the perspective of *both* client and prostitute.

Finally, before leaving this section, we should mention 'Poor Man's Moody Blues', the song which Lees deconstructed from the Moody Blues' 'Nights in White Satin' [1967]. Concerned that the song's lyrics—constrained as they are by the 'Nights in White Satin' template—did not quite resonate as a love song, some fans believed that it might well be about a stalker-prostitute relationship, an interpretation which Lees himself has rejected. It is, however, possible to see how one could securely arrive at such a view of the song, and even find a potential societal event to have instigated such lyrics. The interpretation that 'Poor Man's Moody Blues' is a story about a man stalking a prostitute is not only internally self-consistent, but also resonates with Lees' thematic writing, in particular with that of the particular period in time; the previous two albums had yielded 'One Night' and 'Polk Street Rag', another song about the sex industry, which we shall come to in a moment.

The societal inspiration for the stalker-prostitute theory would have been the Yorkshire Ripper, a serial killer who was terrorising Northern England at the time. A number of gruesome attacks on women—mainly prostitutes—in West Yorkshire during 1975 and 1976 seemed to follow the same pattern, leading police to conclude that one individual was responsible. Four women had already been killed by the beginning of the summer of 1977—the time up to which 'Poor Man's Moody Blues' may have been influenced—and another nine would lose their lives to the Yorkshire Ripper before his arrest at the beginning of January 1981. The Ripper did not just make local, obscure news reports, he made it to the national TV networks—it was big news from early on in the cycle of attacks. Everyone knew about it at the time.

Whilst the chorus is ostensibly "sweet"—"'Cause I need you! / Yes I want you! / Yes I love you!"—the "I want you!" adds a touch of machismo control that is at odds with a natural love and, in conjunction with "I need you!", suggests that the protagonist cannot actually fulfil his desire. This lends a certain frustration to the song's aura that is missable on a distracted hearing. Then, the key that is used to unlock the song as a stalker-prostitute story comes in the second verse:

As I look from my window
to the streets where you stand,
I am gazing through dark glass:
we can't walk hand in hand.

This is the crunch: the woman, the object of the protagonist's lust, is a prostitute—"the streets where you *stand*"—and the protagonist's window does not belong to some building that he is looking from—it is a tinted car window. The protagonist is kerb crawling. The remainder of the song then falls into place, including the associated meaning of the first verse:

> All the nights that I've missed you,
> all the nights without end!
> All the times that I've called you,
> only needing a friend.

These nights that he's missed her are the "nights without end" when he has been driving around and around the streets, kerb crawling, looking for his favourite prostitute and *not finding her*—"missed" would be used in that context, not in that of longing for a loved one. They have possibly had sex at some time in the past: "all the times that I've called you" (he calls out to her from his car, not on the telephone. The protagonist's obsession with the prostitute is growing and her friends, *other prostitutes*, begin to get worried, deflecting him away:

> Though your friends try to tell me,
> though your friends you defend,
> they keep my heart from your heart:
> we must be in the end!

Given the profession's societal standing, prostitutes look after each other; tight communities where each looks after the other's welfare. On the occasions when the stalker does manage to find his favourite, she defends her friends' diversionary tactics. He is angry—"we must be in the end!" would be a threat, not some wishy-washy-lovey-dovey desire!

Other alternative theories destroy this interpretation's internal self-consistency. For instance, the theory that this difficult love might be between two individuals living in bitterly opposed communities—let us say a Protestant and a Catholic in Belfast at the height of the Troubles as that would have wonderful Leesian appeal, breaking the "circle of hate" that he writes about in a number of songs—does not work, because the song's protagonist can quite easily talk to the friends, which would not happen across a divided community. No, she is on the streets, her friends are on the streets; they are prostitutes defending one of their own community against an obsessive stalker-type.

Within this stalker-prostitute theory, the question arises as to whether the prostitute is killed within the song. The one lyrical clue is very ambiguous, even noting that it occurs again in the repeated verse towards the end of the song: "Now your eyes shine with beauty / that I missed long ago." Has the stalker already killed her? Is he finding her still and lifeless eyes reflecting some light that is making him wistful, now that the deed has been done? If the Yorkshire Ripper story had been at the root of the song's inspiration then this sort of depraved pleasure is what one might imagine a serial killer enjoying.

The other two clues are musical. The first is that on the original album version there is a significant "timpani attack" at the end of the drum crescendo approaching the outro. The theory is that this is the musical interpretation of the moment of the fatal attack; however, it does reflect a similar musical moment in 'Nights in White Satin'. Secondly, on the John Lees' Barclay James Harvest *Legacy* tour album and DVD (2007), Wolstenholme cries out "NOW!" at an equivalent point just prior to a musical climax. Can the band not keep time? Does Wolstenholme really have to scream to make sure they're in unison? Finally, Wolstenholme himself stoked the flames of this particular theory when, in an interview published in 2008, he made it clear that he had wanted to increase the sense of drama conveyed by the music:

> I wanted to change the end of 'Poor Man's Moody Blues' but John wasn't for it because he's safety-in-what-you've-done-before. I wanted to do what I did later at the end of 'One Drop in a Dry World' *[hums strident sequence]*,[1] to do that right at the end of 'Poor Man's Moody Blues' *[hums strident end sequence melodramatically and mocks big drum roll ending]*, so that it would have taken all the steam out of it and the final drums would have been out of tempo and it would have been a more dramatic end to it . . . it would have worked.

If this interpretation of 'Poor Man's Moody Blues' had been correct, one would have to say that it would have been entirely consistent with Lees' canon. He would have enjoyed nothing more than putting one over on the journalist by writing such a devious "copy" of a soppy love song.

What, then, does this secure misinterpretation imply for our social history, given that many of the sociological songs require interpretation to a greater or lesser degree? The answer is: nothing. The fact is that 'Poor Man's Moody Blues' always sounded like a love song, albeit with some darkness, and the misinterpretation hinges on one line: "to the streets where you stand." Also, there is no effective contextualisation from other songs. The stalker-prostitute theory, whilst appealing to many—myself included—always lay in the realm of speculation; it was like building an edifice without foundations. There are less than a handful of sociological songs within our social history in which

1. The song's ending is explained in context in the chapter 'Battle for the Mind'.

I have attempted speculation (clearly identified) or—in one instance—hinged the interpretation on a single word. In each of those cases—except for one which appears later, but I'll let you work out for yourself which song it is—the songs would still have earned their specific place in our social history by virtue of the fact of an easily interpretable part of their meaning.

So, our social history is secure! And, dear friends and fellow fans, having bought the music, if we then want to assign a particular significance to ambiguous songs, should we not be able to do so? To paraphrase from 'Nights in White Satin', it is up to us to decide what is right and what is an illusion.

❦

The empathy that Lees shows towards prostitutes on 'One Night' is not always shared by the rest of society and this is reflected in the treatment of the subject elsewhere in rock. For instance, Ian Anderson's jeering depiction of wanton promiscuity in Jethro Tull's 'Cross-Eyed Mary' [*Aqualung*, 1971] is an entirely different approach. Mary is depicted as a young nymphomaniac who would rather chase old men for sex than play with other teenagers of her own age, and Anderson amplifies her oddness of character through her physiognomy. Some might argue that the song is not completely lacking in empathy—Mary is seen as providing a service for men who cannot afford professional prostitutes—but it does lack the compassionate feel of 'One Night'.

A song which does treat the subject with an empathy analogous to Lees' is Elton John's 'Sweet Painted Lady' [*Goodbye Yellow Brick Road*, 1973], the lyrics being written by his most regular songwriting partner, Bernie Taupin. The song is sympathetic to the prostitute in its overall characterisation and through the music. It covers one of the time-honoured professions associated with prostitution—seafaring—and is romantic in feel, the lyrics implying a shared understanding and affection between prostitutes and sailors, who leave behind, almost as a gift, the aroma of the sea perfuming the prostitutes' beds.

Taupin and Lees are accepting of the fact that prostitution is a constant and through the compassion in their characterisation suggest that society as a whole has to recognise the fact and find a different approach to dealing with prostitutes and their clients, irrespective of the fact that, ultimately, prostitution's transient love is unfulfilling for the human spirit, whether it be the client's or the prostitute's.

❦

Pornography

Another facet of the sex industry is pornography: like prostitution, it has almost certainly been a constant throughout history and, like prostitution, more often than not societies have driven it underground. How often has one heard the question "art or pornography?"? The subject of many research grants, I'm sure.

Twentieth-century society in Britain was no different from this generalisation, despite the liberalisation of attitudes that the Fifties Child saw during its second half. Legal regulation controlling pornography in England has its roots in Common Law, which is based on precedent and goes all the way back to the Middle Ages and beyond. Specific legislation covering printed matter and stage performance began to appear in the eighteenth and nineteenth centuries, and legislative control of the movie industry followed in the early twentieth century.

By the time a Fifties Child reached his teenage years, there were considerable societal forces converging that had the effect of liberalising these laws. Amongst the factors contributing to weaken pornographic censorship were the weakening influence of formal religion over people's lives, globalisation and advances in technology.

This weakening of the religious force was an insidious effect that cleared the way for advocates of liberalisation to open up breaches in the state's defence against pornography. A landmark case was that brought against Penguin books in 1961 under the Obscene Publications Act for its publication of D. H. Lawrence's 1928 novel *Lady Chatterley's Lover*. Lawrence used words such as "fuck" and "cunt" that would have been previously impermissible but the court accepted the defence's argument that the literary value of the book merited its publication. Henceforth the Crown would have increased difficulty in bringing cases to trial.

The first legal mass circulation of pornography was to come via the medium of magazines. Probably the most influential in terms of breaking through into the mainstream was *Playboy* magazine. *Playboy* was launched in the United States in December 1953 with Marilyn Monroe featured as its first centrefold model and it was a huge commercial success. Its inclusion of, amongst other things, short-story fiction by notable writers, together with interviews with celebrities and politicians, resulted in giving its pornographic content an air of reflected respectability. The magazine was soon offered for sale in Britain.

Playboy's success spawned inevitable copycat publications in Britain. The naturist magazine *Health & Efficiency*, launched in the early twentieth century, had already overlapped into pornographic tendencies but it was not until *Penthouse* was launched in 1965 that *Playboy* had a direct competitor. *Men Only* and its associated Paul Raymond publication *Club International* appeared in the early Seventies and the pornographic magazine had well and truly arrived. In the years and decades that followed there would be a continuing attempt to increase the explicitness of the images portrayed. The increase in permissiveness also manifested itself in other media, such as television and film.

There was a reaction to this liberalisation. In Britain, possibly the most vociferous campaigner against the relaxation of standards was Mary Whitehouse, who we have already met in the chapter on 'Politics & The Media'. Her fight was doomed. In a bizarre and distastefully contemptuous move, one pornographic publisher even named its magazine *Whitehouse* after her.

Advances in globalisation exerted pressure on standards by exposing the black market to materials imported from abroad. In the late Sixties Denmark relaxed its legislation on what was acceptable to be shown on film and Danish movies began to find their way onto the black market. Whilst it was illegal in Britain to project these films in public, private clubs overcame the restrictions.

Imports from abroad dominated the early push-back of permissive frontiers. In 1968, pressure from playwrights and others led to the abolition of censorship in the theatre via the Theatre Act. Ready to profit from this relaxation was the American musical *Hair*, a powerful rock opera inspired by the hippy culture movement. Its strong theme of breaking free from parental and governmental control led to sub-themes which embraced pacifism and environmentalism, as well as sexual and drug permissiveness. There was profanity, nudity and simulated sex. Oh, and some fabulous music too! The show was a huge hit in London's West End, notching up nearly 2,000 performances on its opening run.

Liberals who favoured relaxing attitudes towards sex (and violence) would be the winners in the battle against conservatism, aided and abetted by the advances in technology that made pornographic material more easily available to the masses, alongside the liberalisation occurring in other countries of the world. The arrival of affordable video players in the Eighties increased the ease with which pornography could be disseminated and effectively meant that the battle had been won by the liberationists. Then, less than twenty years later, with the arrival of the worldwide web, the acceleration of pornographic (and violent) material availability to the public became exponential. The effects of the advances in liberalisation were insidious: for instance, whereas even in the relatively liberalised Seventies sex shops had to operate behind unwelcoming and seedy premises with whitewashed windows, by the twenty-first century the *Ann Summers* chain had brought them to the high street.

An American creation, the film *Deep Throat*, made in 1972 by director Gerard Damiano, is generally regarded as heralding a breakthrough in standards relaxation and features in Barclay James Harvest's songs. It was perhaps the first pornographic film to be shown in American cinemas, by virtue of having a plot. Whilst the film was not actually shown in mainstream cinemas in Britain until the twenty-first century—perhaps to Whitehouse's credit, as she campaigned vigorously against its screening—it had become notorious well before that time. It was the subject of numerous battles in the American courts, as various states tried to ban its screening and soon became a cause célèbre as a number of famous actors and celebrities—Martin Scorsese, Frank Sinatra, Bob Hope and Jack Nicholson amongst them—saw it, in the process legitimising its cause.

One of the states in which the film was screened was California and it was here that Lees saw it in 1976 whilst staying in San Francisco for the (aborted) recording of the *Octoberon* album with Elliot Mazer as producer.[2] 'Polk Street Rag' takes its name from the street in San Francisco's red-light district in which Lees saw the film. The sarcasm pervading the song would seem to indicate that it was an experience that he did not enjoy. Certainly, Lees' suggestion is that the sex was simulated. The film's star, Linda Lovelace (a pseudonym for Linda Boreman), became an ally of anti-pornography feminist campaigners when she claimed in her 1980 autobiography to have filmed the sex scenes under duress. However, some sources claim that she later actively promoted and profited from the sale of *Deep Throat* memorabilia before dying in a car crash in 2002.

On a casual hearing, the lack of compassion in 'Polk Street Rag' seems atypical of Lees' overall opus. However, contextualising from the other songs on this topic and his song canon, it is clear that its sarcasm is purely a means of belittling the pornographic experience. The approach to 1979's 'Skin Flicks' is more in line with his, and the band's, general lyrical style. It tells the story of a loving relationship gone awry after the woman becomes lured into the world of modelling. The song is in two parts: the first is sung in the third person and sets the scene, before the man takes over in the second part, describing their love and its demise, singing as though it is to her. However, it is almost as though he is entrusting his broken-hearted thoughts to his personal diary, or rehearsing what he wants to say to her, rather than it being his part of a dialogue. The model is portrayed as a normal person who, despite starting out with the best of intentions—she is interested in the "art" aspect of the profession—is trapped by the glitzy world of celebrities. In the lyrics, she is referred to as a "page two girl": an interpretation is that this is an intentional slight on the habit of tabloid newspapers like *The Sun*, which, from the beginning of the Seventies, were in the habit of publishing photographs of topless models on page three. This is another example of the liberalisation of standards that the Fifties Child witnessed: these topless models were soon to virtually fill whole "newspapers", accompanied by lurid tittle-tattle. This couple's love is destroyed by her bedazzlement with glitz: the sadness in the

2. Mazer had produced the *Time Honoured Ghosts* album in San Francisco and the band had hoped to use him for the follow-up, but were scuppered by overruns on other Mazer work, and eventually recorded *Octoberon* in Britain.

tale is Lees' way of, once more, heralding the woes of a libertarian lifestyle, a sentiment we have seen echoed in 'Midnight Drug'.

Overall, one could say that Lees' view of the sex industry as seen through these four very varied songs is that, through its apparent easy glamour, it is a dark force capable of destroying truly loving relationships, and that those drawn into it are often victims of circumstance who find it difficult to find true happiness. This view is not an uncommon one for a Fifties Child; and it also has much in common with the views of Mary Whitehouse, who was born in an earlier generation, pre Great-War.

I have chosen to highlight only one contemporaneous song, but it is one that—in direct contrast to Lees' writing—demonstrates the strength of the forces in favour of liberalisation of standards: Roger Waters' 'Pigs (Three Different Ones)' from Pink Floyd's *Animals* [1977], specifically focusing on its third part. The importance here is that it is effectively arguing for more permissiveness in society through its vilification of Mary Whitehouse. The approach is direct: Waters names Whitehouse directly, mocks her and calls her behavioural conservatism a charade, one that—should her arguments win the day—would suppress people's true feelings.

Porn, like conflict, is everywhere. For a Fifties Child, this was a massive societal change. He saw the relaxation in sexual mores bring pre-marital sex, cohabitation, gay marriages and the eruption of pornography into mainstream society. Strangely, one thing this libertarian society has not been able to solve has been the one permanent factor: prostitution. In that respect, its failure is similar to its inability to tackle that other constant "problem": recreational drugs . . .

14

Drugs

There was undeniably a strong drug culture associated with the psychedelic rock scene of the Sixties. In his teens the Fifties Child's senses will have been bombarded with inputs assuring him that tripping on hallucinatory drugs was an essential element of being part of the scene. There cannot have been one teenager from that generation who did not take, or did not pass up the chance to take, hallucinatory or other psychoactive drugs. How many did pass up the opportunity? One will never know the exact answer, although it was not hip to be part of the scene and refuse. From as early as 1965, the Beatles' 'Day Tripper'—"day tripper" in this context is slang for someone who flirts with the hippy/drug lifestyle before rejecting it—reflects that fact. Despite peer pressure, some teenagers who enjoyed that scene were able to resist the temptation of LSD, marijuana and other drugs: for instance, Barclay James Harvest's John Lees is on record as saying that he did resist this type of drugs.

More stringent social histories than that suggested by our three songwriters might point out that the use of drugs is probably as old as man himself. Certainly, opium use goes back thousands of years. Opium poppies contain morphine, and are nowadays used to manufacture heroin. Looking in the history mirror, back one hundred years from today, it is opium use and addiction that we see as the image.

This does not alter the fact that for the Fifties Child, the flower-power psychedelic rock era felt like a revolution of old mores. In the new, post-war world, sex and drug-taking became acceptable within that movement. And, in that world, the psychedelic era acted as the catalyst for the spread of hallucinogenic and other drugs into other realms of society. The Seventies saw increases in more general drug usage and this trend has continued unabated since, unaffected either by the sections of society who condemn it or by the law enforcement agencies who police its prohibition.

Other societies—that of the Netherlands is the most oft-quoted example—

have had some success by decriminalising less-potent drugs, such as marijuana. The arguments for and against decriminalisation are undoubtedly too complex for this book but it is still worth saying that history shows that banning pleasure-seeking in the form of drugs, alcohol, sex or gambling does not prevent people from seeking them. Demand brings supply, even if the resultant business is illegal; all criminalisation does is push up the price to the consumer and create an underworld. The debate will go on, meanwhile the drugs and their use will continue to exist.

All of Barclay James Harvest's songs about recreational drugs are of Lees' authorship. The first was written at the turn of the Sixties, as the psychedelic rock peak was waning. The song 'Hymn' was originally entitled 'Hymn for a White Lady' and had been considered—and rejected—for the band's 1971 album *Barclay James Harvest and Other Short Stories*. "White Lady" was slang for a type of drug and the dropping of that part of the title, along with the song's overt Christian message, has led 'Hymn' to be often misinterpreted as a purely Christian song. This is understandable, and the Christian aspect of the song is covered in the 'Spirituality' chapter.

The drug aspect of 'Hymn's meaning is implicit within the lyrics. One of the oft-quoted interpretive factors is that, during the song's earliest live performances, Lees was in the habit, during the coda, of calling out the names of famous rock stars—Hendrix, Kossoff, Joplin—whose lives had succumbed to drug addiction. However, this could not have happened very often at all. It was certainly missing from the band's performance at Bristol on the *Gone to Earth* tour in 1977.[1] What is usual is for Lees to illicit an audience response by just shouting "Yeah!" a number of times during the final sections of the song: clearly, this does not aid interpretation! Fans will also have become familiar with the song's intended meaning when Lees himself revealed it in an interview at the time of its release. This is what he had to say to the *Daily Mirror* in July 1977:

> People on drugs often say they take them to go on a 'trip'; a flight of spiritual freedom. Well, part of my lyrics say: 'don't try to fly, you know you might not come down'. In other words, you might take an overdose and die . . . all the misery drugs cause prompted me to write this hymn.

With this information, the allusion to drugs in the opening verse becomes clear: Lees' metaphor for the difficulty of finding God—of finding the right spiritual path—is that of trying to reach a very high mountain top from the valley floor, but if you try to reach such dizzy heights by taking drugs then you

---

1. My senility could be deceiving me . . . after all, it was 35 years ago!

are in danger of never being able to regain control of your mind. The remainder of the song's lyrics concentrate on the Christian gospel story, accentuating Jesus's resurrection and ascension to heaven, which Lees interprets as being God's way of saying that it is only through him that one can fly; in the spiritual sense, clearly. As Lees explained in the same interview as that referenced above: "I do believe in God and I also believe that He is preferable to cocaine." Despite the implicit nature of the message on drugs within 'Hymn', there can be little doubt that most, if not all, fans of Barclay James Harvest were aware of it.

Lees' opinion that the spiritual path was the only one capable of liberating the mind will not have been unanimous. Within the Fifties Child generation, and in particular for those who were strict adherents of the psychedelic movement in America, there will have been many who believed the exact opposite. LSD and similar drugs were still legal early in the Sixties, allowing Timothy Leary, an American psychologist, to conduct experiments under controlled conditions, using prisoners and theological students, into the effect of specific dosages of drugs on the mind. He believed that, under the guidance of psychologists, the use of these drugs would be able to affect errant behaviour such as criminality and alcoholism. Additionally, the capability of drugs such as LSD to trigger a spiritual awakening was actively promoted by Leary's advocates. Leary's own advocacy of the benefits of drugs was extensive, gaining much support from sections of the "psychedelic" community. Some of his catchphrases—"turn on, tune in, drop out"—have lasted to this day. Famously, he stood against Ronald Reagan—a future president of the United States—in the 1969 election for governor of California under the slogan "Come together, join the party!" John Lennon's 'Come Together' [1969] was inspired by his support for Leary's campaign; their association was strong, evidenced by Leary's appearance on the Beatles' 'All You Need Is Love' broadcast and his presence during the recording of Lennon and Yoko's 'Give Peace a Chance' [1969], in which he is mentioned. Leary's campaign for governor was interrupted by his incarceration in 1970 for a charge (brought in 1968) of possession of marijuana. He was initially sentenced to ten years in jail; this was increased to twenty whilst he was inside prison because of another previous offence. He escaped but was eventually re-arrested, however he was then granted an early release in April 1976 by Jerry Brown, the governor of California.[2] Leary's ideas continued—and continue—to influence a portion of liberal society.

Moving chronologically through Lees' songs on this topic brings us to

2. Jerry Brown was governor between 1975 and 1983, taking over from Ronald Reagan. He returned to head the state in 2011, this time replacing Arnold Schwarzenegger.

'Midnight Drug' once more. The song issues a warning to a friend about the dangers of the easy lure of the pleasures of nightlife—sex, drugs, and alcohol—and it has a strong parallel with Lees' other songs on drugs in that its main message is that there is a better way to happiness—in this instance, through the love of family of friends. There is a possible allusion to drugs within the song, which is weaker than those to sex or alcohol, and it comes through the lyrics "you spend your life going faster / there's no surviving when you crash at speed", with "speed" being a slang term for a type of drug. Also, the song's closing lyrics, as we discussed in the previous chapter, contain a play on words that equates the addiction to sex with that to drugs.

The reference to drugs in 'Psychedelic Child' is fleeting, but easier to understand. The song is principally an exultation of the late Sixties' psychedelic scene but its chorus carries another warning about the dangers of hallucinogens in the form of a reminder of the terror that a bad session on drugs can cause.

Finally, we come to a late masterpiece, 'Mr E' [1997], which comes complete with a musical and lyrical link to the Beatles' 'Strawberry Fields Forever' [1967]. An interpretation of 'Strawberry Fields Forever' is that it partly references LSD and—not just by association—the context of 'Mr E' also embraces drugs.[3] In fact, a secure interpretation is that the song is about the dangers of ecstasy,[4] also colloquially known simply as E, in a directly equivalent way to the message in 'Hymn'.

Lees was on particularly strong musical and lyrical writing form for 1997's *River of Dreams*, and 'Mr E' is an exceptional song in both respects. It uses common metaphors, sure, but Lees' cunning is twofold. First, he personifies the drug (hence, "Mr E") and, second, the song is sung as though it was the internal, mental dialogue that a young person, struggling to come to terms with life and find happiness, might have in making the difficult decision of which path to follow. The song is about the internal conflict of our inner psyches, between our "good" and "bad" selves, and Lees is offering—yet again—a spiritual answer.

Within our social history, we have already seen how the songwriting stratagem in 'Mr E' appears elsewhere in Lees' writing. We have just seen the use of two different perspectives within a song as in 'The Closed Shop', 'One

---

3. In an interview in 1980, Lennon revealed that Strawberry Fields was a real place that he visited in his youth. However, at the time of writing, he had been experimenting with LSD, and later admitted that drug-taking influenced his songwriting. Despite Lennon's explanation, many people still believe that the song at least partly alludes to drug-taking.

4. Ecstasy is a synthesized drug whose use became socially popular amongst the younger generation in Britain during the late Eighties.

Night' and 'Skin Flicks'. Of more direct relevance to 'Mr E', however, is 'Summer Soldier's specific use of two explicit and contrasting personalities to depict the "good" and "bad" parts of the psyche; and later in our social history we shall see how Lees had previously used such an equivalent explicit contrast in 'Mother Dear'. In 'Mr E', the appearance of these two opposing sides of the psyche is more subtle—one can put this down to Lees honing his songwriting craft in the intervening twenty-five years! What has not changed in that interim period is the fact that it is this internal battle that Lees always seeks to win—and urges others to do so, as in this song—by following a spiritual path.

In the song, the drug—Mr E—is characterised as a braggart: boastful, self-confident and with no compunction about the damage it is doing to the individual living through a crisis of confidence:

> I'll take your truth and give you back a lie:
> my secret lives in your deceit!
> Innocence crumbles in the face of your greed:
> . . .
> I know no magic forest in this part of town;
> no mystic rainbow's end, no gold for free!
> The colours lift you up, I push you down:
> That's why they call me Mr E.

"Magic forest" is an allusion to the hallucinogenic effects of "magic mushrooms", and the line "no mystic rainbow's end, no gold for free" is saying there's no gold "at the end of the rainbow". The personified drug is boasting: you have nothing else, try me!

The other "personality" in the conflict is the personification of the individual's "good", their spiritual side, and it is arguing that the spiritual way, though it may be hard, is ultimately more fruitful than the emptiness of the easy high:

> And every day you're searching hard
> for something you can't find:
> a hollow-hearted love that pays
> with pictures for the blind.
> . . .
> The promise lies in endless dreams:
> a nightmare's what you find!
> My promise is a window to
> the bottom of your soul:

this nightmare is the way you feel
about yourself and no one else.
Let me take you down to the river side:
hold your hand and lead you in.
I can take you down to the river side
but only you can swim.

"Pictures for the blind" is an allusion to the psychedelic mental images caused by the hallucination; by contrast the personified spirit is offering "a window to the . . . soul". The first "nightmare" sounds like the anxiety caused by addiction; the second like the depression which is tempting the individual to try the drug. The final image in the excerpt, which is being offered as the way to cure the individual's depression, is that of the spirit taking the individual to the river and it is an echo of the Christian gospel account of the baptism of Jesus by John the Baptist, when the heavens opened and the spirit descended on Jesus. This path—the spiritual path—is hard: the spirit can show the way but the individual must do the "swimming".

It is worthwhile noting that Lees gives a musical clue to the fact that there are two personalities involved in 'Mr E': the music for the verses of Mr E and "Mr Spiritual" (the good part of the psyche) carries quite a different arrangement, albeit this distinction is lost in the chorus ("let me take you down to the river side . . .").

On the German tour promoting the *River of Dreams* album, Lees said that "E" stood for ecstasy, envy and emulation and that anyone finding all of the meanings within the song would be doing very well. The interpretation given here holds up under both the "envy" and "emulation" monickers. These are characteristics that will lead individuals to follow life-paths which stray from the spiritual one (the "Mr Spiritual" is a constant in the song). Envy of what others have fosters greed and desire. Emulation of one's peers is a potential route to recreational drugs; it is also the quality that traps children into the "circle of hate" that Lees writes about in 'Summer Soldier' and, equally, ensnares the adult "no ones" in 'For No One'.

There is another potential meaning within 'Mr E' that I almost hesitate to mention because I have no stronger argument to offer other than that—and, having read this book, you will certainly agree—it is typically what Lees would do. Despite the fact that only Lees himself could confirm or deny the following interpretation, I have decided to include it because, if true, it adds to the song's wonder. In 1996, a social housing association group based in Liverpool—but wanting to expand further afield beyond Merseyside—changed its name to the Riverside Housing Association. As part of their work they assist in supporting and providing housing for vulnerable and homeless people—in fact, just the sort of people that might otherwise fall in temptation to Mr E. Merseyside is near to the area where Lees lived and local news may well have carried items about the Riverside Housing Association. Also, bear in mind that on the same album as 'Mr E' we find 'Three Weeks to Despair', a moving song about homeless people, so the topic of homelessness and housing was clearly on his mind. Could it be that Lees, knowing that John Lennon had said that 'Strawberry Fields Forever' was inspired by a Salvation Army home called Strawberry Field, used ideas from that Beatles song's melody and lyrics to embed within 'Mr E' his own admiration for the Riverside Housing Association? 'Mr E's lyrics would work with this interpretation. I think that would be stunning writing, and just the sort of thing Lees would do. We might never know . . . Irrespective of whether this last meaning was intended or not, it is clear that 'Mr E' is a brilliant song—it is the 'Hymn' for the Nineties.

One last thing before we move on. So, if 'Mr E' is the 'Hymn' for the Nineties and, as we have seen, the message in both of these songs is the antithesis of Timothy Leary's media-circus extolment of drugs, we should note that 'Hymn' was released in 1977, the year after Timothy Leary's release from prison, while 'Mr E' was released in 1997, the year after his death. Coincidences, surely, but intriguing ones nevertheless.

Typically, Lees' underlying message in these four songs touching on the topic falls short of an outright condemnation of drugs. 'Psychedelic Child' concentrates on the rock scene without developing the drugs aspect, but in the other songs the fundamental message is that there is a way to find happiness that is both safer and more fundamental than drugs. What Lees would also say is that one can enjoy the music without being drugged up, without being spaced out.

✿

Songs about drugs and songs written under their influence are common in rock; what is much rarer are songs that condemn their use. Probably the most famous such song, whilst it does not meet the strict contemporaneous criteria, is worth mentioning: the message of Neil Young's 'The Needle and the Damage Done' reached millions through being on his influential *Harvest* [1972] album.[5] Unlike Lees' illusive writing, Young's message is explicitly blunt and the song draws much of its power from its very directness. Young senses the appeal of drugs but he has seen acquaintances die, and others damaged, from its use—each addict is facing death. It is simple, direct and hard-hitting.

5. Neil Young: born Canada, 1945. It is clear that Neil Young had an influence on Barclay James Harvest: his *Harvest* album, a huge success in Britain, was produced by Elliot Mazer, who later produced *Time Honoured Ghosts*. There will be a significant overlap between fans of both artists.

Another example failing my strict criteria is the Moody Blues' 'Legend of a Mind' [*In Search of the Lost Chord*, 1968], written by Ray Thomas. It merits inclusion on the basis that it demonstrates the reach of Timothy Leary's views on the benefits of LSD. The song deals with Leary and his views in a non-condemnatory way and with only the slightest hint of sarcasm: it is easily interpretable as supportive of Leary's advocacy of LSD.

Redressing the balance and equally explicit as Neil Young's 'The Needle and the Damage Done' is Lemmy's 'Dead Men Tell No Tales' [*Bomber*, 1979], written after he had managed to overcome his own addiction. Because of this, the message is conveyed from a different perspective as Young's, but it is essentially the same: addicts are on a fast highway to death.

The final example is from a surprising source: Black Sabbath. We met 'Hand of Doom', an anti-drugs song, earlier in our social history in the chapter on Vietnam; the surprise stems from the fact that the band were not shy to write other songs that could be interpreted as glorifying drugs, 'Sweet Leaf' [*Master of Reality*, 1971] being an example. 'Hand of Doom' was inspired by Geezer Butler's shock at seeing the mass of needles and syringes littering the floor after the band's shows. The song is, again unlike Lees' songs, explicit. Arguably, it is the deepest of the songs analysed apart from 'Mr E', in that it examines the events that can drive an individual to drugs, potentially then trapping them in an addiction from which it is difficult to extricate themselves. There is an overall consistency with the sociological concerns that affected Barclay James Harvest's songwriters (which, in turn, mirror Fifties Child's society). Individuals with a conscience will have been so appalled by the inhumanity of nuclear weapons, the Vietnam War and other aspects of real life that they will have been driven to try the soothing effect of drugs. At first, the drugs satisfy but, as addiction sets in, the body becomes ill and the individual is cut off from reality forever. Death awaits.

The message conflict in Black Sabbath's drugs songs reflects the same conflict enveloping society: the pressure to take drugs—be it peer pressure, temptation during depression, curiosity etc—versus the pressure to resist from those whose friends had died, from parents, from authorities and—thank you, Mr Lees—from one's inner "good", spiritual part of the psyche.

Overall, what all of the songs presented in this chapter represent is that sizeable portion of society, which has existed since drug use became popular amongst the younger generation, which is concerned for the ultimate damage that these drugs can do through overdosing, misuse and addiction. Lees' own predilection for a spiritual alternative to attaining the highs so often associated with drug usage mirrors a subset of that societal concern.

The gaping sociological omission of the songs lies in actually not reflecting in any depth the issues relating to drug use. They say, "drugs are bad, they'll kill you, there's a better way", but fail to tackle issues such as addiction, overdosing and criminality. These omissions are significant in that they also perhaps reflect why, despite the strong societal concern, drug use has continued unabated, claiming lives down the decades from the psychedelic era. The drugs issue is one of the great unresolved conflicts, not just for the Fifties Child, but for today's generation.

The songs' omissions are also significant when one brings alcohol and anti-depressant drug usage into the equation. Both are legal, yet when used inappropriately—addiction, overdosing, inappropriate prescription—can be as harmful as the drugs which are the subject of the songs in this chapter. This is not mere intellectual frippery: at least two of Barclay James Harvest's songwriters were adversely affected by these drugs—yes, it is appropriate to lump alcohol and anti-depressants in with that term—and this is therefore a subject that we shall return to in our social history in the chapter 'The Battle for the Mind'.

Meanwhile, let us finish looking at sex, drugs and . . .

15

Rock 'n' Roll

Barclay James Harvest's songwriters became professional rock 'n' roll musicians because of their love of the music. They achieved a dream that many aspire to but few achieve: was it worth it? And what of the bands they admired?

Rock Music

The Fifties Child may not have invented rock music but he was there near its beginning, enjoying its first fruits. This music had huge societal significance: it was the way that this generation broke free from the constrained shackles of the past, from the conformity of their parents' lives, it was the key factor that allowed the Fifties Child to exert his individuality. Rock has its origins in the United States, becoming firmly established as the popularity of rock 'n' roll and electric blues grew in the Fifties. In the shrinking post-war world these forms of music soon became popular elsewhere, particularly in Britain.

What needs to be recognised immediately is that in the Sixties and the first half of the Seventies—the key period for the Fifties Child—home-centred forms of entertainment that are hugely popular today, such as computer games and DVDs, were not available, and so rock music had a proportionately greater impact on the lives of adolescents than it does today. Rock music's importance to the Fifties Child is confirmed by Lees himself in a couple of songs—'Panic' and 'Spud-u-Like'—both of which, despite their ostensibly simple lyrics, convey that message admirably.

Possibly the most significant factor to occur in the period leading up to the arrival of rock music was when the electric guitar began to supplant the piano and the saxophone as the lead instrument in rock 'n' roll bands during the latter half of the Fifties. As rock 'n' roll developed, new artists took influences from its style, along with influences from other styles such as blues and folk, to form what became generally known as "rock", a music in which the electric guitar dominated the sound.

The Sixties saw an explosion in this new form of popular music. The Beatles and other British groups led the way, capturing the fervour of the Fifties Child generation. As the decade wore on, electric keyboards in various forms began to be amalgamated into rock bands, with impressive effect. American band the Doors was one of the first to use a Moog synthesizer in 1967, the Mellotron became a staple of the Moody Blues, whilst other bands favoured the Hammond organ, another instrument with a very distinctive sound. Keyboard instruments had, for the first time since the rock 'n' roll bands of the Fifties, earned the right to lead instrument status in some bands.

The Fifties Child was hooked. Along with the new music came new fashions in appearance, attire and intoxicants. In combination these forces led to 1967's Summer of Love and the American flower power movement of the late Sixties, with its attendant psychedelic rock music and protests against the Vietnam War. Despite being centred in America, these events and their music had a big influence in Britain and elsewhere, aided by enhancements in the media and easier world-wide travelling. The anthem of that summer, Scott McKenzie's rendition of 'San Francisco (Be Sure to Wear Flowers in Your Hair)' was a chart-topping single in Britain. However, some British bands were also taking their influences from closer to home and began to fuse folk and European classical music into their rock, developing what became a hugely commercial brand of distinctive progressive rock: King Crimson were as English as Frank Zappa was American. Defining the chasm with American influence is one of the most enduringly popular singles ever, Procol Harum's 'A Whiter Shade of Pale' [1967], which is firmly based on Johann Sebastian Bach's 'Air on the G String', originally composed in the eighteenth century.

This sort of musical development is typified by Barclay James Harvest's own musical history. Prior to the formation of the band, Les Holroyd and Mel Pritchard had been in Heart and Soul and the Wickeds, whilst John Lees and Woolly Wolstenholme had played with the Blues Keepers, both local Oldham bands. Barclay James Harvest's early live performances and their initial recordings—the singles released in 1968 and in the following year—betrayed little of the classical-rock fusion innovations that were to come on their first four albums.

The late Sixties and early Seventies were golden years for rock music. The exponents of this music took full advantage of the relative youth of the electric guitar and electronic keyboards to innovate both in terms of playing technique and composition. The limited competition from other forms of entertainment meant that albums sold well and record companies encouraged artists to be bold. This era lasted less than ten years—one can mark it roughly from the Beatles' *Revolver* [1966], then accelerating sharply from *Sgt. Pepper's Lonely Hearts Club Band* [1967], but it was already petering out by 1975. After this, innovation began to wither. The music did change after this golden period whose fruit the Fifties Child gorged upon. The changes, when they came, were natural, brought on by ageing, by the comfort of money-making, by changes of personnel within bands, by the adoption of new influences and so on. The reasons for the decline are many and varied, while there are arguments for not considering the arrival of punk music as the strongest factor.

Many commentators like to over-dramatize the consequences of the punk revolution by saying that it killed off whole types of music such as "progressive" rock, but nothing could have been further from the truth, even despite such renowned "celebrities" of the genre such as Rick Wakeman stating that it was a fact. What is a fact is that, by 1976,[1] bands such as Barclay James Harvest, Strawbs, Yes, Pink Floyd, Genesis and others had already been making music for many years and were undergoing a natural stylistic development, which was sometimes accelerated by changes in personnel, sometimes not. There were similar instances in other musical genres too: bands such as The Bee Gees and Fleetwood Mac found great success with musical changes of direction that were undented by the punk revolution. Consider the case of Pink Floyd, whose 1979 concept album *The Wall* was a massive popular success in Britain, as well as abroad. Just as progressive was Jeff Wayne's *War of the Worlds*, a partly-spoken, heavily instrumental concept album based on the H. G. Wells novel, which was a huge hit in 1978. Marillion, a progressive rock band in the Genesis mould, did not release their first album until 1983, and it was an immediate chart success. Barclay James Harvest themselves continued to sell well in Britain until the mid-Eighties. Indeed, their biggest British chart success was *Berlin: A Concert for the People*, reaching No. 15 in 1982, and their biggest headlining concert in Britain was at Wembley Arena in 1984.

No, punk did not kill or even displace Barclay James Harvest's music. It had its own musical merits, of course, and brought a politicisation of lyrics that the majority of mainstream rock acts had avoided until that time, and it won new fans who had not been attracted to the older music but it did not replace it. Many fans of the older music, including those of Barclay James Harvest, liked the new bands that sprung up and became fans without feeling the need to abandon their previous heroes. What the punk revolution did do was to alter which music was fashionable, and the music papers of the day—in particular

1. Taking the onset of the punk revolution in Britain as being roughly from the appearance of the Sex Pistols' 'Anarchy in the UK'.

Sounds and *New Musical Express*—stopped writing about the "old" artists almost overnight. That mattered nothing to Barclay James Harvest, who had never had a high profile in the written media in Britain.

The change in fashion did mean that new bands starting out had to favour one particular style over another. However, one can still over-state that aspect. If a band was good enough, it could still transcend the hype of fashion. Dire Straits are a good example: 'Sultans of Swing', a six-minute single that owed nothing to punk rock or New Wave, launched the band on a massively successful career in 1979.[2] Their sound was based around Mark Knopfler's superfluid guitar playing—the very antithesis of the punk rockers—and they made rapid progress, becoming one of the most popular bands of the Eighties.

So, if you are still amongst those who believe that punk rock swept away the past, perhaps you should consider Johnny Rotten's words from 1978, uttered on stage in San Francisco at the end of a performance of 'No Fun': "Ha, ha, ha! Ever get the feeling you've been cheated?"

One thing that punk did in fact do with the arrival of the Sex Pistols was to make it far more acceptable for rock lyrics to carry social comment. That was the real revolution—suddenly, rock songs were replete with sociological content, and this movement would see artists such as Billy Bragg flourish in the Eighties rather than be consigned to the folk clubs. Barclay James Harvest just carried on as usual.

If anything, the revolution which did affect Barclay James Harvest more than punk was the disco revolution, which occurred at roughly the same time. One can detect the influence of this shift in popular music in the opening songs from 1979's *Eyes of the Universe* album: Holroyd's 'Love on the Line' and Lees' 'Alright Down Get Boogie (Mu Ala Rusic)'. Hmm . . .

From the late Seventies, other forms of entertainment began to compete with music for fans' spare cash and, just as important, time. Videos and computer games wormed their way into spaces where previously there had been only music. Competition breeds commercialism. The rock music industry would never be the same again.

※

It is principally the golden era of rock from the late Sixties and early Seventies which is covered by Barclay James Harvest's own music. As Fifties Children, Barclay James Harvest's songwriters were also fans of the music coming out of the rock revolution and their music writing was influenced by it. Therefore, before discussing the references to rock music in their lyrics, it is important to dwell a while on the references in the music itself.

---

2. The year it was a Top 10 hit: it had been originally released in 1978 but failed to chart.

Barclay James Harvest were often accused of being mere copyists, in particular of the Moody Blues. Very early in their career, prior to building up their own repertoire, they would perform 'Nights in White Satin' (a Top 20 chart hit for the Moody Blues in 1967) in their live set. Their adoption of the Mellotron, an instrument pioneered within a rock band context by the Moody Blues' Mike Pinder, assisted in persisted comparisons. Eventually, when one album reviewer (without, he later admitted, having actually heard the album) called them a "poor man's Moody Blues", Lees was livid. In response, he composed his deconstructed version of 'Nights in White Satin' for the band's *Gone to Earth* album in 1977. 'Poor Man's Moody Blues' became one of Barclay James Harvest's most popular songs.

Lees had previously deconstructed another chart hit for the *Everyone is Everybody Else* album [1974]: the Bee Gees' 'New York Mining Disaster' [1967] was adapted musically with lyrics inspired stylistically by the Beatles' 'A Day in the Life'. Whilst both 'The Great 1974 Mining Disaster' and 'Poor Man's Moody Blues' are altered musically and lyrically—they are neither copies nor cover versions—strong echoes of the originating songs remain, so it is doubtful that writing songs based on such recognisable chart hits would have helped to convince a sceptical British music press that Barclay James Harvest were not mere copyists.

Despite the high-profile comparison that the press made with the Moody Blues, arguably the biggest influences on Barclay James Harvest's music were the Beatles. Their influence is reflected strongly, both musically, for instance in direct quotations such as in 'Mr E', as well as lyrically, such as in 'Titles'. From the mid-Seventies, some American bands, notably the Eagles and Chicago, began to influence the band musically.

Criticisms similar to those implied by the preceding discussion of these deconstructed songs are used by some people to dismiss Barclay James Harvest's music as purely derivative. However, anyone who is familiar with the band's musical output will realise that, despite these high-profile influences, their music is quite unique and easily recognisable as their own.[3] The influences are there, for sure but, even on the deconstructed songs, significant personal input and composition has then worked them into what are, undoubtedly, original songs. These techniques are nothing new in musical composition: borrowing and self-borrowing go well back into the classical music periods from centuries ago; it is a common practice.

3. Returning from the Antarctic in 1982, I turned on the car radio. The song that was playing, which I had not heard before, sounded uniquely like Barclay James Harvest, even before the vocals came in. The song was 'Doctor Doctor' from *Turn of the Tide*, which had been released whilst I was away. No one sounds like Barclay James Harvest—they are unique.

In the classical music world, when such influences are stark and clear and the composer chooses to acknowledge them, he might title or subtitle his composition something like "variations on a theme by X". Lees used a similar ruse for 'Titles', which is credited "Traditional, arranged by John Lees". Lees uses direct musical and lyrical quotations from the Beatles in the song but it is nevertheless an original piece and the distinction, in terms of origin, between it and 'The Great 1974 Mining Disaster' and 'Poor Man's Moody Blues'— whilst real—is a subtle one, yet the latter songs are simply credited to Lees alone.

This subtlety is much more than just a theoretical nuance to relish discussing over a pint at the local hostelry. The amount of input that a musician or arranger needs to make to an original song before he is credited as a composer is a matter of serious import as, along with the credit, there may well be remuneration. When Barclay James Harvest did suffer significantly as a result of such a consideration, the source of the legal challenge was rather surprising, in that it arose from someone who had worked closely with the band during its first years: Robert John Godfrey.

Before forming the Enid, Godfrey had worked closely with Barclay James Harvest as a classical arranger for about two years, having met them at the end of 1968. It was a close working relationship and Godfrey provided arrangements for a number of songs that were included on the band's first two albums in 1970 and 1971. These songs were credited either to an individual member of the band or to "Barclay James Harvest". To his chagrin, Godfrey had not been allowed to become the fifth member of the band and therefore his work was neither credited nor would he receive any royalties from the songs. Godfrey's working association with the band ceased in 1971. Barclay James Harvest were therefore shocked when, in 1985, Godfrey issued a writ against the four members who had comprised the band at the beginning of the Seventies, claiming joint copyright of five compositions from each of the band's first two albums.

Barclay James Harvest's songwriters contested the case. With their financial security threatened, the consequent costly legal proceedings would last nearly ten years and blight their lives. The case finally reached the High Court in March 1995 and was judged by Justice Blackburne, whose judgement was that Godfrey had established that he had made a significant and original contribution to the creation of six songs and must be regarded as a joint author.[4] However, the judge prevented Godfrey from obtaining any royalties on the basis that it had been 14 years before he had brought the claim.

The Godfrey vs. Lees case has become something of a legal landmark. The

4. The songs were 'Dark Now My Sky', 'When the World Was Woken' and 'The Sun Will Never Shine' from the first album and 'Mocking Bird', 'Galadriel' and 'Song for Dying' from *Once Again*.

judgement that Godfrey was entitled to be regarded as joint author effectively ruled against the music industry convention, accepted until that time, that it was the composer of the chords, main vocal melody and lyrics who had the right to be identified as author and therefore entitled to the entire musical copyright. The fact that this issue is one of some debate, even in the courts, can be seen from the fact that, whilst a similar judgement was reached in other cases, the judge in the Hadley & Others vs. Kemp case (the Spandau Ballet case) reached a different conclusion. The legal precedent swung back again in the Bobby Valentino case of 1999 and was reinforced and, crucially, extended by the 2006 Fisher vs. Brooker case in respect of 'A Whiter Shade of Pale', which was also judged by Justice Blackburne. Matthew Fisher, who had written the distinctive introductory organ solo, was declared not just co-author of the song but awarded 40 per cent of the musical copyright. This meant that Fisher had a right to claim royalties from the date that the claim had been brought, some 38 years after the song's release! Brooker appealed and Justice Blackburne's decision was overturned, the Court of Appeal deciding that Fisher's claim had indeed been delayed too long for him to profit financially from royalties. However, in a final legal twist, the case was appealed again and heard in the House of Lords in 2009. The Lords reinstated Justice Blackburne's original judgement, leaving Fisher clear to seek royalties from 'A Whiter Shade of Pale'.

The confusion over authorship and copyright is not helped by the fact that the courts themselves are undecided: however, this last 2009 decision by the House of Lords would appear to settle the position. Let us see if we can make our own minds up faster than the courts, shall we? An analogy might help: if I draw a line picture and you colour it in beautifully, adding to its aesthetic appeal, then you have a right to joint "authorship". If the coloured-in line-drawing is then reproduced many times and the copies sold, with your vibrant colours a major highlight, then you have a right to some of the proceeds. Seems fair, doesn't it? However, if I have coloured in the picture already and all you do is add a couple of different hues of yellow to a yellow part of that picture, then your claims to authorship and copyright are significantly less, and you may have none at all. Surely that is fair? Clearly, the law decided that Godfrey's orchestration and Fisher's organ on the original versions of 'Mocking Bird' and 'A Whiter Shade of Pale' were more to do with "vibrant colour" than "subtle shades". One can have prejudices as to whether the Law was right or not, but neither I nor the majority of people reading this book will have had access to all the evidence garnered and presented in court, so it is impossible for us to make an objective assessment.

Perhaps my analogy is over-simplistic, in particular as there will be many musicians who will argue that there are significant precedents against the

House of Lords decision. However, the problem with that precedent argument is that there are quite a few bands out there—including Barclay James Harvest in their early days—who were happy to assign authorship to all band members because of the common input they all had into the songs, irrespective of who had composed the melody, chords and lyrics. And, clearly, there are enough sufficiently dissatisfied musicians who feel that they have not been given adequate compositional credit who are prepared to bring lawsuits. What seems to have happened is that the "industry standard" for rock music composition accreditation, once it has been challenged, has been seen to have fallen out of step with the requirements of modern law and, partly thanks to Barclay James Harvest, it is now catching up. It is deeply ironic, however, that whatever clarification has now been given by the House of Lords judgement, it comes at a time when most rock musicians are complaining bitterly about lost revenue on account of the widespread illegal downloading of music files and unauthorised broadcasting of songs on the internet.

'Mocking Bird' is the most famous and most commercially worthy of the six Barclay James Harvest songs of which Godfrey was judged to have joint authorship. Perhaps surprisingly, in the light of the discussion above, on the 2011 fortieth anniversary edition reissue of the album *Once Again*, the song is still only credited to Barclay James Harvest, although a side-note adds "arranged . . . by Robert Godfrey"—this is hardly different to the original album release, where Godfrey was credited as being the "conductor and director" of the Barclay James Harvest Symphony Orchestra. For his part, Godfrey has recorded 'Mocking Bird' with the Enid for a YouTube video and has also included it in a live performance by the band, dedicating it to the memory of Wolstenholme, with whom he had a good rapport at the beginning of the Seventies. The song also appears on their live recording *The Enid Live With the City of Birmingham Symphony Orchestra* [2012].

The Enid's dedication of 'Mocking Bird' to Wolstenholme will be poisoned with bitterness for many Barclay James Harvest fans, in particular those who were his personal friends. They knew the distress and anxiety that Godfrey's lawsuit had caused him and believe that it was a contributory factor to the bouts of depression that would eventually cost him his life. Godfrey, perhaps disingenuously, claims that because Wolstenholme had left Barclay James Harvest some six years before the legal action was brought, he did not realise that the lawsuit would involve him and, had he realised, he may not have pursued the case. If that really is so, then you, dear reader, may well wonder why he did not then drop the lawsuit, when it quickly became apparent that it did involve his erstwhile friend...

The stress of the lawsuit would affect not only Wolstenholme but the other members of the band, as it had been brought against them all, despite most legal records now showing it as just simply "Godfrey vs. Lees". Many fans believe that Lees' 'Lady Macbeth', one of his most enigmatic songs, is about Godfrey's lawsuit. If so, it is a stinging indictment. The clues seem compelling:

> Like a jester dressed
> in a silly gown,
> . . .
> In the dead of night
> all who'd listen gathered round
> . . .
> By the pricking of my thumbs
> something wicked this way comes.
> Like a fool possessed,
> evil grabbed the blade,
> dripping blood upon the keys.
> With her cheap disguise
> no one realised
> how this jester could deceive.
> . . .
> Time knows the truth
> and her lies linger on
> . . .
> Hush now children:
> don't you worry!
> Lots of young ones
> singing Mahler.
> Lies so deadly,
> wrapped in sugar candy.

For a period during Barclay James Harvest's formative years the four band members lived together in an old farmhouse (Preston House) near Oldham, where they would also write and rehearse. Godfrey first met the band whilst they were still living there and he eventually moved in with them, to enhance his input into the band's music. He liked to wear flowing gowns, hence the first couplet of Lees' excerpt above. He introduced the band, in particular Wolstenholme who was the most receptive listener, to Mahler—hence "all who'd listen gathered round" and "lots of young ones singing Mahler". Lees sees the lawsuit as "evil". "Dripping blood upon the keys" is a reference to the fact that Godfrey was a classically trained pianist. The couplet "Hush now children: / don't you worry!" is a distorted echo from the most commercially valuable song in the lawsuit, 'Mocking Bird': "Hush now baby, don't you cry." It all stacks up. The real cunning twist in the song comes through its title, which then yields the Shakespearean quotations and, of course, *Something Wicked This Way Comes* is the title of the Enid's fifth album [1983]; Lees would have worked back from that title as his origin in piecing the song together. The relevance of arriving at Lady Macbeth reflected the way all of the band must have been feeling over Godfrey's lawsuit: her character is devious, deceitful and power-hungry. Lees is happy with the gender-crossing within the song, and therefore referring to "her" within the lyrics, because of Godfrey's homosexuality. It is no wonder the fans think that 'Lady Macbeth' is about Godfrey.

This might be just mine and the other fans' airy fairy nonsense; a mere supposition. After all, Lees himself will only say that 'Lady Macbeth' is not about Margaret Thatcher. It is surely significant, however, that Godfrey not only believes that 'Lady Macbeth' is about him but has gone so far as suggesting that its writing—the song was released in 1990, before the issue had been settled—was responsible for aggravating the legal position. Irrespective of the true identity of the song's vitriol, it is clear that the Godfrey lawsuit was a significant episode in the Barclay James Harvest story, as well as one with serious consequences for other musicians.

The Beatles's music is a convenient place to continue our discussion of Barclay James Harvest's lyrics. Four of Lees' songs are relevant: 'Titles', 'John Lennon's Guitar', 'Mr E' and 'You Can't Get It'.

The lyrics for 'Titles' are made up of Beatles titles and lyric snippets, as well as borrowing musical phrases, a fitting tribute to Lees' heroes while 'John Lennon's Guitar' provides a different sort of homage. In 1970, during the Abbey Road recording sessions for the album *Once Again*, Lees was given the opportunity to play John Lennon's blonde Epiphone guitar. The song is a straight retelling of a moment which was clearly very special to Lees. Whether it is apocryphal or not, Lees accentuates the significance of the moment by saying that the Beatles, his heroes, would split the day after he played Lennon's guitar. Time passes and the world changes but memories and friends remain: this particular cherished memory is one that will definitely not fade.

In contrast to this very explicit approach is 'Mr E', whose lyric reference to the Beatles is contextualized by its musical quotation from 'Strawberry Fields Forever' [1967] and the fact that both songs, perhaps arguably, partly or wholly deal with hallucinogenic drugs. In that respect, 'Mr E' has been dealt with thoroughly in the 'Drugs' chapter. The lyric reference to the Beatles comes in the first couple of lines of the chorus and it is sung to a melody similar to that of 'Strawberry Fields Forever': "Let me take you down to the river side / hold your hand and lead you in."

The final featured song with lyrical references to the Beatles is 'You Can't Get It', released by John Lees as a solo artist in 1974 but its rarity meant that most fans did not get to hear the song until it was included as part of the bonus material on the reissue of Lees' solo album *A Major Fancy* in 2010. The song also includes a lyrical reference to the Rolling Stones where Lees refers to John Lennon and Mick Jagger directly as superstars. These lyrical references are fleeting but the musical reference to the Stones is more significant in that the song is effectively Lees' third deconstruction, this time of that band's 'You Can't Always Get What You Want' [1969]—Lees' song's rarity has perhaps helped to maintain its anonymity. As a final remark before abandoning the subject of Lees' deconstructions, it should be noted that he makes no attempt to hide their provenance, with the title of all three clearly pointing the way to the originating artist.

Lees' citations of musicians, who clearly affected him in mostly positive ways, is significant throughout his career. The first of such songs to appear, 'Thank You', preceded 'Titles' by some years, appearing in 1972. The song's lyrics are an unexciting list of "thank yous", mainly to people in the rock music business. Of most interest here are the references to Eric Stewart, Kevin Godley and Lol Creme, three of the four members of the band Hotlegs—also referenced directly in the song—and which had become 10cc in the year before the song's release. These musicians, like Barclay James Harvest, were from the Manchester area. Stewart later helped the band out when they were out of contract with EMI, offering them good advice that assisted them with the move to Polydor, with whom they were to remain. Godley and Creme are thanked for their "Gizmo", a guitar effects device that they were developing and which they later used on their recordings. The device enabled a guitar player to obtain orchestral string effects from his instrument. It was clearly a whacky invention and it takes Lees back to his childhood days of watching the BBC children's series *Billy Bean and his Funny Machine*.

'The Great 1974 Mining Disaster', a song we have already met, actually begins with a positive reference to David Bowie's chart hit 'A Space Oddity' [1969]:

Heard a song the other day
about a major out in space;
and though the song was kind of grey,
it took me far away;

Later on Lees then refers to another of Bowie's songs, 'The Man Who Sold the World' [1971] with: "heard a song just yesterday / about a man who sold the world away."

'A Tale of Two Sixties' and 'Psychedelic Child' also feature what might just appear to be long lists of names and titles, but both actually convey more meaning than 'Thank You'. The first of the pair, 'A Tale of Two Sixties', suggests Lees' dissatisfaction with the music scene that, despite the punk movement of a couple of years before, is failing to produce the inspirational music of his youth. The song's title is a play on the title of Charles Dickens' novel *A Tale of Two Cities* (1859) and, as in the novel, two different areas of the world are the focus for our "story". In 'A Tale of Two Sixties' Lees uses famous bands from the original rock revolution—both from Britain and the United States—to argue that "modern" music has reached an impasse and is just repeating the old. The writing technique, which he uses elsewhere, is to meld snippets of names, titles and plays on words to construct his meaning. Here is an extract from the opening verse and chorus:

I'm hitting the road to heading nowhere,
got no place to go.
I'm stuck inside my generation:
round and round I go.
    . . .
Give me the sound of Arthur Lee with
'Forever Changes'—I'll remember!
'Andmoreagain': don't leave me ever!
Buddy Holly say 'Baby, please be mine' -
all the time!

'Andmoreagain' is the title of a track on Love's *Forever Changes* album, a seminal recording of the psychedelic rock era, while Arthur Lee was the band's lead vocalist. The revelation of the dissatisfaction with (the then) modern music is cemented in the second verse:

I'm cutting out now before the New Wave
takes my surf board flair:
remember the time when Zappa said:
'Punk, where you going with that flower in your hair?'[5]
There's so many Who's Whos, Rolling Stones,

5. This is a misquote—almost certainly intentional—from the Mothers of Invention's 'Flower Punk' (1968). The final word that Zappa sings is "hand". Incidentally, 'Flower Punk' is an uncredited parody of the famous Sixties song 'Hey Joe': this reinforces the point I was making earlier about "borrowing".

Rod Stewarts and Small Faces
and Tommy's the king of the pinball flings
that chased my generation.

The "New Wave" refers to a genre tag that branded much of the music that had been ushered in by (or, arguably, arrived coincidental with) the "punk revolution". "Surf board flair" is a reference to the Beach Boys' inspirational sound. "Tommy", "pinball flings" and "my generation" are, of course, further references to the Who after the initial "so many Who's Whos".

At the time of 'A Tale of Two Sixties', the Who were heavily influencing the Jam, a band that had broken through commercially on the crest of the "New Wave". One can now understand that the lyric "I'm stuck inside my generation", which appears in the song's opening verse, is actually the first of the references to the Who's 'My Generation' [1965]. There is therefore a cunning circularity in Lees' lyrics, accentuating the suggestion (not forgetting the "round and round I go", which follows that first reference to the Who) that the constant repetition of imitators never actually comes up to the same standard as the innovators. Other notable names mentioned in 'A Tale of Two Sixties' are Bob Dylan, David Bowie and the *Easy Rider* film [1969], which had a stunning rock soundtrack featuring such classics as Steppenwolf's 'Born to be Wild' and Roger McGuinn's 'Ballad of Easy Rider'.

'Psychedelic Child' is similar in design, in that its deeper meaning—that drugs are bad—is shrouded by what appears to be a namechecking of personal heroes and notable "psychedelic scene" icons. It is perhaps not surprising that casual listeners dismiss the lyrics as simply a list. Amongst the highlighted items are 'My Little Red Book' [1966], the first single by Love, the band that Lees had already namechecked in 'A Tale of Two Sixties', the Beatles' 'Day Tripper' [1965], the Grateful Dead and the Charlatans (the latter being an American band from the psychedelic rock period, not to be confused with the British new wave band of the same name that originated in Manchester). The UFO Club and Crawdaddy, famous music venues of these halcyon days of rock, also get a mention: the UFO hosted bands like Pink Floyd and Soft Machine, whereas the Rolling Stones played their first gig at the Crawdaddy. Finally there are references to aspects of psychedelic rock fashion, including the transcendental meditation guru Maharishi Mahesh Yogi, who was famously consulted by the Beatles, Donovan and other celebrities, thus himself becoming a symbol of the psychedelic era.

As in other areas, Holroyd's writing in this topic area is less expansive than that of Lees, with the only explicit lyrical reference to the music that influenced him coming in 'African Nights', a song replete with happy reminiscences from the band's tour to South Africa in 1972. One of these is the joy of driving in the early morning, enjoying the beauty of the scenery as the sun rises, a moment cemented in Holroyd's mind by the Eagles' 'Take It Easy' playing over the radio, a song that clearly made an impact on him. This is still an important reference call, despite being Holroyd's only one. In particular, with respect to Barclay James Harvest itself, it identifies a point in time at which such music was already beginning to influence Holroyd's writing. We have also already seen plenty of evidence from Lees' songs that, from an earlier time, he was happy to listen out for and enjoy music coming from across the Atlantic. This influence, and in particular the connection to the Eagles, was cemented by his decision in 1974 to record their song 'Best of My Love' as a single release under his own name. Also, it was only three years after the South African tour referenced in 'African Nights' that the band travelled to San Francisco to record *Time Honoured Ghosts* with the legendary Elliot Mazer producing. Considering them sociologically, these references to The Eagles echo the popularity that such music found in Britain.

Before we go on to explore how some other songwriters express their love for music and adulation for their heroes, let us just first make a very quick mention of a couple of songs which are as close to their root songs as Lees' own deconstructions. The first may perhaps surprise: take a listen to the Beatles' 'Sun King' and Fleetwood Mac's 'Albatross'. Both were released in 1969: which came first? In 1987, George Harrison claimed that 'Sun King' does not sound like 'Albatross', despite being based on it—he was, of course, wrong. As an illustration of the circularity and sharing of ideas in music, we then find that 'Oh! Darling', another Beatles song from the same album as 'Sun King'—*Abbey Road*—becomes the sure template for 10cc's 'Donna'. I'm sure you can think of others in this vein—the examples are not few and are certainly not just the province of Barclay James Harvest.

Now, there can be no better song to start our sample of other artists' exultation of music and heroes than John Miles' fabulous 'Music'. The song is a stylistic musical extravaganza, the lyrics are simple but strike the heart of the matter. Music—past, present and future—is Miles' first and unending love, giving him the strength to face the world and all its troubles—he cannot imagine living without it. John, I'm with you, mate!

There are three songs by Chris Adams that have a deep resonance with Lees' writing on the rock music topic.[6] Adams was a founder member of the

---

6. Chris Adams was born in Scotland. He has confirmed that he meets my "contemporaneous" criterion but without revealing his exact date of birth!

golden era band String Driven Thing. His most recent album, *Songs from Another Country* (2009), has been released under the foreshortened name of String Driven. No less than three songs from this latest album fit snugly up against Lees' own writing on the topic. The first is 'Idol', a homage to Adams' own inspirational hero, Alex Harvey, whose sublime control of the dynamics within the Sensational Alex Harvey Band inspired Adams to take up rock music. Harvey is not named explicitly within the song and Adams admits that his persona could be morphed with that of other heroes such as Dylan and Presley.

'Place to Lie' is similar to Lees' lists of heroes, but is cleverly done:

> Yeah I gotta find me a place to lie:
> some little churchyard, shady and green,
> in some little village that I've never seen;
> down with the beetles [sic], down with the stones,
> down with the zombies, in the dead zone.

Subsequent verses have the place of his repose as the ocean and above the clouds; which introduces other bands—subtly disguised of course—such as the Turtles, the Sharks, the Eagles and the Byrds.

Finally, 'Die Without It' stresses not only the importance that rock music has had to Adams but also his disillusionment at what he perceives as today's soulless music. It is a sort of an amalgam between 'A Tale of Two Sixties', 'Panic' and 'Spud-u-Like':

> When I first heard that magic sound
>   . . .
> well I knew that was where I belonged.
>   . . .
> Call me a crazy dreamer
> but the music has stayed in my soul;
> and I'll get by without sex,
> I'll get by without drugs,
> but I'd die without rock and roll.
>   . . .
> But the times they are a changin'
>   . . .
> for the Philistines have claimed it,
> with their samplers and machines.
> And their regurgitated muzak
> comes spillin' from our screens

. . .

Don't let them take your music
or else they'll take your soul
and you'll die without it

. . .

without rock and roll.

As you can see, there is quite a synergy in the respective songs of Adams and Lees.

As not all the musings of this chapter have been happy ones, it seems appropriate to finish on a lighter note, for which we call on Nick Lowe and his song 'Rollers Show' [US release of *Jesus of Cool*, 1978; expanded CD re-issue, 2008]. Lowe is wildly excited because he's going to see the Bay City Rollers and it's going to be fantastic. He's going to scream and sing along and he can't wait to hear Les singing 'Money'. Now, I'll leave you to decide for yourselves whether Lowe is referring to Barclay James Harvest's Les Holroyd singing along in the audience to the 'Money Honey' hit [1976] or whether it's just a straightforward namecheck of the Bay City Rollers' lead singer of the time, Les McKeown . . .

Our social history has therefore shown how, for a Fifties Child, rock music was an important form of entertainment. As he grew older, the Fifties Child could see how the standard and value of popular music was being degraded by media manipulation and other forms of entertainment that he saw as soulless. This saddened him but, by now, society itself saw him as a dinosaur. Time now to see how the rock 'n' roll life turned out for those Fifties Children who were so hooked by the music that they too wanted to become rock stars.

The Life of a Rock 'n' Roll Star

Stepping through the door from the corridor into the wings, the intensity of the sound slaps me like a rushing wind and I cover my ears until the all-clear comes from the stage controller. There is pain in my head from the noise as I finally step onto the stage in view of the massive and ardent crowd. Waving briefly to acknowledge the hordes, I launch into the power riff of 'Rock 'n' Roll Dream', one of my world-wide chart-topping songs. Head-banging riffs, sweet sing-along melodies, magic stuff!

The reaction is awesome and the crowd's fervour grows with each song. At the end, they aren't sated by the three encores I've already done and manager Bill has to come and drag me from the dressing room: they have carried on chanting my name for ten minutes after the lights-on and I must go back and play again or there will be a riot. The trials of being a star . . .

Later, in the plush suite that occupies the top floor of the Ritz, I sip cocaine-laced champagne cocktails whilst begrudgingly giving interviews to a unanimously adoring

*press. I've had enough adulation by about 2 a.m. and my heavies usher them out, then
bring in a couple of pretty maidens, who are extremely nice and polite and would like
to help me fill the hours before dawn in my otherwise lonely hotel room. I consent.*

Ah! Bliss.

Same again tomorrow.

Adulation. Wealth. Drugs. Sex. The chances are, given that you are reading this book, that you have had your own rock 'n' roll daydream and some of
you may even have gone on to write songs and play in a band, taking that first
step towards fulfilling the fantasy. You will know, then, that the rock 'n' roll
dream becomes reality for only a very few who set off on that road. More often
the experience is one of hard work and graft for little if any financial reward.
However, that image of fabulous success and wealth remains the dream of
many. We have just seen in the previous section how Barclay James Harvest
and other artists expressed adulation for their own heroes through their music,
and we can now taste the kind of rock 'n' roll life that their love of music led
them to follow.

In essence, from the financial perspective, the rock 'n' roll life is no different to any other business. If we think about "normal" work, then at the very
top we have, for example, the bankers who earn extraordinary sums of money,
party on sumptuous yachts, fly everywhere on their private jets and generally
lark about in Paradise, whereas you and I—most of the population—work
almost certainly as many hours and assiduously as they do, but are paid wages
that go to cover, we hope, the cost of the mortgage and heating, and—if we're
lucky—we spend a week in Costa del Spagbol, cramped round the pool, battling for sunloungers with hordes of other dreamers.

This spectrum of success is reflected in rock music, as is perhaps not surprising, although it may still have been a misconception of the Fifties Child
that all rock stars were living the Dream. They were not. One only has to consider artists such as Caravan—who, arguably, have a better musical reputation
in many quarters than Barclay James Harvest—who abandoned the music
business in the early Eighties because they could not earn a living from it.

To surf the wave of fickle fashion you need to have spread your tendrils into
so many markets, so that at any point in time, somewhere in the world, you
will be *it*. Not many rock musicians who have worked virtually uninterrupted
through all the decades from the Sixties achieve that: Eric Clapton and the
Rolling Stones have done it, but are there many others? Another contender is
Ray Davies—one of the most brilliant songwriters of any generation—but
how many British youngsters have heard of him today? Many other musicians,
like Caravan's Geoffrey Richardson, adapt to survive in the industry, working
as session musicians, writing jingles and TV music and the like, but few have
managed to lead a career continuously off their own brand.

Our misconception of the rock 'n' roll life possibly stems from the concept of the celebrity megastar. Popular musicians and singers have always been held in high regard by societies and enjoyed lavish lifestyles. Mozart— although he died in financial insecurity—was courted by royalty in the eighteenth century, while Caruso, the operatic tenor from the turn of the nineteenth century, and the first recording artist to have sold a million copies, enjoyed fabulous wealth and a glitzy life. In the second half of the twentieth century, film and television acted together to enhance the cult of the celebrity. Elvis was followed by the Beatles, whose 1965 Shea Stadium concert brought in "stadium rock". It all seems so easy, so attainable—after all, I can play and sing too! This aspect of the rock 'n' roll dream, the goal of becoming a celebrity, is fundamental in luring many to follow the life. The successful ones, such as Barclay James Harvest, manage to eke a living from their music, whilst the others just fade away and have to find another way of paying the mortgage. The bankers are few, though they have a flamboyant profile.

Let us try to put some very rough numbers on this in today's money. Say a four-piece band records an album that does pretty well, going platinum in the UK and selling a few copies abroad, although does not break the American market. Four hundred thousand copies sold in its first year—very good indeed. The average retail price is £10 and the band gets ten per cent of this. So, that's £400,000 in their pockets, a lot of money. Hang on, there's four of them, and out of that they have to pay the producer, their managers, etc, so let's say they end up with 60 per cent, or £240,000 between them. £60,000 each: a good salary, you might think, particularly if you add the income from touring in support of the album. However, many bands playing the college and small concert hall circuit in the Seventies would say that there was no money to be made from touring, it was just something you had to do to pro- mote the album. What we are left with, then, is a reasonable salary for an album that has sold very well, but, don't forget, that's just this year. Our band members need to pay the mortgage next year too, and for the next couple of decades; and what use to an employer can you be when you've been bashing the drums for ten years?

So, on comes the pressure to reproduce the same performance next year, and the next, in a world of rapidly changing musical fashions. Suddenly, despite there being other forms of income for the songwriters, such as radio airplay and cover versions, it seems not so easy to make a living from rock 'n' roll. To realise the dream, to become that banker in paradise, you really do have to write a huge hit song. For instance, someone like Steve Harley can make a living from the royalties to a time-honoured favourite such as 'Make Me Smile (Come Up and See Me)' [1975] despite the fact that, in many respects, neither he nor his band, Cockney Rebel, were as successful as Barclay James Harvest.

✻

The careers of Barclay James Harvest's songwriters now span more than forty years so their experience reflects many aspects of the rock 'n' roll life (those already covered in the previous section will not be repeated here). At the very beginnings as a band, Barclay James Harvest were a five-piece: Rod Buckley had joined as vocalist from one of the originating bands in the merger that formed them. However, he barely registers as a member of the group—much less so than Pete Best with the Beatles, for instance—because he was soon sacked and, for the next twelve years, until Wolstenholme's musical differences with the other songwriters fuelled his own departure in 1979, the remaining four would maintain a stable line-up. This very stability was unusual, if not unprecedented, for a rock band. It is not that there were no pressures to split during that time—penury was one—but, in a strange twist of fate, the band found themselves in such heavy debt by 1973, courtesy of the massive financial cost of touring with an orchestra, that they decided that the most propitious way of resolving their financial predicament was to achieve success in the music industry, and the most likely way that each one of them had of doing that was to capitalise on the reputation that they had already made for the Barclay James Harvest brand. Hence, the band lived on. The strategy paid dividends and they went on to commercial success within a short time of signing a contract with the Polydor record company, even having their own taste of stadium rock. Detractors may say that the massive Berlin concert doesn't count, because it was a freebie, but they had previously headlined a 1979 four-date German stadium tour over a 'Sultans of Swing'-fuelled Dire Straits, as well as over Whitesnake and the Police, finishing off in front of 28,000 fans in Munich, in what was to be Wolstenholme's last gig with the band.

Soon after, Holroyd, Lees and Pritchard, encouraged in a more financially acute world by their record company, capitalised on the commercial base that the band had built up as a four-piece by tailoring their sound to their biggest market, which by that time was in Germany and other countries of mainland Europe. However, Lees soon became uncomfortable with the musical shift and tensions within the band grew. Pip Williams, producer of the commercially successful *Ring of Changes* [1983] and *Victims of Circumstance* [1984] albums, has said that Holroyd and Lees were barely on speaking terms at the time. Despite this, it would be another thirteen years before Holroyd's and Lees' differences became irreconcilable: Barclay James Harvest disintegrated in 1997, leaving a palpable sense of acrimony between the two.

Rock music fans love to analyse their favourite bands' post-split lyrics for evidence of a slanging match between the protagonists. Equally, rock musicians write such lyrics carefully enough so that they remain ambiguous, and then vigorously deny any specific insult was intended. In this regard, Barclay James Harvest's songwriters and fans are no different and strongly reflect that characteristic.

The one exception to the generalisation above is 'Sail Away', which Wolstenholme openly admitted was written about his split from the band. This is a gentle song, without recriminations, accentuating that he simply had to leave to follow his own direction. Wolstenholme is also responsible for two of the least ambiguous songs dealing with disaffection within the band. The first, 'Sea of Tranquility' was written when he was still on board and the second, 'Carpet', a quarter of a century after he left.

'Sea of Tranquility's link to the band comes through use of the word "harvest". Within the lyrics' ambiguity the interpretation then becomes that the song traces the band's career up to that time, from Wolstenholme's standpoint. Starting off full of high ambition and ideals, they hope that they will reach the top and that their songs will always last. Finding that the pinnacle is proving too difficult to reach, they then abandon their musical ideals in a desire to achieve commercial success.

Most fans of the band would agree that this is a harsh indictment of the music. Bearing in mind that the song appeared on *Gone to Earth*—a beautifully crafted album in what was an archetypal Barclay James Harvest style—and that predecessor albums had as yet shown no leanings towards the more commercial direction that the band *would* follow, it seems a surprising criticism. The truth almost certainly lies in the fact that, whereas Holroyd and Lees had begun to be influenced by the new music coming from across the Atlantic— we have recently seen their connection to the Eagles—Wolstenholme eschewed this new direction that he could sense the music developing towards. His music remained rooted in the English pastoral tradition and he would have wanted the band to continue in that vein, following a steady progression from their Harvest-era albums. His song 'Mæstoso (A Hymn in the Roof of the World)'—rooted in that pure Englishness—was omitted from the first post-Harvest era album—*Everyone is Everybody Else*—because it didn't fit with the feel of any of the other songs, all of whose music was by Holroyd and Lees. After that they all went to America to record the follow-up, a decision that Wolstenholme was dissatisfied with. To add insult to injury, producer Elliot Mazer then decided to delete the coda from 'Beyond the Grave', Wolstenholme's only composition on the album, and simply stopped the tape, with the effect that the song ended abruptly. One has to say that Mazer's solution is musically impressive, but Wolstenholme was aggrieved. One can sense, therefore, that his dissatisfaction with the band had been growing from at least 1974. 'Sea of Tranquility' is understandable in this light.

'Carpet' is vicious, musically as well as lyrically. The suggestion that the song is about the Barclay James Harvest split comes in what seems an obvious quotation from Holroyd's song 'I'm Like a Train'. Wolstenholme then adds accusations of fratricide and of pursuing the lure of money and fame. Nevertheless, direct quotation aside, the lyrics are sufficiently ambiguous to be interpretable in other ways, for instance as though they deal with Wolstenholme's split from his wife.

Three songs on Holroyd's only studio album to date since the 1997 split, 2001's *Revolution Days*, have been interpreted by some fans as dealing with topics similar to the ones just referenced by Wolstenholme, making his own position clear and taking a swipe at former colleagues. 'It's My Life' and 'That Was Then This Is Now' would belong the former category, whereas the vitriolic 'Quiero el Sol' would fall into the latter. All of these songs are more ambiguous than Wolstenholme's own and, as Holroyd himself has decried interpretations linking them to the band, there is no reason to identify them as sociological songs. Here's what he told the fan club magazine about such an interpretation of 'Quiero el Sol': "It's not about anybody. It's just generally about a lot of people in the business . . . no one in particular, just a rock 'n' roll thing really."

Similarly, Lees' added verse to the revisited version of 'Titles', from his 1999 Barclay James Harvest through the Eyes of John Lees *Nexus* album, has been interpreted as referring to the personal difficulties between him and Holroyd. However, much more likely explanations are that it continues the oft-interpreted theme of the original song from *Time Honoured Ghosts* by being about the difficulties between John Lennon and Paul McCartney or that it is a parallel commentary written by Wolstenholme about his own difficult position within the original band.

Frustration with the inability to achieve the rock 'n' roll dream features in Barclay James Harvest's writing via Holroyd and Lees, and this is occasionally couched as a criticism of the record industry. Record companies are often criticised for taking such a large slice of artists' earnings, but it should be appreciated that they take a fair slice of the risk in signing on an artist. If the artist fails to ignite the public's interest, the record company will make a loss. Despite the frustrations of Barclay James Harvest and other contemporaneous artists with the inequities of the music industry, the attitude of artistic freedom allowed by record companies in the late Sixties and early Seventies is often praised by the younger generation of recording musicians, who are seeing their income streams slashed by internet piracy.

During the band's early years they made a concerted effort to write a hit single and their inability to do so, despite the undoubted quality of some of the attempts, caused friction between those with a stake in the Barclay James

Harvest brand. Lack of success and financial disarray are sure to catalyse dissension in any endeavour. Lees writes about his dissatisfaction with this difficult period in two songs, clearly written around the same time: 'Blue John's Blues' and 'You Can't Get It', the B-side of his solo 1974 'Best of My Love' single release, which we mentioned in a different context in the earlier section. Of the two songs, 'Blue John's Blues' has a greater lyrical ambiguity and its interpretation as expressing dissatisfaction with the music industry requires contextualisation from 'You Can't Get It', with which it shares sufficient similar phrasing to allow the linking of the songs' themes.

A common metaphor in both songs is that of travelling down a road, representing the life's journey—encompassing the rock 'n' roll life—that Lees and others are on. A second link is that in both songs there are people that Lees meets on this road who, metaphorically, will not share their load. The meaning of this second metaphor is not totally clear but in 'You Can't Get It' the people that Lees "meets" are John Lennon and Mick Jagger and, in context, Lees is unable to reach the lofty heights of these "stars", alluding to himself as a "comet" that just spins round them, never coming close, despite other stars being formed and dying all the while. Essentially, the message one infers from 'You Can't Get It' is that the "rock 'n' roll dream" has turned sour; for all his efforts, he is not going to get close to the "load" of wealth that is carried by these "stars".

Contextualising the metaphors into 'Blue John's Blues', one can sense an equivalent message—this is perhaps not surprising given their proximity in compositional time. A reference to "Joe" within the song is thought to refer to John Crowther, the band's manager at the time, who had signed them up as fledglings and who had invested significant time and money in their development—including allowing them to move in to his newly acquired, but dilapidated, old farmhouse so that they could bond, write songs and rehearse, whilst he and his wife stayed with his parents—but who was becoming disaffected with the lack of return on his investment. Lees too is becoming disaffected and urges Joe to take back his money, recalling that his parents had warned him that he would find the rock 'n' roll life a let-down. It must be said though, that musically this fine slow-burning rocker—and in particular its stonking coda—is sufficient to hold most people's blues at bay.

Lees' strong musical opener to the *Time Honoured Ghosts* [1975] album, 'In My Life', is often interpreted as referring to the perceived inequities prevalent in the music industry and, taking into account contextualisation from the preceding songs and 1997's 'River of Dreams'—with which we shall close this discussion later—it seems likely that its subject matter, as a minimum, embraces the issue:

Seen the stars plant their seeds and watch them grow
just to keep Mister reap but never sow.

. . .

Grace is for God,
greed is to know.
Mister middle of the road
reaps what you sow.

These lyrics in particular now resonate with his other writing on the topic, clearly revealing that he thinks that rock stars' artistic endeavours are keeping a number of interlopers in a profitable financial situation that they themselves don't actually enjoy. "Mister reap but never sow" and "Mister middle of the road" do not necessarily represent the same people: the former refers to record industry executives, whereas "middle of the road" is a term, more popular at the time than now, that is used, often disparagingly, to refer to commercial, radio-friendly pop music. So, in the latter case, Lees is implying that the hard work and financial earnings of "serious" bands such as Barclay James Harvest are being fleeced by the record industry to subsidise their investment in this other music, in which they anticipate even greater profits.[7]

Incidentally, 'In My Life' is not a spiritual song, but it is interesting to note how Lees is still tempted into using biblical imagery within it to make his point; the sowing of seeds recalls Christ's parable. By using such a biblical reference, Lees is reinforcing the iniquities of the music industry by effectively declaring it an immoral business.

Holroyd, too, has felt frustrated with the industry throughout his career. 1976's 'Rock 'n' Roll Star' from the *Octoberon* album—the band's only single to trouble the British Top 50—sees him in an atypical straightforward mood; there is no interpretation needed here. Holroyd taunts those would-be future stars who think that writing a hit song is easy: when you first set off on that task, no trouble is too great on this exciting adventure but, after you've taken a few knocks, reality sets in and the dream pales. Yes, unless one hits the rock 'n' roll jackpot, the dream is difficult to sustain through the years of graft and penury.

Holroyd uses a couple of metaphors that are common with Lees' writing. The first—that of the rock 'n' roll life being like a journey—is common to this topic amongst other songwriters. Holroyd does not use the example of a road but likens it to a journey across rivers, valleys and mountains and wonders if it

7. It is less likely that Lees was referring directly to Middle of the Road, a Scottish band who had a trio of million-selling singles in the early Seventies. I am sure, however, that readers will remember 'Chirpy Chirpy Cheep Cheep' with some fondness. I myself saw the band live—though it was not my fault, I hasten to add. As a boy, I was taken to the panto one Christmas—Dick Whittington I think—and there they were. The experience has not marked me for life . . . or has it?

all goes wrong whether the way home can be found. You may have spotted the second coincidence already, hidden in the previous sentence: the high mountain-low valley metaphor is identical to Lees' in 'Hymn'. Who was cribbing who? Don't forget that 'Hymn' dates back to 1971, and whilst the lyrics of that song as a whole changed significantly before its 1977 release, the first verse itself—with that metaphor—is unchanged. Despite that, the answer is probably no one, it is a fairly common metaphor after all. More importantly, the usage of this metaphor demonstrates that the frustrations of the music industry affected Holroyd in a similar way to Lees.

Equally as significant is the tension between colleagues and peers that cribbing, or simply even the perception of cribbing, can cause. We have already seen how such tensions can lead to acrimonious disputes that seem destined to remain unresolved—certainly in the protagonists' minds—and which lead to the ludicrous use of the courts, in which only the lawyers are enriched. However, the litigious examples discussed in the previous section must just be a publicly visible demonstration of much rancour which exists between musicians working together on a daily basis. An illustration of this characteristic of the rock 'n' roll star's life is the bitterness that Lees felt over Holroyd's use of his "victims of circumstance" phrase to compose his title-bearing song on the band's 1984 album. During an interview in the summer of 2012 for the band's fan club, Lees revealed that his annoyance ran so deep that he seriously considered quitting the band, but was persuaded to remain by David Walker, their manager at the time.

Listening to the interview, one can sense that the issue still rankles with Lees. This feeling of angst might seem surprising to some people, given that Holroyd's song—despite the legitimate inspiration that he took from that particular phrase—is a completely original composition that owes nothing musically to 'Rebel Woman', the song in which he had heard the lyric excerpt. Furthermore, Lees himself was not shy of taking inspiration from other artists' songwriting, as we have already discovered in our social history: 'The Great 1974 Mining Disaster', 'Titles', 'You Can't Get It', 'Poor Man's Moody Blues'. Clearly, Lees' rancour was so great that his compassion—which reached as far as terrorist bombers—could not extend to his own colleague.

I suspect that it would be naive to think that this sorry story is unique amongst rock 'n' roll stars as it demonstrates the intense rivalry which exists within bands. Sometimes—such as when there is a court case—we get to hear about it, but more often than not it is just one of the hidden aspects of the daily rock 'n' roll routine. What this story also illustrates, by demonstrating the bitterness that can occur over what many outsiders to the situation will consider a triviality, is the difficulty that humanity—despite all the compassion which exists in the world—will always encounter in lifting itself out of conflict.

Holroyd returns to the theme of disaffection with this rock 'n' roll life in the title track to 1990's *Welcome to the Show* album. 'Welcome to the Show' is a strong song with, as we have already seen, interpretable lyrical depth. The aspect to draw out in this chapter, however, is an important one in the life of a rock 'n' roll star: though the work can be a drudge, reflected in the song as the tedium of touring, and there are setbacks through not being fashionable, there remains something about the rock 'n' roll life that acts almost like a drug, and one becomes addicted:

It's a long journey
we travel on.
Gypsies of the night,
riders of the storm:
though it's heartbreaking
we must go on!
Wrong place!
Wrong face!
Somewhere on the road:
keep playing
and saying
"Welcome to the show!"
. . .
We started something:
now we can't get away from it all.

Barclay James Harvest built up their strong reputation as a live band by means of some vibrant performances and extensive touring during their early years; this helped them to attract audiences in excess of the expectation suggested possible by their studio album sales. This aspect was manifested by the fact that their first taste of the chart success part of the rock 'n' roll dream was the *BJH Live* album, released in 1974. It will therefore seem extraordinary to realise that it was during these early years that Lees had to resort to prescribed drugs to overcome the anxieties of live performance. Later in the band's career he would obtain sufficient succour from prayer and from audience response and participation. Two of his songs, 'Sperratus' and 'For Your Love', are thought, within their ambiguities, to refer to audiences' habit of igniting and waving lighters during a performance, allowing the band to see and obtain support from the crowd.

The band's fans' website describes 'Sperratus' as being "about the complex relationship between stars and the fans who put them in that position". That much certainly appears to be true. Consider the chorus:

Shout it, shout it, shout it out loud!
Sing it, sing it, sing to the crowd!
Call out, call out, call out from afar:
make them, make them, make you superstar!

However, I believe that the song is intentionally ambiguous and contains more insights into Lees' spiritual beliefs—we shall address this aspect in the appropriate chapter of our social history later in the book. Similarly, 'For Your Love' is credited with being purely about European fans' habit of holding up flames during concerts. Lees was certainly inspired to write the song by this, but it has a wealth of meaning and imagery beyond the relationship between performer and audience, so I shall again defer a fuller analysis until later.

The thrill of the adulation and the buzz of the adrenaline rush are best encapsulated in Holroyd's 'Back in the Game', in which the addictive aspect is evident in the tension to continue re-experiencing the highs of the rock 'n' roll life, even in one's later years. The song opens the *River of Dreams* album and is immediately followed by Lees' title track—both songs are undoubtedly autobiographical. The conjunction of the two is lyrically interesting, encapsulating in a microcosm the tensions between artists that can lead to a band breaking up. Shortly after this, of course, the tensions finally took their toll: Barclay James Harvest would not work together again after the tour promoting the album.

'River of Dreams' is, in effect, the lyrical antithesis of 'Back in the Game'. Lees recalls his youth, contrasting the experiences and feelings he had as a young man with what he now knows. It has all turned sour. In his youth he valued the lure of the money, adulation and celebrity status that came with the rock 'n' roll life but now, looking back, these hopes are all sullied by reality. Worse still, he values music, and following its path gave him all he wanted from life but now he can see that all of the things it promised never really materialised. There is no sense here that Lees wants to continue, that he misses the buzz of playing live or the rock 'n' roll life. Quite the opposite, he has awoken from the rock 'n' roll dream despite, by his own admission within the song, the good times that it gave him. If read literally, it is actually quite an extraordinarily despondent song and a surprising one given the length of Lees' career before *and* after it was written. Is Lees really that unhappy with his life, with his career, as the song might appear to suggest?

This is unlikely, and a more plausible explanation lies in the fact that—as we shall soon see in more detail in forthcoming chapters—Lees' spiritual strength grew throughout the Seventies and beyond. This growth was significant to the extent that, for instance, later in his career he no longer needed psychiatric drugs to combat mental anxiety. So, it is possible that by the time of 'River of Dreams' he was able to place his life in a spiritual perspective and the highs of money, adulation, adrenaline rush and music—all referred to in the song as having been sullied—were now paling against the succour of spiritual strength and conviction. Lees is, in effect, saying that yes, he had the rock 'n' roll dream, it was good, it helped him in early adulthood but the spiritual life has shown him that there is a fundamentally more satisfactory way to happiness. This is diametrically opposite to the meaning of 'Back in the Game'— it is no wonder that the band ended its career at that point! Despite his disaffection with the industry, Lees has continued to work—though sporadically when compared with Holroyd's frequent live appearances—under the Barclay James Harvest brand, but one gets the sense that it is now very much on his own terms, much more so than it would have been working for the original band, pulled and twisted by the forces of media, record companies, management, and a host of others.

Wealth, penury, fame, obscurity, exultation, frustration, disaffection, vendettas, as wide a range of experiences to be had from the rock 'n' roll life as any other, this was the Barclay James Harvest experience. Not always as sweet as the dream but surely better than a life in the mills, eh?

Rock stars often write about the rock 'n' roll life, and for this social history I have selected songs by other songwriters that, like Barclay James Harvest, tell of their relationship with the music industry.

First up are the perennial underground heroes Hawkwind, with Dave Brock's and Robert Calvert's reminiscences of their earliest days from the late Sixties in 'Days of the Underground' [*Quark, Strangeness and Charm*, 1977]. Dave Brock, one of Hawkwind's principal songwriters, is not a contemporary of Barclay James Harvest's lyricists but Robert Calvert was.[8] The song looks back at their time spent high on drugs, making music, participating in protest movements and wonders—even as relatively early as 1977—what happened to that carefree innocence. The song also fondly remembers some of their friends who did not make it past the daze of drugs.

In the previous section we had a laugh with Nick Lowe's 'Rollers Show' and here are a couple of other songs of his in which his sense of humour shines through, whilst still making some very serious observations about the music industry. 'I Love My Label' is one glorious joke, replete with sarcasm.[9] His

8. Born Pretoria, South Africa, 1944. Moved to England with parents when aged two: hence, societally, qualifies as a Barclay James Harvest contemporary. As well as working with Hawkwind in the Seventies, Calvert released much work under his own name Died in 1988.

9. First released on a Stiff records compilation in 1977, *A Bunch of Stiff Records*. Included on the 2008 re-issue of *Jesus of Cool*.

label loves his music, but tells him exactly what to write! The song was written when Lowe was still signed to United Artists, whom he wanted to leave. United Artists refused so Lowe began to deliberately write songs that he thought would get him fired. 'Bay City Rollers We Love You' was one such song; unfortunately the plot backfired on Lowe when it became a hit in Japan!

The other song is, well, it is two songs really. 'Shake and Pop' was also recorded as the near identical 'They Call It Rock': the former appeared on the original UK issue of *Jesus of Cool*, with 'They Call It Rock' appearing as a one-sided 45 r.p.m. bonus single packaged with the album, as well as replacing 'Shake and Pop' on the US version. The only difference between the songs is the interchangeability in the lyrics of the words in their titles. The song addresses the ephemeral nature of rock 'n' roll fame. It starts off describing how wonderfully a fictitious band's record is received by the record companies and the press, it makes them lots of money and places them on the pedestal of celebrity but, come the second record, it's all change. The reviewers say it's shit and it flops.

The last word on the matter goes to 10cc's Lol Creme and Eric Stewart on 1970's '4 Percent of Something' [B-side to 'Johnny Don't Do It'].[10] Clearly, this was written early in their career—and hopefully they were soon able to negotiate better contracts—but at this stage they are moaning about the fact that pop impresario Jonathan King will only give them 4 percent on their sales and that is making them feel depressed. Here they are, working their fingers to the bone, barely eking out a living from their music, and this man won't even offer them ten per cent!

So, there you have it. The ups and downs of the rock 'n' roll life neatly encapsulated through songs: in real life, the dream has its nightmarish side.

Sociologically, rock music was very important for many Fifties Children: it defined their individuality, their break with the strictures of their parents' generation, informed them about what was happening in the world in a myriad ways and, not least, formed one of the principal sources of their leisure time. Rock music defined who they were.

In the final chapter of the Life is for Living section we shall move on to look at some of the other sources of leisure that were popular with Fifties Children.

10. All members of 10cc are not only contemporaneous, but are from Barclay James Harvest's local environs.

16

Elves, Aliens and Other Forms of Escapism

We have already seen how Barclay James Harvest's songwriters described aspects of popular culture in their songs. This chapter completes the review of our social history as suggested by these songs. The first part deals entirely with fantasy and science fiction—-progressive rock music lyrics of the Seventies are often derided, perhaps unjustly, for just being about elves and other flights of fancy, and Barclay James Harvest, in their most progressive period, often partook of that particular pleasure—while the second wraps up other popular culture references, allowing us as full a sociological picture as possible.

Fantasy and Science Fiction

As genres, fantasy and science fiction may have been born earlier, but it was only through the popularisation of tales by the likes of Jules Verne—*20,000 Leagues Under the Sea* and *From the Earth to the Moon* amongst them—and H.G. Wells—with classics such as *War of the Worlds* and *The Time Machine*—that it became fully established in the late nineteenth century, before exploding into the mainstream through American pulp fiction in magazines such as *Amazing Stories* and *Astounding Science Fiction*. The main market for such magazines was the United States, but what they did was to provide an economic platform for a number of hugely influential authors, making it commercially viable for them to write professionally. Soon, the bookshelves on both sides of the Atlantic were packed with novels and short story collections by the likes of Isaac Asimov, Ray Bradbury, Phillip K. Dick, Arthur C. Clarke and others. These writers carved out golden seams of imagination in teenagers' minds. And yet, despite the interest in these genres, they have always been perceived by many as the sole province of pimply adolescent males and have therefore never gained the acceptance of the literati. No matter to us!

The interest in science fiction in particular was fuelled by the launch of spacefaring rockets in 1957 and the ensuing space race between the United States and the Soviet Union, the highlight of which was the first man to walk on the moon in 1969. The space race was, effectively, a spin-off of the Cold War, one of the ways in which the Soviet Union and the United States attempted to achieve a technical and propaganda superiority over each other. Having lagged behind in the nuclear arms race, the Soviets took the lead in the space race when they launched the world's first artificial satellite, Sputnik 1, in the autumn of 1957. In these early days, before the technology and confidence had been developed for manned space flight, animals were used to gather data. The Soviets again beat the United States in placing an animal into earth orbit when, a month after Sputnik 1, the second Sputnik carried a dog into space. At this time, this was a tit-for-tat competition and the United States scored a first in 1959 when they were actually able to return space-travelling animals—two monkeys—alive to earth. The pair survived a short non-orbital trip aboard a Jupiter-class Intermediate Range Ballistic Missile (IRBM), but the Soviets again superseded them the following year when another Sputnik flight carried two dogs into earth orbit and returned them safely home. In 1961, in one of the more bizarre publicity coups of the Cold War, the Soviet leader Khrushchev presented United States President Kennedy's wife with a puppy dog that had been born to one of the dogonauts after its mission had been completed!

The Soviets were also in the lead in the more serious business of manned space flight: Yuri Gagarin became the first man to achieve orbital flight, aboard Vostok 1, in April 1961. The Americans were stung by the Soviets' persistent technological lead and the propaganda victories they were amassing and their response was to launch the manned moon programme. Kennedy's inspirational speech in 1962 fired the imagination of the Fifties Child generation: "We choose to go to the moon in this decade and do the other things, not because they are easy, but because they are hard!" The United States achieved its goal when the Apollo 11 mission landed Neil Armstrong and Buzz Aldrin on the moon in July 1969. Cameras mounted on the spacecraft's lunar module transmitted the images back to earth: man's first moonsteps were witnessed by a massive world-wide television audience. Armstrong's words in making those steps have likewise become famous: "That's one small step for man, one giant leap for mankind." Contrast that with the modern day's lack of scientific and technological adventure: it is as though the human soul has folded in on itself and lost its imagination.

To a Fifties Child, the remainder of the space race was anti-climactic. There were six more moon-landing missions, one of which, the Apollo 13 mission, became famous when the spacecraft's malfunction led to the abandonment of the planned lunar landing as the three astronauts and staff at mission control concentrated all efforts on returning the crew safely to earth. Apollo 17 was the final manned mission to the moon, landing in December 1972. In the Seventies, Soviet efforts were directed at developing space station technology whilst, post-Apollo, the Americans concentrated on developing unmanned space probes and a re-useable space shuttle. Exciting as some of these post moon-landing projects were to some people, they lacked the necessary factor to spark the imagination of mankind. The two superpowers began to co-operate on some space projects in a new spirit of detente and the fizzle went out of the space race, petering out even before the collapse of the Soviet Union in 1991.

Where then is the manned mission to Mars? The moon-landing of 1969 was more than forty years ago! This staggering loss of ambition is best dissected in music by Andy Tillison—his song 'Not as Good as the Book', from the Tangent's album of the same name (2008) describes the issue to perfection: "They went to space in an old tin of beans haphazardly strapped to a firework, with less than a ZX81 to direct them back home . . . we sit here with gigs [abytes] and just twiddle our thumbs, while personalising our desktops."

Fantasy and science-fiction's popularity was also reflected in a number of hit films and TV series. *Star Trek* [1966] first appeared on television in Britain in 1969 and has been hugely popular since, spawning a number of blockbuster films. *Dr Who*, arguably the British equivalent to *Star Trek*, first appeared in 1963. At the height of the space race, in 1968, the film *2001: A Space Odyssey* was released, becoming a huge success. Despite an initially mixed critical reaction, Stanley Kubrick's film is now widely acknowledged as one of the greatest of all time. It was based on a short story by Arthur C. Clarke, *The Sentinel*, which had first appeared in 1951 in *10 Story Fantasy* magazine. Clarke contributed to the film's script. Works by other contemporaneous science fiction authors have also yielded hit films, through adaptation of ideas rather than strict following of the originals' plots: Phillip K. Dick's *Do Androids Dream of Electric Sheep?* [1968] became the superb *Blade Runner* in 1982 and Isaac Asimov's legendary *I, Robot* (first published in 1950 as a collection of short stories) finally inspired a film in 2004.

The world of fantasy writing was also popular for the adolescent Fifties Child, not least of which were authors such as J. R. R. Tolkien and Michael Moorcock. Moorcock wrote dozens of hugely popular fantasy books from the Sixties onwards, but none was as uniquely successful as Tolkien's *The Lord of the Rings* (initially published as three volumes in 1954 and 1955) which is one of the world's best-selling books, finally making it onto the big screen in three films corresponding to the book's volumes, between 2001 and 2003.

It is Tolkien who first provokes Barclay James Harvest's interest in song, with one of his heroines being the inspiration for Lees' ethereal 'Galadriel'. Lees' characterisation, musically as well as lyrically, evokes a deep sense of light—both in the sense of luminosity and mass, and, despite the reference to snow, warmth both in the sense of temperature and affection. Ostensibly a disarmingly simple song, it has a priceless melodic quality that is able to convey so much of the fantasy of its subject, making it an enduring favourite beyond the established fan-base forty years after its first release.

The Tolkien connection is maintained in Lees' 'Long Ships', released on his solo album, *A Major Fancy*, in 1977. As in 'Galadriel', in which the explicit link comes only through the title, in 'Long Ships' Lees provides only a brief reference to Tolkien's characters, although in this instance it occurs during the course of narrating his story, which merges characters from several sources. As a song, 'Long Ships' owes its origin to the long tradition of sea-faring storytelling in British folk music. There are some who would therefore describe the song's arrangement on *A Major Fancy* as folk-rock, but musically it actually shows less empathy with folk tradition than some of Lees' other forays into storytelling. Nevertheless, one can hear, with little difficulty, in one's mind's ear, a great folk traditionalist such as June Tabor singing 'Long Ships' a cappella. Elrond and Legolas—characters from Tolkien's *The Hobbit* and *The Lord of the Rings*—are aboard an exciting longship expedition of discovery into uncharted waters, in the search for rich lands of legend, which their people believe the gods have made it their destiny to find and prosper from. Borne aimlessly by the tides and the wind, the journey progresses without sight of this promised land. Eventually, battered by storms, the ships have sustained damage beyond repair; the adventurers' spirits are broken and they prepare for death, offering their souls to the Norse god Odin,[1] and consign their bodies to the depths of the sea.

There is a third Tolkien link in Barclay James Harvest's history. In 1972, frustrated at their inability to score a chart hit single, they released a double A-side under the pseudonym of Bombadil, another character from *The Lord of the Rings*. This ruse did not change the band's luck though, and chart compilers have never been troubled by Bombadil.

Still with its roots in the fantasy fiction world is another of the band's most popular songs, 'Medicine Man'. Lees takes his inspiration from Ray Bradbury's *Something Wicked This Way Comes*, which was first published in Britain in 1963. This fantastical story tells of the adventures of two boys in small-town America when a mysterious travelling carnival fairground arrives near their town, announced by an eerie calliope (a steam organ). Bradbury's

1. Although the Tolkien character Gandalf has been compared to Odin . . .

fantasy worlds are often tinged with horror: there are spooky characters aplen-
ty, magic mirror mazes and a carousel that, if one is tempted to ride it, can
transform people back through time into their younger selves as it spins. Of
course, there is a price to pay: they will then fall under the control of Mr Dark.
There is no "medicine man" in Bradbury's story though—as elsewhere, Lees
adapts the characters and situation to tell his own version of the tale. Let me
show you—here's an excerpt from Bradbury:

> "It's not true, anyway," Will gasped. "Carnivals don't come this late in the year.
> Silly darn-sounding thing. Who'd go to it?"
>   "Me." Jim stood quiet in the dark.
>   Me, thought Will, seeing the guillotine flash, the Egyptian mirrors unfold
> accordions of light, and the sulphur-skinned devil-man sipping lava, like gun-
> powder tea.
>   "That music . . . ," Jim murmured. "Calliope. Must be coming tonight!"

And here's Lees:

> The Medicine Man sits on the stage;
> eats fire and water, earth and air while we all stare.
> The silver blade burns bright
> and tells us to beware
> of mirrored passages
> that throw a thousand images
> of younger days.

This is not simple paraphrasing, it is a leap of the imagination, a wonderful
adaptation come to life. And there is one more connection between Ray
Bradbury and the band: he performed as support act at one of their concerts
in Los Angeles in 1976 by reading from his books.

Barclay James Harvest's six remaining forays into the imaginary world
classify as science fiction. Two of them, 'One Hundred Thousand Smiles Out'
and 'Negative Earth', deal with the same topic: that of a lost spaceman,
marooned in space without a hope of returning home. This was a period in
time when space exploration was in focus. Possible inspiration for both these
songs includes any or all of the following: the *2001: A Space Odyssey* film, the
1969 moon landing by the United States' Apollo 11 crew, and the tense, sus-
penseful days lived out in real-time when television screens across the world
announced that the Apollo 13 mission had technical problems on its outward
journey to the moon, ensuring that the aim of the hopes and prayers of millions were these bold pioneers travelling through the vast emptiness. Another

potential influence, of course, was David Bowie's 'Space Oddity'—almost certainly inspired by *2001: A Space Odyssey*—which was released in 1969 on his debut album. The single release reached No. 5 in the British charts.

'Negative Earth' is one of only two of the band's songs to have lyrics written by drummer Mel Pritchard.[2] This is a shame, because he clearly had a talent:

> For fifty-five days, I've been flying around the world.
> Here in syncopated time, while my tangled web of rhyme
> dangles aimlessly, time drips slowly by,
> and all I've got to do is sit and cry!

There is similar despair in the words of Holroyd's astronaut in 'One Hundred Thousand Smiles Out': he appears to be drifting aimlessly in space and has lost contact with mission control. Loneliness and depression are affecting him and he doesn't think that he can survive much longer on his own.

The astronauts in 'Negative Earth' and 'One Hundred Thousand Smiles Out' are both lone travellers, so perhaps the influences come more from the *2001: A Space Odyssey*/'Space Oddity' direction than from the Apollo missions, which were all manned by three men: other than in science fiction, it was only the first few sub-orbital and orbital space flights that were undertaken solo.[3]

Lees' 'Nova Lepidoptera' is composed very differently from all of the band's other forays into fantasy and science fiction: its lyrics are written using the time-honoured rock lyricist's technique of throwing a whole load of disconnected phrases into a pile on the desk, then trying to form them into a coherent lyric. On this occasion the phrases are sourced from Lees' literary science-fiction collection. Coherence in a rock song lyric is not always necessary for the success of the song of course, and in this instance Lees succeeds in building the proper sense of musical mystery for his galactic nonsense.

A semblance of lyrical order returns for 'Origin Earth', inspired by Greg Bear's novel *Eon* [1985]. This emotive song tells the tale of space travellers in the far future whose genetic memory of home is rekindled by photographs accessed from their ship's memory banks. Once seen, visions of Earth haunt the travellers' thoughts and dreams, driving their ambition to find their way back. It may just be me,[4] but I find the song's last verse, repeated three times

---

2. Except for the opening words "for fifty-five days", which were provided by Holroyd, who also wrote the music for the song. Pritchard's other lyrical contribution, 'Paper Wings', follows on from 'Negative Earth' on the *Everyone is Everybody Else* album.

3. Although the spaceship in the film started off with a crew of five, three of which were in cryogenic stasis. Those three and another astronaut were killed by the space-ship's computer, HAL.

at the end, deeply moving in an almost spiritual way, as Lees draws inspiration from the magnetism created by the Earth's evocative beauty and the anticipation of returning home:

> Star bright, your light
> guiding us back to a new tomorrow!
> Star bright, your light
> bringing us peace and an end to sorrow!

This may have been an inspirational passage from *Eon*:

> He began to chant.
> "In the name of Star, furnace of our being, forge of our substance, greatest of all fires, Star give us light, give us even in darkness the gift of right creation . . . In Fate we lay our trust, in the Way of Life and Light, in ultimate destiny's pattern, which we cannot deny, whatever we choose, however freely we choose."
> . . . Patricia clenched her hands together in front of her, realizing that she was making a gesture of prayer.

In a sense, the feelings expressed through this science-fiction tale have a resonance with Lees' strong sense of home and family, which are so important to him and which we have already covered earlier in our social history, only that to these space travellers in the future, "home" is represented by the long-lost origin planet.

Before leaving Barclay James Harvest's fantasy and science fiction songs, we need to mention again, for the sake of completeness, 'After the Day' and 'Death of a City', which were discussed in the chapter 'Spectre of a Nuclear Holocaust'. Both of these songs were written in a story form which would classify as science fiction.

Considering all of these songs by Lees together, one can draw the conclusion—which is consistent with that which we drew in the previous chapter regarding his musical influences—that even when the influence has been something specific, like Bradbury's *Something Wicked This Way Comes*, Lees' resulting work is entirely original. He makes these stories his own, they are not copies. The same applies to songs falling into other categories, such as 'May Day', which is reminiscent of Orwell's *1984*. There is another such song in Lees' canon which will not be categorised sociologically in this book, 'Leper's Song', which is inspired by two books: Graham Greene's *A Burnt Out Case* [1960] and Joseph Conrad's *An Outcast of the Islands* (1896).

---

4. Although the experience of life teaches that it never is "just you".

Lees' love of books and skill at storytelling leads one to speculate that, had Barclay James Harvest been a failure, he may have taken up writing fiction professionally. It would be churlish not to point out that 'One Hundred Thousand Smiles Out' and 'Negative Earth' are also written as stories, and very successfully too. However, in Holroyd and Pritchard's case there are insufficient other songs of this nature to allow conclusions or further speculation.

As if to stress the significance of fantasy and science fiction to Fifties Children, it is not hard to find other contemporaries' musical contributions. David Bowie's 'Space Oddity' has already been mentioned, but equally often compared to 'One Hundred Thousand Smiles Out' and 'Negative Earth' is Elton John's 'Rocket Man', with lyrics again written by his songwriting partner, Bernie Taupin. However, it is unlikely that 'Rocket Man' could have influenced 'One Hundred Thousand Smiles Out' as the two songs were released within six months of each other. The similarity of these themes accentuates the societal importance of space travel at that time. The treatment of the subject matter in 'Rocket Man' is very similar to that of the Barclay James Harvest and Bowie songs: the astronaut is desperately lonely and affected by depression.

In another league altogether are Hawkwind, many of whose songs are fantasy or science fiction related; indeed, some albums have a specific science-fiction concept. Hawkwind even collaborated with the fantasy writer Michael Moorcock for many years. Robert Calvert's lyrics for 'Spirit of the Age', first released on *Quark, Strangeness and Charm* [1977], are a particular favourite of mine. The lyrics are actually sourced from two separate poems but their humour, in particular that of the first verse, lifts the song. It deals with the space traveller theme again: travelling far out into space he wishes that his girlfriend, who has been left behind on earth, had been put into cryogenic sleep so that she would not be dead on his return. There is spice in the verse's "twist": the girlfriend was still underage when he left and he carries an android replica of her on the trip but it malfunctions, calling out someone else's name during sex.

'Fahrenheit 451'[5] links up with Barclay James Harvest via the Ray Bradbury connection. The 1953 book, in which a fireman's job is to burn all books, which have been banned by society, instead of putting out fires, achieved widespread popularity, reaching beyond the fantasy and science-fiction community, and was adapted into film by François Truffaut in 1966. Calvert's own

5. 'Fahrenheit 451': *Choose Your Masques*, 1982. Credited to Calvert/Brock; the lyrics are by Calvert.

adaptation locates the book burning in Lexington, a place that had previously featured in his 'Damnation Alley' [*Quark, Strangeness and Charm*], another song firmly rooted in science fiction, being based on Roger Zelazny's short story and novel of the same name. It is worth mentioning that these adaptations by Calvert lie much closer to the feel of the original stories than Lees' adaptations of *Something Wicked This Way Comes* and *Eon*.

Yet another Hawkwind song worth mentioning is Lemmy's 'The Watcher', first released on *Doremi Fasol Latido* [1972] and then subsequently by Motörhead—the band Lemmy formed after leaving Hawkwind—on their eponymous debut album in 1977. This is a much darker song than those already featured in this chapter, concerning as it does an all-powerful being—another manifestation of God, similar to those in Black Sabbath's 'Electric Funeral' and 'War Pigs', both of which we have already looked at—watching over the Earth. The Watcher is disappointed with humanity and destroys the Earth.

This recurring theme of the world being watched by all-powerful beings is a variant on the disputably factual extrapolations of Erich von Daniken, whose *Chariots of the Gods* [1968] and other books claiming that the earth had been often visited by astronauts in the ancient past were extremely popular with the same Fifties Children who were interested in fantasy and science fiction.

A softer variant derived from the same basic premise can be found in the Sutherland Brothers' 'Space Hymn', written by Gavin Sutherland and released in the same year as 'The Watcher' on the band's *Lifeboat* album. This features an alien space traveller who arrives on Earth to try and help mankind live with greater equanimity. He says that he shall show us what we have to do, but we will then have to do it for ourselves. The space traveller is not convinced that we will follow his advice because the last time he came it did not have much effect. Chris de Burgh's 'A Spaceman Came Travelling' [1976] is disqualified from this consideration, not because of its close thematical similarity to 'Space Hymn', but because de Burgh is not a contemporary of Barclay James Harvest's.

It is clear then that fantasy and science fiction was an important aspect of popular culture for Fifties Children, one that clearly motivated their own imagination, opening up vast daydream worlds. No need for them of the cheap, easy lure of the video nasty and the computer game. This form of entertainment was all about one's own imagination—it had no limits!

A Popular Culture Miscellany

The remainder of Barclay James Harvest's songwriters' sociological songs nearly all fit under a "TV & Movies" banner, but they are quite varied thematically, so it is more appropriate to sweep them up in this miscellaneous section, drawing out any relevant sociological aspects as we go.

Holroyd's 'Jonathan' takes inspiration from the allegorical, million-selling novel *Jonathan Livingston Seagull* [1970] by Richard Bach. The book was made into a popular film in 1973, with a soundtrack by Neil Diamond. 'Jonathan', like its root derivatives, is a spiritual fable and so we shall deal with the song again in the 'Spirituality' chapter.

'The Streets of San Francisco' [1978] is the first song we come to chrono-logically that is not covered elsewhere in the book. This again finds Lees in story-telling mode, using a setting familiar to him, not only from the band's visits to the city to work with Elliot Mazer in 1975 and 1976, but also from the popular film and TV detective series of the same name. American detective series such as this were hugely popular on British television in the Seventies, whether they featured solo sleuths such as *Kojak*, *Columbo* or *Banacek*, or part-ners such as *Starsky and Hutch* and, in *The Streets of San Francisco* itself, Stone and Keller. Many of the actors in these series became huge celebrities, as was the case with teenage heart-throb David Soul, who played Hutch, and Michael Douglas, who played Keller.[6] In the song 'The Streets of San Francisco' a woman, jilted and beaten up by her lover, wreaks her vengeance on manhood in general by assassinating men at random in Golden Gate Park.

Cinematic influences also have a high profile in the band's popular culture songs and, in 'Marlene', Holroyd sings an emotional eulogy to Marlene Dietrich (1901-92), who became an icon of the twentieth century, not just as a result of the erotic image developed over a series of sultrily filmed movies, but also, despite being wooed by the German authorities in the years pre-ceding the Second World War, because of her renouncement of the Nazi regime. Born a Berliner, Dietrich, who had moved to Hollywood under con-tract to Paramount Pictures, became an American citizen before their involvement in the Second World War began and she became an avid and morale-boosting entertainer of front-line troops during the War. These rebuffs caused some consternation amongst many fellow Germans, and it has taken many decades for her native nation to fully embrace her again, sadly too long for Dietrich, who died in Paris in 1992. Holroyd uses his lyrical skill to draw out many facets of her life in his plaintive eulogy: he recalls her days in cabaret, the success of her time in Hollywood and the lonely final years in Paris. Now, in death, her war finally over, she leaves us with memories of her soul-touching, bewitching smile and with the sadness of knowing that, in life, she would never be blessed with the reconciliation that she most eagerly

6. In 1976, when Barclay James harvest were in San Francisco, waiting in vain for Elliot Mazer to produce the follow-up to *Time Honoured Ghosts*, they used up some of their time by recording backing vocals for 'Black Bean Soup', a track on the album which David Soul—riding on the wave of *Starsky and Hutch*'s success—released in that year.

craved: the renewed friendship of her own people—the Berliners, the Germans.

Wolstenholme's 'Blood and Bones' also references a couple of films. This is a complex song to interpret lyrically, dealing as it does with the nature of reality and fundamental questions of existence; like 'Jonathan', it appears again in the 'Spirituality' chapter. Inspired by a trip to a Bodyworlds exhibition in Venice, Wolstenholme uses that city as a backdrop to his musing and, in so doing, refers to two works of fiction based there: Nicolas Roeg's film, the 1973 psychological occult thriller *Don't Look Now*, and Thomas Mann's novel *Death in Venice* [1912], which was subsequently transferred by Luchino Visconti to the big screen in 1971, starring Dirk Bogarde.

There is no cinematic connection whatever in our final example, Wolstenholme's 'Love Is . . .', which is clearly inspired by Kim Casali's extremely popular cartoon strip of the same name. The cute, single-frame cartoons, first published in 1970, quickly became admired by newspaper readers the world over. British cartoonist Bill Asprey took over drawing the strip in 1975, publishing them under Casali's pen-name Kim. The cartoon strip's typically sugary philosophy is given short shrift by Wolstenholme's sombre mood and the lyrics, the vast majority of which start "love is", tend towards bitter rather than sweet. The song's twist comes the only time that Wolstenholme, having lulled the unsuspecting listener into the cartoon's groove with some saccharine music, breaks the lyrical pattern:

> Love is sun,
> love is rain.
> Love has gone,
> love is pain.
> Love is kind:
> not one bit.

'Love Is . . .' provides a classic example of Wolstenholme's late period habit of mixing sumptuously melodic writing, often associated with pure love, with themes of loss of love or difficulties in relationships. It makes for an absorbing musical experience, but it is never going to be a style that provides a Top 10 hit because, unlike a song such as 'Make Me Smile (Come Up and See Me)', which has similar contrasting emotions between the lyrics and music, the lyrics of 'Love Is . . .' are literal enough to be easily interpretable as an experience of emotional pain, and the conflict in the associated lyric-music messages then detracts from the casual listener's enjoyment.

You will be pleased to know that it is possible to finish this part of our social history on a light note. Ignoring this section's cinematic centre of gravity, I have plumped instead for a song that—like Wolstenholme's 'Love Is'—demonstrates the importance of print media in shaping the culture of the Fifties Child: 10cc's 'Sand in My Face' from their eponymous debut album [1973]. Credited to Godley, Creme and Gouldman, this is a wonderful, jokey adaptation of the famous Charles Atlas bodybuilding advertisements that appeared in comics for decades from the Forties onwards. A nine-stone weakling has sand kicked in his face and loses his girlfriend to a hunk, takes up bodybuilding—the Charles Atlas way of course—and gains revenge on the hunk by retaliating in kind and winning the girl back. It is a subject matter made in heaven for 10cc, and in particular the Godley-Creme songwriting partnership, which was noted for its humour. Given the success of the advertisements, there must have been many Fifties Children who signed up for Mr Atlas' campaign!

It is easy to see through the songs in this part of our social history that Barclay James Harvest's songwriters' tastes in popular culture reflected that of large portions of society, in particular that of their contemporaries. Their enjoyment of rock music through the Sixties lured them to try the rock 'n' roll life themselves, a venture at which they were successful, but not to the point of becoming the kind of millionaire songwriters who can afford to sit back at leisure, waiting for the royalty cheques to be delivered to their poolside on silver trays courtesy of haughty butlers. Their rock 'n' roll lifestyle was less hedonistic than that made notorious by some other bands, but the fact that Lees' songs explicitly reject drugs culture indicates that it was possible to try and survive—and even enjoy—life without embarking on the journey of assisted daydreams, an addictive trip from which some of their friends would not return. However, coping with life without the help of recreational drugs did mean that the Battle for the Mind would have to be fought with other resources . . .

Mel Pritchard

Part 5
Echoes and Shadows

17

The Battle for the Mind

Let's face it, *what* really does matter to you? At the time of writing, three million haven't got jobs—well, the poor will be with you always. Arab populations are revolting against ruthless leaders who are prepared to deploy tanks against civilians in an attempt to quash resistance—well, it's a local dispute, let them sort it out amongst themselves. Pigs and other animals (your food) are teased, taunted and tortured in our slaughterhouses—well, they're only animals, get over it. Gangsters are making parts of our cities no-go areas—well, lock the buggers up. My husband is doing a load of unpaid overtime at the office these days (really a bit too often, it seems) in order to keep in with the boss—well, I'm sure he'll be bringing in more cash soon. You're a vegetarian and you eat cheese—well, at least they keep the cows alive a little longer. Your work colleague has been unjustly (surely, anyone could see that!) promoted over you—well, it's a dog-eat-dog world. The government has just invented a new tax to stave off the deepening recession—well, it's only money. Those palpitations in your chest are becoming more persistent—well, the gym is now offering discounted memberships. Your six-year-old daughter has contracted leukaemia—well . . .

Come on! Relax, breathe deep, sort yourself out. After all, it's only life, this is living. Can you not cope? Too much work? Not enough money? Can't get enough sex? Fed up with the depressing TV news? World a piece of shit?

Perhaps you are one of the few who floats through life like a seed on the breeze, unconcerned with your destination or future. For most of us, however, at some moments in time, life causes some mental angst, for a variety of reasons that vary from individual to individual. Within that large sub-set of the population, there is another sub-section of people—perhaps because their bodies are predisposed to it—for which life *always* causes some mental angst. And all of us who live into adolescence and adulthood will—again to varying degrees—come face to face with our mortality and ponder on the meaning of that particular journey.

So, how do *you* cope with your mind's ventures into unanswerable questions and depression? Where to now, my friend? Drugs? Or alcohol? Religion, perhaps? No, let's ask the quack—he's a trustworthy fellow—I'm sure he'll prescribe some medication to help you out. Maybe try the lot, why not?

This chapter and the next, 'Spirituality', are in many ways the most important chapters of this social history because they deal with how Fifties Children have coped—or not, as the case may be—with the imponderables and misfortunes that life has thrown at them. Their success or failure in dealing with the ravages of the mind would, like in countless generations before them, dictate whether they would consider their lives a happy or a sad one.

For the Fifties Child, this battleground of the mind and spirituality would be waged very differently to that of *all* previous generations. It is not the fact that the Fifties Child would have access to mind-altering drugs and alcohol that would make this battleground unique for his generation—arguably, similar substances would also have been previously part of the arsenal—but more so the facts that psychiatric drugs were, effectively, new and that the Fifties Child would be the guinea-pig for their trial. These were the really significant changes. Just as importantly, one of the effects of world-shrinkage would be the easy dissemination of new spiritual ideas from around the globe that would help to accelerate, and fill the spiritual gap caused by, the drop in formal Christian observance. These two factors would ensure that the Fifties Child's potential weaponry for battling mental distractions of all kinds would be greater in scope than his predecessors. Whether this made it easier or not for him to find mental solace is debatable, but lies beyond the scope of our social history. As always, we shall be guided by our songwriters. Let us then see how they coped with the ravages besetting the mind.

In the 'Drugs' chapter, we saw the different attitudes towards recreational drugs that were buffeting Fifties Child's society: they ranged from unabashed advocates of drugs, such as Timothy Leary, to its total detractors, such as our own John Lees. However, even some of those Fifties Children who managed to resist the lure of recreational drugs still succumbed, under medical pressure, to partake in another sort of mind-altering experience. From the Fifties onwards, drugs to combat depression and other mental illnesses were, perhaps too commonly, prescribed by the medical profession. At least two members of Barclay James Harvest have been affected by such drugs, and they deserve a place in our social history.

Is alcohol so different? Those of you who are, or who have known, alcoholics will know that it is not. Indeed, its popularity almost certainly stems from the fact that it *is* capable of altering the mind's perception of the world. Short term, it can bring a high. Long-term addiction brings dullness, depression. Again, at least two members of Barclay James Harvest have been affected by this drug and it must therefore also feature on our social history.

The material that follows is not indicated for those of a nervous disposition... but then, is life?

✄

Alcohol

Alcohol has never been prohibited in Britain although, of course, it has in the United States, where it was prohibited for over ten years between the two World Wars.[1] As the meshing of the popular cultures of the two countries increased during the twentieth century, the consequences of this prohibition, as retold principally through the cinematic medium, became all too clear to the Fifties Child. People want to drink, and prohibition does not work. All that happens is that an illicit industry is built up as a result of profiteering from the ban, providing the alcohol illegally. Criminals were organized into competing gangs that were occasionally in violent dispute. Aspects of this illicit trade, buoyed by the power of cinema, have become icons of the age: the Chicago gangster Al Capone, the speakeasy, the Valentine's Day Massacre. One wonders whether any parallels exist between this situation and the current prohibition of drugs . . .

The prohibition in the United States was motivated by religious considerations. A movement backed by evangelical Protestant churches garnered the support that persuaded the government to implement prohibition. Religious considerations have also been the prime motivator behind prohibition in other countries at various times, such as the prohibitions in place today in many Muslim countries. The concern arises not only from the possibility that overindulgence is harmful to health or causes anti-social behaviour but, perhaps more importantly from a spiritual perspective, also from the fact that an intoxicated mind is incapable of effective prayer, as this excerpt of a translation from the Quran exemplifies: "Indeed Satan seeks only to sow enmity and hatred among you by means of wine and gambling, and to keep you from the remembrance of God and from prayer. So will you not desist?"

The issue about clouding of the mind is also important in Buddhism, in which of one of the Five Precepts—which can be interpreted as equivalent to the Ten Commandments of Christianity—is the abstinence from intoxicating substances such as drugs and alcohol. Without a clear mind, one cannot meditate or be in full awareness of the present, meaning that one cannot approach

---

1. However, a Quaker-influenced area in Birmingham, the Bournville Village Trust, has been voluntarily "dry" for more than one hundred years.

nirvana. The origins of these various religious considerations are of course echoed in Lees' songs about drugs and we shall touch on the issue again in the following section on anti-depressants.

However, religious considerations are by no means the only ones that persuade many people of the dangers of alcohol. With overindulgence come problems such as domestic violence and rowdy and intimidatory public behaviour; and with dependence come associated health issues, all of which cost public service providers—and therefore you, dear taxpayer—many billions of pounds each year. Whilst it is also true that most of the cost of legally bought alcohol is tax revenue, the public cost is greater, meaning that either the deficit is being provided by general, including non-drinking, taxpayers or, depending on how you look at these things, drinkers are partly responsible for spiralling the country into debt.

Government statistics on alcohol-related deaths show a near doubling of the rate (for men; the increase for women is less) since the early Nineties, to about 18 per 100,000 of the population in 2009. Coincidentally, this rate is virtually equivalent to that from suicide. The recreational-drug related death rate is about a fifth that of the alcohol rate. Whether these figures are shocking or not depends on personal perspective: in context, society is quite happy to accept a road-traffic accident death rate comparable to that from recreational drugs, presumably because the advantages of road traffic to both individuals and society outweigh the risks. Again, perspective—many consumers of alcohol and recreational drugs would argue that there are benefits to them.

The debate on the best way to control alcohol and its relation to the drug situation is undoubtedly more complex than can be covered in this book but, irrespective of the societal costs and risks, it is clear that, like drugs, alcohol will continue to be consumed, whether by those who are just after a good night out or those who want to blot the mind to reality and depression.

✦

The two Barclay James Harvest musicians known to have fallen prey to the lure of alcohol are drummer Mel Pritchard and Wolstenholme. Pritchard only penned the lyrics for two songs, and unsurprisingly neither deals with the issue, but two of Wolstenholme's songs for his band Mæstoso do. Like Lees' songs about drugs, neither attempts to deal with the many intricacies of the alcohol issue: both limit themselves to morose observations of its consumption.

Whilst referring to Barclay James Harvest's early period in a 1988 interview, Wolstenholme confided: "I was not then quite such a bibber of alcohol." His near-twenty year absence from the rock industry perhaps explains why his first song dealing directly with alcoholism, 'One Drop in a Dry World', did not appear until 2004, many years after his interview admission.[2] The song describes a bingeing session, its hangover and muses that an occasional enjoyable drink is no longer enough. In so doing, it describes perfectly how that inoffensive drink with your mates can develop into an addiction, almost without one noticing the shift. The musical effect at the end of the song, which Wolstenholme refers to in the interview excerpt in the 'Sex' chapter, is significant whichever way one interprets it. The grandiose coda turns into a weak whimper, then an explosive sound from a drum. The protagonist has become unconscious, the interpretation of how and how badly he is injured is left to the listener's imagination.

The reflective 'Blossom Hill' from 2007 almost feels like a follow-up, suggesting that addiction has set in, partly as a panacea for the worries of life:

On Blossom Hill
day's curtains close,
and troubled man
finds his repose.
Farewell the sun:
his last embrace
runs deepest red;
now all is said
we drink our fill
on Blossom Hill.

Despite his various difficulties, Wolstenholme was in extremely strong writing form for the three Mæstoso albums that appeared between 2004 and 2007, and the finale of 'Blossom Hill' contains an example that is worthy of recording, for the wit of its ambiguity:

Stars shine for all
until they fall;
and fall they will
on Blossom Hill.

The "fall they will" refers, of course, as much to the drunks' inability to stand upright on the hill as it does to shooting stars, giving the song's ending a wonderful bite of Wolstenholme's legendary sense of humour. In fact, the whole

2. It is believed that Wolstenholme was not actually addicted to alcohol himself but had drinking friends who were. The songs covered in this section, whilst sung in the first person, may actually relate to someone else's alcoholism. This does not affect their relevance to our social history.

song is a cunning play on words as "Blossom Hill" is one of Britain's top selling wines! However, neither of these two songs carries the hope of Lees' sallies
into the drugs topic—the image is of alcoholism as a fact of life. In this regard
these songs do, unfortunately, reflect the modern increase in consumption.

Returning briefly for completeness to Lees' 'Midnight Drug', which we
have already met a couple of times, its alcohol reference comes in the lyric:
"You spend your day in an in-joke / pouring your life in a glass of ice." This
reference is fleeting, as was its reference to recreational drugs: the stronger
focus for the song's warning is prostitution, as has already been discussed in
the 'Sex' chapter.

There are many drinking songs in British vocal music history, reflecting alcohol's popularity through the ages. What is more difficult to find, as in the drugs
topic, are songs that deal with the issue of alcohol in a less celebratory fashion.
A couple of such songs come from the pen of Ozzy Osbourne, the former
leader of Black Sabbath, who went on to a successful solo career in the Eighties
and beyond. Osbourne has managed something that none of Barclay James
Harvest's songwriters have done, which is to become a "celeb" in today's media
world, known to people who have never even heard a note of his music. Some
may call it notoriety rather than fame, but to a celeb that is a trifling difference.
Irrespective, Osbourne was addicted to alcohol for long periods during his life
and his struggle for rehabilitation has become part of his celebrity portfolio.

'Suicide Solution', issued on his first solo album in 1980, has suffered the fate
that was highlighted in this book's introduction and which writers must fear,
that of severe misinterpretation. In 1984 an American nineteen-year old teenager, John McCollum, shot himself in the head whilst listening to the album that
contains 'Suicide Solution'. Subsequently, his parents brought a lawsuit claiming that Osbourne was responsible for their son's death. The lawsuit was rejected by a Los Angeles court in 1986 as some of the plaintiff's claims—for instance,
the fact that there were "hidden" lyrics in the song saying "get the gun and try
it: shoot, shoot, shoot"—were unsustainable. However, even if one just considers the verse that bookends the song, one can perhaps understand a degree of
confusion arising in many listeners' minds: the protagonist would appear to be
directing the listener to kill himself through alcoholism. Elsewhere too, it is easy
to interpret the meaning as being that alcohol leads inevitably to death. It cannot have helped that the song title is ambiguous, with the word "solution" being
interpretable both as a "liquid" and as the "answer". Whilst Osbourne certainly
intended the song to mean that alcohol addiction is a sure road to death, he was
probably not exhorting people to commit suicide through its use—the unfortu-
nate incident of John McCollum goes to show how anything can take on a life
of its own once it reaches the public domain.

In fact, there is an interpretation of 'Suicide Solution's bookends verse that can easily explain how the greatest confusion arises: the protagonist of this verse, unlike that of the remainder of the song, is Alcohol personified. Like Lees in 'Mr E' years later, Osbourne has used the rare rock songwriter's technique of switching personas mid-song. As we have seen with Lees' examples, this can be very difficult to detect, even when one is familiar with the songwriter's technique. In 'Suicide Solution', the "main" song is sung by an observer, who describes the effect of alcohol and how it can lead to death, but the bookends verse is sung by "Mr Alcohol" himself, and it makes a crucial difference to interpretation. Once this is understood, it becomes abundantly clear that Osbourne is saying how evil alcohol is, without any ambiguity whatsoever.

Mr Alcohol returns in 'Demon Alcohol' [*No Rest for the Wicked*, 1988]. This time there is only one protagonist and the personification is much clearer— Osbourne sings "I am", and the song is impossible to misinterpret. There is a neat reference back to the controversial song that we have just discussed when Mr Alcohol refers to "suicide solutions". He is boastful and uncompromising; revelling in teasing his victim and looking forward to a good binge, knowing that he has won over his victim—addiction has set in!

A songwriter possessing perhaps greater musical affinity with Barclay James Harvest's songwriters than Osbourne is Gerry Rafferty, who was in the band Stealers Wheel. After they had disbanded, Rafferty went onto a successful solo career, most notable for penning the massive-selling, Top 10 chart hit 'Baker Street' [1978], where the protagonist and his friend are both caught in the trap of alcoholism, having strayed to drink to escape the harsh reality of city life and the consequent depression. Despite the slight hint of hope towards the song's end, with the friend's intention to abandon the drink and his own intention to leave the city, the inference is that these hopes are forlorn and that neither will succeed in liberating themselves that easily.

It is a feature of these songwriters that, unlike Lees with his songs on recreational drugs, none of them offer any hope of redemption. However, what the songs reflect societally is the depth of the addiction that alcohol can lead individuals to. In particular, Wolstenholme's 'One Drop in a Dry World' identifies the almost inconspicuous, innocuous way that the drink lulls you in, maintaining a sense of security and control in the individual even whilst the addiction is taking hold. The lure, the power and the danger of alcohol is centred in this insidious burrowing of the mind that ultimately defeats the good part of the psyche. This characteristic is no different to that of recreational drugs, though perhaps less strong, which is maybe why alcohol is legal and recreational drugs are not. But then . . . because it is legal, it inevitably affects more people. But then . . . if you criminalise, society is faced with a host of other significant problems. It is a conundrum as old as society itself.

Depression and Psychiatric Drugs

The Fifties Child—fortunately or not, the debate remains open—has witnessed at first hand the explosion in the prescription of psychiatric drugs that began its unprecedented acceleration in the first half of the Fifties itself. Drugs had only occasionally been used in the treatment of mental illnesses prior to that time; never in the same concerted, determined and, some would say, haphazard way that would become the norm once their prescription had become fashionable in psychiatry. They are now prescribed not just by professional psychiatrists but also by general practitioner doctors (GPs) for many illnesses including depression and insomnia.

Psychiatry itself has a shady reputation as a science, despite the fame—or is it infamy?—of practitioners such as Sigmund Freud. Conditions in nineteenth-century mental "hospitals" were notoriously bad: overcrowding and abuse of patients being common. Even in the early twentieth century, prior to the Second World War, the drugs that were administered were mostly for sedation, providing "chemical restraint" of the patient. "Treatments" did begin to appear in the first half of the twentieth century, though they were often given as much in hope as in expectation of a cure.

Some of these "treatments" were grisly in nature. One, which is still in use today, was electroconvulsive (ECT) therapy—used to combat mood disorders such as depression and mania by giving the patient an electric shock to induce fits. Severe side-effects affect a significant proportion of patients, with estimates of the numbers affected varying between 10% and nearly 100% of those treated, depending on whether the surveys are conducted by proponents or detractors of the procedure. Another treatment, popular in the Fifties but which lost favour from the mid-Sixties, was insulin coma therapy (ICT), which had become established as a treatment against schizophrenia. A large dose of insulin would be administered, putting the patient into a coma. After a few hours, the coma would be terminated by administering glucose. A course of treatment might involve up to 60 induced comas. Perhaps not surprisingly, the mortality rate was high, up to 10 percent in some clinics that offered the treatment.

The explosion in the use of drugs for psychiatric treatments began in the Fifties when French hospitals began to oust ICT with chlorpromazine for the treatment of patients with schizophrenia. In the five years after 1952, when the drug was introduced, its use in France multiplied around 5,000-fold. Chlorpromazine quickly caught on in the United States, where the power of the pharmaceutical companies began to manifest itself with Smith, Klein & French investing heavily in promoting it as Thorazine.

Let's just digress a moment to consider this aspect: chlorpromazine is perceived to work so a big company comes in and calls it something else—Thorazine—with the aim of making a profit. This aspect—the market power of the brand—took on a new dimension for the Fifties Child, in this as well as in other areas of life: after all, is advertising Thorazine any different to promoting the Conservative Party or selling the *News of the World*? Perhaps in detail, but not in essence, and the effect on the target audience is identical. Why pay less for Ibuprofen when you can buy Nurofen for five times the price? It's the same active drug in both—what you are buying into is the brand, the comfort of the group, the status that your mind ascribes to it. If you struggle with Nurofen as the concept, then think Nike, or think Audi, or think "circle of hate". We buy into them because of the status that we perceive that they give us. The power of the media pervades the Fifties Child's generation.

Despite their high level of usage in modern treatment, there is a strong body of opinion that believes that many psychiatric drugs are ineffective—or much less effective than billed—and that they are, in general, over-prescribed. One of the factors leading to over-prescription is the pressure on medical professionals to prescribe such drugs, even if a cure is not foreseen, in order to reduce the numbers needing to be treated in mental hospitals at a time when government funding of public services is being squeezed. This is reminiscent of the use of drugs in sedation/chemical restraint in the nineteenth century.

One must also remember that many of the drugs used in psychiatric treatment are the same as those used recreationally—and illegally. This aspect has a long history, with opium and LSD amongst the drugs that have been used in psychiatry. The significant point here is that addiction to psychiatrically prescribed drugs is as undesirable as that to drugs used recreationally, although arguably that shouldn't happen as the individual is under the supervision of a professional psychiatrist or doctor.

In defence of psychiatry, mental illness is very common—one in four people will suffer from it at some point in their lives. Mixed anxiety and depression are the most common form of the illness in Britain, and so seeking to cure such illnesses has to be a worthwhile endeavour. There can be few people, who have been lucky enough to escape mental illness, who do not know of a close relative or friend who is either suffering or has suffered from the affliction. My own mother was prone to depression: as an alcoholic, this made for a potent brew of drugs. She died in hospital from pneumonia after an alcohol-induced fall in the home. I am sure that you will have your own stories. Who would not seek to cure such illnesses?

Depression might be the most common form of mental illness, but it was only recognised as an actual illness in the twentieth century and it is only since the Fifties that attempts have been made to cure it in earnest. However, mental illness is still not perfectly understood, so diagnosis and treatment continue to have high failure rates. It might seem harsh to say that Fifties Children were often the guinea pigs for new psychiatric ideas and drugs, but that is indeed what they were.

There is a burden on those willing to take psychiatric drugs. Side-effects are often severe which means that other drugs are needed, with more potential side-effects, to combat their consequences. How does one then know oneself when under the influence of such a cocktail? How does one reclaim a drug-free body and mind? Is one then trapped in a never-ending cycle of different drugs and dosages? Can the ordinary man in the street, without access to a large bank account, command the same attention of the medical profession as the wealthiest rock stars who can afford the best doctors and rehabilitation centres? These issues are pertinent, of course, not only to psychiatric drugs but to alcohol and recreational drugs as well. There are undoubted benefits to all of them, as well as dangers, which is why society will continue to debate their use into the future.

Both Lees and Wolstenholme suffered from mental illness during their lives and in the latter's case it was to eventually cost him his life, a tragedy that mirrors many in our society. It may be coincidental, but there are many songs that clearly deal with aspects of depression in the Barclay James Harvest canon and others, including some by Holroyd, which could be (less securely) interpreted as such.[3] These songs start appearing right from the very beginning of the band's career, with Wolstenholme's 'Mr Sunshine' [1968], the B-side of the band's first ever single, introducing the theme of mental anguish. The song is sung in the first person and whilst it might be foolish to categorically ascribe the feelings of depression that the protagonist feels to Wolstenholme himself, it is tempting—given the significant run of career-spanning songs in a similar vein that 'Mr Sunshine' presages—to conclude that this song, together with the others stemming from his pen that are covered in this section, encompasses some of his own personal experience. Sociologically, of course, it does not matter whether the songs are auto-biographical or not; Wolstenholme is writing about someone's experiences: that is what matters. In 'Mr Sunshine', the protagonist is in a daze: people and the world all around seem unreal. He can cope with most things but not the sunshine, which he has to hide away from. The sunshine's not for him. Despite the early-career simplicity, there's a couple of worthy nuances to the lyrics. The first is, clearly, that sunshine is used as a metaphor for happiness; and the second, the ambiguity between

3. For instance, 'When the World Was Woken' (1970), 'The World Goes On' (1976) and 'Believe In Me' (1976).

"sunshine's" and "sun shines"—whilst it is not necessary for interpretation—does cement the idea that the protagonist will never be blessed with happiness—the sun shines not for him.

Wolstenholme then follows this up with 'The Sun Will Never Shine' on the band's 1970 eponymous debut album, in which the presence of the theme of mental anguish is more arguable, but surely present, at least metaphorically in a very similar way to that just explained for 'Mr Sunshine'; and then again—twice—in 1971 with 'Ball and Chain' and the broken love lament 'Someone There You Know'. This is already—four years into a songwriting career ten times that long—a significant run of songs on the theme of mental anguish: you should now understand the temptation to—given that we also know how his illness affected him in later life—mark the songs as at least partly autobiographical.

'Ball and Chain's cry for help is almost desperate, and it should be said that the musical treatment is perfectly suited to the topic—this is an early Barclay James Harvest classic. Again, we have a protagonist singing in the first person, distressed because his life is full of bad luck and misery. He bemoans the fact that he has never had any good times and makes a desperate plea for God to help him. The inference is that the "ball and chain" are a metaphor for his unhappy life. However, Keith and Monika Domone's biography *The Barclay James Harvest Story* refers to a "lost" verse—not recorded because of time constraints—that makes it clear the protagonist of the song is in a prison car. It is therefore possible that 'Ball and Chain' is strictly literal, but there is sufficient precedent from other songs to favour the metaphorical interpretation. Notwithstanding, such a run of songs as otherwise described is still very significant, in particular if one adds another lost recording of Wolstenholme's from 1968, 'State of Mind', which the same reference states is about "loneliness".

By contrast with 'Ball and Chain', 'Someone There You Know', whilst still musically muscled, is gentler in both lyrical and musical respects. The song is inspired by lost love: its relevance to this part of our social history lies in the verse in which the protagonist admits having experienced loneliness and states that the warmth of a friend is needed to help him through difficult times.

Also rich in metaphor is the song that precedes 'The Sun Will Never Shine' on the debut album: Lees' 'Mother Dear'. What is most intriguing in retrospect about this song is that it is the first time that Lees introduces the stark duality of "good and evil" of the psyche, that is also to feature in his later writing in 'Summer Soldier', 'Mr E' and, less obviously, 'For No One'. 'Mother Dear's dream sequence has a certain resonance with its slightly distorted echo in 'Summer Soldier's own dream sequence. This is the metaphor in 'Mother Dear':

I awoke in the light of a vision in white—
the prettiest girl that I have ever seen!
'Lately my love', said the lady in white,
'I have watched from afar, but love draws me near.'

  . . .

Was it just another dream in the night?

  . . .

On that same silver night,
saw a figure in black by the lady in white:
he said his name was Death, was he right?
Do you know what this could mean, mother dear?

  . . .

It's so cold by your side, no don't cry, can't you see?;

This becomes sharpened by the horrors of the Troubles in 'Summer Soldier':

I thought I saw a summer soldier, helmet on his brow:
his silver rifle clutched beneath his armour-plated shroud.
'I fire in hate', he cried aloud,

  . . .

'My shield's my cause, my cause is war!'

  . . .

I dreamt I saw an angel bright, a halo on his brow:,
his golden sword lay in its sheath, beneath his silver shroud
'I draw thee not', he cried aloud,

  . . .

'My shield's my love, my cause is peace!'

However, the significance of 'Mother Dear's dream sequence in the particular context of this section on psychiatric drugs is that it demonstrates that Lees had suffered mental anxiety from a young age and that his spiritual development, that relentless mental battle between the good and evil sides of the psyche, had been ongoing during Barclay James Harvest's formative years.

Our social history has already mentioned this battle for the mind a number of times and it is now appropriate—also noting that Lees had a formal Christian upbringing in his childhood before straying away from the church in his teens—to reveal a potential source for his thinking on the matter. Consider this following excerpt from the New Testament:[4]

4. St Paul's Epistle to the Romans, Chapter 7 (twenty-first century King James version).

18 For I know that in me (that is, in my flesh) dwelleth no good thing; for to will is present with me; but how to perform that which is good, I find not.

19 For the good that I would do, I do not; but the evil which I would not do, that I do.

20 Now if I do that which I would not do, it is no more I that do it, but sin that dwelleth in me.

21 I find then a law that, when I would do good, evil is present with me.

22 For I delight in the law of God according to the inward man.

23 But I see another law in my members, warring against the law of my mind and bringing me into captivity to the law of sin which is in my members.

24 O wretched man that I am! Who shall deliver me from the body of this death?

25 I thank God—through Jesus Christ our Lord! So then, with the mind I myself serve the law of God, but with the flesh the law of sin.

Lees' thinking may have been influenced by St Paul, or he may have developed the ideas himself: what is clear is that, societally, this duality of human nature and the constant battle between good and evil would have been part of the Fifties Child's Christian upbringing.

So, if this constant battle between our good and bad parts of the psyche is present in each of us—and many, if not all of us, will recognise the characteristic struggle within our own minds—then conflict between humans must inevitably result, because at any one time not all of us will have the "good" part of the psyche winning the internal battle. It must now seem clear then why conflict is intrinsic to humanity, as we identified in the chapter on 'The Second Iraq War'.

Whilst Lees never wrote specifically about psychiatric drugs himself, he did refer to them in some interviews during his career. His illness manifested itself in extreme anxiety, making it difficult for him to work. In his instance, of course, the work involved going on tour and performing live shows. In his early adulthood, Lees resorted to prescribed psychiatric drugs: in 1977, at the time of the release of 'Hymn', he explained to an interviewer that the only drugs he had ever taken were "those prescribed by my psychiatrist to keep me working. You see, I suffer from an anxiety complex: it started seven years ago when I had a nervous breakdown . . . but I would never dabble with [recreational] drug taking."

Lees is one of those lucky people who has managed to find a way back out of the morass of psychiatric drug taking. It is not that his mental anguish has vanished—one of the things that life teaches is that we all suffer from it to some degree throughout our lives—but Lees has found a way to develop the mental solace that he had always found through the power of prayer—which he had used even when he was uncertain in his own spiritual beliefs—to help him overcome the need for psychiatric drugs.[5] Interviewed in 2006, he explained his changed attitude thus: "I wouldn't [now] go down the route of taking prescribed drugs to keep me doing the job. If I'd have been strong enough mentally, I would've overcome that." The difficulty in resolving this problem, i.e. finding a natural solution to mental illness, is covered by Lees in 'Doctor Doctor':

> Doctor, doctor, why am I alone
> listening to my heart
> beating through the cold dark night?
> . . . I'm shaking in the gloom!
> Could this be defeat?
> . . .
> Doctor, doctor, help me through the day:
> give me something natural I can depend on
> . . . it's something that I need -
> it's a natural panacea
> like a cure for every fear . . .

The twist in the song is that Lees himself then goes so far as to define the "panacea":

> It's some of her sweet love
> mixed up with her young blood:
> true love and devotion—
> what a wonderful potion!

Now, at face value, this is no more than an archetypal rock song's love theme, and perhaps that is all that it is. However, contextualising from Lees' interview statements, as well as from all of his many spiritual songs—which are covered in full in the next chapter—it would not be inconsistent if the love that he was referring to was a spiritual love: that of Jesus' mother, Mary. In the Christian tradition, Mary is revered for the depth of her faith and love, which is highlighted in the Gospel stories from the time that she was visited by the Archangel Gabriel and agreed to be the virgin mother of Jesus. The use of the word "devotion" is key in this context:[6] Lees is seeking the mental strength

---

5. This use of prayer is in no way contradictory. For "prayer" read "meditation"; the absorption into the inner self where mystics such as Jesus, Muhammad and Buddha would point the way to "happiness".

6. "Devotion" is a word with strong religious connotations and is often used during Christian teaching and worship.

that a love, devotion and faith like Mary's would give in the struggle against anxiety. Furthermore, Mary will almost certainly have been a teenager when agreeing to be the mother of Jesus, hence "young blood, true love and devotion". Assuming that the song is autobiographical—a fairly safe assumption—this interpretation appears more likely than the alternative "sexual love" possibility, after all 'Doctor Doctor' appears on the same album as 'How Do You Feel Now?' and 'In Memory of the Martyrs'. In the first of these, he delights in his daughter's birth and expresses how it has strengthened his marriage; and in the second he demonstrates a deep spirituality, as we shall soon discover in the next chapter.

Irrespective of whether it is a sexual or spiritual love that is the panacea in 'Doctor Doctor', it is clear that the mental strength that had originally allowed Lees to resist recreational drug taking has developed during his lifetime to the extent that he has also been able to combat mental anguish and resist travelling the scree slope of more psychiatric drugs. It may well be that this was already developed by the time of 'Doctor Doctor'—after all, Lees is *telling* the doctor what he needs, not vice versa! The depth of his belief and inner strength at this time can also be gauged from the pure spirituality inherent within 'In Memory of the Martyrs'.[7]

Speaking in the latter half of the Eighties, Lees told an interviewer: "A year and a half ago I was going through a crisis in my life. The only thing I could think of was praying and my prayers have always been answered in a miraculous sort of way." This is the process—prayer helping to relieve mental anguish—which is alluded to in 'Doctor Doctor'. It is referred to again by Lees in 'For Your Love', a song with greater depth of meaning than many fans of the band have credited, and to which we shall return again in more detail in the 'Spirituality' chapter. This excerpt, from the opening of the song, describes the torture of sleeplessness through mental distress:

> For your love I cry
> the long lonely hours
> before the dawn.
> In my dreams I try
> to hold back the dark,
> to hold back my fear.
>
> . . .
>
> I have hope, I pray . . .

7. The analysis of this aspect of 'In Memory of the Martyrs' is included in the chapter on Spirituality.

Perhaps surprisingly, praying for relief from mental anguish had actually already been the topic of one of Holroyd's songs, 'Sweet Jesus'. Holroyd's songs are the least autobiographical—in an interpretive way, certainly—of the three Barclay James Harvest songwriters, so the surprise stems from the fact that he should write, in the first person, such personal-sounding lyrics. This is surely one of the most explicit Christian prayers to be found in rock music: the protagonist is suffering from mental anxiety and asks Jesus to help him. Of course, the difficulty with interpreting 'Sweet Jesus' as a personal song is that there is very little else to back up the interpretation. With many of Lees' and Wolstenholme's songs there are others to aid in contextualisation, or there are key interview statements, but with Holroyd there is no really significant "key" to assist with unlocking the true meaning.

Arguably, the following year's 'The World Goes On'—another first person song—is a follow-up to 'Sweet Jesus', in which the protagonist has meditated on the whys and wherefores of life and resolved his mental anxiety. If the two songs are connected in some way—but because of Holroyd's desire to protect his innermost personal thoughts and life private, even in his songwriting, this can only be supposition—then one would say that the balance of probability is that they are autobiographical and suggestive of the fact that in his early life Holroyd, like his fellow songwriters, also suffered from some kind of mental anguish. Whilst both songs appear highly personal, the fact that they are sung in the first person may simply be the very common writer's device for giving them more impact. Whether they are personal or not, they are worth recording here as part of the band's sociological songs, as they reflect individuals suffering mental anguish and, in the case of 'Sweet Jesus', using prayer as a help.

We shall now return to Wolstenholme's songwriting to see how his mental torture is reflected in his post-Barclay James Harvest songs. 'Why Remain', recorded in 1982 but not released until 2004, is replete with the angst of depression, full of mental pain. Shuttered at home, too depressed to do anything, shunning the world, the afflicted wonders what is the point of living, when the world is full of pain, sadness and bad things.

Taking his oeuvre as an indicator, it would seem that Wolstenholme's spiritual life journey lacked Lees' conviction about the strength of prayer, perhaps leaving him more vulnerable than his friend to the effects of mental anguish, which he again describes in 'The Devils That I Keep', a song which also provides his first reference to the psychiatric drugs that helped him to cope. Wolstenholme describes how the mental angst instils a feeling of hopelessness and individual worthlessness, noting that it is not life's events that cause this but the devils that torture his mind. God, creator of the universe, cannot help him, so he resorts to sleeping pills for some respite.

The lyrics and the music of all of these songs are very fine things. One can listen to them in a half-attentive state and never really pick up on the depth of feeling that has prompted the songwriters to, perhaps in a cathartic attempt, share their thoughts. However, away from our stereos and sound systems, the songwriter is possibly still battling the sapping illness, with whatever tools and strength are at his disposal.

During a particularly low period in 2003, Wolstenholme attempted suicide by taking an overdose of sleeping tablets. After the immediate recovery in hospital, he spent a period recuperating and restoring his health at Bootham Park, a hospital in York specialising in mental health issues. Helped by this recuperative experience, he reformed the Mæstoso band. Early in this period of renewed creativity, Wolstenholme recorded his experience at the hospital in 'Bootham Park Elegy', a song that was originally released on *Black Box Recovered* [2004]. The peace and tranquility that he found during that period of repose is eloquently evoked through the music and near repetition of lyrics within the song. In describing a new day Wolstenholme makes the subtlest of changes to words between otherwise identical verses, for instance where "faceless" becomes "blameless".

Sleep deprivation induced by mental anguish such as Lees wrote about in 'For Your Love' is a dire and common consequence of mental illness, and one to which Wolstenholme also refers in the appropriately titled '2 a.m.', which we have already met in the 'The Second Iraq War' chapter. The song's main theme relates the process of endless mental loops that torture those afflicted, whether it be caused by work or family pressures, or by illness. One of the most striking and enduring metaphors that Wolstenholme conjures is that of a million sleepless people, all fighting their despair, as if struggling to avoid falling off a precipice into the depths of hell. Meanwhile, others manage to sleep, unconcerned, through the worst of troubles. '2 a.m.' is another eloquent description of the depths of despair to which mental anxiety drives people.

The final Mæstoso studio album, 2007's *caterwauling*, contains a couple more songs dealing with depression and psychiatric drugs. The first, 'Quicksand', is an entirely metaphorical composition describing the tenuous nature of the grasp on sanity for people with such illnesses. Inexorably disappearing into quicksand is the first metaphor, this is then followed by others depicting a struggle to float in the deep end of a pool and, finally, balancing on a tightrope. In each case, he is hoping for some help to save him but the final lyric destroys that hope.

Finally, 'pills' provides a sobering and chilling reminder of the fact that people who suffer from depression consider suicide as a realistic option. Ostensibly a Pythonesque piece typical of Wolstenholme's wacky sense of humour, 'pills' is composed as a pastiche on a musical, featuring a sketch in a psychiatrist's consulting room before the music opens up. When it does, what Wolstenholme has to say through the lyrics, in the persona of the psychiatrist, must make all those who have been afflicted by mental illness wince:

> My friend, I recommend something completely new:
> think Freude, not paranoid, uh?,
> and we're certain to pull you through!

"Something completely new"—dreaded words to sufferers. Worse is to follow:

> Take one, take two
> and I'm sure a cure you'll find!
> . . . but, if not, just take the lot
> and your troubles will be behind you!

The satire in this excerpt indicates a degree of scepticism about the effectiveness of psychiatric drugs, as well as reinforcing lyrically that Wolstenholme, in common with many suffering from depression, had himself soberly contemplated the option of suicide.

Sadly, this section must end by recording that Wolstenholme did lose his battle with his inner demons, committing suicide in December 2010. He is surely one of the most under-rated English musicians of his generation. His musical and human legacy will be fondly remembered by all those who were lucky enough to be touched by his aura. May he find peace in his next life.

Songs alluding to depression and mental anxiety are common. What is rarer are ones in which psychiatric drugs are covered, perhaps reflecting the fact that their usage was still accelerating through the period when most of these songwriters were active.

At this stage of our social history, as we approach the 'Spirituality' chapter, George Harrison starts to take a prominent role in proceedings. Introducing him this early might perhaps seem premature but his 'Beware of Darkness' is relevant to some of the issues raised in this section.[8] Most obvious is the metaphorical use of darkness as depression which Harrison urges listeners to watch out for, especially in the depths of night when it can bring deep despair. He believes that being trapped by feelings of hopelessness is not our purpose

---

8. *All Things Must Pass*, 1970. "Darkness" is often used by Fifties Children to express depression.

in this life and alludes to what we should be striving for when he then warns us to beware of Maya. "Maya" has many meanings but in Hinduism, and in this particular song, it refers to the illusion of reality. Essentially, then, Harrison is inferring that our purpose in this life is to meditate and so begin to understand that illusion. In so doing, we can start to comprehend our true place in the universe. If you seek out the depth of meaning behind Harrison's specific religious imagery, then what you will understand is that the mental battle that an individual needs to go through to understand the duality that Maya represents is not hugely different to that mental battle of the psyche that Lees also alludes to in his own songwriting, although he uses Christian-derived duality imagery. Our social history will draw another comparison between Harrison's 'Beware of Darkness' and Lees in the 'Spirituality' chapter.

More straightforward is Roger Waters' writing for Pink Floyd's *The Final Cut* [1983], which deals conceptually with the disillusionment of the post-Second World War hope. It is a bleak Cold War-period concept album, nevertheless absorbing, and provides a couple of examples for our social history: 'Paranoid Eyes' and the title track itself. 'Paranoid Eyes' could also have been included in the section on alcohol, as its protagonist resorts to drink in order to combat his own mental demons. Knowing the social stigma attached to mental illness and depression, this sufferer manages to put on a show of bravado to hoodwink his friends and acquaintances, and nips over the road to the pub, where he overplays the mirth and jollity card. In essence, alcohol is the panacea for his illness. Accordingly, Waters feels tempted to include three alcohol-related wordplay nuances in the final verse. First, he uses the word "haze" as an aid to the idea that the victim is spending all his time in pubs, drinking his life away—remember that pubs were smoky places back in 1983; second, he uses the popular expression "pie in the sky" as an allusion to the common pub meal; and finally, he describes the victim's eyes as "brown and mild"—these are, of course, types of ale.

'The Final Cut' carries an even bleaker message, as depression and paranoia have taken hold of the protagonist. He wonders if he would still be loved if it was obvious he was suffering mentally. He is barely struggling through life. The wordplay in this song is the "final cut" itself: an attempt at suicide by slitting his wrist . . . which failed because he heard the phone ringing and lost his nerve. Lyrically, it is a harrowing song.

The theme of sleeplessness is also covered by contemporaneous songwriters. Appearing on the Kinks' 1966 album *Face to Face*, 'Too Much On My Mind' by Ray Davies—well, how could we omit one of the foremost English sociological songwriters from our history, after all?—is probably the first such example. It is a straightforward song—and almost certainly autobiographical—describing how the rattling, unstoppable thoughts inside the protagonist's mind are disrupting his sanity and stopping him from sleeping.

There are many modern rock songs that deal with psychiatric drugs. An example is 'Paroxetine—20mg' from the Tangent's album *Down and Out in Paris and London* (2009).[9] We have already met its songwriter Andy Tillison in our social history. Like many people, Tillison has battled with mental anxiety and deals with the drug issue directly in the song. Tillison describes the depression caused by a feeling of helpless detachment from our modern high-speed world and the inability of doctors and psychiatrists to help him, together with the numbing effect of the Paroxetine they prescribe: it dulls his mind to the point that he no longer feels himself. This illustrates one of the downsides of taking these drugs: they may help the anxiety, but by numbing the senses to the extent that the user no longer knows himself.

Not knowing oneself, this is indeed the hub of the problem with drugs, whether they are recreational, alcohol or prescribed. There are undoubted benefits to all, as there are dangers, and not just from abuse and addiction. When under the influence, one does not really know oneself. How much is me and how much is the drug? How do I get off?

Can there be many Fifties Children that have avoided the pitfalls in all of these mind-affecting substances? Many will surely have avoided recreational drugs, but alcohol and psychiatric drugs as well? There cannot have been many and, as all of these substances affect the mind and body, the distinctions between them are, to some degree, arbitrary. Clearly, some Fifties Children who have been trapped by their lure, like Lees, have subsequently managed to extricate themselves and have benefited from the inner strength needed to win that battle. Others have succumbed to the pitfalls of drugs, including many who will have dabbled innocently and inoffensively for years, a little here and there, before suddenly finding or, perhaps more to the point not realising, as Wolstenholme points out, that one fix is no longer enough. Once addiction has caught hold, it is a long climb out of the pit.

When thinking about drugs in a societal context, two things are certain: the Fifties Child was not the first to have to deal with mental anxiety or with drugs and he will certainly not be the last; and, whether legal or otherwise, drugs and their use—recreational, alcohol, psychiatric—are here to stay, both as a panacea to those who are seeking respite from the world, as well as to those who just want a good night out. Society, as well as each of us individually, has to accept that and determine the best way to deal with the fact. Ostracising and criminalising users may not be the most efficient way. As for psychiatric drugs, there are certainly many people who need treatment for their mental

9. Paroxetine is an antidepressant drug.

illnesses. One can only hope that medical knowledge advances sufficiently to allow better understanding, targeting, dosage control and monitoring.

Whilst the Fifties Child was not the first to have to wage this time-honoured battle for the mind, his access to these various mind-altering substances was almost certainly greater than in previous generations. Another significant factor affecting the Fifties Child's battle for the mind was that he was unshackled from the strictures of ritualistic Christianity and introduced to the teaching of many other religions from across the world. This development was significant, in that it allowed individuals greater confidence and freedom to develop their own spirituality at a pace that suited them. We have already seen how spiritual strength helped Lees and, by contrast, how Wolstenholme eventually succumbed in the battle for the mind. Whether or not spiritual life provides the only avenue for successfully defeating the evil part of the psyche is a subject beyond the remit of this book, but what must already be clear from our social history is that it does provide at least one of the important avenues.

Barclay James Harvest's songwriters' experiences on this spiritual journey are sufficiently diverse to suggest that they might be generally representative of Fifties Children. The spiritual aspect of each of their life's journeys, as represented through song, was significant, and merits close discussion as we approach the culmination of our social history.

18

Spirituality

Choosing a title for this key chapter has been troublesome. "Religion" does not quite capture the essence of what many of Barclay James Harvest's songs lead one into, as the word implies a formality that does not quite fit the "spirituality" prevalent in a significant number of them.[1] True, a couple of these songs appear to vouch a strict Christianity but, when one places them in the context of the overall canon, it is clear that "spirituality" is a better title.

In a sense, choosing spirituality over religion reaffirms the Fifties Child's rejection of authority. The rituals and unquestioning allegiance demanded by organised religion were rejected by the Fifties Child's generation, who—despite having been given a formal Christian education—viewed religion and its leaders as complicit in the shocking events of the first half of the twentieth century. *God*, King and Country.

Almost certainly because of its rejection by the Fifties Child, religion and rock music are not a comfortable combination. Many fans find religious lyrics sanctimonious and offputting. This dichotomy between the two—organised religion and spirituality—is analogous to that between enslavement to authority and freedom. Freedom, that cherished hope of the Fifties Child!

One can quickly demonstrate the distinction further within the rock world itself by reference to George Harrison, who was at the vanguard of the spiritual rock song's genesis and is indisputably one of the greatest spiritual songwriters of the Fifties Child generation. Discussing the inspiration for his hit song 'My Sweet Lord' [*All Things Must Pass*, 1970] in his autobiography, he says:

I thought a lot about whether to do 'My Sweet Lord' or not, because I would be

---

1. The New Oxford Dictionary defines "spiritual" as: *of, relating to, or affecting the human spirit or soul as opposed to material or physical things.*

committing myself publicly and I anticipated that a lot of people might get weird about it. Many people fear the words "Lord" and "God"—makes them angry for some strange reason.

Now, 'My Sweet Lord' was not the first spiritual song that Harrison had written, nor even the first song about "Lord" or "God", but previously—such as on 'Long Long Long' [*The Beatles (White)*, 1968], which sounds like a standard rock "love song" but in which Harrison is actually singing about his love for "God"—the subject was carefully shrouded.

So, "spirituality" it is!

The spirituality pervading Barclay James Harvest's songwriting is one of the strongest elements which can explain how these individuals managed to work together for so long. The band had been together as a foursome for more than ten years when Wolstenholme departed in 1979—this longevity was extremely unusual for a rock band at the time. Holroyd and Lees, despite any differences they might have had, then worked together for nearly twenty more years. Of course there will have been disagreements—there are in any marriage—but there must have been elements about their common outlook that kept them going through all that time—and not just the Barclay James Harvest brand name and the need to make a living. If you really can't stand the person next to you, then you move on. A certain shared spirituality, despite differences in the detail of its expression, was surely one of the unifying elements.

In our modern age, it has become customary to label everything, including music types, and Christian rock has emerged as a distinct genre that draws its own fans, whilst discouraging many others. Barclay James Harvest were not a Christian rock band but their most popular song, 'Hymn', is undoubtedly a Christian song. Despite its popularity, its explicit Christianity alienates some hardcore fans whilst simultaneously—and for the same reason—attracting many others. Nevertheless, even their two most overtly Christian songs are fundamentally spiritual messages rather than ritualistic preaching. Therefore it makes sense, within our social history, to consider Barclay James Harvest's spiritual songs together with the Christian ones within the following section.

The Spiritual Journey

In the Fifties, Great Britain was a Christian country. It still is, but the numbers paying more than lip service to Christianity, such as by adherence to formal churchgoing, has waned significantly in the ensuing decades. Other factors changing the demographic nature of religion have been immigration and "world-shrinkage", which has allowed for greater ease in the dissemination of new ideas and cultures. There is now less societal respect for organised Christianity than at any time since the Fifties.

Nevertheless, a Fifties Child would undoubtedly have been formally educated in the Christian tradition; a tradition that would have endured strongly at least into their teenage years. Hence it is perhaps not surprising that when writing about spiritual matters, it is mostly Christian imagery that often comes to the fore in Barclay James Harvest's songwriting, even if the songwriters are not seen to formally follow a particular religion or to be churchgoers.

There is less of a contradiction here than might immediately seem to be the case. Imagine, for instance, a self-proclaimed Christian who is active in sectarian violence. Is such an individual really a Christian, really a spiritual person? All Christian religions, indeed many religions, as well as non-godhead "ways of life" such as Buddhism, systematically preach a system based on love—including for one's own enemies—compassion and non-violence. No, calling oneself a Christian or even observance of that church's rituals do not automatically make someone a Christian, certainly not in the spiritual sense. Conversely, one can be a deeply spiritual person without formally observing the tenets of a particular religion. 'Summer Soldier' exemplifies this distinction perfectly. Lees was not a formal churchgoer at the time that it was written, yet it is a deeply spiritual song. In fact, one could argue that 'Summer Soldier's spirituality is purer and deeper than that contained within 'Hymn's overt Christianity. And yet, 'Summer Soldier' has never been exposed to the same sort of criticism as 'Hymn'. Why? Because Jesus is not mentioned? God is mentioned briefly, but with such a brief mention God can mean many things to different people; Jesus, on the other hand, is a concrete proposition and plays a leading role within 'Hymn'. This is the George Harrison conundrum: how to mention Jesus in a song such as 'Hymn' without being considered to be preaching? Anathema to the Fifties Child!

As the twentieth century wore on, people tended to abandon formal religion, which is not to say that they became less loving or compassionate. People have not become less spiritual, they have simply tended to abandon formal worship. Barclay James Harvest's songwriting reflects that trend in society for a Fifties Child, which was the move away from formalised religion to life systems based less on formal worship. Societally, this trend is manifested in different ways, such as in religious education and church attendance.

Immediately post-war, religious teaching and worship in schools, whilst non-denominational unless in a specific church school, was based on the Christian Bible. Bible teaching went into decline in the Sixties and by the Seventies humanism and world religions began to be taught. By the late Eighties religious teaching in non-denominational schools no longer assumed or sought to impose a religious system on pupils. In 1988, the Education

Reform Act required that religious teaching should cover the principal faiths represented in British society, whilst noting that the majority were Christian based. The Nineties saw a shift into an exploratory approach, seeking to enable children to develop an understanding of their own inner life and spirituality.

Christian church attendance figures, in particular those of the Church of England and Roman Catholics, have dropped steadily from the Fifties until recent times, leading some researchers to suggest that faiths such as Islam and Hinduism will soon have more formal worshippers in Britain than Christianity. Our next king may well become "Defender of Faith" rather than "Defender of *the* Faith", which is how that aspect of Queen Elizabeth II's formal role is presently defined.

Another indication of the diversification in religious demographics is that, since 2001, the state census has begun to monitor the population's religious beliefs.[2] The top three in 2001 were:

Christian	37,046,500
Muslim	1,546,626
Hindu	552,421

About eight million people gave answers that either indicated no religion or atheism. These figures are quite startling compared with the research prediction on formal worship: clearly, the only explanation is that many people calling themselves Christian do not attend church services.

Having received a Christian Bible-based religious education, the Fifties Child has been subjected to various other influences during his life. One of the most significant for our songwriters, as well as for other fans of popular music, will have been the Beatles' well publicised trips to India in the Sixties to meet with Maharishi Mahesh Yogi, and Harrison's subsequent conversion to Hinduism. It is worth repeating that, in this respect, the Fifties Child is unique: his was the first generation to have been exposed, in its formative years, to the idea that there were satisfactory, non-Christian spiritual life paths.

The resulting decline in formal Christianity was reflected within Barclay James Harvest, with Lees being the one who most obviously allowed his

2. Also indicative of the decline in religious observance is the fact that, due to a concerted internet campaign, the fourth highest religion in the UK was voted as being "Jedi Knights". Such ribaldry would have been blasphemous in the Fifties. The 2011 census data pertaining to this issue has not yet been released: pre-census surveys carried out in 2011 indicate there is no return to formal Christian observance.

denominational belief to be reflected in his songwriting. This profligacy may have led to some disquiet within the band, as reflected in Holroyd's comments to a radio interviewer at the time of the release of 'He Said Love' in 1986: "John writes all of those: he wrote 'Hymn' and he wrote 'He Said Love'. It's not necessarily the way that the rest of the band feel. It's not something that I would like to get into." This is not to say that Holroyd is not a spiritual person—the fact that his songwriting is replete with compassion would suggest otherwise—simply that he might choose to express it less explicitly. Having said this, of Barclay James Harvest's Christian songs, his 'Sweet Jesus', introduced in the previous chapter 'The Battle for the Mind', actually comes across as a perfect Christian prayer:

> Sunday morning comes, I'm feeling kind of down:
> I can't see back to where it all began,
> and I know you'd help me if you only could:
> I don't know why or where or who I am.
> Oh sweet Jesus hear me cry:
> let me see a clearing sky!
>   . . .
> so take the shadow from my eyes.

Again, as pointed out earlier, whether 'Sweet Jesus' is autobiographical or not does not affect its sociological value, as it is generically representative of a Fifties Child praying to Christ.

Interestingly, and reinforcing the stresses on formal Christianity as a way of life, Holroyd's very next song to feature on *Time Honoured Ghosts* is the equally atmospheric 'Jonathan', another song that we have already met in our social history. The gull, Jonathan, breaks free of his restrictive upbringing by taking delight in the joy of acrobatic flight, finding freedom of thought and expression far away from his flock. The message—of book, film and song— is that one should not be afraid to break free of the strictures of the past in order to progress on one's own spiritual journey. 'Jonathan' exemplifies the thinking that was assisting the move away from formalised religion. On *Time Honoured Ghosts*, its juxtaposition with 'Sweet Jesus' and Wolstenholme's 'Beyond the Grave'—which immediately follows it and categorically states that our spirits live on after our death—may be accidental but is nevertheless thought-provoking and revealing of the societal spiritual issues of the day.

Included in this section are no less than *sixteen* of Lees' songs, four of which are Christian—although admittedly 'Sperratus' and 'Doctor Doctor' require some interpretation—and twelve whose spirituality is not denominationally focused. This is a significant number by any measure pertaining to contemporaneous rock musicians and gives a good insight into the course that a Fifties Child's spiritual life might take. Generally, what we know factually is as follows: Lees was formally educated as a Christian and attended church in his youth. That attendance then lapsed as he grew into adolescence, although he never lost his faith in prayer, and he started attending a Christian church again in the Eighties after his children had been born. Those are the dry facts—let us see if his songs, most of which we have already discussed in connection with other topics, reveal more of interest. We shall start with the Christian songs.

As we have already seen in the 'Drugs' chapter, 'Hymn' is implicitly about the dangers of drug abuse, warning that it is not through their use that one reaches ultimate satisfaction. However, without that foreknowledge the song's Christian stance becomes even stronger, through being the only explicit theme. Irrespective of the drug issue in the song, the Christian message is strong and does dominate, with aspects of the Gospel story being retold.

However, this was not always the case: the lyrics for the 1971 demo version differ markedly in this respect and this difference therefore provides a clue as to how Lees' spiritual development was progressing. In the demo version, Lees continues the theme of the opening metaphor, making the link to drugs stronger than in the released version due to a wordplay on the word "grass". From a spiritual viewpoint, a reference to what you must do to commune with "your God" in the unreleased lyrics indicates that, at that time, Lees was thinking more generically about everyone's own individual spirituality. The "your" is missing from the final version and, coupled with the inclusion of the mini Gospel story, this hardens the specific Christian message. An inference that could be drawn from this is that in the intervening years Lees' spiritual journey had led him back in the direction of Christianity and he was now confident and joyful of the fact, to the extent that he was content to take the "Harrison risk" and sing about it. Lees has not spoken about his reasons for writing 'Hymn' in such a way, but Harrison did so about 'My Sweet Lord', and the interesting thing about what he had to say is that, in one's imagination, one can sense Lees' total empathy with his words: "Well, it was what I felt, and why should I be untrue to myself? I came to believe in the importance that if you feel something strong enough then you should say it."

'Hymn's ultimate, unequivocal message is a Christian one: it is through observing Christian tenets that one finds happiness. Lees uses the simile of Christ's ascension into heaven to signify that it is only through God that one can "fly". Lees pauses for a whole bar before the culmination of his drug-implicated—through the word "fly"—simile, giving the meaning more emphasis. The song's music supports this interpretation: building from acoustic guitars, other instruments are added and intensified, resulting in a subtle crescendo, and the song ends in a final solo keyboard chord climax. The effect is truly epiphanic.

We do not know whether 'Hymn' has saved lives in the same way that Harrison believed that 'My Sweet Lord' did, but one thing is sure: despite its detractors, there are many fans who find the song spiritually enhancing. Music is undoubtedly a societal force, part of which is a spiritual force—songs such as 'My Sweet Lord' and 'Hymn' have a significant influence on many of their listeners.

Before we move on to discuss the remainder of Barclay James Harvest's spiritual songs, it is worthwhile—given the high profile of recreational drugs culture in the life of the Fifties Child—to dwell a little longer on this synergy between Harrison and Lees. Harrison, as is well known, experimented with LSD during the Sixties, whilst still with the Beatles. Fortunately—and unlike other rock stars we have mentioned—his spiritual journey quickly took him to a place where he found true happiness, so he was clearly delighted to learn that 'My Sweet Lord' had the effect of saving some addicts from the perils of drugs. This experience of his, i.e. spirituality as an alternative to drugs, is very close to that which Lees is describing in 'Hymn' and so it should come as no surprise to learn that Harrison also committed it to song, coincidentally at around the same time as Lees wrote the demo to 'Hymn'. There is, however, one major difference between Harrison's 'Try Some, Buy Some' [*Living in the Material World*, 1973] and 'Hymn', which is that Harrison shrouds his meaning—the spiritual source of true happiness is not given Lees' explicitness. Nevertheless, his meaning is clear to anyone who knows about his drug experimentation and who listens attentively and openly; it is, undoubtedly, his 'Hymn'.

Lees' other explicitly Christian song, which we briefly mentioned earlier on in this discussion, 1986's 'He Said Love', is lyrically more straightforward than 'Hymn'. If Lees had developed the confidence to write 'Hymn' as an exultation of his Christian belief by 1977, then he had certainly not lost that confidence in the intervening nine years. In fact, as we shall see, other evidence suggests that his faith had strengthened. The song recalls several episodes from the Gospels, in a very orthodox retelling. It was Lees' way of thanking Jesus for seeing his prayers answered, as he explained to an interviewer: "'He Said Love' is a memorandum and a thank you because Jesus has helped me." Despite the obfuscation caused by the comparatively long verses retelling the Gospel, the song actually carries a similar message to 'Hymn', in that—effectively—Lees says that Jesus will change people's lives if only they will welcome Him into their psyche. Nevertheless, of greatest interest to us in 'He Said Love' are the lyrics that link most directly to many of Lees' other songs, demonstrating the driving force behind much of his writing. The chorus and its adaptation at the end of the song repeatedly accentuate the power of love—spiritual love—and "understanding"—empathy and compassion—as being the only things that will help people reach the ultimate goal of "happiness". This will not come as a surprise since it is a motto that shines brightly in much of his songwriting.

Interpretation is required to classify 'Sperratus' and 'Doctor Doctor' as Christian songs. 'Sperratus' is one of two songs that will be analysed in this section that takes its inspiration from Lees' rapport with the crowd at concerts, in particular those who showed their presence and support for the band by igniting lighters. Whilst that is the origin of its inspiration, the song itself is lyrically subtle and, contextualizing from Lees' spiritual oeuvre, it solicits an interpretation beyond the Lees-audience relationship.

The song's title is an anagram of "superstar", and this is also an allusion to Tim Rice and Andrew Lloyd Webber's 1970 album, later to become a hit musical and film, *Jesus Christ Superstar*. The concept for this adaptation of the Gospels was that it was the interaction between Jesus and his disciples that elevated Him to the status of "superstar" and it was this—the elevation to stardom—as much as his religious teaching, that led to his execution. Lees, in enmeshing these various ideas with his own exhortation of large crowds from the stage, writes a complex lyric that touches on deeply held beliefs. It is another song sung in the first person and, within the song's ambiguity, one of the personas is Christ himself. Here is the opening of the song:

> Look in my eyes:
> see the light of the universe!
> I'm man, born of God,
> not a clown in disguise.

Even if other aspects of my interpretation are unfounded, and the song is purely about Lees and his audience, then the line "I'm man, born of God" is sufficient to qualify this as a spiritual song, as the only interpretation would then be that Lees was saying that he was "born of God". This is a common belief of spiritual people, as well as—in the song's parallel Jesus–disciples theme—reflecting the specific Christian teaching that Jesus was the son of God, as well as being a man. In this parallel meaning, the lines "look in my eyes / see the light of the universe" are another indication that Christ is imbued with the essence of the universe. By implication of this parallel approach, Lees is suggesting that he and the rest of us of course, all have this essence within our psyche. This theme of the essence of the universe, i.e. God, being present in us all is continued in the second verse:

Look in my face:
see the light
of a thousand stars shine bright
in the night
as I step
from the stage.
Don't burn your hands
on my skin:
you can't touch what's deep within—
that's my soul,
reaching my final goal!

The beginning of this excerpt continues on from the opening verse. Individual words, as in that first verse, take on subtly different meanings in the parallel threads: for instance, "stage" is literal in the Lees–audience theme but is metaphorical in the Jesus–disciples, as well as possibly being an allusion to the *Jesus Christ Superstar* stage musical/film. One can push the interpretation (possibly unwisely!) into tenuous areas, such as nuances suggesting that the Jesus–disciples theme is based on the trial before Pilate in *Jesus Christ Superstar*. In the film, the trial scene is held in an arena, with Jesus standing on the stage; Pilate says that Jesus is mad, and calls Him a fool—Lees uses the expression "clown in disguise"—and Jesus' only riposte to all the accusations is that Pilate has no room for manoeuvre, that any power that he has comes from "far beyond", as if to say—in Lees' words—"you can't touch what's deep within / that's my soul / reaching my final goal!" Irrespective of the accuracy of that particular interpretation, the lines just quoted again cement the song as spiritual even in the—unlikely, to my mind—event that the song is purely about the Lees–audience interaction, because Lees is clearly saying that he has a soul.

Before we move on from 'Sperratus', it is worth spending a little time on some speculation concerning the song's title. Why not simply call the song 'Superstar'? After all, that word carries the punch in its chorus: "make them, make them, make you superstar!" Why go to the trouble of deriving and then titling the song with a meaningless anagram? Could it be that there is something special about the word "Sperratus" that caused Lees to choose it as the title? Possibly: if we treat the word phonetically, rather than as the anagram itself, then two intriguing avenues of thought reveal themselves. The first of these is the fact that, in Latin, "speratus" is the perfect passive participle of "spero", a word used in the Latin Mass to indicate hope in God. As the single word of the title, its translation might be "having been awaited", which does not jar contextually with the fact that one of the personas within the song's ambiguities is Christ. The second avenue of possibility reveals Paul Speratus, a German Catholic priest born in the fifteenth century, who became a devotee of the Protestant reformer Martin Luther. Speratus' name has lived on through the centuries by virtue of the fact that he wrote hymns, some of which were still being published in hymnals and music books that the Fifties Child would have access to. Speratus' most enduring hymn, 'Es ist das Heil uns kommen her', was one of three of his authorship that formed the *Achtliederbuch*, the first Lutheran hymnal,[3] which was the forerunner for all Protestant hymnals. The hymn has been translated into English both as 'Salvation unto us has come' and 'To us salvation now is come': the hymn espouses the Lutheran doctrine of salvation by faith alone, which has become a tenet of Protestant creeds. Now, let us remind ourselves of the strength of faith of the persona in 'Sperratus':

> you can't touch what's deep within—
> that's my soul,
> reaching my final goal!

Could it be that Lees, who had a Protestant upbringing and whose most celebrated song is 'Hymn', chose to honour Speratus, one of the two forefathers of hymn-writers, by naming 'Sperratus' after him, or is this similarity in the song's title just a zany coincidence? Either way, quite remarkable!

'Doctor Doctor' is the final song in which Christianity is explicit. I say explicit, but it does require the interpretation that I provide in the chapter 'The Battle for the Mind', one that I feel secure in. Essentially, in 'Doctor Doctor' Lees aspires to a "pure love and devotion" similar to that of Jesus' mother, Mary. Our confidence in this interpretation stems from contextualisation from the other spiritual songs as well as from our knowledge of the fact that Lees prayed his way out of depression—'Doctor Doctor' deals with his fight against it.

Prior to discussing Lees' remaining spiritual songs, it is worth recapping briefly the evidence which we already have which shows how Lees simplified for himself the internal mental and emotional battle for man's psyche (or soul, or spirit) and how he himself succeeded in the battle against his internal demons. This is important because, having fought and won that internal

---

3. The *Achtliederbuch* (literally "Eight Song Book") was first published in 1524 and was immediately popular. Of the other hymns, four were written by Luther himself and the remaining one has been attributed to Justus Jonas, a priest who similarly became a follower of Lutheranism.

battle, he emerged stronger spiritually and with a renewed formal Christian observance. This must be reflective of the experience of many Fifties Children who, having strayed, found their way back to the flock.

The (approximate) chronology of Lees' spiritual battle diary in song—to which you, dear reader, will be able to add to once you have absorbed the remainder of this chapter—with interview progress milestones is as follows:

1970	Mother Dear	*lady in white—love* *figure in black—death*
1972	Summer Soldier	*there's a man by your side with a knife and a gun in each hand—you're one and the same—it's time to stop and decide: is it love or hate?*
1972	Summer Soldier	*summer soldier—fire in hate* *angel bright—cause is peace*
1974	For No One	*lay down your thoughts of being no one, concentrate on what you ought to be*
1974	For No One	*everyone's a no one till he wants to make a stand*
1977	Interview (Hymn)	Lees has been taking psychiatric drugs to combat anxiety
1977	Hymn	Following God is the only way to reach the freedom and happiness that some people think that recreational drugs can provide
1981	Doctor Doctor	*a natural panacea like a cure for every fear: it's some of her sweet love mixed up with her young blood, true love and devotion.*
1984	For Your Love	*I pray that someday we'll all have love of our own. In the long, lonely night, I'll hold to the fire that's burning so bright.*
1987	Interview (He Said Love)	. . . I was going through a crisis in my life. The only thing I could think of was praying and my prayers have always been answered in a miraculous sort of way.

1997	Mr E	*Mr E—my secret lives in your deceit . . . the colours lift you up, I push you down; (the good part of the psyche)—my promise is a window to the bottom of your soul.*
2006	Interview	I wouldn't [now] go down the route of taking prescribed drugs to keep me doing the job. If I'd have been strong enough mentally, I would've overcome that.

The stark contrasts in the metaphors of the early writing represent the internal battle he himself must have been having: the struggle between the "good" and the "evil" parts of the psyche, which Lees sees as being present in us all. Whether we are conscious of it or not, we are constantly fighting this battle. If the evil side is winning then we stray towards conflict, drugs and other easy pleasures—sex, alcohol, gambling—with no depth of feeling. As the good side gains the ascendancy, we can resist the peer pressure that is leading us to fight on the streets for "ideals aged and past their time", we can resist the drugs and focus on what we "ought to be". Lees would appear to have won this internal battle through the power of what he calls prayer. You and I might call it something different: meditation, perhaps. Essentially, it does not matter what you call it, the technique has worked but, because of his upbringing as a Fifties Child, these are the words that Lees has used to rationalise it and the vehicle for his spiritual security has become Christianity.

The subject of prayer returns us to 'For Your Love', neatly allowing us to firm up on the extract used in the chronology above. Lees himself has confirmed that 'For Your Love' was inspired by the fans who waved lighters and sparklers at the end of live shows. However, like 'Sperratus', this is another song inspired by Lees' relationship with his audience that contains more depth than a casual listener might gleam. Let us start with Lees' own description:

'For Your Love' is about the kids who hold up lighters at the end of our concerts. When I used to get depressed and feel nobody cared, I used to think of those kids who must really like the music. In the darkest moments of everyone's life, if they could just hold a flame up and everyone else did it too, it might force all the black and dark to go away.

This "flame" has a metaphorical meaning, as well as the literal one which inspired the song and becomes the "flame of love" within the song. The fans' love of his music was clearly a factor that helped Lees relieve his mental anxiety and depression: if that love, that energy, could be kindled in all our psyches and directed to help all people suffering similar problems then the world would be a happier, peaceful place. Sounds good, but what makes 'For Your Love' a spiritual song? Well, the fact that, suffering anxiety in the sleepless night, Lees *prays* that such love will fill the world, and he uses the force of that love to help him through his own dark spell:

> I have hope; I pray
> that someday we'll all
> have love of our own.
> In the long lonely night
> I'll hold to the fire
> that's burning so bright.

We are now familiar enough with Lees' songwriting to know that "pray" is meant literally. Effectively, the whole song is a prayer: a prayer for peace in the world. Lees' Christmas 1983 message to the fans follows the theme of 'For Your Love':

> Light up the flame of love,
> whenever fear and darkness surround you.
> For only, with all our flames
> joined together in one great light
> can we hold back the cold night
> and bring peace to all mankind.

This is the hope of the Fifties Child rekindled, the hope that Lees prays will be realised, when each person defeats the bad part of his psyche, the "circles of hate" are broken and mankind can live harmoniously in peace. This is Lees' motto, what his soul yearns for, and the message you find repeated in different guises in many of his songs. 'For Your Love' is often called a torch song. It is indeed that, as Lees expresses that message through song, by asking everyone to help him fulfil his life's dream by rekindling the love of the Fifties Child:

> We're not alone tonight,
> so help me turn the tide:
> light up the flame of love
> and let it shine!
> Let it shine!
> Let it shine!

I want a world without starvation, without wars and without destruction of the environment, and a world in which people get on well with each other.[4]

And if I may be allowed another diversion into tenuous interpretation, then I would point out the resonance between the "flame of love" image and the ritual of many Christians of lighting a candle in church as an offering of love and evocation of the symbol of the Light of Christ,[5] when making a special prayer.

For me, 'For Your Love' is clearly a spiritual song that describes an aspect of Lees' struggle and victory over mental anxiety and depression, as well as expressing his hope for the peace of mankind. One can feel the depth of his supplication and *force of emotion* conveyed through the powerful vocal and musical performance. It is a song straight from the soul!

Lees' hope for mankind—the hope of the Fifties Child—had been the subject of the previous year's 'Fifties Child', the song that inspires the title of this book. The song is perhaps the most surprising inclusion in this section. It does, however, sound to me very much like another *prayer*. Here is the opening:

> Love was a lesson we tried to learn:
> there were no exams to pass or fail,
> only heartbreaks.
> Renew our faith!

"Renew our *faith*", what's that about? We continue:

> Life was a lesson we've tried to learn:
> there were no tests to pass, no licence to gain;
> only win or lose.
> Renew our faith!
> Renew our faith, let us see
> Fifties child was right to believe
> peace and love were our needs;
> the need to be free!

The "renew our faith" can be one of two things: an exhortation to everyone— "come on everyone, shall we all renew that belief we had?"—or it can be a

---

4. This is a statement that Lees made in an interview for *Hurricane* magazine in 1987; it demonstrates the desire that drives songs such as 'For Your Love'.

5. "I am the Light of the world. Whoever follows me will never walk in darkness, but will have the light of life." (John c.8, v.12)

prayer from someone in his thirties who has been through some bad times and wants his old, perhaps idealistic, values to reassert themselves in his (and everyone else's) psyche(s). I favour the latter interpretation, particularly when you place the song in the context of its timing with respect to Lees' spiritual journey. Lees is not careless with his words and the choice of *faith* has religious connotations. He is praying, and when he says "let us see", the meaning of *let* is "allow us". So, paraphrasing the prayer: "Allow us to see that we were right and reaffirm these values in our psyche." Incidentally, it does not now take a great leap to realise that the "love" referred to in the opening verse is not a sexual love but, indeed, the same sort of love that is the aim of 'For Your Love'. This is the love and peace between mankind: the "heartbreaks" refer to the Fifties Child's disillusionment as, growing older, the cold reality of the world began to oppress his psyche.

'Fifties Child' represents the crux, the turning point, of the Fifties Child's life. Full of hope and anticipation of a peaceful world during his teens, his hopes take a pounding from the late Sixties—Northern Ireland, Vietnam, the Bomb, racial hatred, famine—and our Child's psyche wilts under the barrage of life's thorny twists. Now, in his fourth decade, the Child's emberish hopes could fade forever. He is at the crossroads of life. Having fought his demons valiantly through his twenties, this particular Fifties Child—Lees—takes all that is wonderful in the world, in nature, in his fellow men and he finds his faith, and he exults! Renew our faith! I was right! Peace and love! Let that always be the Fifties Child's motto.

In that respect, Lees' 'Taking Some Time On', the first track on the band's first album, deserves a mention in our social history, not as a spiritual song but because, now that we have sufficient knowledge to place it into perspective, it introduces a number of concepts that are vital to his spiritual development. Even now, at the very beginning of the Seventies, Lees is already yearning for a return to the values of the Fifties Child's dream, expressed in 'Taking Some Time On' as a return to the value of freedom. The song also drops a hint of the ravages of the mind that troubled him and which we have been discussing since the previous chapter. Finally, Lees uses imagery related to nature, which is key to his spirituality, an aspect which we shall discuss presently.

So . . . let us recap: love and understanding are the goal of life; I pray that some day we'll all have love of our own; peace and love are our needs . . . which brings us seamlessly to another spiritual song *par excellence*, 'In Memory of the Martyrs'. A long way back in our social history, in the chapter on Berlin, I made the assertion—which you may have thought a little implausible at the time—that spirituality was at the core of the song, and I have teased you with it since. Enough—it is appropriate to address the issue now.

'In Memory of the Martyrs' is an example of holistic spirituality. The inspiration for the song may have been the despair of the people of East Berlin and those who died trying to cross its Wall, but Lees' approach to the topic is spiritual and, in that sense, notably different from Holroyd's, who also dealt with the same theme in a number of songs. There is no sense of spirituality—other than compassion perhaps—in Holroyd's approach, which was, effectively, to encourage the people to have hope in the power of their unified belief as a catalyst for political change. Lees approaches the issue from a purely spiritual angle. Consider the song's opening:

> Life is like a tall ship
> drifting gently from the shore;
> time is like a fair wind
> with a lifetime to explore.

This is a metaphor for life. The opening couplet represents a child's birth, and the following one describes how our lives might have to steer this way and that at the mercy of destiny's wind, tacking and jibing in order to make progress, sometimes only with great difficulty, sometimes having to heave to, sometimes with a favourable wind driving us along. Crucially, this strong opening is immediately followed by:

> The beauty that surrounds you
> was meant to be adored;
> the problems that surround you
> were meant to be ignored.
> We are love, we are, we are love.
> We are love, we are, we are love.

We are love. We are. We are love. Repeated and repeated throughout the remainder of the song. Clearly—because they open the song!—these metaphors, together with their unequivocal message about beauty and problems, occur before Lees actually develops the metaphors that deal with the subject that is normally ascribed to this song, namely the martyrs that died trying to escape across the Berlin Wall. This actually makes Lees' prime message abundantly clear: focus on the spiritual, accentuate the beauty of the (spiritual) natural world within your psyche, and the rest will follow naturally. No matter what trials life throws at you, there is beauty and love to be found. Make compassion your life's work. The fair wind of time will take its course. Accentuate "love" in your life. This is as deep a spiritual message—and very different to Holroyd's approach to the subject of Berlin—as you will find anywhere in popular music.

It is a message that has a strong thematic resonance in 'Sideshow'—which, incidentally, I am not classifying as a spiritual song—as Lees berates the TV news companies for continually accentuating the wrong message. They show us death, destruction and the evil ways of man—mankind's "sideshow"—when they should be concentrating on showing all of the peace, love and compassion that is present in the world, and which represents the life worth celebrating, worth shouting about, worth transmitting on TV. To do so would be to inspire such love in others, and help the entire world. In fact, precisely the same theme had already manifested itself in 'For No One':

> Please lay down your thoughts of being no one:
> concentrate on what you ought to be!
> . . .
> God alone knows how we will survive!

The subject matter of 'For No One' was different, hence the different words, but the underlying message is essentially identical: sort yourselves out mentally, get the good side of your psyche to triumph and God (or nature, or destiny) will look after the rest.

It is clear from his songs that Lees derived much energy for his spiritual force from nature. We have just read about the "beauty that surrounds you [that] was meant to be adored" and another example worth recalling from further back in our social history is 'Knoydart', in which Lees describes how the beauty of the Scottish Highlands powers his spiritual psyche. The final verse of 'Paraiso dos Cavalos' also gives that sense of spiritual recharging, this time from communing with horses on Algarvian beaches. 'Sperratus', too, imparts the notion that we are intrinsically part of nature: "Look in my eyes: see the light of the universe. I'm man, born of God."

Yet another in this important series, one which we have not yet met in our social history, is 'Hymn for the Children'. Lees' assertion in the song is that the optimal way to live is written all around us—nature shows us the way, if we would only stop and look. The treatment of this aspect in 'Hymn for the Children' is quite modern, approaching holistic teachings, demonstrating how far the progression from a strict Christian upbringing has been for a Fifties Child:

> Life is a bird in the sky,
> life is the breeze blowing by.
> . . .
> Life is the rain from on high,
> life is the sun in the sky.

Time picked the words,
time picked the songs.
We were the choir
but we sang them wrong!

The message is wrapped up in another of Lees' perennial messages—that of
equality between all human beings; the inference in this case being that if we
manage to live all of our lives by honouring that equality then inevitably this
will result in less harm to children. The treatment of equality in 'Hymn for
the Children' is enshrined in the belief that our spirits are inextricably linked
with nature—we are all part of one whole nature, we are all *one*:

Their spirits with the rain
that feeds the wheat and weeds the same,
your love and mine.
The sun their spirits light
that feels and warms both black and white,
your love and mine.
. . .
Their spirits bless the cruel,
the intellectual, the fool,
your love and mine.

Many fans of the band may have wondered at the meaning of the oft-repeated line "your love and mine" within the song. That meaning should now have
become clear given the contextualisation from this very significant run of
songs that we have just been discussing, going all the way back to 'He Said
Love'. The "love" that Lees is referring to is that love that is the strength of
the good part of the psyche, that love that can lead to the defeat of one's inner
demons, that "flame of love" that if we all foster and hold up will help
mankind live peacefully. What Lees is saying is that the food for that love, the
energy for that love, is contained in nature all around us—and each and every
one of us can tap into it to enhance our own spirit.

The systematic message is that we are one, and we are one with the universe, with nature. "Look in my eyes, see the light of the universe", that is a
spiritual message that transcends religious denominational borders, and it is a
truly momentous shift from the Fifties Child's orthodox religious education.

This spiritual shift towards drawing strength from the natural world should
really not be surprising as it is present in the most obvious way—though I
suspect we often gleam over its significance—in religious education. Where
does Jesus go to pray to enhance his own spiritual strength? To the desert. To

the Garden of Gethsemane. Where does Moses, another ascetic, go? To Mount Sinai. This the Fifties Child will have learnt at school. Since then he may have discovered for himself that Muhammad retreated to a cave in the mountains and that Buddha abandoned his family to seek spiritual truth by meditating in the forest. Beyond the glibness of my words, there is a significant synergy of approach, suggesting that to enhance one's spiritual strength one needs to detach from worldly concerns and commune with nature.

What chance, then, for humanity's spirituality as the world population approaches nine billion? Retreats and open churches may be part of the answer but there is still a real challenge for organised religion, which urgently needs to find leaders with spiritual power sufficient to break the "circle of hate" that is denominational fundamentalism, and unify mankind.

'Blow Me Down' [1983], another song that we are meeting for the first time, completes our review of the spiritual link between nature and the psyche. Lyrically, this is an intriguing song in that Lees repeats common metaphors that he has used previously and, given the contextualisation from all of the other songs that we are now familiar with, they unlock the song's meaning. The song is again written from the perspective of the first person, and I think that by now we can be certain that the song is autobiographical. In the first verse, Lees observes that some people use drugs to "fly"—the metaphor is used in an analogous way to its usage in 'Hymn'—whereas others struggle through life's journey without the use of mind-altering substances. Then, in the second verse, he describes a meeting with a man whose characteristics are very similar to that of the Christ persona in 'Sperratus': this is clearly a manifestation of the emergence of the good, spiritual side of Lees' own psyche because the "man" speaks to him in words that are his own. Finally, his spiritual force renewed, the third verse describes how he can "fly" or "walk" through life at will even if depression comes (the metaphor used for this is the grey sky). Essentially, 'Blow Me Down' is a brief metaphorical description of Lees' spiritual life journey, starting off when he is struggling through life without drugs, then the transformation caused by the emergence of his spiritual force and, finally, the strength that his spirit has given him to withstand and enjoy life.

There is also an element of this confident spiritual strength about Holroyd's late-period 'Revolution Day'. This song needs interpretation, so this makes the analysis riskier as there are fewer of his songs to contextualise from. Nevertheless, Holroyd's writing is sufficiently consistent on this theme to venture an explanation. The difficulty arriving at a satisfactory meaning to 'Revolution Day' arises because of the lines "we don't want to change the world / just looking to survive." Perhaps because of the ill feeling between

Holroyd and Lees which surrounded the band's break-up, together with their different writing styles, many fans interpret this as a reference to Lees' greater tendency to write clear sociological songs, with Holroyd's response as something like "never mind all that protest in your songs, we really just want to make some money from this venture". This then sits in apparent contradiction against the clarion call of "waiting for the revolution day" and other similar lyrics. In fact, a close examination reveals that 'Revolution Day' is not about the band at all. The trick to overcoming the barrier of that contradiction and so understanding the song comes through divining what Holroyd's theme really is, and for that we need some contextualisation. Within the song, the key lyrics that demonstrate the strength of spirit that I referred to earlier are:

> Our voices will be heard:
> we'll stand up for our rights.
> Our spirit will awake
> and something deep inside
> will help us find the way.
>   . . .
> Hold on to your beliefs:
> don't think about what people say.
> Got to be the light to show the way.

Remember 'Victims of Circumstance', in which Holroyd berated politicians for making decisions without consulting the people, thereby making them the victims? 'Revolution Day' is the sequel. The song actually starts like this:

> There's something in the air:
> a feeling if uncertainty.
> I see it everywhere:
> don't let those bad times fall on me;

This is then followed sequentially by the lyrics we have already quoted. That is more or less it. There is a bit of repetition but that's the basis of the lyrics. The interpretation, then, is that Holroyd continues to be dissatisfied with what is going on all around in the world but his strength of spirit is such that his belief in the Fifties Child's values are unshaken. He does not necessarily "want to change the world", but he does want to live in peace without becoming a "victim of circumstance" and it is his strength of spirit, his belief in those values of peace, love and freedom, which give him the confidence to continue to speak out and wait with hope for the day when the world will change itself for the better. If 'For Your Love' was Lees' torch song for the world, then 'Revolution Day' is Holroyd's own, and very powerful, torch song. You can't touch me, and others like me, our strength of spirit makes us impregnable! It is the same strength of spirit that inspired 'Berlin' and 'Back to the Wall'. It may have taken time, but we knocked the Wall down, and I'm going to continue standing up for what is right until the world changes for the better! Powerful stuff indeed.

Returning now to Lees, but adopting a chronological approach rather than the thematic one we have been following in order to complete the review of his spiritual songs, we arrive at 'Child of Man', which was released some six months ahead of 'Summer Soldier' and is actually Lees' first overt spiritual song to be released. Its unambiguous message of loving one's neighbour and making them "understand", we can now see, is one that would recur throughout his songwriting career.

The timeline then again yields what has surely become a firm favourite: 'Summer Soldier'. Our previous analysis of this song has already revealed all of its spiritual clues. Essentially, what drives Lees to his extraordinary message in 'Summer Soldier' is a spiritual force:

> The Lord God said love thy neighbour:
> break the circle, free the hater,
> call him a friend . . .

There can be little doubt about 'Summer Soldier's spirituality, its compassion is breathtaking. However, in essence, the song reflects the whole of Fifties Child's society's spiritual shift. The temptation is to think of the "God" in 'Summer Soldier' as the Christian God, because of Lees' Christian upbringing and re-assimilation back into that Church in later life, despite the fact that Lees was not a churchgoer at the time. However, the crux is that in 'Summer Soldier' it actually would not matter one iota whether God was mentioned or whether He is a Christian God. The crux actually is "break the circle, free the hater". In this context the "hater" can mean more than another individual. Remember that in its second phase 'Summer Soldier' moves into a (metaphorical) dream sequence with the "summer soldier" and the "angel bright" respectively representing the evil and good parts of the psyche. "Hater" as a word was chosen to some extent because Lees had to find something appropriate to rhyme with "neighbour". I think that, as well as the meaning which we have already explored in the 'Troubles in Northern Ireland' chapter, the "hater" can also represent the evil part of the psyche. Lees is urging everyone involved in the conflict to feel compassion by overcoming the "hater" that is in their—and indeed all of our own—psyches, by overcoming the "summer soldier" and making the spirit pure, making the spirit "angel bright".

There is no ambiguity at all about 'Back to Earth', written in memory of Lees' father, who died in 1992. The song's spiritual credentials come in the suggestion of a belief in an afterlife.

Finally, we return to 'Mr E', analysed in detail in the 'Drugs' chapter but which needs inclusion here for completeness. In 'Mr E' the good part of the psyche, the spirit, is trying to persuade the protagonist to resist the lure of drugs and other ultimately unsatisfactory pleasures by promising "a window to the bottom of your soul". I termed 'Mr E' the 'Hymn' for the Nineties, an accolade that it richly deserves. Its spiritual credentials are reinforced by contrasting the different approaches taken by 'Mr E' and Ozzy Osbourne's "Mr Alcohol" in 'Suicide Solution', a song that was discussed in the 'Battle for the Mind' chapter. Both songs feature two personalities, one of which is "bad": these are Mr E and Mr Alcohol. However, whereas in 'Mr E' Lees offers a spiritual solution to the problem, Osbourne does not do so in 'Suicide Solution', in fact there is no solution of any kind offered at all, either in this song or in the related 'Demon Alcohol', in which Mr Alcohol is the only persona.

So there we have it, that rounds off all sixteen of Lees' songs dealing with a Christian or strong spiritual theme, and some readers may now be wondering " . . . but what about such-and-such a song?"

These spiritual songs form a quite extraordinary testament from a songwriter working in a non-religious rock band, even one with such a long history as Barclay James Harvest. The spirituality in most of these songs is purposefully shrouded and one can enjoy the songs without even noticing the message running through their heart. Even if you notice it, you really have to try quite hard to decipher it. Fortunately—for me at least—the message in Lees' songs *is* worth deciphering.

Even when Christian imagery is used explicitly in these songs, listening carefully to their message, it is clear that the main intent is to convey the importance of compassionate love to obtaining happiness, rather than the preaching of Christianity per se. It is the *message*, rather than the *religion*, which is the key factor. I suspect that Lees would have written the same songs using Islamic imagery had he been born in Basra instead of Oldham.

Now, should you wish, you can fill in the gaps and complete for yourself the chronology which I started earlier. You may then wish to speculate as to what the exact shape of Lees' spiritual life journey is in song and where that crucial turning point occurred when his spiritual confidence had grown to the extent that he could subdue the ravages of his bad psyche. Was it in the run-up to the 1977 version of 'Hymn', giving him the confidence to sing the overtly

Christian words? Or was it a few years later, in his early thirties? Certainly, 'Blow Me Down', released in 1983, suggests that he had already reached the plateau of confident spiritual strength. And how can you write such a supremely confident song oozing in spiritual vision such as 'In Memory of the Martyrs' [1981] without having already succeeded in the fight against the inner demons? Ultimately, from the standpoint of our social history, it is the shape of the journey that matters, not the specific timings. Yes, Lees is just one Fifties Child, but his spiritual journey, with its ability to deliver or withhold happiness, must have been similarly reflected in the lives of so many other Fifties Children.

Of course, other Fifties Children may have had less satisfactory spiritual life journeys. Sufficient is known about Wolstenholme to conclude that, unfortunately, he was unable to find a spiritual solution that satisfied his own needs. However, there is no denying that Wolstenholme was a spiritual person: he released fewer songs than Holroyd or Lees but there is ample evidence of compassion in his writing as well as a demonstrable, ongoing search for a spiritual solution. We have already dealt with his battle against mental illness in the previous chapter, so let us now review what we can of his spiritual search.

Earlier in the chapter we mentioned that about eight million people in the 2001 British census had indicated that they had no religion or were atheists. In fact, atheists were only a very small proportion of the eight million, leaving a sizeable proportion of the population claiming "no religion". This does not mean that these eight million are not spiritual or compassionate. Many might simply still be looking for an answer that makes sense to them, and they have not yet found it in formal religions. Fifties Children were as susceptible to these doubts as younger people and, within Barclay James Harvest's writing, it is Wolstenholme who is searching.

If one has rejected the call to unquestioning faith of a formal religion like Christianity then it is clear that, if one has a spiritual element, then one will search wide for an answer that resonates with one's own spirit. Within Wolstenholme's songwriting that search manifests itself in an eclectic, occasionally humorous, and sometimes deeply questioning approach to spirituality. We shall begin with his first spiritual song, 'Mæstoso (A Hymn in the Roof of the World)'. His "magnum opus"—in his own words—was originally recorded by Barclay James Harvest in 1974 for the *Everyone is Everybody Else* album but was eventually omitted from the album on the grounds that it would have disrupted its musical cohesiveness. Wolstenholme eventually released the song on his 1980 solo album, *Mæstoso*. The song deals with the key Fifties Child dream of unifying mankind. Its inclusion as a spiritual song rests on the interpretation that the protagonists—soldiers from opposing nations who have died during a battle—have ended up being reconciled at the gates of heaven. There, far above the world, the clouds begin to shield the earth from view and, as they do so, the pure heavenly air sweeps away any trace of man's doings, they discard the useless symbols of their warring nations and unite in rejoicing and thanking God that they are alive. Clearly, the intended message is that we should do the same whilst here on earth, and not wait until we are in the next life.

Early on in this chapter we mentioned 'Beyond the Grave', which also suggests a belief in an afterlife and we have also previously met—in 'The Soldier as Victim' chapter—'Gates of Heaven', another song which does the same, this time by saying that the soldiers killed in the First World War heard sweeter music at the gates of heaven. Then, nearly a quarter of a century after the *Mæstoso* album that contained two of these three songs, we hear another song—'Blood and Bones'—which again suggests that Wolstenholme believed that there must be something more than just this earthly life.

'Blood and Bones' hints at, if not some uncertainty about man's spirituality, then at least some confusion and also perhaps some angst. It is the refrain, which contains the title, which suggests that Wolstenholme still believes in a human soul, even if simply because he is incredulous that otherwise we would just be "blood and bones". The song's verses, however, reveal an interest in the writing of the nineteenth-century German philosopher Friedrich Nietzsche, as well as in other material that deeply questions reality. There is a direct reference to Nicolas Roeg's 1973 film, the psychological occult thriller *Don't Look Now*. Nietzsche's indirect reference comes through a reference to Thomas Mann's book *Death in Venice* [1912]—later made into a film—which deals with Nietzschean philosophical ideas. Wolstenholme was to make another, explicit, reference to Nietzsche in 'Location, Location, Location'. These references cement the importance that Wolstenholme gave to his thinking at the time. 'Blood and Bones' is a lyrically rich but complex song. It is clear, even for a non-expert, that aspects of Nietzsche's philosophy— nihilism, say—have no synergy with the kind of spirituality that we have seen Lees espousing. However, it is now difficult to present an objective analysis on the exact significance and impact of Nietzsche on Wolstenholme's spiritual development.[6] What does remain clear cut from 'Blood and Bones' is that, in his fifties, he was still looking for a satisfactory answer to the meaning of life.

Wolstenholme's last song in this section has elements of humour: 'The Collector' is sung in the persona of the Grim Reaper, one of the most popular personifications of death since the time of the Black Death in the Middle Ages. In the song, the Grim Reaper warns that all one's lifelong wishes

6. Wolstenholme committed suicide in December 2010.

ultimately count for naught when he comes calling. Despite the song's jestful nature, it does have a serious side in that, intentionally or otherwise, the lyrics almost offer a vision of the attainment of nirvana. In the Buddhist teaching, it is necessary to abandon all attachment to worldly things prior to reaching that ultimate, desired state and, within the song, that is when the Grim Reaper comes to collect you.

The contrast between Wolstenholme's and Lees' spiritual songs could not be starker. Sociologically, these contrasts between friends reflects the broadening of the belief spectrum for Fifties Children as they developed into middle age and approached the time at which their mortality comes more sharply into focus. From a Christian education in their teens, globalisation and other pressures opened up new spiritual vistas. Many abandoned ritualistic Christianity but few of those abandoned spirituality altogether. Most adapted the ideas of Christianity to suit their own individualities, finding a solace that the blind, hypocritical pretence at faith could never bring. For others still, the fruitless search continued until their death from this life.

✁

It is not easy to find comparable songs to 'Hymn' and 'He Said Love' from contemporaneous songwriters because overt Christianity in British rock music, unlike its American counterpart, has never been popular.[7] Cliff Richard is probably the best known British rock/pop star with a Christian belief, but he wrote relatively few songs during his career and, in any case, is not a contemporary of Barclay James Harvest, having been born in 1940.

Therefore, it is appropriate to begin a review of other artists' songs by returning to George Harrison, who probably did as much as anyone to promote the cause of spirituality outside of formal Christianity. He seemed to be the main spiritual beneficiary of the well publicised visits by the Beatles to India and this renewed vigour found its way into his songwriting, never more so than when the break-up of the Beatles served to unshackle his songs from the iron grip of the Lennon-McCartney syndicate. His run of solo albums in the first half of the Seventies was replete with spiritual material to add to songs in that vein—such as 'Within You Without You'—that he had already released with the Beatles. Harrison therefore has a strong claim to be recognised as the first British spiritual rock star.

We shall start by returning to 'Beware of Darkness', the song which we discussed in the 'Battle for the Mind' chapter. The last verse is particularly

---

7. The strength of American Christian rock reflects that society's very different attitude to religion. Adherence to faiths and church attendance are higher than in the UK and do not show a similar decline. This disparity is fertile ground for sociologists and psychologists but any attempt at its explanation is beyond the remit of this book.

intriguing: Harrison warns against the temptation to follow leaders—any leaders, they do not have to be political, they could be family for instance, trying to persuade you to maintain the "circle of hate"—along the wrong path of life, and then immediately sings about weeping atlas cedars that want to keep on growing. This is not the non sequitur that it seems: it is clearly meant to indicate that one should not focus on the day to day problems of life, but meditate on the natural world, for it is there that the real answers to life are to be found. This is a message as stark and as compelling as that of Lees' 'In Memory of the Martyrs'.

'Awaiting on You All' is also taken from Harrison's first solo release, *All Things Must Pass* (even the title choice has a spiritual connotation) from 1970. The song is not only abundantly clear in its spiritual message but also contains some swipes at his erstwhile band colleagues, at the same time as being sprinkled abundantly with Liverpudlian humour. The break from the conventional religious worship prevalent in his childhood is immediately clear, but so is the fact that it does not imply an abandonment of spirituality. The Fifties Child's attitude to spirituality is neatly encapsulated by the fact that Harrison denigrates the Pope's spiritual leadership, having already mentioned Jesus in a positive way, this after he had adopted Hinduism and in the same song where he extols the virtues of a mantra used in Japa yoga meditation ("chanting the names of the Lord") of which he was a devotee. The key here is the reinforcement of the realisation that as Fifties Children abandoned the unquestioning allegiance to catechism and formal worship, their adopted spirituality drew influences from any number of sources becoming, arguably, purer. Harrison himself explained it like this in an introduction to Swami Prabhupada's book *Krsna*: "All religions are branches of one big tree. It doesn't matter what you call Him, just as long as you call."

Reading this now, your attitude might be one of shrugful indifference, but at the time this represented the cusp of an astounding spiritual revolution, one that liberated the souls of the Fifties Child's generation—and those to follow—from shackled ritual. It was not a passing fancy either, since Harrison repeats the message in 'Life Itself' [*Somewhere in England*, 1981].

This development towards syncretism, retaining some elements of Christianity, has also been demonstrated by Jon Anderson, most known for being the lead singer of Yes. Anderson has written many spiritual songs during his long career but his absorption of influences from different religions is perhaps best demonstrated by a fairly recent song, 'Big Buddha Song' [*Survival & Other Stories*, 2011], in which Buddha, Jesus, Muhammad and Krishna are all praised in equal measure.

Another artist abandoning conventional worship was the other famed Anderson of rock music, Ian. Within Jethro Tull's 1971 album *Aqualung*,

Anderson systematically espouses a view of Christianity which slightly overlaps with that in Barclay James Harvest's songs.[8] He does this without demonstrating a strong spirituality; in fact, some might argue without demonstrating *any* spirituality whatever. The emphasis of the album sleeve's mock-Genesis "creation of God" story, followed by a sequence of several songs on the "My God" side, is more about exposing the hypocrisy of the formal Church than about compassion, which is the overriding message in Barclay James Harvest's spiritual writing. Nevertheless, despite that stark difference, there is an overlap of opinion, which is best seen by considering 'Wind Up', the powerful album finale. This is a stonking condemnation of the Fifties Child's parents, teachers and religious leaders, who conspired to give him a rigid, rule-based education that in no way prepared him for the realities of life. Sung in the first person to enhance its effect, the protagonist claims that he has communicated with God, who has confirmed that He does not have to be worshipped on Sundays. The protagonist lambasts his headmaster and anyone else who cares to listen that their rigid, ritualistic spirituality is totally missing the point. This is entirely consistent not only with Lees' approach but also to that of many Fifties Children: one can be spiritual without the formality of church ritual observance. In other songs on the album, 'My God' and 'Hymn 43', Anderson takes a huge swipe at the hypocrisy of the formal church and those people whose Christianity does not go beyond lip service.

More than thirty years later, another Fifties Child—Ray Davies—put it even more starkly than Anderson had done, rejecting formal religion and, seemingly, modern spirituality in 'Hymn for a New Age' [*Working Man's Café*, 2007]. Davies reviews the paltry state of the world and of mankind's evil behaviour, says he wants to pray but does not know what to. The world desperately needs an infusion of new spirituality—and he can see none. Clearly, Davies' spiritual journey continues.

Societally, the reactions of Anderson and Davies were quite common in British Fifties Children. We have already covered one of the reasons why, without having drawn out the particular implication, i.e. the Troubles in Northern Ireland where Christians were quite content to perpetrate horrific acts against each other. If this is what Christians do to each other, would I wish to call myself one? Subsequently, mankind has done little to redeem itself. People absorb the headline-grabbing bad news and see no further. The lyrical approach of Anderson and Davies is very different to that of Lees in songs such as 'Summer Soldier' and 'For No One', by choosing to accentuate

---

8. His exploration of the issue is sufficiently strong for many commentators to have called *Aqualung* a concept album; a fact which Anderson himself strongly denies.

religious hypocrisy and problems rather than being compassionate. In fairness, theirs was probably the more common societal approach.

Van Morrison is another artist whose spirituality is more important than the worship of any specific formal religion, though occasionally he does choose to use Christian imagery. His frequent exultation of the spiritual power of nature resonates with some aspects of Lees' lyrical writing. 'Whenever God Shines His Light' [*Avalon Sunset*, 1989], possibly his most orthodox and overtly Christian song, was performed as a duet with Cliff Richard. There are strong echoes of the power of prayer, as in many of Barclay James Harvest's songs, and also of the power and energy that God can transmit to a believer.

There are other songwriters who wrote extensively about spirituality who could feature at this juncture in our social history—Supertramp's Roger Hodgson, Yusuf Islam/Cat Stevens and others—but as ours is a general social history of the Fifties Child, rather than a study on the spirituality of his generation *per se*, we shall leave it there. Suffice to say, as we shall see in the next section, that the spirituality expounded by other songwriters is not as complete as that contained in Barclay James Harvest's songs, in that it is lacking in what is surely one of its principal characteristics: compassion.

Compassion

By this stage of our social history, it will have become abundantly clear how compassion features strongly in Barclay James Harvest's songs—we have already met 'Summer Soldier', 'Child of the Universe', 'Copii Romania', 'One Night' and others. It is a potent list.

Compassion is one of the key characteristics of spiritual people and considering it as a specific topic for discussion reveals a number of other songs that have not yet been covered which are important within the band's spiritual canon. These are best dealt with as a group in this section, together with some reminders of the strength and subtlety of the message in some others.

Measuring compassion societally is difficult. One index might be charitable giving. In this area Britain is consistently ranked very highly amongst the world's countries, so perhaps it is no surprise that, for the societally conscious Barclay James Harvest songwriters, compassion should feature strongly in their songs. One of the targets of the band's compassion was high on the agenda for a Fifties Child: the vulnerability and plight of children, even when living away from zones of conflict, came into widespread public view when photographs and film images from famines in Africa hit the headlines. The Kenyan famine in 1965 was possibly the first whose effects were transmitted on British screens, and this was followed by the Ethiopian famine of 1970 and the Bangladeshi floods and conflict of the same year.

It was the Bangladeshi situation which prompted George Harrison's renowned Concert for Bangladesh in 1971, the first time that a superstar rock concert had been organised as a charity event. Harrison was joined by other rock luminaries, including his fellow ex-Beatle Ringo Starr and Eric Clapton, who would later also go on to feature in 1985's Live Aid, which was organised to help victims of the Ethiopian famine that was raging at the time. The cinematic overage that these Sixties and early Seventies famines raised, together with the extra media attention garnered by the galvanization of two ex-Beatles was key in opening up the world as a subject for compassion to the Fifties Child.

Protecting children as the focus for compassion is not just a Christian concept. Their innocence and reliance on adult help for well-being, comfort and development makes their protection an almost universal precept. A view of their innocence is vocalised by Lees in 'African':

> Through the eyes of a child
> there's no wrong or right;
> no reason to hate,
> no need for a fight;
> no colour, no creed,
> no malice, no greed.

This may sound naive as expressed for the lyrics, but the central point for our social history is that children's innocence makes them a focus for compassion. Despite this, children everywhere are disadvantaged by the actions of adults and this is an aspect that is irksome to both Holroyd and Lees, as evidenced by their songwriting.

The plight of children was one of the focus points of Lees' wistful 'Hymn for the Children' which, as we have just seen, is a highly spiritual song without a hint of Christianity, demonstrating that for Lees, like many other Fifties Children, religion is much more than strict orthodoxy. The focus on children comes, of course, through the song's title, as well as through its closing verse:

> Life is a soft lullaby
> soothing a child as it cries;
> but it cries in pain.
> Time wrote the songs:
> we hear the cry
> and still we sing wrong!

The sentiments in this closing verse have a soulful echo in Holroyd's plaintive

'Copii Romania', which we first discussed in the 'Break-Up of the Soviet Empire' chapter. Holroyd is moved by their plight and incredulous that others might ignore the problem. Holroyd and Lees have a common frustration at how societies continually disadvantage children, despite there being no doubt that they should know how to organise themselves differently.

Famine may be one of the most common instigators of rock musicians' compassion but is addressed specifically only once within Barclay James Harvest's canon, by Wolstenholme in 2004. Wolstenholme shows his sharp wit and anger at humanity's inability to tackle the problem efficiently by choosing to use a single, oft-repeated lyric, which is also the title, in Mæstoso's song 'The Starving People of the World All Thank You for Your Time'. The continuous repetition of the sole lyric carries greater impact than many verbose songs!

Reinforcing the band's Eastern European connection is Holroyd's 'Kiev', written in the aftermath of the world's worst nuclear disaster at Chernobyl in the Ukraine.[9] The power station's Reactor 4 exploded during an experimental procedure in April 1986 and the subsequent fire in the exposed graphite moderator sent a radioactive plume high into the atmosphere, seriously contaminating the surrounding countryside. The fallout was so severe that it reached places as far off as Britain and some sheep farmers in Britain were still restricted in their activities into the twenty-first century as a consequence of the accident. Kiev, the capital of that Soviet state, is situated only sixty miles or so south of Chernobyl but escaped the worst of the local fallout due to the prevailing wind direction. In fact, the neighbouring state of Belarus was overall more seriously affected than Ukraine itself. However, given the nature of radiation and its effects, these facts only came to light a long time after the event. What was clear at the time, from the immediate effects of local radiation and the deaths of power station and recovery workers, was that this had been a horrendous accident.

Holroyd's response is typical of the band: full of empathy and compassion for the people of the area who—let us not forget—at this time belonged to the enemy in the Cold War. Holroyd sees through all that fluff and expresses his sympathy, noting our ideological differences, and says that we would help if we only knew what to do. 'Kiev' is a supremely compassionate song, driven by empathy with people, no matter who they might be, or what their political allegiances might be. Rather than focus on the grisly effects of nuclear power, or accentuate the radiation issue, which might have made for greater headline grabbing, Holroyd has chosen to focus on the human impact, and the result is a great Cold War-busting song!

9. Ukraine was then part of the Soviet Union.

Lees deals with another section of people struggling to survive in society—the homeless—in 'Three Weeks to Despair'. The approach, lyrically and musically, is soft and gentle, typically Leesian in that it makes no explicit judgements. How much of their desperate situation is of their own making, and how much is it of ours? The song uses recordings, superimposed on the music, from a conversation that Lees and the album's producer, Martin Lawrence, had with a homeless man on the streets of Stockport. The effect is profound, managing to draw out all of the homeless individuals' humanity in a touching way. Lees had been inspired to write the song having read a couple of articles by Margaret Driscoll in *The Sunday Times* and the following quote from her, accentuating the humanity in the song, is included in *River of Dream's* sleeve notes: "Behind every tatty sleeping bag and cardboard box there is a human being with a family, a history and a personality."

Whilst it is true that the song makes no explicit judgements, the last couplet of the refrain, which changes slightly on each of the three iterations, contains the same, piercing image. The first verse deals with a homeless woman, the second deals with a man and the third deals with their combined predicament. The woman's luck has run dry: as night comes and the rain falls she huddles in the shadows of some dark porch, as if hiding, shielding herself from the light, and we walk by, not seeing, averting our eyes. The man's grandiose schemes of improving himself and rejoining "normal" society all come to nought; as night falls and the rain pours he shields himself in the shadows of a mingy alley, as if hiding, running away from the lies, and as we step closer we cross to the other side of the road. An empty cardboard box for a bed, a paper cup to drink from, hunger rumbles: their morale is at its lowest ebb as the day darkens into night and the rain lashes down. They hide in the shadows, running away, their fight for self-esteem all but lost. We approach, feel, see unseeingly, look down, walk on. It is a chilling song with as powerful a condemnation of our indifference as Holroyd's had been in 'Copii Romania'.

Equally moving and, in conjunction with these songs' acerbic remarks, providing a sobering and thought-provoking close to this section on the band's compassion songs, is Wolstenholme's 'Shoes'. Inspired by the horrors of the Nazi death camps, it oozes pathos as the discarded shoes and bones of the countless victims are mournfully observed before noting that, despite their grisly provenance, they are now only inanimate objects with no story to tell of what might have been had humanity not been so brutal. The song is a testament to the fading hope of this Fifties Child: yes, man should forgive and forget, but the human condition is so full of deficiencies that our frail humanity is at risk of failing completely.

Yes, after all we are just men, and all of us are on our own spiritual journeys. All of us are tall ships blown hither and thither by the wind of life, which sometimes helps, sometimes hinders us on our way; all of us trying to gather some sense from the constant wash of the mental battle between our good and bad psyches.

May your own journey be a successful one.

✤

For our discussion of other artists' songs dealing with compassion, let us return to Ian Anderson and his depiction of the homeless in Jethro Tull's 'Aqualung' [*Aqualung*, 1971]. Its shocking opening lyric is accompanied by one of the greatest and most recognisable guitar riffs in rock history, but it is totally lacking in compassion as it paints the image of an unwashed, lecherous, snotty-nosed man wearing ragged clothes.[10] Anderson hardly eases up, representing Aqualung very much as society's cast-off and, when he is called "friend" in the final verse, it almost seems to me as if it is the Grim Reaper or—let us be fair to Anderson because of the album's concept[11]—God talking to him just before he splutters to his death. Aqualung also receives an unflattering mention in the next song, 'Cross-Eyed Mary'. As far as our social history is concerned, there is certainly no compassion accompanying the description of Aqualung as "friend". Any emotion is shrouded in its battle with Aqualung's repulsive depiction. This is in sharp contrast to Lees' approach in 'Three Weeks to Despair', for instance, which serves to stress the humanity of the homeless in Stockport.

As we noted at the close of the previous section, it is actually difficult to detect much compassion in the writing of the other artists who otherwise qualified as spiritual songwriters. However, Ralph McTell's 'Streets of London' [*Spiral Staircase*, 1969] is a good example of a compassionate song. His treatment of homelessness is similar to Lees' in that the compassion shines through musically as well as lyrically, and is non-judgemental, acting as a reminder to all those of us who are lucky enough to have a roof over our heads not to go around griping about our misfortunes. McTell may have been inspired to write the song by the sight of homeless of Paris rather than London, but the choice of city is immaterial, it is the compassionate message that is the focus.

Before we move on to discuss other compassionate songs, it is worth drawing a societal observation from three of the songs which we have already discussed in this chapter—'Streets of London' [1969], 'Aqualung' [1971] and 'Three Weeks to Despair' [1997]—which is that society clearly failed to solve the problem of homelessness in the near thirty-year period spanned by these songs. Indeed, the issue persists to this day.

---

10. Anderson based his lyrics for 'Aqualung' on photographs taken by his wife at the time, Jennie Franks. She also contributed part of the lyrics to the song and is given a joint composing credit.
11. My words, not his.

Graeme Edge and Ray Thomas were both born in 1941 and so fall slightly outside my self-imposed definition but their 'Balance' for the 1970 Moody Blues album *A Question of Balance* is an interesting example of textbook spirituality. It describes perfectly a spiritual life journey's awakening to understanding, and with that understanding comes love and compassion. This message finds loud echoes in Harrison's and Lees' writing, not because they are cribbing, but because they too have, individually, found their own way. Note how these post-War children are all finding their spirituality without the aid of Christianity or another religion even when, as in Lees' case, they end up returning to that formal worship. Another example, showing how the spectrum of spiritual experience mushroomed for the Fifties Child is how Yusuf Islam's spiritual quest, as Steven Georgiou and Cat Stevens, took him back into formal religion—not the Christianity of his education, but Islam.

We shall finish the discussion with Donovan's 'No Hunger' [*Neutronica*, 1980]. One of its subjects is clear from the title, and the song also encompasses disease, poverty and quality of life. Its message is simple and very typical of the artist, resonating with aspects of Holroyd's and Lees' writing in songs such as 'Copii Romania' and 'African'. Donovan is shocked by the burning of food for economic reasons, the use of taxes for armaments and the purloining of happiness by too few in society—and what are you going to do about it?

Despite not being a popular subject for rock songs—other than for Barclay James Harvest's visionaries—these songs demonstrate that the compassionate streak that the Fifties Child was born with has not waned. The number of Barclay James Harvest's own songs featured in this chapter is significant, even for a band with a career as long as theirs. It is by far the largest number of songs in any chapter of our social history. Some have been complex, others simply retell the Gospels, some are prayers, others ooze compassion.

Barclay James Harvest were not a Christian rock band but they were one of the most spiritual bands, if not *the* most spiritual, to have graced our shores. I would venture that this very fact is pertinent in explaining not only their popularity through the Seventies and Eighties, in the face of a generally hostile music media—press and radio—but also the survival of their music to this day. Even when listeners have not understood the detailed nuances of the words, they have been able to *hear* the love and compassion in the music. Fans going through their own battles for the mind will have found a helpful resonance in these many songs. Subliminally or otherwise these songs will have acted as a catalyst for developing their own spiritual strength. Barclay James Harvest's continuing fan base is an indication that the spirit and the hope of the Fifties Child remains alive in the world.

The spiritual journey is, arguably, the most important we make in our lives. Extrapolating from the diversity of the band's spiritual songwriting to wider society as a whole, one begins to perceive how very different—and potentially richer—all of our spiritual journeys are now that, released from the strictures of centuries-old ritualistic worship, we are at last free to fumble on our own way.

Christianity has survived the rejection of authority and, despite its waning influence, continues to be a useful point of reference for a Fifties Child, a way of shaping and understanding his own spirituality. We have seen how the demographics of religion have changed, and how the questioning of beliefs thought unassailable at the Fifties Child's birth has led different people down very different avenues but without necessarily affecting the strength of their compassion or spirituality. Formal religion may have lost out, humanity has not.

19

Ring of Changes

When Barclay James Harvest's songwriters were born, the life expectancy for a man was about 66 years. By the turn of the century this had risen by about ten years and there had been a corresponding improvement in general health.

Therefore, it is almost certain that when our songwriters started their rock careers in 1967, they had no expectation that they would still be writing in the twenty-first century. After all, the rock adage of the age was summed up by the likes of Peter Townshend who, in 1966's 'My Generation', proclaimed that he wanted to die before getting old. Jethro Tull's Ian Anderson took a slightly different view; he had no wish to die before his dotage, but the title of his 1976 song 'Too Old to Rock 'n' Roll, Too Young to Die' makes it quite clear that he did not envisage celebrating the fortieth birthday of 1972's *Thick as a Brick* album by recording a follow-up! What's more—and strangely enough around the same time as Ian Anderson's song—many thought that the punk revolution would quickly silence songwriting such as Barclay James Harvest's.

It was not to be. Barclay James Harvest were never the darlings of the British music press and the punk revolution—a media-driven phenomenon—simply bypassed them. Album and concert ticket sales in their home country did not suffer from the New Wave's splash, rather their fortunes were dictated only by life's normal twists. Even so, the band's songwriters would have been surprised at the longevity of their rock 'n' roll life. Perhaps, when you think about it, this is not so remarkable. I can remember being shocked, as a teenager, by my parents dancing around the room to a Frank Sinatra concert on the TV, so why should our own heroes not have the same effect on us as we grow older? There is some infiltration of Barclay James Harvest's music into younger generations, but the main market for these songwriters continues to consist of the same fans who followed their careers in the Seventies and

Eighties. Societally, it is a manifestation of the fact that most of us are living healthily for longer—hence we continue to enjoy listening to music, which makes enough of a market for our heroes to record and play live.

As has often turned out to be the case when such artists continue writing, in their later years, that writing turns to reflecting and pronouncing on the state of the modern world which, human nature has it, is never as good as in the Good Old Times. Our society is full of such pronouncements from our elder citizens, so much so that television programmes such as *Grumpy Old Men* (first shown 2003) and *Grumpy Old Women* (2004) have become popular.

This final chapter of our social history therefore looks at the aspects of modern life that grate with Barclay James Harvest's songwriters, as well as at the loss of their youthful, idealistic innocence.

The Loss of Innocence

Our social history has already revealed that, in his youth, the Fifties Child dreamt of . . . nay, he actually *believed* that he could transform humanity so that we all lived in a peaceful world where man lived in harmony with his fellow man and with his environment. That belief was shattered all too quickly. A song such as Lees' 'Taking Some Time On', released in 1970, shows that the belief had already turned, and really was now back in the realm of hopeful dreaming.

This turning point is consistently repeated through Barclay James Harvest's songs and through those of other songwriters: the flower that had bloomed so brightly in the Sixties was cruelly battered down by the lashing rain of Vietnam, Altamont, Northern Ireland, and by the ignominious death, within three weeks of each other, of rock heroes Jimi Hendrix and Janis Joplin. By the end of 1970, the party was over.

'The Joker', a 1972 songwriting collaboration between Holroyd and Lees, recognises the loss of belief in a better world. The "joker"—sardonically named because people laugh at his continuing hope for a loving, peaceful world—does not think that it is too late to regain that prize if people will only slow the pace of life down and focus on supporting each other. The people just sneer and continue their busying, egoistic activity. For me, this song is significant not just for its sociological message, but also for the fact that it is a joint Holroyd/Lees composition. Clearly, they both still had a trace of the Fifties Child's dream in their spirit, they had not totally lost their hope and their idealism. Holroyd takes the lead vocal and the lyrics are written more in his style than Lees', but one can easily envision them having been written by either songwriter. This evident resonance of spirit within 'The Joker' acts to reaffirm our conviction that it was surely a factor, despite other differences, that contributed to Barclay James Harvest making music for so long.

Barclay James Harvest's 1997 album, *Ring of Changes*, was fertile ground for songs battling for the right of inclusion in this chapter. Two of Holroyd's songs have made the final cut. OK, you think there should have been more and you're probably right: but the ones making it to our social history are 'Do You Believe in Dreams (Same Chance for Everyone)' and 'Time of Our Lives'.

Interpretation of Holroyd's songs is not usually straightforward and 'Do You Believe in Dreams (Same Chance for Everyone)' is no exception. The clue that it is about the downward path of the band's own career comes in a clear reference to their famous Berlin concert of 1980, when they performed on the steps of the Reichstag to an audience of a quarter of a million. As budding rock stars when they set up the band in 1967, that would have been their dream: fame and fortune. So where did it all go from there, in the space of a few short years? Seventeen years on, where is the music? Where are the fans and why did they desert the band? Holroyd is phlegmatic about the fact that everyone has the same chance to make it and Barclay James Harvest were more successful than most but, nevertheless, the rock 'n' roll dream—as we have already seen in an earlier chapter—turned out to be an illusion.

The band's first ever release, the 1968 'Early Morning' single, has not quite made it into our social history, although some fans might argue that it merited inclusion in the 'Nature and the Environment' chapter, but their last album track, 'Time of Our Lives', has. This also refers to dreams, although in this instance the dream is the Fifties Child's idealistic one of peace, love and freedom that we have become so familiar with. This is a fitting song with which to draw the curtain on Barclay James Harvest's career. It recognises the peril facing the Fifties Child's dream as, worldwide, the law of the gun seems to be winning the battle against righteous values. All seems despair, the dream is surely over but, just like in endings of the best novels when the author leaves the reader on tenterhooks for the sequel, right at the end Holroyd rekindles a small, glimmering flame of hope: those that have the dream, if they wake up in time and unite, could still triumph . . . perhaps. This is the time. The time for change is now.

The next two songs to be discussed are both of Lees' authorship and were released on the 1999 *Nexus* album.[1] Accordingly, 'Brave New World' becomes, in some respects, one of the most intriguing songs in Lees' canon. Its theme of lost innocence is clearly laid out: having enjoyed the simple pleasures of play around the safety of home and the ones he loves, the boy grows into manhood and finds that the world is a dangerous place filled with

---

1. *Nexus* was released under the "Barclay James Harvest Through the Eyes of John Lees" brand.

evil. By the age of twenty-four, the violence in the world is enough to make him cry. Growing into his grey years, the continuing violence has dried the tears as his and his peers' own death approaches. The old man then philosophises on the imponderables of life, reflecting on how events just unfold without anyone appearing to be in control, and wonders whether expecting anything more is unreasonable. These sentiments may all appear very similar to older readers, who will themselves almost certainly have mused on the whims, coincidences and trials of life. The extraordinary thing, then, is that Lees wrote these words in 1971, when he was in his early twenties! A demo version of 'Brave New World' exists which, although it has slightly different lyrics that serve to accentuate the link with Lees' boyhood, retains the key verse in which the protagonist has grown old. It is therefore unclear whether Lees is extrapolating his own thoughts into a possible future or whether he is writing about the experiences of his father, or some other family member. In essence, from a sociological viewpoint, it does not matter if the song is not completely autobiographical, because what Lees has already described (he *was* twenty four in 1971) reveals how the Fifties Child was not immune to having his carefree happiness eroded with the passing of only a few short years.

In the 1999 *Nexus* version of 'Brave New World', the song's last verse—an addition from the 1971 demo—returns to a theme that Lees had visited before in 'River of Dreams', that of his disillusionment with the rock 'n' roll life which had promised so much when he had been a young man. Then he had dreamt of untold riches, only to be disillusioned, in the same way that the idealistic vision of the triumph of nature over the evil ways of man would collapse. The metaphor used for the crumbling of that hope is that of the ageing of—and he refers to the song directly—'Brother Thrush'. Clearly, when that song was released in 1969, this vision of a better world was still tangible.

Musically, 'Star Bright' is quintessential Barclay James Harvest, the tempo slowed to a meditative step, allowing the focus to dwell on the melody and the orchestration, and enabling it to seep into and mesh with the soul. If you go with it, allow yourself to be enmeshed by it, then when the music ends, gently, softly, imperceptibly, it can feel like its warm hand has just set you back down to earth from some other, finer world. If, having arrived at this juncture of our social history, you still think this band might be derivative, then you need to go and listen to this song now—it is like no one else. Lyrically, the theme is similar to that of 'Brave New World', except the emphasis of the loss in 'Star Bright' is the pure ("star bright") love of a mother, that the child distanced himself from when the pull of life lured him away from home. Metaphorically, this might also be interpreted as a yearning for a return to that confident idealism of the youth. Thematically, the song has an affinity not only with 'Brave New World' but also, more remotely, with 'River of Dreams'.

This trio of late-period songs then—'River of Dreams', 'Brave New World' and 'Star Bright'—are all about looking back on life from the vantage point of experience and, essentially, noting how the Fifties Child's youthful hopes and aspirations were so quickly dashed.

Holroyd's 'Ring of Changes' is very different in approach to all of these preceding songs and yet, despite this, shows an equal degree of world-weariness. It targets no specific subject, simply noting that, as the old saying goes "nothing ever changes, nothing's ever quite the same".[2] Look back through history—the same as now, think of tomorrow—it'll be the same. This reinforces the view that Holroyd's idealistic hopes of a better world, as originally evidenced by 'The Joker', had faded. Of course, we now know from the suggestion of songs such as 'Time of Our Lives' and 'Revolution Day' that whilst the hope might have faded, it has not completely vanished.

This loss of innocence features prominently in the work of other songwriters. A consistent theme is how early the disillusionment set in: Ray Davies' '20th Century Man' [*Muswell Hillbillies*, 1971], a song decrying the technological, insensitive, stressful world that Fifties Child finds himself in, was written when he was still comparatively young. Unfortunately, he complains about so much that the song turns into a bit of a rant. Strangely he omits to complain about one thing which many people would have on their list: noisy rock bands! Davies clearly feels strongly enough that he still gives the song prominence in his twenty-first century live shows.

'Lies Through the Eighties' was written for Manfred Mann's Earth Band's 1981 *Chance* album by Denny Newman.[3] The lyrics have synergy with themes that we have discussed throughout this book but it is the disaffection with technological progress that cements its place in this chapter. Super-video, super-fast information, but will it really help us all? Youngsters look sad, there is nowhere left to play and they have already lost their hope of a bright future, as though the onset of the loss of innocence had accelerated through the Seventies.

It may seem extraordinary but, nevertheless, these Fifties Children had by their twenties seen enough of the twentieth century to have had their

2. This is precisely the phrase that John Peel uttered immediately after playing 'Friend of Mine' and 'Poor Man's Moody Blues', from the newly released *Gone to Earth* album, on his late night Radio 1 show in 1977. I am sure he meant it kindly, he liked the band.
3. Not certain of exact birth date, but Newman meets the criteria for a contemporaneous artist.

innocent, youthful hopes crushed. Television—not impressed. Technological wizardry—not interested. Mechanisation—not impressed. Improvements in transport—not interested. Faster, bigger, better, more, more, more—not impressed! What has become of the sweet, green fields of England? The hope of the Fifties Child lies in ruins.

The societal inference is that this was a common experience for Fifties Children in general. By the time the Sixties faded away, so did their hopes of a Brave New World. Considering the lyrics of these songs, and the way that the world developed from the Seventies through to the twenty-first century, it is clear to see that there would be little to come in the ensuing decades, save for a brief glimmer as the Soviet empire fell, to rekindle that hope. All the Fifties Child would have to protect him from the strictures of life would be his strength of spirit. But life's journey towards developing a spiritual strength sufficient to withstand the ravages of reality was, as we have already witnessed in our social history, a perilous one and, despite their bravest efforts, not all Fifties Children would succeed.

Grumpy Old Men

Foul! Referee! How unfair to end our social history with a section entitled "Grumpy Old Men". Well, there are contributions from all three of our song-writers, so they only have themselves to blame!

'Children of the Disappeared' is a song that we met all the way back in the very first chapter, in 'Family and Environs'. Lees' explicit complaint that children of today have nowhere safe left to play, as in his own youth, is typical of the Fifties Child generation. It was better in his day. This theme is, in essence, similar to one of the themes of 'Spud-u-Like', which also bemoans how society's progress has affected the leisure time of youths and adults alike. Instead of listening to some fine rock 'n' roll on the radio, like Lees did, they are assimilated into the virtual reality world of computer games, disconnected from the reality that surrounds them. 'Spud-u-Like's future-shock differs from that of 'Children of the Disappeared' in that its technical origin was also able to inflict a zombifying effect on adults. Rock 'n' roll was much better. Well, that's not what his mum and dad said!

Despite having previously noted the "ring of changes" that is all life, Holroyd was still tempted to have a moan in 'Welcome to the Show'. Written in the same societal period as 'Spud-u-Like', it shares a thematic similarity, in that it disparages the way that video razzamatazz is taking over the music scene which, by implication, was better in Holroyd's day. Of course it was!

Wolstenholme's reformation of his Mæstoso band in the twenty-first century gave him the opportunity to write and record his trio of studio albums, mostly replete with either his own songs or collaborations with other band members. As we have already seen, many of these modern songs are sociological in nature and there are three, two of which have not yet been discussed in our social history, that fit neatly into this chapter's topic.

The first, the one which we have met very briefly, is 'Location, Location, Location', and it is thematically linked to the songs of Holroyd and Lees that we have just discussed, in particular 'Spud-u-Like' and 'Welcome to the Show', in that it berates the moronisation of television, with a consequential effect on the viewing public, as its power has grown down the decades from its introduction. Whereas once television would educate, its programming now seems to consist entirely of glitzy and banal light entertainment shows. Clearly, Wolstenholme perceived TV programmes, and their many spin-offs, such as *Location, Location, Location* (first aired in 2000), *Ready Steady Cook* (first aired in 1994) and *Wife Swap* (first aired in 2003) as torpor-inducing! I don't have the time to comment on this right now as I'm too busy watching repeats of *Come Dine With Me* . . .

Another facet of the commercialism hinted at in Holroyd's 'Welcome to the Show' is also evidenced by Wolstenholme in his 'A Waiting Game'. There he was, enjoying the autumn colours of October whilst waiting at a bus stop in London, when his peace was disturbed by the sounds of Slade's 'Merry Xmas Everybody' spilling loudly out into the street—the shops all around him in New Oxford Street were already into their full Christmas swing! In his website's notes on the song, Wolstenholme muses that if Jesus was to return now, even He would have the greatest of difficulty in defeating this rampant consumerism.

The moronisation of modern society hinted at by Lees' 'Spud-u-Like' and Wolstenholme's own 'Location, Location, Location' is reinforced and then dealt a sarcastic metaphorical slap on the cheek by the biting 'A.N.S.S.', another song from Wolstenholme's *One Drop in a Dry World* album. Wolstenholme parodies the behaviour of British youth on their package holidays in the sun. Behind the mock-reggae and lyrical ridicule is the serious message that modern youth's loutish behaviour is simply self-degrading. One of the generational contrasts within the song comes through the youths' urge to text rather than write. This is generally seen—in particular the alterations to the standard English language—by Fifties Children as a degradation of standards.[4] Wolstenholme's constant repetition of "nothing" within the song cements the idea that the moronisation of society is complete.

The attack of our Fifties Children songwriters on the negative impact of technological advance reflects the concern of many of their contemporaries

---

4. In fairness, many Fifties Children, perhaps in an attempt to continue communicating with their grandchildren, have adapted well to texting and email.

but it does carry a degree of irony. After all, it is almost certainly the advances in communications technology—in particular that of the internet—that have acted as the catalyst for the late period blossoming of their careers, by enabling vastly easier and more efficient dissemination of information regarding their activities.

Even if other contemporaneous rock artists have rarely continued to work as steadily as Barclay James Harvest's, it is still possible to gleam some of the grumpy-old-men syndrome coming through in their writing. We shall, however, content ourselves with just one example by returning to Ray Davies and 'Stand Up Comic', released on his solo album, *Other People's Lives* (2006). The complaint here is about the moronisation of comedy, as a symptom of the wider adoption of yob culture and, as such, there are echoes of Wolstenholme's bemoaning in 'Location, Location, Location'. Gone are the wit and wordplay of Shakespeare and Coward, instead they have been replaced by belching, farting, shouting and swearing. Fed up, Davies sneaks off down the pub for a quiet pint.

Sociologically, then, what the combination of these songs shows is that the Fifties Child generation has itself not been immune to these developments of character as the shadow of its years lengthens. The good old days, the good old days! As the demographics of society changes to include a greater weighting of older people, this in turn will mean that society's dynamic will come under greater influence from such thinking. Admittedly, the effect is still fairly recent, so we do not yet know what the outcome will be. That particular social history will be one for the next generation of conscious rockers to delight our ears with.

In Conclusion

So, we have come to the end of our social history. It is, I am sure you will agree, a broad and insightful view into the life of the Fifties Child, encompassing as it does major twentieth century events from British and world history, as well as revealing much about the culture of the period from the Fifties to the present day. That such a valuable social history can be suggested by the songwriting of the original members of Barclay James Harvest is truly remarkable and a compliment to their canon of songs. The breadth of its insight makes these songwriters' sociological songs unique—and worthy of special recognition—in the history of British rock.

Despite its fascination, the social history we have derived is not complete. This should not be a surprise from a sample of just three Fifties Children; indeed, the bigger surprise lies in how broad the history actually is. One gap that I will mention, because it affects their home town of Oldham, is how the demographics of the population have changed during the lifetime of a Fifties Child. Commonwealth workers, lured to Britain by post-War governments in order to rebuild the country and to man industry for an economic recovery, came to settle in this country with their families. For their children and grandchildren, Britain is their only home. Another major wave of migration has resulted from the break-up of the Soviet empire, where the subsequent liberalisation and amalgamation into the European Union of countries previously under Soviet influence has allowed an influx into Britain of workers from Eastern Europe. These migrations have been significant enough to impact on the cultural demographics of Britain. Not everyone is happy about this: ethnic tensions in Oldham—where Commonwealth citizens were welcomed to work in the cotton mills—are by no means unique and led to riots in 2001. We should, however, remember that although this major change, on their own doorstep, has not yet been covered by our songwriters, Holroyd and Lees have not yet retired, so the scope of Barclay James Harvest's social history may yet come to encompass it!

Our social history has been a good way to review many of Barclay James Harvest's songs, but one could have chosen a different way to have done so. For instance, a way of opening their canon up to analysis would be to review against themes. In that way, one might actually encompass more songs, because themes such as "birds" or "love" open up songs not captured by this social history. Nevertheless, we have not done badly: readers will undoubtedly have identified themes along the way, such as "victims", "innocence" and—arguably the strongest theme in the whole of Barclay James Harvest's writing—"spirituality". Let me give you just a quick example of thematic analysis (and it will be quick because writing this book has been tough enough!) by considering the trio of songs that closes one of the band's most revered albums, 1974's *Everyone is Everybody Else*. The songs have all been covered topically in our social history: 'Poor Boy Blues' and 'Mill Boys' were considered as a song cycle in the 'Family and Environs' chapter, and 'For No One' was analysed in 'The Troubles in Northern Ireland'. Topically, that is where they belong for the purpose of relating a social history but they share a common theme: "breaking free of the strictures of the past". In 'Poor Boy Blues', the protagonist wants economic freedom, so he leaves the town behind—where only low-paid work can be found; 'Mill Boys' warns against being trapped working in the mills and advises getting an apprenticeship in some other trade; and 'For No One' urges individuals to free themselves from peer pressure and break the "circle of hate". Perhaps it is their common theme that has led the songs to be unified musically on the album, with 'For No One' segueing on seamlessly from the 'Poor Boy Blues'/'Mill Boys' song cycle. Finally, one could say that their common theme—freedom from the norms of the past—defines the Fifties Child.

The band's songwriters could quite easily have become "victims" themselves. Born in Oldham, a drudge-labour mill town on the decline, they could have found themselves scraping a living by slogging away at repetitive, mind-numbing work, or been struggling to find any job at all as the town wilted, or even having to leave their roots for some glitzy city in search of fortune. They did none of those things. Empowered by the spirit of the Fifties Child, these songwriters found their own freedom, flying on the wings of their hope. And what soaring flight! How boldly it extended their horizons! They looked up from the microcosm of routine, they looked up from the decaying north and glanced far, far beyond. The spirit of the Fifties Child imbued them with the vision of how we are all one as humanity, just one part of an integrated natural world, all of us worthy in our own ways of attaining happiness and love, and of living in harmony with our environment. They shared this vision through song: our follies, our loves, stories of our fellow man in parts of the globe near and far. They shared a vision not only of the frailty of the human mind but also of how to overcome our fears and strengthen our spirit. All this they have done at the same time as entertaining us with some fabulous music!

The platform of music enabled Barclay James Harvest to enrich not only their own lives, but those of many others. In this, they were certainly not helped by the rock press, who consistently slated them. Despite the barrage of criticism, they found their own musical niche, writing rich, melodic music with lyrics of immense vision. Their songs have, for more than forty years, reflected many of the key societal aspects facing their generation. Clearly, the impact of the view they provide is greatest when looked at retrospectively from the standpoint of the totality of the songs, but attentive fans will have realised that such a view was developing album by album. Indeed, this is one of the aspects of Barclay James Harvest's music which has made it so appealing. Listening to these songs down the years has been like listening to a friend, for that is what this music has become, sharing views and opinions on the world, its problems and its joys.

People are not daft. They recognise beautiful music and meaningful lyrics, despite what the press might say. The band's music has survived in much the same way that dissident movements survive in totalitarian states. You *feel* the message, it resonates with your soul, you become inseparable from its own soul. It fosters loyalty, passion and comradeship. *That* is why Barclay James Harvest's music survives. They have always been, and still are, a people's band.

Enhancing the value of this collection of sociological songs is the fact that the Fifties Child's social history is itself unique. Born into the wake of two cataclysmic World Wars, the Fifties Child threw off the shackles of Empire, rejected the values of his fathers and forefathers and, free of those burdens from the past, initially saw a bright future for himself, full of peace, love and understanding; the embodiment of the Summer of Love. It was not to be. As his adolescence turned to adulthood, the realities brought on by the empire's death throes clouded his hopes: terrorism on his door step as trouble flared in Ireland, a bleak financial situation at home and, further afield—or was it just next door?—Cold War conflicts painting his TV screens and newspapers with images of woeful suffering.

And yet, compared with many other generations, the Fifties Child was lucky, at least he saw that glimmer of hope, he saw the future as a free, equal world. Me? Born just a few years later, my teenage consciousness awoke to bombings, napalm, three-day weeks, the nuclear threat. I saw no Summer of

Love. By itself, this stark difference is a virtually sufficient explanation as to why the Fifties Child sang about peace and love, whereas the Sixties Child sang about anarchy in the UK. The Fifties Child's social history is unique indeed.

The Fifties Child has seen vast and fundamental changes during his lifetime: the fall of empires, the infiltration of the power and influence of television into his home, the meshing of politics and the media, the relaxation in sexual morality, the weakening of the family unit, the desertion of organised Christianity. Just pause and consider these for a moment, either in totality or individually, and reflect on how they impact on how life is lived. Life. Yes, that life that the Fifties Child's parents lovingly taught him about and prepared him for. His parents were mistaken: their life would never exist for him, the Fifties Child would have to find his own way.

Amidst the tumultuous changes, there would be two constants during the Fifties Child's life. The first, sadly, was conflict but the second was the force and strength of his spirit and compassion. This strength varies between individuals, as we have seen, but it is the constant that has allowed many Fifties Children to survive the constant conflict and fundamental, fast paced change. It is precisely this spiritual quality which provides the hope that humanity is not beyond redemption.

Look . . . you will find that hope there, amidst the chaos. Listen . . . you will find that hope there, in Barclay James Harvest's songs.

Our spirit will awake
and something deep inside
will help us find the way.

Barclay James Harvest, 1987 –
Mel Pritchard, John Lees, Les Holroyd

Appendices

List of Principal Sources

General sources used throughout the book
en.wikipedia.org/wiki/
www.bjharvest.co.uk—this is the most comprehensive Barclay James Harvest website, and includes links to the splinter bands' own websites.
The Barclay James Harvest Story, Keith & Monika Domone, 2005

Chapter specific sources
INTRODUCTION
  Classic Rock Presents Prog, #18.

CHAPTER 1: FAMILY AND ENVIRONS
  thedisappearedni.co.uk
  www.bbc.co.uk
  www.gingerbread.org.uk
  www.murderuk.com
  www.telegraph.co.uk
  Child Abductions: Understanding Police Recorded Crime Statistics, Newiss and Fairbrother, Home Office Publications, 2004
  Households and Families, Jen Beaumont, Office for National Statistics, 2011
  Monsters and Angels: Visual Press Coverage of Child Murders in the USA and UK, 1930-2000, Wardle, 2007

CHAPTER 2: NATURE AND THE ENVIRONMENT
  www.aip.org (American Institute of Physics)
  www.bbc.co.uk
  www.greenpeace.org
  www.theozonehole.com
  www.un.org
  Global Warming and Global Politics, Matthew Paterson, 1996

CHAPTER 3: THE SOVIET THREAT
  www.independent.co.uk
  1984, George Orwell, 1949

CHAPTER 4: SPECTRE OF A NUCLEAR HOLOCAUST

www.atomicbombmuseum.org
www.cnduk.org
www.fsmitha.com (Macrohistory & World Report)
www.gwu.edu (The National Security Archive)
www.washingtonpost.com
Consequences of Using Nuclear Weapons, Babst and Krieger, 1997
One Minute to Midnight: Kennedy, Khrushchev, and Castro on the Brink of Nuclear War, Dobbs, 2008

CHAPTER 5: VIETNAM
www.britishpathe.com

CHAPTER 6: BERLIN
The Berlin Wall: Life, Death and the Spatial Heritage of Berlin, Dumont

CHAPTER 7: BREAK-UP OF THE SOVIET UNION
www.time.com

CHAPTER 8: THE TROUBLES—NORTHERN IRELAND
cain.ulst.ac.uk/issues/violence
irishconflict.webs.com/britishmilitary
news.bbc.co.uk
www.bloody-sunday-inquiry.org
www.coldstreamguards-boro.org
www.guardian.co.uk
www.historyonthenet.com/Chronology/timelinenorthernireland.htm
www.wesleyjohnston.com/users/ireland/past/troubles/major_killings.html

CHAPTER 9: SOUTH AFRICA UNDER APARTHEID
dustyspringfieldsoul4u.com/dusty-in-south-africa
overcomingapartheid.msu.edu
uk.oneworld.net
untreaty.un.org/cod/avl/ha/cspca/cspca
www.anc.org.za

CHAPTER 10: THE SECOND IRAQ WAR
www.jewishvirtuallibrary.org/jsource/History

CHAPTER 11: THE SOLDIER AS VICTIM
www.aftermathww1.com
www.bbc.co.uk/history

www.bbc.co.uk/news
www.britishlegion.org.uk
www.guardian.co.uk
www.independent.co.uk
www.parliamentarybrief.com
www.rfc-rnas-raf-register.org.uk/
www.shotatdawn.info
www.ukpolitical.info

CHAPTER 12: POLITICS AND THE MEDIA
www.barb.co.uk
www.ier.org.uk
www.redflag.org.uk/frontline/13
Nova Lepidoptera (International Barclay James Harvest Fan Club magazine),
#6

CHAPTER 13: SEX
www.bl.uk
Mellotron: The Machine and the Musicians that Revolutionised Rock, Nick
Awde, 2008
Paying the Price Again: Prostitution Policy in Historical Perspective, Julia Laite
Wolfenden Report, 1957.

CHAPTER 15: rock 'n' roll
www.5rb.com
www.theroot.com
www.virginmedia.com/music
Classic Rock Presents Prog, issue with Pip Williams feature (#22?)
Nova Lepidoptera (International Barclay James Harvest Fan Club magazine),
#56

CHAPTER 16: ELVES, ALIENS and OTHER FORMS OF ESCAPISM
Eon, Greg Bear, 1985
Something Wicked This Way Comes, Ray Bradbury, 1962.

CHAPTER 17: THE BATTLE FOR THE MIND
articles.latimes.com
www.mentalhealth.org.uk
www.quransearch.com
www.telegraph.co.uk
www.winmentalhealth.com

I Me Mine, George Harrison, 1980

The Story of The Kinks: You Really Got Me, Nick Hasted, 2011

Feel So Real, Tony Jasper, 1991

Drug Treatment in Modern Psychiatry: The History of a Delusion, Joanna Moncrieff, 2002

Drinking in the UK: An Exploration of Trends, Smith and Foxcroft, 2009

CHAPTER 18: SPIRITUALITY

www.christian-research.org

www.guardian.co.uk

www.whychurch.co.uk

Hurricane magazine interview, 1987.

Teaching Religion: Sixty Years of Religious Education in England and Wales, Terence Copley, 2008

Feel So Real, Tony Jasper, Marshall Pickering, 1991

CHAPTER 19: GRUMPY OLD MEN

The Story of The Kinks: You Really Got Me, Nick Hasted, 2011

Appendix 1:
A Brief History of
Barclay James Harvest

A detailed history of the band is available in Keith & Monika Domone's excellent, detailed book *The Barclay James Harvest Story*. This short appendix gives a personal view of their music over the course of their, as yet continuing, history.

Barclay James Harvest were formed in Oldham in 1967. More than 40 years on their music survives in good health and two offshoots of the band still remain musically active. Whilst they did become European superstars in their heyday, they never quite made it to English rock's premier league. The band split in 1998, leaving a strong musical legacy of 17 studio albums. Often accused of being highly derivative by the English music press, their sound is nevertheless quite unique and easily identifiable; the strongest influence to consistently shine through being that of the Beatles.

The story of the band's history can be divided into five musically distinct periods: "Harvest" (1967-1973), "English Rock" (1974-1977), "European Conquest" (1977- 1984), "Slumber" (1985-1998) and "Offshoots" (post 1998).

Harvest (1967–1973)

John Lees (guitar, vocals); Les Holroyd (bass, guitars, keyboards, vocals); Woolly Wolstenholme (keyboards, vocals) and Mel Pritchard (drums) came together from the remnants of two bands from the Oldham area in Lancashire.

Very early on in the band's career they impressed an impresario named John Crowther, who became their backer and manager. He installed them in his own farmhouse in Diggle—Preston House—so they could concentrate on writing and rehearsing material. Crowther negotiated the release of their first single 'Early Morning' in 1968. The band's use of the Mellotron—which has become one of *the* iconic instruments of progressive rock—marked out a feature of their soundscape that was to remain for a decade or more.

Shortly afterwards they befriended Robert Godfrey (later of the Enid), who moved into Preston House with them. Godfrey was pivotal in the decision for the band to employ their own orchestra not only for recording but also to tour. Whilst hugely expensive and landing the band with heavy financial losses, the music from this period—where the band developed their own unique brand of *very* English pastoral symphonic rock—was often exciting, inventive and inspirational. The approach worked well, whether on short, quiet numbers like 'Galadriel', or on state-of-the-art rock-orchestra fusions like 'Dark Now My Sky', on conscience songs like 'After The Day' or 'Summer Soldier', as well as on love songs such as 'Mocking Bird'. The latter song was to become one of the band's most famous but would also be the cause of some major hassle and angst many years after its first release.

Godfrey had considerable input into the arrangements of a few of the band's songs at this time, not the least of which was 'Mocking Bird', but his involvement ceased in 1971. More than ten years later, after the band had begun to enjoy considerable commercial success, Godfrey issued a writ seeking to share in the profits from the songs he claimed to have co-written, but for which he had not been credited. The resulting High Court case was a predecessor to the now more famous Fisher vs. Brooker case in respect of Procol Harum's 'A Whiter Shade of Pale'. In fact, the same judge presided over both cases and the Godfrey vs. Lees case was quoted in the judgment of Fisher vs. Brooker. Whilst the judge agreed that Godfrey had a justifiable claim to authorship of six songs, he judged that the band's commercial success was as a result of all the hard work that they had put in since his involvement ceased. So no royalties for Godfrey, a hollow victory with no financial reward, save for the lawyers.

In 1969, EMI launched a brand new label in order to fully capture the benefits of the changing, "progressive" music scene. Barclay James Harvest were amongst the first acts to be signed, along with acts such as the Pretty Things and Pink Floyd. The new label's name, Harvest, was derived from the band's own name.

The band's first release for Harvest was 'Brother Thrush' c/w 'Poor Wages'. Like 'Early Morning', the single did not chart. This inability to find a hit single would continue to haunt the band for many years to come. As well as a few non-charting singles, the band recorded four studio albums for Harvest, which also failed to chart. The second of these, 'Once Again' [1971], is still heralded in progressive music circles as one of the hallmark albums of the era.

Tribulations mounted for Barclay James Harvest from 1972. Musical differences between the three songwriters began to manifest themselves from the time of the fourth album, *Baby James Harvest* [1972], leading Lees to take a break from the band to record a solo album, *A Major Fancy*. The band's lack of commercial success, mounting debts and other pressures, such as the ill-advised tour of South Africa at a time when anti-apartheid feeling was running high, led to them losing their record contract and management team in the summer of 1973.

It is likely that the band would have split were it not for the fact that the most likely way of repaying their debts was to try to make the best possible use of their brand name rather than restarting as individuals.

■ *Recommended listening from the period:* the live *BBC In Concert 1972*. Not released until 2002, this vibrant recording of the band with the orchestra is an excellent showcase for their material from this period and is an ample demonstration of why the band built up a reputation and fan base through live performance.

English Rock (1974–1977)

The band's debts made the task of seeking a new manager and contract all the more difficult. Eventually, Lees turned to his friend, 10cc's Eric Stewart, for advice. Finding a new management team as a result, a new recording deal was eventually signed with Polydor in December 2003. Refreshed, the band launched into what was to become a halcyon period. Whilst short, "English Rock" is a distinctive period in the band's musical history and, for the majority of English fans, is when the band was at its peak. The change of soundscape from the Harvest years was significant—gone was the orchestra and any pretension to symphonic progressive rock. The band hired Rodger Bain (famous for producing bands such as Black Sabbath and Budgie) for their first studio album for Polydor, *Everyone is Everybody Else* [1974] and a darker, heavier rock sound resulted, closer to the band's live persona.

Despite their lack of commercial success the band had been steadily winning fans on the English touring circuit, playing to larger and larger audiences as the years went by. It was no surprise then, when their second album for Polydor, *BJH Live* was their first album to reach the UK charts. Once you were won over to the band, it was not easy to let go and their popularity at home continued to increase over the next few years, each of their remaining studio albums as a foursome charting.

This short period in the band's history was one of rapidly changing soundscape, enhanced by a change in producer on each release. *Time Honoured Ghosts* [1975] was produced by Elliot Mazer (renowned for his work, amongst much else, on Neil Young's famous *Harvest* album) in San Francisco. The success of the album prompted the band to fly back out to San Francisco for Mazer to produce the follow-up, but he let them down and so *Octoberon* [1976] ended up being self-produced by the band.

This successful period saw any musical differences smoothed over by good studio production that was able to extract the synergy from the band's varied songwriting approaches. However, the singles market in the UK continued to be a problem, as it always would, but it was in this period that Barclay James Harvest achieved their greatest singles success at home, reaching No. 49 with the Live EP recording of 'Rock 'n' Roll Star' (a song from *Octoberon*) c/w 'Medicine Man' (a perennial favourite of the band's live set). They even managed an appearance on the legendary TV singles programme of the era, *Top of the Pops*.

■ *Recommended listening from the period:* A single recommendation from this period is difficult in that all three studio albums and the *BJH Live* album are excellent. so it depends on your musical leanings: for the more progressive of you, pick *Octoberon*, those with a heavier rock leaning go for *Everyone is Everybody Else*, whereas *Time Honoured Ghosts* is a wonderful fusion of English flavoured rock with whiffs of prog given an American West Coast production—it's a simply gorgeous album! *BJH Live* has a strong set of the band's material up to that point in time and is a wonderful example of the Mellotron's integration into a rock band.

European Conquest (1977–1984)

Gone to Earth [September 1977], marks the launch of the band's conquest of Europe, a period of sustained commercial success lasting through to *Victims of Circumstance* [1984]. The difference in sound from *Octoberon* was subtle but significant. There was a continuing mellowing with a move towards the pop end of the musical spectrum and the disparity in the writing styles of Lees, Holroyd and Wolstenholme was not only continuing to grow but becoming more evident in their recorded output.

Gone to Earth was a great success, particularly in Germany where it stayed on the chart for 202 weeks. These album sales translated well into demand for live shows. The band had toured to Europe before but the tours of the Continent became more extensive after this time.

Not surprisingly, after ten years of penury, and given this commercial success, the band did not veer back towards the more progressive rock territory for their next album, *XII* [1978]. Whilst this again sold well the musical differences and resulting frustrations deepened to the extent that Wolstenholme quit the band to pursue his own musical career just as the recording of the following album, *Eyes of the Universe* [1979], was getting under way.

Wolstenholme's foray in the music world without the Barclay James Harvest brand name to support him was not too successful. The excellence of the *Mæstoso* album [1980] did not translate into significant sales and Polydor were unwilling to issue a second, already recorded, album that was planned to be released as a band album (the band also being named Mæstoso). Wolstenholme quit the music business entirely in 1982, resurfacing, a bit like the proverbial phoenix, refreshed and enthusiastic some twenty years later.

Meanwhile Holroyd, Lees and Pritchard continued from strength to strength as a three-piece band, using session musicians to add depth to the sound both live and in the studio. *Gone to Earth* eventually sold over 750,000 copies in Germany; *Eyes of the Universe* sold over 500,000 and *Live Tapes, XII, Turn of the Tide, Berlin, Ring of Changes* and *Victims of Circumstance* all sold over 250,000.

The band's main market was in Germany. In 1980, as a thank-you gesture to their German fans, the band played a free concert in front of the Reichstag in Berlin to a crowd of around 250,000. The gesture was repeated in East Berlin in 1987, when they played to 150,000 fans at Treptower Park.

But, by then, Barclay James Harvest were in slumber.

■ *Recommended listening from the period: Victims of Circumstance*, produced by Pip Williams, is an excellent pop-rock album. However, if forays into pop aren't your thing then *Gone to Earth* would be a safer bet, retaining as it does some shreds of Wolstenholme's progressive influence.

Slumber (1985–1998)

At the time of *Victims of Circumstance* Barclay James Harvest was still a major attraction in Europe, as well as in the UK. There then followed a sabbatical period of period of nearly three years before the release of their next studio album *Face to Face* in 1987.

Clearly, the band was now receiving sufficient income from royalties that they could afford the luxury of such a lengthy break. Unfortunately, the music business is fickle and waits for no man. At such a stage in their career, with the fan base ageing, marrying, having children, getting weighed down with the stress of jobs and life, having such a long interval since the previous album was not a good idea and *Face to Face* was not the album to propel the band back to the heights that it had forfeited in 1984.

The polarisation between Holroyd and Lees' writing styles was still evident and, if anything, had deepened with Lees seeming to revert back to a Seventies feel on his songs, Holroyd continuing the lighter vein of his early Eighties output. As a result, the album did not altogether gel as a unit. Unsurprisingly, sales and tour attendances were down and this was a trend that would continue to the end of the band's existence.

From having issued 13 studio albums since 1970, the 13-year slumber period saw the issue of only four more studio albums. Due to falling sales their last studio album, *River of Dreams* [1997] was not even released in the UK, although imported copies were widely available in high street record shops.

The Godfrey litigation hung over the band like some Damoclean sword for most of this period, having been brought in 1985 and not resolved in their favour until 1995!

Given the circumstances, the *Welcome to the Show* album [1990] proved to be quite superb, reminding fans of the days of the band in its prime. Their most pleasing albums had always been those when an outside producer had managed to harmonise the different styles of the songwriters into a homogeneous soundscape (Norman Smith, Rodger Bain, Elliot Mazer, Pip Williams). This time, Jon Astley and Andy McPherson were to be the band's slumber period saviours, and *Weclome to the Show* was well received by fans on both sides of the English Channel and is still highly regarded today. It is the only studio album from the period to have topped the 250,000 sales mark.

■ *Recommended listening from the period:* *Welcome to the Show*, where the production weaves a harmonious "Barclay James Harvest sound" for the Nineties.

Offshoots (1998–present)

The band more or less fell apart in 1998, Lees beginning to work on a project called "Barclay James Harvest through the Eyes of John Lees" whilst the band were supposedly in a sabbatical period. It soon became clear that Holroyd's and Lees' musical and personal differences had worsened to the extent that there was no way back for them to perform again as Barclay James Harvest.

The activity of Barclay James Harvest through the Eyes of John Lees has been sporadic, their only studio album being *Nexus* [1999]. There have also been tours in 1999, 2000, 2001 and regularly from 2006 (since then under the name John Lees' Barclay James Harvest—same band though). Live recordings of the band are available on both CD and DVD. This offshoot's choice of live material is unashamedly culled almost exclusively from the band's first ten years. At the time of writing, another studio album is currently being recorded.

Lees had recruited Woolly Wolstenholme to his own version of Barclay James Harvest from the start, having reportedly missed his input into the arrangements for his own songs following his departure in 1979. Wolstenholme's life had reached a crossroads in 1998 and the thought of becoming involved in the music scene again appealed. However, when the *Nexus* album and early touring failed to materialise into routine activity, Wolstenholme decided to reform his own band, naming it after his original album from 1980, Mæstoso. The other members had all been associated with Barclay James Harvest through the Eyes of John Lees except Steve Broomhead, who had been the guitarist for Wolstenholme's solo work in the early Eighties. Wolstenholme has been the most prolific of the three Barclay James Harvest offshoots in terms of new material. The band's third and last album, *caterwauling*, was released three years before his premature death from depression in 2010. Two other fine albums had preceded it: *One Drop in a Dry World* (2004) and *Grim* (2005).

Les Holroyd was slower off the mark with his offshoot than Lees and, although only one studio album has arisen from his "Barclay James Harvest featuring Les Holroyd" band (2002's *Revolution Days*), Holroyd has more than made up for it by touring extensively in Europe. His band suffered a setback when its drummer, original band member Mel Pritchard, died in 2004. Holroyd rekindled some of the old Barclay James Harvest spirit by touring with the Prague Philharmonic Orchestra. Whilst the orchestra was not used in quite the same innovative and vibrant way as during the band's early years, it did complement the band's sound: a CD and DVD of the concert at Amneville in France, *Classic Meets Rock* (2006) shows Holroyd's band on top form.

It is interesting to compare the musical work of the three offshoots, as a reflection of the tensions that affected the band during its period as a four-piece. Lees' output strongly reflects that era whereas Holroyd's balance of material is chosen from the post-Wolstenholme period, showing Barclay James Harvest's poppier side. Wolstenholme's Mæstoso, on the other hand, shows the spirit of the original Barclay James Harvest, venturing into adventurous progressive rock territory but always retaining a sharp, keen eye for beautiful melody. It really is as if, as Lees once said, "Wolstenholme is the soul of Barclay James Harvest".

■ ***Recommended listening from the period***: Mæstoso's *caterwauling*. This is pure English classic rock at its best: whimsical, humorous, eclectic, progressive and with some exquisite musical moments. The segued couplet of songs 'Soldier of Fortune/Road to Nowhere' is worth the price of the disc several times over on its own for the way that the force of its message is accentuated by the music.

Legacy

The overall impression is that, whilst successful, the band under-achieved in the UK. There might have been a number of factors for this: the press, the band's generally soft-rock album sound, the punk revolution, their lack of hipness. They were not pretty, did not get drunk and smash up hotel rooms or guitars on stage, didn't do the drug culture trip. Their inability, despite many attempts, to hit the Top 30 singles charts must have been a factor. Equally significant perhaps was the fact that they never fixed on one producer, hence their sound, although easily identifiable, was always subtly changing.

So . . . what musical legacy does the band leave the future? Will there be anything beyond the enjoyment of their music by our generation and perhaps a few of our children? Whilst ten million is a sizeable number of records to have sold, the band's most original and innovative music, arguably from the Harvest period, did not reach anything like such an audience and the band's unique (though derivative) sound has not been claimed as a major influence in any of the headlining acts of today, unlike peers of theirs such as Pink Floyd and Yes.

Despite this, their opus is such that, as a minimum, they should be considered as worthy as other contemporaneous classic English rock bands such as Procol Harum, Strawbs, Caravan, Camel and Renaissance. Perhaps they deserve much more as their songs contain a unique chronicling—for a rock band from this period—of the societal concerns and history of the age. They take us all the way from factory workers in Lancashire, through a gamut of minority and underprivileged groups in society to the destruction of the environment. They share our fears about the power of the media, our concerns about violence and war and our joy at the break up of Eastern Europe. It is a legacy that deserves to survive.

As in all things, the writers of history will be their judge.

CHART POSITIONS

	UK	Germany	Switzer-land	France	Nether-lands	Norway

Albums

	UK	Germany	Switzer-land	France	Nether-lands	Norway
Live	40	–	–	–	–	–
Time Honoured Ghosts	32	–	–	–	34	–
Octoberon	19	40	–	–	–	–
Gone to Earth	30	10	9	–	–	37
Live Tapes	–	33	–	–	–	–
XII	31	18	–	–	–	–
Eyes of the Universe	–	3	–	–	–	6
Turn of the Tide	55	2	1	–	–	4
A Concert for the People: Berlin	15	1	–	–	–	14
Ring of Changes	36	4	2	–	26	7
Victims of Circumstance	33	4	1	1	34	13
Face to Face	65	9	7	–	–	14
Glasnost (Live)	–	47	30	–	–	–
Welcome to the Show	–	10	7	–	–	24
The Best of BJH	–	9	13	–	–	–
Caught in the Light	–	82	33	–	–	–
River of Dreams	–	71	33	–	–	–

Singles

	UK	Germany	Switzer-land	France	Nether-lands	Norway
Titles	–	–	–	–	9	–
Rock 'n' Roll Star (Live EP)	49	–	–	–	–	–
Love on the Line	63	–	–	–	–	–
Life is for Living	61	2	1	–	49	–
Child of the Universe (Live)	–	27	–	–	–	–
Just a Day Away	68	40	5	–	–	–
Victims of Circumstance	–	46	19	1	–	–
Stand Up	92	–	–	–	–	–

Appendix 2:
Anoraks' Corner

Number of Sociological Songs by Songwriter

Holroyd   28
Lees   65
Wolstenholme   37

Song Incidence

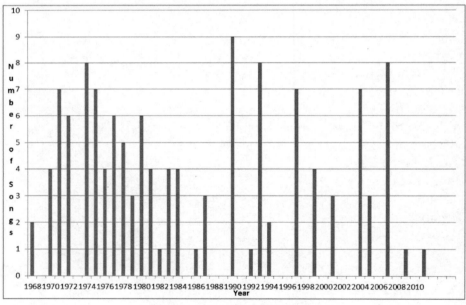

Incidence chart of sociological songs

The Anti-Hunting Suite
   Spirit on the Water (Holroyd)
   The Will to Fly (Sport ohne Mord) (Wolstenholme)
   Shadows on the Sky (Holroyd)
The Berlin Suite
   Berlin (Holroyd)
   Back to the Wall (Holroyd)
   In Memory of the Martyrs (Lees)

The Troubles Suite
  Summer Soldier
  Child of the Universe
  For No One
  Cheap the Bullet

A Fifties Child's Spiritual Song Journey

This is my own effort at completing the table depicting Lees' spiritual journey that I presented part of the way through the 'Spirituality' chapter. Words in *italics* in the third column signify actual lyrics. Where lyrics are paraphrased, then they appear in a normal font.

I have split the spiritual-related elements into four categories:

1. **Values.** These are the key spiritual values, the "drivers" that causes one to search for a satisfactory spirituality. From Fifties Child, it is clear that the three key values are peace, love and freedom.
2. **Duality of the Psyche.** This is the recognition that within our minds there is a constant battle between good and evil. Recognising this aspect of the mind allows one to work to enhance the good part of the psyche.
3. **Spirituality.** This describes how the spirituality manifests itself within the song. Songs without this category listed are not considered spiritual songs, although they are important in deciphering how the search for spirituality is progressing.
4. **Influence of Nature.** Identifies the elements of the natural world that have helped the search for, or reinforced, a satisfactory spirituality.

Temporally, the spiritual journey is split into three phases:

1. searching
2. crystallisation: in other words, paraphrasing, I think I've found the answer but I just need to make sure.
3. rock solid: total spiritual confidence.

There is an argument for placing the transition to the third phase even earlier than I have suggested, by anchoring the start of the "confidence" phase to 'Sperratus' but, despite the momentous 'In Memory of the Martyrs', I have chosen instead to delay the onset of this period to the 'Fifties Child'–'Blow Me Down' axis. Remember, the exact shape of the transition is a little speculative, based as it is on my interpretation of the songs, although the overall spiritual journey still has sociological interest because it reflects the sort of journeys that many Fifties Children will have had.

The Search for a Satisfactory Spirituality

1970	Taking Some Time On	Establishes values and hints at the duality of the psyche and influence of nature. Values = let's remember the days when we were **free**; Duality of the Psyche = the hidden meanings of the mind; Influence of Nature = the sky joins with the sea.
1970	Mother Dear	Duality of the Psyche = *lady in white*—represents love (compassion, empathy); *figure in black*—represents death (evil)
1971	Hymn (demo)	Spirituality = as in the song released in 1977, the message of the lyrics of this demo are that there is a better way to happiness than through drugs. However, the demo lacks a Christian message, referring only to "your God" as the source of that more satisfying happiness. There is no retelling of aspects of the Gospel story.
1971	Child of Man	Values = **love** (for brother, sister, neighbour i.e., everyone). Spirituality = the child of God's message is that you should love your neighbour and help him to "understand". "Understand" is a word used many years later in 'He Said Love' to denote empathy and compassion.
1972	Summer Soldier	Values = **peace, love.** Spirituality = *The Lord God said love thy neighbour* Duality of the Psyche = (1) *there's a man by your side with a knife and a gun in each hand—you're one and the same—it's time to stop and decide: is it love or hate?*; (2) *a summer soldier – I fire in hate; an angel bright – my cause is peace*
1974	For No One	Values = **peace** Spirituality = (1) *then pray God we can live in peace;* (2) *God alone knows how we will survive* Duality of the Psyche = (1) *lay down your thoughts*

of being no one, concentrate on what you ought to be;
(2) everyone's a no one till he wants to make a stand
Influence of Nature = *take a look at what lies all*
around you

1975 Hymn for the Children	Values = *Your **love** and mine.* This is the strength of faith in equality, in freedom and in peace, which can bring about a happy world if we all apply it. It leads to compassion and empathy and is the same "love" that appears later in 'In Memory of the Martyrs', 'Fifties Child', 'For Your Love' and 'He Said Love'.

Spirituality = This is a holistic spirituality, represented by the metaphor *time picked the words, time picked the songs.*

Influence of Nature = This song is replete with examples demonstrating how nature influences spiritual thinking: the first, *their spirits soar on high, they wing with birds that float on by*, is just one of many.

1977 Interview (Hymn)   In the past, Lees has had to take psychiatric drugs to combat anxiety.

Crystallisation of Faith

1977 Hymn   Spirituality = The straight retelling of aspects of the Gospel makes this—for the first time—an overtly Christian song, as it is much more significant in terms of impact than the inferred Christianity of 'Child of Man's "child of God".

1977 Interview (1987)   "I was a Christian at the time [1977], although my belief was a bit split . . . but in spite of different beliefs I was convinced that it was better to believe in something spiritual than to take the risk of getting involved with drugs and killing yourself."

1979 Sperratus   Spirituality = *You can't touch what's deep within: that's my soul. Reaching my final goal!* The means of faith as the as the sole route to salvation was a teaching of Martin Luther, one of whose first adepts was Paul Speratus, who contributed three of the eight hymns to the first Protestant hymnal. Influence of Nature = *Look in my eyes: see the light of the universe.*

1981 Doctor Doctor

Spirituality = *Help me through the day. Give me something natural I can depend on… it's a natural panacea like a cure for every fear: it's some of her sweet love mixed up with her young blood: true love and devotion.* Lees admitted in interviews that he prayed when depressed. In 'Doctor Doctor' he yearns for a faith as deep as that of the Holy Mary, to help him when he is depressed.

1981 In Memory of the Martyrs

Values & Spirituality = *We are love.* This is our purpose in life: to demonstrate compassion and empathy, to help each other, and we can do these things wherever we are, irrespective of the trials we live under.
Influence of Nature = *The beauty that surrounds you was meant to be adored.*

Standing on the Rock of Faith
1983 Fifties Child

Values = *Fifties Child was right to believe **peace** and **love** were our needs; the need to be **free**.* This is perhaps the most important song in Lees' canon from the perspective of understanding his oeuvre, because it underscores unambiguously his values and therefore helps to unlock the meaning to many songs. Whilst there has been a spiritual development during his life, these values—peace, love, freedom—have been a constant for Lees.
Spirituality = The song is a prayer, from someone who is now confident in his Christian faith, asking that all people of the world should adopt the values of peace, love and freedom. *Renew our faith: let us see—young and old—we're right to believe peace and love are our needs, the need to be free.* In this way, it predates 'For Your Love', which is a similar prayer.

| 1983 | Paraiso dos Cavalos | Influence of Nature = the song demonstrates how communing with nature (riding horses along the beach) has recharged Lees' spirit. |

1983 Blow Me Down

Spirituality = The song relates, in metaphor, Lees' spiritual life journey. The final verse confirms that Lees is now confident in his faith. The song therefore anchors the start of the "Standing on the Rock of Faith" period.

Influence of Nature = In the middle verse's "epiphany metaphor", Lees meets a man in whose eyes he sees the world and a clear blue sky.

1984 For Your Love

Values = *For your **love***.
Spirituality = *I pray that someday we'll all have love of our own.*

1985 Interview (1987)

"A year and a half ago, I was going through a crisis in my life. The only thing I could think of was praying and my prayers have always been answered in a miraculous sort of way."

1987 Interview

"I want a world without starvation, without wars and without destruction of the environment, and a world in which people get on well with each other."

1987 He Said Love

Values = **Love**. In this song, Lees also uses the word "understanding" to denote the compassion and empathy that he implies by the use of the word "love".

Spirituality = An unambiguously Christian song.

1993 Knoydart

Influence of Nature = The beauty of the Scottish Highlands heals Lees' soul.

1993 Back to Earth

Spirituality = Lees believes that he will be reunited with his father after his own death.

1997 Mr E

Duality of the Psyche = *Mr E—my secret lives in your deceit; (the spirit)—my promise is a window to the bottom of your soul.*

Spirituality = (1) following the good part of the psyche will lead to the discovery of one's soul; (2) *Let me take you down to the riverside* is an echo of the baptism of Jesus by John the Baptist.

2006 Interview

"I wouldn't [now] go down the route of taking prescribed drugs to keep me doing the job. If I'd have been strong enough mentally, I would've overcome that."

Sociological Songs by Studio Album

Sociological songs are identified in **bold**, along with the chapter in which they appear. *Early Morning Onwards* is taken as a studio album as this became the introduction to the band for many fans and was counted by the band themselves in the run-up to *XII*. Singles releases are only identified when the song does not appear on one of the albums listed.

BARCLAY JAMES HARVEST
  Taking Some Time On [Spirituality]
  Mother Dear [The Battle for the Mind]
  The Sun Will Never Shine [The Battle for the Mind]
  When the World Was Woken
  Good Love Child
  The Iron Maiden
  Dark Now My Sky [Nature and the Environment]

ONCE AGAIN
  She Said
  Happy Old World [Nature and the Environment]
  Song for Dying
  Galadriel [Elves, Aliens and Other Forms of Escapism]
  Mocking Bird
  Vanessa Simmons
  Ball and Chain [The Battle for the Mind]
  Lady Loves

. . . AND OTHER SHORT STORIES
  Medicine Man [Elves, Aliens and Other Forms of Escapism]
  Someone There You Know [The Battle for the Mind]
  Harry's Song
  Ursula (The Swansea Song)

Little Lapwing
Song With No Meaning
Blue John's Blues [Rock 'n' Roll]
The Poet
After the Day [Spectre of a Nuclear Holocaust]

EARLY MORNING ONWARDS
Early Morning
Poor Wages
Brother Thrush [Nature and the Environment]
Mr Sunshine [The Battle for the Mind]
Taking Some Time On [Spirituality]
Mother Dear [The Battle for the Mind]
Mocking Bird
Song With No Meaning
I'm Over You
Child of Man [Spirituality]
After the Day [Spectre of a Nuclear Holocaust]

BABY JAMES HARVEST
Crazy (Over You)
Delph Town Morn [Family & Environs]
Summer Soldier [The Troubles in Northern Ireland; The Battle for the Mind; Spirituality]
Thank You [Rock 'n' Roll]
One Hundred Thousand Smiles Out [Elves, Aliens and Other Forms of Escapism]
Moonwater

'Rock 'n' Roll Woman' b/w **'The Joker'** [Ring of Changes]

EVERYONE IS EVERYBODY ELSE
Child of the Universe [Introduction; Vietnam; The Troubles in Northern Ireland; South Africa Under Apartheid; Politics & The Media; Spirituality]
Negative Earth [Elves, Aliens and Other Forms of Escapism]
Paper Wings
The Great 1974 Mining Disaster [Politics & The Media; Rock 'n' Roll]
Crazy City [Nature and the Environment]
See Me See You
Poor Boy Blues [Family & Environs]
Mill Boys [Family & Environs]
For No One [The Troubles in Northern Ireland; Spirituality]

TIME HONOURED GHOSTS
    In My Life [Politics & The Media]
    Sweet Jesus [The Battle for the Mind; Spirituality]
    Titles [Rock 'n' Roll]
    Jonathan [Nature and the Environment; Elves, Aliens and Other Forms of Escapism; Spirituality]
    Beyond the Grave [Spirituality]
    Song for You
    Hymn for the Children [Spirituality]
    Moongirl
    One Night [Sex]

OCTOBERON
    The World Goes On [The Battle for the Mind]
    May Day [The Soviet Threat]
    Ra
    Rock 'n' Roll Star [Rock 'n' Roll]
    Polk Street Rag [Sex]
    Believe In Me
    Suicide?

'Hymn' [Drugs; Spirituality] c/w **'Our Kid's Kid'** [Family & Environs]

GONE TO EARTH
    Hymn [Drugs; Spirituality]
    Love is Like a Violin
    Friend of Mine
    Poor Man's Moody Blues [Sex; Rock 'n' Roll]
    Hard Hearted Woman
    Sea of Tranquility [Rock 'n' Roll]
    Spirit on the Water [Nature and the Environment]
    Leper's Song
    Taking Me Higher

XII
    Loving is Easy
    Berlin [Berlin]
    A Tale of Two Sixties [Rock 'n' Roll]
    Turning in Circles
    The Closed Shop [Politics & The Media]
    In Search of England [The Soldier as Victim]

Sip of Wine
Harbour
Nova Lepidoptera [Elves, Aliens and Other Forms of Escapism]
Giving It Up
The Streets of San Francisco [Elves, Aliens and Other Forms of Escapism]

EYES OF THE UNIVERSE
Love on the Line
Alright Down Get Boogie (Mu Ala Rusic)
The Song (They Love to Sing)
Skin Flicks [Sex]
Sperratus [Rock 'n' Roll, Spirituality]
Rock and Roll Lady
Capricorn
Play to the World

MÆSTOSO (Woolly Wolstenholme solo album)
Sail Away [Rock 'n' Roll]
Quiet Islands [Nature and the Environment]
A Prospect of Whitby [Nature and the Environment]
Lives on the Line
Patriots [The Soldier as Victim]
Gates of Heaven (14/18) [The Soldier as Victim]
American Excess
Mæstoso (A Hymn in the Roof of the World) [Spirituality]
Waveform

TURN OF THE TIDE
Waiting on the Borderline
How Do You Feel Now? [Family & Environs]
Back to the Wall [Berlin]
Highway for Fools
Echoes and Shadows
Death of a City [Spectre of a Nuclear Holocaust]
I'm Like a Train
Doctor Doctor [The Battle for the Mind; Spirituality]
Life is for Living
In Memory of the Martyrs [Berlin; Spirituality]

RING OF CHANGES
Fifties Child [Spirituality]

Looking From the Outside
Teenage Heart
High Wire
Midnight Drug [Sex; Drugs; The Battle for the Mind]
Waiting for the Right Time
Just a Day Away (Forever Tomorrow)
Paraiso dos Cavalos [Nature and the Environment]
Ring of Changes [South Africa Under Apartheid; Ring of Changes]

'Waiting for the Right Time' c/w **'Blow Me Down'** [Spirituality]

VICTIMS OF CIRCUMSTANCE
Sideshow [Politics & The Media]
Hold On
Rebel Woman [The Soviet Threat]
Say You'll Stay
For Your Love [Rock 'n' Roll; Spirituality]
Victims of Circumstance [Spectre of a Nuclear Holocaust]
Inside My Nightmare
Watching You
I've Got a Feeling

FACE TO FACE
Prisoner of Your Love
He Said Love [Spirituality]
Alone in the Night
Turn the Key
You Need Love
Kiev [Spirituality]
African [The Soviet Threat; South Africa Under Apartheid; Politics & The Media]
Following Me
All My Life
Panic [Rock 'n' Roll]
Guitar Blues
On the Wings of Love

WELCOME TO THE SHOW
The Life You Lead
Lady Macbeth [Rock 'n' Roll]
Cheap the Bullet [The Troubles in Northern Ireland]
Welcome to the Show [Politics & The Media; Rock 'n' Roll]

John Lennon's Guitar [Rock 'n' Roll]
Halfway to Freedom [Berlin]
African Nights [South Africa Under Apartheid; Rock 'n' Roll]
Psychedelic Child [Rock 'n' Roll]
Where Do We Go
Origin Earth [Elves, Aliens and Other Forms of Escapism]
If Love is King
Shadows on the Sky [Nature and the Environment]

'Stand Up' (released in various versions) [Nature and the Environment]

CAUGHT IN THE LIGHT
Who Do We Think We Are? [Nature and the Environment]
Knoydart [Nature and the Environment; Spirituality]
Copii Romania [Break-up of the Soviet Empire; Spirituality]
Back to Earth [Family & Environs; Spirituality]
Cold War [Break-up of the Soviet Empire]
Forever Yesterday
The Great Unknown
Spud-u-Like [Rock 'n' Roll; Ring of Changes]
Silver Wings
Once More
A Matter of Time
Ballad of Denshaw Mill [Family & Environs]

SONGS FROM THE BLACK BOX (Woolly Wolstenholme solo album)
Has to be a Reason
Down the Line
All Get Burned
Too Much, Too Loud, Too Late
Even the Night
Deceivers All
The Will to Fly [Nature and the Environment]
Sunday Bells [Family and Environs]
Open
(Why Remain [The Battle for the Mind])—added on 2004 re-issue)

RIVER OF DREAMS
Back in the Game [Rock 'n' Roll]
River of Dreams [Rock 'n' Roll; Ring of Changes]
Yesterday's Heroes

Children of the Disappeared [Family & Environs; Spirituality]
Pool of Tears
Do You Believe in Dreams (Same Chance for Everyone) [Ring of Changes]
(Took Me) So Long
Mr E [Drugs; Rock 'n' Roll; Spirituality]
Three Weeks to Despair [Spirituality]
The Time of Our Lives [Ring of Changes]

NEXUS (Barclay James Harvest Through the Eyes of John Lees)
Festival! [Nature and the Environment]
The Iron Maiden
Brave New World [Ring of Changes]
Hors d'Oeuvre
Mocking Bird
Sitting Upon a Shelf
Hymn [Drugs; Spirituality]
The Devils That I Keep [The Battle for the Mind]
Titles [Rock 'n' Roll]
Float
Loving is Easy
Star Bright [Ring of Changes]

REVOLUTION DAYS (Barclay James Harvest Featuring Les Holroyd)
It's My Life
Missing You
That Was Then . . . This is Now
Prelude
January Morning [Break-up of the Soviet Empire]
Quiero el Sol
Totally Cool
Life is for Living
Sleepy Sunday
Revolution Day [Spirituality; Concluding Remarks]
Marlene [Elves, Aliens and Other Forms of Escapism]

ONE DROP IN A DRY WORLD (Mæstoso)
The bells, The Bells!
Blood and Bones [Elves, Aliens and Other Forms of Escapism; Spirituality]
A Waiting Game [Ring of Changes]
It's You (Sixties Mix)
Souk

One Drop in a Dry World [The Battle for the Mind]
ANSS [Ring of Changes]
The End of the Road
Explorers
2 a.m. [The Second Iraq War; The Battle for the Mind]
The Starving People of the World All Thank You For Your Time [Spirituality]
Carpet [Rock 'n' Roll]

GRIM (Mæstoso)
Coming Soon to a Cinema Near You
Through a Storm
Love Is . . . [Elves, Aliens and Other Forms of Escapism]
A Lark
That's the Price You Pay
The Iceman Cometh
Hebden Bridge [Nature and the Environment]
Loot
Harp and Carp
Birds
Location, Location, Location [Spirituality; Ring of Changes]
Abendrot
Marsch Burleske
Pas de Deux
A Scene From a London Flat

Caterwauling (Mæstoso)
Caterwauling
Soldier of Fortune [The Second Iraq War; The Soldier as Victim]
The Road to Nowhere [The Soldier as Victim]
Matilda Yarrow
The Collector [Spirituality]
Closure [Family & Environs]
Always
I Don't Like You
Tonight Could Be the Night
Shoes [Spirituality]
Strange Worlds
Quicksand [The Battle for the Mind]
Blossom Hill [The Battle for the Mind]
Pills [The Battle for the Mind]

List of Barclay James Harvest's Songwriters' Sociological Songs

1) **2 A.M. (Wolstenholme), 2004**
Appears in the following chapters:
The Second Iraq War
The Battle for the Mind
Song profile:
One Drop in a Dry World—CD—2004
Uneasy Listening—Compilation CD—2009

2) **AFRICAN (Lees), 1987**
Appears in the following chapters:
The Soviet Threat
South Africa Under Apartheid
Politics & The Media
Song profile:
Face to Face—LP—1987
Live set list: 1987
Live recordings, 2: Glasnost; Glasnost/Victims of Circumstance
Compilation albums, 2: All is Safely Gathered In; Sea of Tranquility

3) **AFRICAN NIGHTS (Holroyd), 1990**
Appears in the following chapters:
South Africa Under Apartheid
Rock 'n' Roll
Song profile:
Welcome to the Show—LP—1990

4) **AFTER THE DAY (Lees), 1971**
Appears in the following chapter:
Spectre of a Nuclear Holocaust
Song profile:
Barclay James Harvest and Other Short Stories—LP—1971
Live set lists: 1971, 1972, 1973, 1974, 1975, 2006, 2009, 2010, 2011, 2012
Live recordings, 5: Live; BBC In Concert 1972; After the Day—The Radio Broadcasts 1974-1976; Legacy; Rock Legends Filmed Live at Metropolis Studios
Compilation albums, 7: Early Morning Onwards; The Best of Barclay James Harvest Volume 3; Another Arable Parable; The Harvest Years; Mocking Bird—The Best of Barclay James Harvest; All is Safely Gathered In; Taking Some Time On

5)   ANCIENT WAVES (Lees), 2011
Appears in the following chapter:
The Second Iraq War
Politics & The Media
Song profile: ——
Live set lists: 2010, 2011
Live recordings, 1: Rock Legends Filmed Live at Metropolis Studios

6)   A.N.S.S. (Wolstenholme), 2004
Appears in the following chapter:
Ring of Changes
Song profile:
One Drop in a Dry World—CD—2004

7)   BACK IN THE GAME (Holroyd), 1997
Appears in the following chapter:
Rock 'n' Roll
Song profile:
River of Dreams—CD—1997
Live set lists: 1997, BJHFLH
Live recordings, 1: Classic Meets Rock
Compilation albums, 3: Mockingbird; Evolution Years—The Best of Barclay
James Harvest Featuring the Songs of Les Holroyd; All is Safely Gathered In

8)   BACK TO EARTH (Lees), 1993
Appears in the following chapters:
Family & Environs
Spirituality
Song profile:
Caught in the Light—LP—1993
Live set list: 1993

9)   BACK TO THE WALL (Holroyd), 1981
Appears in the following chapter:
Berlin
Song profile:
Turn of the Tide—LP—1981
Live set lists: 1981, 1982

10)   BALL AND CHAIN (Wolstenholme), 1971
Appears in the following chapter:

The Battle for the Mind
Song profile:
Once Again—LP—1971
Live set lists: 1971, 2011, 2012
Live recordings, 1: High Voltage 23rd July 2011
Compilation albums, 5: The Best of Barclay James Harvest Volume 3; Another Arable Parable; The Harvest Years; Mocking Bird; Taking Some Time On

11) **BALLAD OF DENSHAW MILL (Lees), 1993**
Appears in the following chapter:
Family & Environs
Song profile:
Caught in the Light—LP—1993
Compilation albums, 2: All is Safely Gathered In; Sea of Tranquility

12) **BERLIN (Holroyd), 1978**
Appears in the following chapter:
Berlin
Song profile:
XII—LP—1978
Live set lists: 1978, 1979, 1981, 1982, 1984, 1987, 1990, 1992, 1993, 1995, 1997, BJHFLH
Live recordings, 5: A Concert for the People (Berlin); Glasnost; Classic Meets Rock; The Best of Barclay James Harvest Live; Glasnost/Victims of Circumstance
Compilation albums, 8: The Compact Story of Barclay James Harvest; Alone We Fly; The Best of BJH (1992); Master Series; Mockingbird; Evolution Years—The Best of Barclay James Harvest Featuring the Songs of Les Holroyd; All is Safely Gathered In; Sea of Tranquility

13) **BEYOND THE GRAVE (Wolstenholme), 1975**
Appears in the following chapter:
Spirituality
Song profile:
Time Honoured Ghosts—LP—1975

14) **BLOOD AND BONES (Wolstenholme), 2004**
Appears in the following chapters:
Elves, Aliens and Other Forms of Escapism
Spirituality
Song profile:

One Drop in a Dry World—CD—2004
Compilation albums, 1: Uneasy Listening

15)   BLOSSOM HILL (Wolstenholme), 2007
Appears in the following chapter:
The Battle for the Mind
Song profile:
caterwauling—CD—2007

16)   BLOW ME DOWN (Lees), 1983
Appears in the following chapter:
Spirituality
Song profile:
Single B-side c/w 'Waiting for the Right Time'—1983
Compilation albums, 2: Alone We Fly; Master Series

17)   BLUE JOHN'S BLUES (Lees), 1971
Appears in the following chapter:
Rock 'n' Roll
Song profile:
Barclay James Harvest and Other Short Stories—LP—1971
Compilation albums, 1: Taking Some Time On

18)   BOOTHAM PARK ELEGY (Wolstenholme), 2004
Appears in the following chapter:
The Battle for the Mind
Song profile:
Black Box Recovered—CD—2004
Compilation albums, 1: Uneasy Listening

19)   BRAVE NEW WORLD (Lees), 1999
Appears in the following chapter:
Ring of Changes
Song profile:
Nexus—CD—1999
Live set lists: 1999, 2000
Live recording, 1: Revival—Live 1999
Compilation albums, 1: Taking Some Time On (1971 demo version)

20)   BROTHER THRUSH (Lees), 1968
Appears in the following chapter:

Nature and The Environment
Song profile:
Single, A-side—1968
Live set lists: pre-1970, 1999
Live recordings, 1: Revival—Live 1999
Compilation albums, 8: Early Morning Onwards; The Best of Barclay James Harvest (1977); The Harvest Years; The Best of BJH (1997); Mocking Bird; Mocking Bird—The Best of Barclay James Harvest; All is Safely Gathered In; Taking Some Time On

21) **CARPET (Wolstenholme), 2004**
Appears in the following chapter:
Rock 'n' Roll
Song profile:
One Drop in a Dry World—CD—2004
Compilation albums, 1: Uneasy Listening

22) **CHEAP THE BULLET (Lees), 1990**
Appears in the following chapter:
The Troubles—Northern Ireland
Song profile:
Welcome to the Show—LP—1990
Live sets: 1990, 1992, 1993, 1999, 2000, 2006, 2009, 2010, 2011
Live recordings, 2: Legacy; The Best of Barclay James Harvest Live
Compilation albums, 4: The Best of BJH (1992); Master Series; All is Safely Gathered In; Sea of Tranquility

23) **CHILD OF MAN (Lees), 1972**
Appears in the following chapter:
Spirituality
Song profile:
B side to 'I'm Over You'—Single—1972
Compilation albums, 8: The Best of Barclay James Harvest (1977); Another Arable Parable; The Harvest Years; The Best of BJH (1997); The Collection; Mocking Bird—The Best of Barclay James Harvest; All is Safely Gathered In; Taking Some Time On

24) **CHILD OF THE UNIVERSE (Lees), 1974**
Appears in the following chapters:
The Vietnam War
The Troubles—Northern Ireland
South Africa Under Apartheid

Politics & The Media
Spirituality
Song profile:
Everyone Is Everybody Else—LP—1974
Live sets: 1975, 1976, 1977, 1978, 1979, 1982, 1984, 1987, 1990, 1992, 1993, 2000, 2006, 2009, 2010, 2011, 2012
Live recordings, 8: Live Tapes; A Concert for the People (Berlin); Legacy; Classic Rock Legends; Victims of Circumstance; The Best of Barclay James Harvest Live; Caught Live; Glasnost/Victims of Circumstance

25) CHILDREN OF THE DISAPPEARED (Lees), 1997
Appears in the following chapters:
Family & Environs
Ring of Changes
Song profile:
River of Dreams—CD—1997
Compilation albums, 2: All is Safely Gathered In; Sea of Tranquility

26) THE CLOSED SHOP (Lees), 1978
Appears in the following chapter:
Politics & The Media
Song profile:
XII—LP—1978
Compilation albums, 2: All is Safely Gathered In; Sea of Tranquility

27) CLOSURE (Wolstenholme), 2007
Appears in the following chapter:
Family & Environs
Song profile:
caterwauling—CD—2007

28) COLD WAR (Holroyd), 1993
Appears in the following chapter:
Break-up of the Soviet Empire
Song profile:
Caught in the Light—LP—1993
Compilation albums, 1: Evolution Years—The Best of Barclay James Harvest Featuring the Songs of Les Holroyd

29) THE COLLECTOR (Wolstenholme), 2007
Appears in the following chapter:

Spirituality
Song profile:
caterwauling—CD—2007

30) COPII ROMANIA (Holroyd), 1993
Appears in the following chapters:
Break-up of the Soviet Empire
Spirituality
Song profile:
Caught in the Light—LP—1993

31) CRAZY CITY (Holroyd), 1974
Appears in the following chapter:
Nature and the Environment
Song profile:
Everyone is Everybody Else—LP—1974
Live set lists: 1974, 1975, 1976, 1977, 1980, 1981, 1982, 1990, 1992, 1993, BJHFLH, 2012
Live recordings, 4: Live, Live Tapes, After the Day—The Radio Broadcasts 1974-1976; Caught Live
Compilation albums, 4: Alone We Fly, Evolution Years—The Best of Barclay James Harvest Featuring the Songs of Les Holroyd; All is Safely Gathered In; Sea of Tranquility

32) DARK NOW MY SKY (Lees), 1970
Appears in the following chapter:
Nature and The Environment
Song profile:
Barclay James Harvest—LP—1970
Live set lists: pre-1970, 1970, 1971, 1972, 1973, 1974
Live recordings, 1: BBC In Concert 1972
Compilation albums, 3: The Harvest Years; All is Safely Gathered In; Taking Some Time On

33) DEATH OF A CITY (Lees), 1982
Appears in the following chapter:
Spectre of a Nuclear Holocaust
Song profile:
Turn of the Tide—LP—1982
Live set lists: pre-1970, 1981, 1982, 2011, 2012

34) DELPH TOWN MORN (Lees), 1972
Appears in the following chapter:
Family & Environs
Song profile:
Baby James Harvest—LP—1972
Compilation albums, 4: The Best of Barclay James Harvest Volume 3; The Best of BJH (1997); The Collection; Taking Some Time On

35) THE DEVILS THAT I KEEP (Wolstenholme), 1999
Appears in the following chapter:
The Battle for the Mind
Song profile:
Nexus—CD—1999

36) DO YOU BELIEVE IN DREAMS (SAME CHANCE FOR EVERYONE) (Holroyd), 1997
Appears in the following chapters:
Ring of Changes
Song profile:
River of Dreams—CD—1997

37) DOCTOR DOCTOR (Lees), 198
Appears in the following chapters:
The Battle for the Mind
Spirituality
Song profile:
Turn of the Tide—LP—1981

38) FESTIVAL! (Lees/Wolstenholme), 1999
Appears in the following chapters:
Nature and the Environment
Song profile:
Nexus—CD—1999
Live set lists: 1999, 2000, 2001
Live recordings, 1: Revival—1999

39) FIFTIES CHILD (Lees), 1983
Appears in the following chapter:
Spirituality
Song profile:
Ring of Changes—LP—1983

Live set list: 1984, 2012
Compilation albums, 3: Alone We Fly; All is Safely Gathered In; Sea of Tranquility

40) FOR NO ONE (Lees), 1974
Appears in the following chapters:
The Troubles—Northern Ireland
Spirituality
Song profile:
Everyone Is Everybody Else—LP—1974
Live set lists: 1974, 1975, 1976, 1990, 1999, 2000, 2006, 2009, 2010, 2011, 2012
Live recordings, 6: Live, Live Tapes, After the Day—The Radio Broadcasts 1974-1976; Revival—Live 1999; Legacy; Caught Live
Compilation albums, 3: Alone We Fly; All is Safely Gathered In; Sea of Tranquility

41) FOR YOUR LOVE (Lees), 1984
Appears in the following chapters:
The Battle for the Mind
Spirituality
Song profile:
Victims of Circumstance—LP—1984
Live set list: 1984
Live recordings, 2: Victims of Circumstance; Glasnost/Victims of Circumstance
Compilation albums, 1: All is Safely Gathered In

42) GALADRIEL (Lees), 1971
Appears in the following chapter:
Elves, Aliens and Other Forms of Escapism
Song profile:
Once Again—LP—1971
Live set lists: 1970, 1971, 1972, 1973, 1974, 1975, 1999, 2000, 2006, 2009, 2010, 2011
Live recordings, 6: Live, BBC In Concert 1972, After the Day—The Radio Broadcasts 1974-1976; Revival—Live 1999; Legacy; High Voltage 23rd July 2011

43) GATES OF HEAVEN (14/18) (Wolstenholme), 1980
Appears in the following chapter:
The Soldier as Victim
Spirituality
Song profile:

Mæstoso (Woolly Wolstenholme solo album)—1980
Compilation albums, 1: Songs From the Black Box

44) THE GREAT 1974 MINING DISASTER (Lees), 1974
Appears in the following chapters:
Politics & The Media
Rock 'n' Roll
Song profile:
Everyone is Everybody Else—LP—1974
Live sets: 1974, 1975, 2006, 2009
Live recordings, 4: Live, After the Day—The Radio Broadcasts 1974-1976;
Legacy; Caught Live
Compilation albums, 2: All is Safely Gathered In; Sea of Tranquility

45) HALFWAY TO FREEDOM (Holroyd), 1990
Appears in the following chapter:
Berlin
Song profile:
Welcome to the Show—LP—1990
Live set list: 1990
Compilation albums, 1: Evolution Years—The Best of Barclay James Harvest
Featuring the Songs of Les Holroyd

46) HAPPY OLD WORLD (Wolstenholme), 1971
Appears in the following chapter:
Nature and The Environment
Song profile:
Once Again—LP—1971
Live set list: 1971
Compilation albums, 2: The Harvest Years; Taking Some Time On

47) HE SAID LOVE (Lees), 1986
Appears in the following chapter:
Spirituality
Song profile:
A side—Single—1986
Face to Face—LP—1987
Live set list: 1987
Live recordings, 1: Glasnost
Compilation albums, 1: Alone We Fly

48) HEBDEN BRIDGE (Wolstenholme/Broomhead), 2005

Appears in the following chapter:
Family & Environs
Song profile:
Grim—CD—2005
Compilation albums, 1: Uneasy Listening

49) HOW DO YOU FEEL NOW? (Lees), 1981

Appears in the following chapter:
Family & Environs
Song profile:
Turn of the Tide—LP—1981
Live set lists: 1981, 1982

50) HYMN (Lees), 1977

Appears in the following chapters:
Drugs
Spirituality
Song profile:
A side—Single—1977
Gone to Earth—LP—1977
Re-issued as a single—1977
Live set lists: 1977, 1978, 1979, 1980, 1981, 1982, 1984, 1987, 1990, 1992, 1993, 1995, 1997, 1999, 2000, 2006, 2009, 2010, 2011, BJHFLH, 2012
Live recordings, 13: Live Tapes; A Concert for the People (Berlin); Glasnost; Revival—Live 1999; Legacy; Rock Legends Filmed Live at Metropolis Studios; Classic Meets Rock; Victims of Circumstance; The Best of Barclay James Harvest Live; Caught Live; 25th Anniversary Concert; The Ultimate Anthology; Glasnost/Victims of Circumstance
Compilation albums, 7: The Compact Story of Barclay James Harvest; Alone We Fly; The Best of BJH (1992); Master Series; Mockingbird; All is Safely Gathered In; Sea of Tranquility

51) HYMN FOR THE CHILDREN (Lees), 1975

Appears in the following chapter:
Spirituality
Song profile:
Time Honoured Ghosts—LP—1975
Live set lists: 1975, 1976, 2011, 2012
Live recordings, 1: Live Tapes (expanded CD version)
Compilation albums, 3: Master Series; After the Day—The Radio Broadcasts

1974-1976; Sea of Tranquility

52) IN MY LIFE (Lees), 1975

Appears in the following chapter:
Rock 'n' Roll
Song profile:
Time Honoured Ghosts—LP—1975
Live set list: 1975
Compilation albums, 2: All is Safely Gathered In; Sea of Tranquility

53) IN MEMORY OF THE MARTYRS (Lees), 1981

Appears in the following chapters:
Berlin
Spirituality
Song profile:
Turn of the Tide—LP—1981
Live set lists: 1980, 1981, 1982
Live recordings, 1: A Concert for the People (Berlin)
Compilation albums, 2: All is Safely Gathered In; Sea of Tranquility

54) IN SEARCH OF ENGLAND (Wolstenholme), 1978

Appears in the following chapter:
The Soldier as Victim
Song profile:
XII—LP—1978
Live set lists: 1978, 1979, 2000, 2004, 2006, 2009, 2010
Live recordings, 2: Legacy; Fiddling Meanly
Compilation albums, 2: All is Safely Gathered In; Sea of Tranquility

55) JANUARY MORNING (Holroyd), 2001

Appears in the following chapter:
Break-up of the Soviet Empire
Song profile:
Revolution Days—CD—2001
Live set list: BJHFLH
Live recordings, 2: Live in Bonn; Classic Meets Rock

56) JOHN LENNON'S GUITAR (Lees), 1990

Appears in the following chapter:
Rock 'n' Roll
Song profile:

Welcome to the Show—LP—1990
Live set lists: 1990, 1992
Live recordings, 2: The Best of Barclay James Harvest Live; one version of the CD single release of 'Stand Up'
Compilation albums, 3: Endless Dream; All is Safely Gathered In; Sea of Tranquility

57) THE JOKER (Holroyd/Lees), 1972

Appears in the following chapter:
Ring of Changes
Song profile:
Single B-side, c/w 'Rock 'n' Roll Woman'—1972
Compilation albums, 5: The Best of Barclay James Harvest; The Collection; The Harvest Years; Mocking Bird; All is Safely Gathered In

58) JONATHAN (Holroyd), 1975

Appears in the following chapters:
Nature and the Environment
Elves, Aliens and Other Forms of Escapism
Spirituality
Song profile:
Time Honoured Ghosts—LP—1975
Live set lists: 1975, 1976, 1977, 1978, 1979, 1980, 1990, BJHFLH
Live recordings, 1: Live Tapes
Compilation albums, 3: The Compact Story of Barclay James Harvest; All is Safely Gathered In; Sea of Tranquility

59) KIEV (Holroyd), 1987

Appears in the following chapter:
Spirituality
Song profile:
Face to Face—LP—1987
Live set list: 1987
Live recordings, 2: Glasnost; Glasnost/Victims of Circumstance
Compilation albums, 2: Mockingbird; Evolution Years—The Best of Barclay James Harvest Featuring Les Holroyd

60) KNOYDART (Lees), 1993

Appears in the following chapter:
Nature and The Environment
Song profile:

Caught in the Light—LP—1993

61) LADY MACBETH (Lees), 1990
Appears in the following chapter:
Rock 'n' Roll
Song profile:
Welcome to the Show—LP—1990
Compilation albums, 2: All is Safely Gathered In; Sea of Tranquility

62) LOCATION, LOCATION, LOCATION (Wolstenholme), 2005
Appears in the following chapter:
Spirituality
Ring of Changes
Song profile:
Grim—CD—2005

63) LONG SHIPS (Lees), 1977
Appears in the following chapter:
Elves, Aliens and Other Forms of Escapism
Song profile:
A Major Fancy—LP—1977

64) LOVE IS . . . (Wolstenholme), 2005
Appears in the following chapter:
Elves, Aliens and Other Forms of Escapism
Song profile:
Grim—CD—2005

**65) MÆSTOSO—A HYMN IN THE ROOF OF THE WORLD
(Wolstenholme), 1980**
Appears in the following chapter:
Spirituality
Song profile:
Mæstoso—LP—1980
Songs From the Black Box (Woolly Wolstenholme double album, including a
re-release of Mæstoso)—CD—1994
Compilation albums, 1: Uneasy Listening

66) MARLENE (Holroyd), 2001
Appears in the following chapter:
Elves, Aliens and Other Forms of Escapism

Song profile:
Revolution Days—CD—2001
Live set list: BJHFLH
Live recordings, 1: Live in Bonn

67) **MAY DAY (Lees), 1976**
Appears in the following chapter:
The Soviet Threat
Song profile:
Octoberon—LP—1976
Compilation albums, 1: Sea of Tranquility

68) **MEDICINE MAN (Lees), 1971**
Appears in the following chapter:
Elves, Aliens and Other Forms of Escapism
Song profile:
Barclay James Harvest and Other Short Stories—LP—1971
Live set lists: 1971, 1972, 1973, 1974, 1975, 1976, 1977, 1978, 1979, 1987, 1990, 1992, 1993, 1999, 2000, 2006, 2009, 2010, 2011, 2012
Live recordings, 11: Live; Live Tapes (expanded CD version); Glasnost; BBC In Concert 1972; After the Day—The Radio Broadcasts 1974-1976; Legacy; Rock Legends Filmed Live at Metropolis Studios; The Best of Barclay James Harvest Live; 25h Anniversary Concert; The Ultimate Anthology; Glasnost/Victims of Circumstance
Compilation albums, 12: The Best of Barclay James Harvest; The Best of Barclay James Harvest (Volume 2); Another Arable Parable; The Harvest Years; Endless Dream; The Best of BJH (1997); Mocking Bird; The Collection; Mocking Bird—The Best of Barclay James Harvest; All is Safely Gathered In; Sea of Tranquility; Taking Some Time On

69) **MIDNIGHT DRUG (Lees), 1983**
Appears in the following chapters:
Family & Environs
Drugs
The Battle for the Mind
Sex
Song profile:
Ring of Changes—LP—1983

70) **MILL BOYS (Lees), 1974**
Appears in the following chapter:

Family & Environs
Song profile:
Everyone is Everybody Else—LP—1974
Live set list: 2012

71) **MOTHER DEAR (Lees), 1970**
Appears in the following chapters:
The Battle for the Mind
Spirituality
Song profile:
Barclay James Harvest—LP—1970
Live set lists: pre-1970; 1970
Compilation albums, 6: Early Morning Onwards; The Best of Barclay James Harvest (Volume 2); Another Arable Parable; The Best of BJH (EMI, 1997); Mocking Bird—The Best of Barclay James Harvest; Taking Some Time On

72) **MR E (Lees), 1997**
Appears in the following chapters:
Drugs
Rock 'n' Roll
Spirituality
Song profile:
River of Dreams—CD—1997
Live set lists: 1997; 1999
Live recordings, 1: Revival—Live 1999 (expanded version)
Compilation albums, 1: Sea of Tranquility

73) **MR SUNSHINE (Wolstenholme), 1968**
Appears in the following chapter:
The Battle for the Mind
Song profile:
B side to *Early Morning*—1968
Live set list: pre-1970
Live recordings, 1: The Ultimate Anthology
Compilation albums, 5: Early Morning Onwards; The Best of Barclay James Harvest (Volume 2); The Harvest Years; Mocking Bird; Taking Some Time On

74) **NEGATIVE EARTH (Pritchard/Holroyd), 1974**
Appears in the following chapter:
Elves, Aliens and Other Forms of Escapism
Song profile:

Everyone Is Everybody Else—LP—1974
Live set lists: 1974; 1975
Live recordings, 2: Live; After the Day—The Radio Broadcasts 1974-1976
Compilation albums, 2: All is Safely Gathered In; Sea of Tranquility

75) NOVA LEPIDOPTERA (Lees), 1978

Appears in the following chapter:
Elves, Aliens and Other Forms of Escapism
Song profile:
XII—LP—1978
Live set lists: 1978, 1979, 1980, 1981, 1982, 1987, 1995, 2009, 2010, 2011
Live recordings, 2: A Concert for the People (Berlin); Rock Legends Filmed Live
at Metropolis Studios
Compilation albums, 2: All is Safely Gathered In; Sea of Tranquility

76) ONE DROP IN A DRY WORLD (Wolstenholme), 2004

Appears in the following chapter:
The Battle for the Mind
Profile:
One Drop in a Dry World—CD—2004
Compilation albums, 1: Uneasy Listening

77) ONE HUNDRED THOUSAND SMILES OUT (Holroyd), 1972

Appears in the following chapter:
Elves, Aliens and Other Forms of Escapism
Song profile:
Baby James Harvest—LP—1972
Live set lists: 1973, 1974
Compilation albums, 4: The Best of Barclay James Harvest (Volume 2); The
Harvest Years; All is Safely Gathered In; Taking Some Time On

78) ONE NIGHT (Lees), 1975

Appears in the following chapters:
Sex
Spirituality
Song profile:
Time Honoured Ghosts—LP—1975
Live set lists: 1975, 1976, 2011, 2012
Live recordings, 1: Live Tapes

79) ORIGIN EARTH (Lees), 1990
Appears in the following chapter:
Elves, Aliens and Other Forms of Escapism
Song profile:
Welcome to the Show—LP—1990

80) OUR KID'S KID (Lees), 1977
Appears in the following chapter:
Family & Environs
Song profile:
Single B side to *Hymn*—1977
Compilation albums, 2: Alone We Fly; Master Series

81) PANIC (Lees), 1987
Appears in the following chapter:
Rock 'n' Roll
Song profile:
Face to Face—LP—1987

82) PARAISO DOS CAVALOS (Lees), 1983
Appears in the following chapter:
Nature and the Environment
Song profile:
Ring of Changes—LP—1983
Live set list: 1984
Live recordings, 2: Victims of Circumstance, Glasnost/Victims of Circumstance
Compilation albums, 1: The Compact Story of Barclay James Harvest

83) PATRIOTS (Wolstenholme), 1980
Appears in the following chapter:
The Soldier as Victim
Song profile:
Mæstoso (Woolly Wolstenholme solo album)—1980
Songs From the Black Box (Woolly Wolstenholme double album, including a re-release of Mæstoso)—CD—1994
Compilation albums, 1: Uneasy Listening

84) pills (Wolstenholme), 2007
Appears in the following chapter:
The Battle for the Mind

Song profile:
caterwauling—CD—2007

85) **POLK STREET RAG (Lees), 1976**
Appears in the following chapter:
Sex
Song profile:
Octoberon—LP—1976
Live site lists: 1976, 1977
Live recordings, 2: Live Tapes; Caught Live
Compilation albums, 1: After the Day—The Radio Broadcasts 1974-1976

86) **POOR BOY BLUES (Holroyd), 1974**
Appears in the following chapter:
Family & Environs
Song profile:
Everyone is Everybody Else—LP—1974
Live set list: 2012
Compilation albums, 2: Alone We Fly; Sorcerers and Keepers

87) **POOR MAN'S MOODY BLUES (Lees), 1977**
Appears in the following chapters:
Sex
Rock 'n' Roll
Profile:
Gone to Earth—LP—1977
Live set lists: 1977, 1978, 1979, 1980, 1981, 1982, 1984, 1987, 1990, 1992, 1993, 1995,
1997, 1999, 2000, 2006, 2009, 2010, 2011, 2012
Live recordings, 10: Live Tapes; Glasnost; Revival—Live 1999; Legacy; Rock
Legends Filmed Live at Metropolis Studios; Victims of Circumstance; The Best
of Barclay James Harvest Live; 25th Anniversary Concert; The Ultimate
Anthology; Glasnost/Victims of Circumstance
Compilation albums, 5: The Compact Story of Barclay James Harvest; The Best
of BJH (1992); Mockingbird; All Is Safely Gathered In; Sea of Tranquility

88) **A PROSPECT OF WHITBY (Wolstenholme), 1980**
Appears in the following chapter:
Nature and the Environment
Song profile:
Mæstoso—LP—1980
Songs From the Black Box (Woolly Wolstenholme double album, including a

re-release of Mæstoso)—CD—1994
Live set lists: 1981, 1982, 2004
Live recordings, 1: Fiddling Meanly
Compilation albums, 1: Uneasy Listening

89) PSYCHEDELIC CHILD (Lees), 1990
Appears in the following chapters:
The Vietnam War
Drugs
Rock 'n' Roll
Song profile:
Welcome to the Show—LP—1990

90) QUICKSAND (Wolstenholme), 2007
Appears in the following chapter:
The Battle for the Mind
Song profile:
caterwauling—CD—2007

91) QUIET ISLANDS (Wolstenholme), 1980
Appears in the following chapter:
Nature and The Environment
Song profile:
Mæstoso—LP—1980
Songs From the Black Box (Woolly Wolstenholme double album, including a
re-release of *Mæstoso*)—CD—1994

92) REBEL WOMAN (Lees), 1984
Appears in the following chapter:
The Soviet Threat
Song profile:
Victims of Circumstance—LP—1984
Live set list: 1984
Live recordings, 2: Victims of Circumstance; Glasnost/Victims of Circumstance

93) REVOLUTION DAY (Holroyd), 2001
Appears in the following chapters:
Spirituality
Song profile:
Revolution Days—CD—2001
Live set lists: BJHFLH

Live recordings, 1: Live in Bonn

94) RING OF CHANGES (Holroyd), 1993
Appears in the following chapters:
South Africa Under Apartheid
Ring of Changes
Song profile:
Ring of Changes—LP—1983
Live set lists: 1984, BJHFLH
Live recordings, 1: Classic Meets Rock
Compilation albums, 5: The Best of BJH (1992); Endless Dream; Evolution Years—The Best of Barclay James Harvest Featuring the Songs of Les Holroyd; All is Safely Gathered In; Sea of Tranquility

95) RIVER OF DREAMS (Lees), 1997
Appears in the following chapter:
Rock 'n' Roll
Song profile:
River of Dreams—LP—1997
Live set lists: 1995, 1997, 1999, 2000, 2009, 2012
Live recordings, 1: Revival—Live 1999

96) ROAD TO NOWHERE (Wolstenholme), 2007
Appears in the following chapter:
The Soldier as Victim
Song profile:
caterwauling—CD—2007

97) ROCK 'N' ROLL STAR (Holroyd), 1976
Appears in the following chapter:
Rock 'n' Roll
Song profile:
Octoberon—LP—1976
Live set lists: 1976, 1977, 1978, 1979, 1992, 1993, 1995, 1997, BJHFLH
Live recordings, 4: Live Tapes; Live in Bonn; Classic Meets Rock; Caught Live
Compilation albums, 7: Alone We Fly; The Best of BJH (1992); Master Series; Evolution Years—The Best of Barclay James Harvest Featuring the Songs of Les Holroyd; All is Safely Gathered In; After the Day—The Radio Broadcasts 1974-1976; Sea of Tranquility

98) SAIL AWAY (Wolstenholme), 1980

Appears in the following chapter:
Rock 'n' Roll
Song profile:
Mæstoso—LP—1980
Songs From the Black Box (Woolly Wolstenholme double album, including a re-release of *Mæstoso*)—CD—1994
Live set list: 1982
Compilation albums, 1: Uneasy Listening

99) SEA OF TRANQUILITY (Wolstenholme), 1977

Appears in the following chapter:
Rock 'n' Roll
Song profile:
Gone to Earth—LP—1977
Compilation albums, 3: Sorcerers and Keepers; All is Safely Gathered In; Sea of Tranquility

100) SHADOWS ON THE SKY (Holroyd), 1990

Appears in the following chapter:
Nature and The Environment
Song profile:
Welcome to the Show—LP—1990
Live set lists: 1990, 1992, 1993, 1995, 1997, BJHFLH
Live recordings, 2: Classic Meets Rock; The Best of Barclay James Harvest Live

101) SHOES (Wolstenholme), 2007

Appears in the following chapter:
Spirituality
Song profile:
caterwauling—LP—2007

102) SIDESHOW (Lees), 1984

Appears in the following chapter:
Politics & The Media
Song profile:
Victims of Circumstance—LP—1984, 2012
Live set list: 1984
Compilation albums, 1: Alone We Fly

103) SKIN FLICKS (Lees), 1979
Appears in the following chapter:
Sex
Song profile:
Eyes of the Universe—LP—1979

104) SOLDIER OF FORTUNE (Turner/Wolstenholme), 2007
Appears in the following chapters:
The Second Iraq War
The Soldier as Victim
Song profile:
caterwauling—CD—2007
Compilation albums, 1: Uneasy Listening

105) SOMEONE THERE YOU KNOW (Wolstenholme), 1971
Appears in the following chapter:
The Battle for the Mind
Song profile:
Barclay James Harvest and Other Short Stories—LP—1971

106) SPERRATUS (Lees), 1979
Appears in the following chapters:
Rock 'n' Roll
Spirituality
Song profile:
Eyes of the Universe—LP—1979
Live set lists: 1980, 1981, 1982
Compilation albums, 2: All is Safely Gathered In; Sea of Tranquility

107) SPIRIT ON THE WATER (Holroyd), 1977
Appears in the following chapter:
Nature and The Environment
Song profile:
Gone to Earth—LP—1977

108) SPUD-U-LIKE (Lees), 1993
Appears in the following chapters:
Rock 'n' Roll
Ring of Changes
Song profile:
Caught in the Light—LP—1993

109) STAND UP (Bolland & Bolland), 1992

Appears in the following chapter:
Nature and the Environment
Song profile:
Stand Up—EP—1992
Live set list: 1992
Live recordings, 3: The Best of Barclay James Harvest Live; 25th Anniversary
Concert; The Ultimate Anthology
Compilation albums, 1: The Best of BJH (1992)

110) STAR BRIGHT (Lees), 1999

Appears in the following chapter:
Ring of Changes
Song profile:
Nexus—CD—1999
Live set list: 1999
Live recordings, 1: Revival—Live 1999

**111) THE STARVING PEOPLE OF THE WORLD ALL THANK YOU
FOR THEIR TIME (Wolstenholme), 2004**

Appears in the following chapter:
Spirituality
Song profile:
One Drop in a Dry World—CD—2004

112) THE STREETS OF SAN FRANCISCO (Lees), 1979

Appears in the following chapter:
Elves, Aliens and Other Forms of Escapism
Song profile:
XII—LP—1978

113) SUMMER SOLDIER (Lees), 1972

Appears in the following chapters:
The Troubles—Northern Ireland
Drugs
The Battle for the Mind
Spirituality
Song profile:
Baby James Harvest—LP—1972
Live set lists: 1972, 1973, 1974, 2009, 2010, 2011, 2012
Live recordings, 4: Live; BBC In Concert 1972; After the Day—The Radio

Broadcasts 1974-1976; Rock Legends Filmed Live at Metropolis Studios
Compilation albums, 5: Another Arable Parable; The Harvest Years; Mocking
Bird; All is Safely Gathered In; Taking Some Time On

114) THE SUN WILL NEVER SHINE (Wolstenholme), 1970

Appears in the following chapter:
The Battle for the Mind
Songs Profile:
Barclay James Harvest—LP—1970
Live set lists: pre-1970, 1970
Compilation albums, 2: All is Safely Gathered In; Taking Some Time On

115) SUNDAY BELLS (Wolstenholme), 1994

Appears in the following chapter:
Family & Environs
Songs Profile:
Songs From the Black Box—CD—1994
Live set list: 2004
Live recordings, 1: Fiddling Meanly
Compilation albums, 1: Uneasy Listening

116) SWEET JESUS (Holroyd), 1975

Appears in the following chapters:
The Battle for the Mind
Spirituality
Song profile:
Time Honoured Ghosts—LP—1975
Live set list: 1975
Compilation albums, 3: All is Safely Gathered In; After the Day—The Radio
Broadcasts 1974-1975; Sea of Tranquility

117) TAKING SOME TIME ON (Lees), 1970

Appears in the following chapter:
Spirituality
Song profile:
Barclay James Harvest—LP—1970
Live set lists: pre-1970, 1970, 2011, 2012
Compilation albums, 7: Early Morning Onwards; The Best of Barclay James
Harvest Volume 2; The Harvest Years; The Best of Barclay James Harvest;
Mocking Bird—The Best of Barclay James Harvest; All Is Safely Gathered In;
Taking Some Time On

118) A TALE OF TWO SIXTIES (Lees), 1978

Appears in the following chapter:
Rock 'n' Roll
Song profile:
XII—LP—1978

119) THANK YOU (Lees), 1972

Appears in the following chapter:
Rock 'n' Roll
Song profile:
Baby James Harvest—LP—1972
Compilation albums, 1: Taking Some Time On

120) THREE WEEKS TO DESPAIR (Lees), 1997

Appears in the following chapter:
Spirituality
Song profile:
River of Dreams—CD—1994
Compilation albums, 1: All is Safely Gathered In

121) TIME OF OUR LIVES (Holroyd), 1997

Appears in the following chapters:
Ring of Changes
Song profile:
River of Dreams—CD—1997

122) TITLES (Lees), 1975

Appears in the following chapter:
Rock 'n' Roll
Song profile:
Time Honoured Ghosts—LP—1975
Live set lists: 1975, 1976, 2012
Compilation albums, 5: The Best of BJH (1992); Sorcerers and Keepers; Master Series; All is Safely Gathered In; Sea of Tranquility

123) VICTIMS OF CIRCUMSTANCE (Holroyd), 1984

Appears in the following chapter:
The Threat of a Nuclear Holocaust
Song profile:
Victims of Circumstance—LP—1984
Live set list: 1984

Live recordings, 2: Victims of Circumstance; Victims of Circumstance/Glasnost
Compilation albums, 4: The Compact Story of Barclay James Harvest; The Best of BJH (1992); Master Series; Evolution Years—The Best of Barclay James Harvest Featuring the Songs of Les Holroyd

124) A WAITING GAME (Wolstenholme), 2004
Appears in the following chapter:
Ring of Changes
Song profile:
One Drop in a Dry World—CD—2004
Compilation albums, 1: Uneasy Listening

125) WELCOME TO THE SHOW (Holroyd), 1990
Appears in the following chapters:
Politics & The Media
Rock 'n' Roll
Ring of Changes
Song profile:
Welcome to the Show—LP—1990
Compilation albums, 1: The Best of BJH (1992)

126) WHO DO WE THINK WE ARE? (Holroyd), 1993
Appears in the following chapter:
Nature and The Environment
Song profile:
Caught in the Light—LP—1993

127) WHY REMAIN (Wolstenholme), 2009
Appears in the following chapter:
The Battle for the Mind
Song profile: ——
Compilation albums, 1: Uneasy Listening

128) THE WILL TO FLY (Wolstenholme), 1994
Appears in the following chapter:
Nature and the Environment
Song profile:
Songs From the Black Box—CD—1994
Live set list: 2004
Live recordings, 1: Fiddling Meanly
Compilation albums, 1: Uneasy Listening

129) THE WORLD GOES ON (Holroyd), 1976

Appears in the following chapter:

The Battle for the Mind

Song profile:

Octoberon—LP—1976

Live set list: 1976, BJHFLH

Live recordings, 1: Live Tapes (expanded edition)

Compilation albums, 2: All is Safely Gathered In; Sea of Tranquility

130) YOU CAN'T GET IT (Lees), 1974

Appears in the following chapters:

Rock 'n' Roll

Song profile:

B side to "Best of My Love"—Single—1974

List of Other Lyricists Referenced

The place and year of birth are only given where this has not been covered in the text.

10cc (Creme, Godley, Gouldman, Stewart) [Rock 'n' Roll; Elves, Aliens...]

Adams, Chris (with String Driven) [Rock 'n' Roll]

Anderson, Ian: born Dunfermline, 1947: with Jethro Tull [Spectre of a Nuclear Holocaust; Sex; Ring of Changes; Spirituality]

Anderson, Jon: born Lancashire, 1944: solo and with Yes [Family and Environs; Nature and the Environment; Spirituality]

Barrett, Jonathan: with The Tangent [Politics and The Media]

Black Sabbath [Spectre of a Nuclear Holocaust; The Vietnam War; The Soldier as Victim; Drugs]

Bowie, David: born David Jones, London, 1947: solo [Berlin]

Butler, Geezer: with Black Sabbath [Spectre of a Nuclear Holocaust; The Vietnam War; The Soldier as Victim; Drugs]

Caddick, Bill: born Wolverhampton, 1944 [The Soldier as Victim]

Calvert, Robert: with Hawkwind [Rock 'n' Roll; Elves, Aliens...]

Cousins, Dave: born Hounslow, 1945: with Strawbs [The Second Iraq War]

Davies, Ray: born London, 1944: solo and with The Kinks [The Battle for the Mind; Spirituality; Ring of Changes]

Edge, Graeme: born Staffordshire, 1941: with The Moody Blues [Spirituality]

Ford, John: born London, 1948: with Strawbs [Politics & The Media]

Gabriel, Peter: born Surrey, 1950: solo [South Africa Under Apartheid]

Gilmour, David: born Cambridge, 1946: with Pink Floyd [Berlin]

Hammill, Peter: born London, 1948: with Van der Graaf Generator [Politics & The Media]

Harrison, George: born Liverpool, 1943; died 2001: solo and with the Beatles [The Battle for the Mind, Spirituality]

Hoover, Susan: for Camel [Berlin]

Hudson, Richard: born London, 1948: with Strawbs [Politics & The Media]

Hugg, Mike: born Hampshire, 1942: with Manfred Mann's Earth Band [Nature and the Environment]

Islam, Yusuf: born Steven Gergiou, London, 1948: as Cat Stevens [Family & Environs]

Kilminster, Ian ("Lemmy"): born Stoke-on-Trent, 1945: with Hawkwind and with Motörhead [The Soldier as Victim; Drugs; Elves, Aliens...]

Leitch, Donovan: born Glasgow, 1946: as Donovan [The Soviet Threat; Spectre of a Nuclear Holocaust; The Vietnam War; Spirituality]

Lowe, Nick: born Surrey, 1949: solo [Rock 'n' Roll]

McTell, Ralph: born Farnborough, 1944 [Spirituality]

Miles, John: born Jarrow, 1949 [Rock 'n' Roll]

Morrison, Van: born Belfast, 1945: solo [Family & Environs; Spirituality]

Newman, Denny: for Manfred Mann's Earth Band [Ring of Changes]

O'Riordan, Dolores: born Limerick, Republic of Ireland, 1971: with the Cranberries [Break-Up of the Soviet Empire]

Osbourne, Ozzy: born Birmingham, 1948: solo [The Battle for the Mind]

Rafferty, Gerry: born Paisley, 1947: solo [The Battle for the Mind]

Rea, Chris: born Middlesbrough, 1951 [Family & Environs; Politics & The Media]

Saint-Marie, Buffy: born Canada, 1941 [Preface to Barclay James Harvest's Conflict Songs]

Softley, Mick [The Vietnam War]

Sutherland, Gavin: born Aberdeenshire, 1951: solo and with The Sutherland Brothers [Politics & The Media; Elves, Aliens...]

Sutherland, Iain: born Aberdeenshire, 1948: with The Sutherland Brothers [The Troubles in Northern Ireland]

Taupin, Bernie: born Lincolnshire, 1950: for Elton John [Sex; Elves, Aliens...]

Thatcher, Betty: born London 1944, died 2011: for Renaissance [The Soviet Threat]

Thomas, Ray: born Stourbridge-on-Severn, 1941: with The Moody Blues [Drugs; Spirituality]

Tillison, Andy: with The Tangent [Politics & The Media; Elves, Aliens and Other Forms of Escapism; The Battle for the Mind]

Townshend, Peter: born London, 1945: with The Who [Ring of Changes]

Waters, Roger: born Surrey, 1943: with Pink Floyd [The Soldier as Victim; Sex; The Battle for the Mind]

Weller, Paul: born Woking, 1958: with The Style Council [Politics & The Media]

Wetton, John: born Derbyshire, 1949: with Asia [The Second Iraq War]

Young, Neil: born Canada, 1945: solo [Drugs]

Appendix 3:
The Ones That Got Away

A number of other songs were strong contenders for inclusion in this social history but were ultimately omitted. This section explains why . . .

'American Excess' (Wolstenholme) [*Mæstoso*, 1980]
Of the three Barclay James Harvest songwriters, Wolstenholme was the one not enamoured with Americana. This song can be read as the disillusionment that quickly set in during the band's visit to San Francisco to record *Time Honoured Ghosts*. The title's similarity to the American Express credit card—which was heavily advertised in the Seventies—made this a strong contender for the chapter 'Other Popular Culture Songs'. Its omission is simply due to the fact that I have insufficient understanding of the lyrics.

'Forever Yesterday' (Lees) [*Caught in the Light*, 1993]
This is undoubtedly a sociological song but its subject matter—it deals with the Scottish Highland clearances in the nineteenth century—covers a period outside the scope of this book.

'If Love is King' (Lees) [*Welcome to the Show*, 1990]
Some fans find a spiritual meaning within this song's cryptic lyrics. I sense that they might be right, but I am unable to extract sufficient meaning, even with contextualisation, to warrant including it within the 'Spirituality' chapter.

'Leper's Song' (Lees) [*Gone to Earth*, 1977]
In typical storytelling fashion of adapting from others' material, Lees merges two novels into this one song. The novels are Graham Greene's *A Burnt Out Case* and Joseph Conrad's *An Outcast of the Islands*. The connection between the books is that their central character is an individual who is living cut-off from his normal civilization. For me, there is more of *A Burnt Out Case* in Lees' song and if that was the only input then there might have been an argument for including the song under Spirituality, but that line of thinking is muddied by the allusion to *An Outcast of the Islands* in the second verse. Lees' lyrics are not sufficiently developed to give me the confidence to interpret his intended meaning and so, as neither Graham Greene nor Joseph Conrad fit

into the Fifties Child's popular culture, the song has been omitted. It would, however, have fitted into a thematic analysis of the band's songs.

'Song for Dying' (Lees) [*Once Again*, 1971]

This is often interpreted as an anti-war song, but I struggle to interpret it to my satisfaction. The setting speaks to me of the First World War and soldiers waiting to charge the enemy trenches as dawn approaches. They charge in many pairs and each dies. However, the song's most oft-repeated lyric, as we pass from the verses into the long coda section, almost feels like the antithesis of everything the Remembrance movement stands for; it suggests they died for us but we should now forget about them. It can be also be interpreted differently, depending on who exactly is telling whom to forget. One could be bold and leap to a spiritual reading, deciding that it's Lees' earliest attempt at a similar message to 'In Memory of the Martyrs'. However, as it stands, the song really fails to reveal its meaning and so did not warrant inclusion in the 'Soldier as Victim', or any other, chapter.

Over their long careers, Barclay James Harvest's songwriters have released more than 250 songs into the public domain; and we have already seen that a staggering proportion—about half—are sociological in nature. The lyrics of the remaining songs in the Barclay James Harvest canon are either unspecific, uninterpretable or fall into other categories not covered by this social history; the largest of which would be "love songs". This set of songs includes classics such as 'Mocking Bird', which we have mentioned in the book in reference to the groundbreaking court case brought by Robert Godfrey against the band, as well as a number of others—very few, such as 'Breathless' and 'Alright Down Get Boogie'—that are rarely regarded as classics even by the most ardent of fans.

Hey! You want more? Get real!

Acknowledgements

The author acknowledges the following for permission to quote lyrics in this book:

'African': written by John Lees, published by Bucks Music Group. Used with permission.

'Ancient Waves': written by John Lees, published by Bucks Music Group. Used with permission.

'Cheap the Bullet': written by John Lees, published by Bucks Music Group. Used with permission.

'Children of the Disappeared': written by John Lees, published by Bucks Music Group. Used with permission.

'Fifties Child': written by John Lees, published by Bucks Music Group. Used with permission.

'For Your Love': written by John Lees, published by Bucks Music Group. Used with permission.

'Lady Macbeth': written by John Lees, published by Bucks Music Group. Used with permission.

'Mr E': written by John Lees, published by Bucks Music Group. Used with permission.

'Origin Earth': written by John Lees, published by Bucks Music Group. Used with permission.

'Rebel Woman': written by John Lees, published by Bucks Music Group. Used with permission.

'Back to the Wall': words and music by Richard Leslie Holroyd © 1981. Reproduced by permission of EMI Music Publishing Ltd, London W8 5SW.

'Death of a City': words and music by John Lees © 1981. Reproduced by permission of EMI Music Publishing Ltd, London W8 5SW.

'Doctor Doctor': words and music by John Lees © 1981. Reproduced by permission of EMI Music Publishing Ltd, London W8 5SW.

'In Memory of the Martyrs': words and music by John Lees © 2010. Reproduced by permission of EMI Music Publishing Ltd, London W8 5SW.

'Midnight Drug': words and music by John Lees © 1983. Reproduced by permission of EMI Music Publishing Ltd, London W8 5SW.

'Mother Dear': words and music by Les Holroyd, John Lees, Melvyn

'In My Life': written by John Lees. Published by RAK Publishing Ltd. Used with permission.

'May Day': written by John Lees. Published by RAK Publishing Ltd. Used with permission.

'Medicine Man': written by John Lees. Published by RAK Publishing Ltd. Used with permission.

'Mill Boys': written by John Lees. Published by RAK Publishing Ltd. Used with permission.

'Negative Earth': written by Les Holroyd and Mel Pritchard. Published by RAK Publishing Ltd. Used with permission.

'One Night': written by John Lees. Published by RAK Publishing Ltd. Used with permission.

'Summer Soldier': written by John Lees. Published by RAK Publishing Ltd. Used with permission.

'Sweet Jesus' Words: written by Les Holroyd. Published by RAK Publishing Ltd. Used with permission.

'Die Without It'; copyright Chris Adams; used by permission.

'Four Egos, One War'; copyright Andy Tillison; used by permission.

'Not as Good as the Book'; copyright Andy Tillison; used by permission.

'Place to Lie'; copyright Chris Adams; used by permission.

Index